AI Approaches to Literacy in Higher Education

Oscar Oliver Eybers
University of Pretoria, South Africa

Alan Muller
University of Pretoria, South Africa

A volume in the Advances in
Educational Technologies and
Instructional Design (AETID) Book
Series

Published in the United States of America by
    IGI Global
    Information Science Reference (an imprint of IGI Global)
    701 E. Chocolate Avenue
    Hershey PA, USA 17033
    Tel: 717-533-8845
    Fax: 717-533-8661
    E-mail: cust@igi-global.com
    Web site: http://www.igi-global.com

Library of Congress Cataloging-in-Publication Data

Names: Eybers, Oscar Oliver, 1972- editor. | Muller, Alan, 1987- editor.
Title: AI approaches to literacy in higher education / edited by Oscar
    Eybers, Alan Muller.
Other titles: Artificial intelligence approaches to literacy in higher
    education
Description: Hershey, PA : Information Science Reference, [2024] | Includes
    bibliographical references and index. | Summary: "The objective of this
    book is to provide new research on AI approaches used in the context of
    literacy in higher education. It aims to bring together research
    studies, case studies, and theoretical perspectives to foster a deeper
    understanding of the potential of AI in promoting and enhancing literacy
    skills"-- Provided by publisher.
Identifiers: LCCN 2023051994 (print) | LCCN 2023051995 (ebook) | ISBN
    9798369310540 (h/c) | ISBN 9798369310557 (eISBN)
Subjects: LCSH: Artificial intelligence--Educational applications. |
    Literacy--Study and teaching (Higher)
Classification: LCC LB1028.43 .A376 2024 (print) | LCC LB1028.43 (ebook)
    | DDC 418.0071/1--dc23/eng/20231121
LC record available at https://lccn.loc.gov/2023051994
LC ebook record available at https://lccn.loc.gov/2023051995

This book is published in the IGI Global book series Advances in Educational Technologies and Instructional Design (AETID) (ISSN: 2326-8905; eISSN: 2326-8913)

British Cataloguing in Publication Data
A Cataloguing in Publication record for this book is available from the British Library.

For electronic access to this publication, please contact: eresources@igi-global.com.

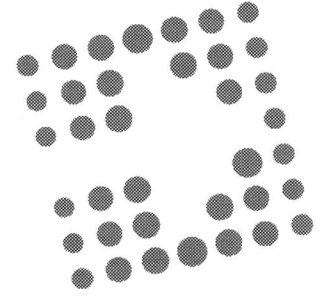

Advances in Educational Technologies and Instructional Design (AETID) Book Series

ISSN:2326-8905
EISSN:2326-8913

Editor-in-Chief: Lawrence A. Tomei, Robert Morris University, USA

MISSION

The **Advances in Educational Technologies & Instructional Design (AETID) Book Series** explores new research and theories for facilitating learning and improving educational performance utilizing technological processes and resources. The series examines technologies that can be integrated into K-12 classrooms to improve skills and learning abilities in all subjects including STEM education and language learning Additionally, it studies the emergence of fully online classrooms for young and adult learners alike, and the communication and accountability challenges that can arise. Trending topics that are covered include adaptive learning, game-based learning, virtual school environments, and social media effects. School administrators, educators, academicians, researchers, and students will find this series to be an excellent resource for the effective design and implementation of learning technologies in their classes.

COVERAGE

- Game-Based Learning
- Instructional Design
- Collaboration Tools
- Web 2.0 and Education
- Online Media in Classrooms
- Curriculum Development
- Classroom Response Systems
- Hybrid Learning
- Educational Telecommunications
- Social Media Effects on Education

IGI Global is currently accepting manuscripts for publication within this series. To submit a proposal for a volume in this series, please contact our Acquisition Editors at Acquisitions@igi-global.com or visit: http://www.igi-global.com/publish/.

Titles in this Series

For a list of additional titles in this series, please visit:
http://www.igi-global.com/book-series/advances-educational-technologies-instructional-design/73678

Effective and Meaningful Student Engagement Through Service Learning
Sharon Valarmathi (Christ University, India) Jacqueline Kareem (Christ University, India)
Veerta Tantia (Christ University, India) Kishore Selva Babu (Christ University, India) and
Patrick Jude Lucas (Christ University, India)
Information Science Reference • copyright 2024 • 293pp • H/C (ISBN: 9798369322567)
• US $275.00 (our price)

Integrating Cutting-Edge Technology Into the Classroom
Ken Nee Chee (Universiti Pendidikan Sultan Idris, Malaysia) and Mageswaran Sanmugam
(Universiti Sains Malaysia, Malaysia)
Information Science Reference • copyright 2024 • 425pp • H/C (ISBN: 9798369331248)
• US $300.00 (our price)

Embracing Technological Advancements for Lifelong Learning
Mahmoud M. Kh. Hawamdeh (Al-Quds Open University, Palestine) and Faiz Abdelhafid
(Al-Istiqlal University, Palestine)
Information Science Reference • copyright 2024 • 365pp • H/C (ISBN: 9798369314104)
• US $230.00 (our price)

Unlocking Learning Potential With Universal Design in Online Learning Environments
Michelle Bartlett (Old Dominion University, USA) and Suzanne M. Ehrlich (University of
North Florida, USA)
Information Science Reference • copyright 2024 • 286pp • H/C (ISBN: 9798369312698)
• US $240.00 (our price)

Navigating Innovative Technologies and Intelligent Systems in Modern Education
Madhulika Bhatia (Amity University, India) and Muhammad Tahir Mushtaq (Cardiff
Metropolitan Univesity, UK)
Information Science Reference • copyright 2024 • 307pp • H/C (ISBN: 9798369353707)
• US $245.00 (our price)

For an entire list of titles in this series, please visit:
http://www.igi-global.com/book-series/advances-educational-technologies-instructional-design/73678

701 East Chocolate Avenue, Hershey, PA 17033, USA
Tel: 717-533-8845 x100 • Fax: 717-533-8661
E-Mail: cust@igi-global.com • www.igi-global.com

For the educators and researchers who are working to bridge the gap between traditional academic rigor and the emerging challenges and potentials of artificial intelligence in higher education. You are an inspiration in navigating the future of teaching and learning.

Table of Contents

Detailed Table of Contents

As artificial intelligence (AI) models become widespread, South African universities need policies that balance access and uphold standards. Literature shows generative AI offers opportunities like personalised support, but risks like plagiarism require addressing. Current university guidance focuses narrowly on misconduct, not innovation. Principles proposed for policies include recognising AI's value if governed well; developing inclusive policies through participation; regular updating as AI advances rapidly; effectively communicating policies; anticipating AI's impact across teaching, learning, research, and assessment; and partnering between universities and AI companies. Case studies show involving stakeholders is vital. Comprehensive policies outlining ethical use across contexts are lacking. Guidance tends to emphasise constraints, not possibilities. However, responsible leveraging can expand access without compromising literacy development. This needs evidence-based governance upholding enduring educational values amid emerging tools.

The chapter explores the transformative potential and challenges of integrating large language models (LLMs) into higher education. It highlights the opportunities

AI presents for enhancing academic literacy, writing, and pedagogy, while also acknowledging the risks to traditional educational values and practices. It proposes a framework, developed with the guidance of academic literacy, information literacy, digital literacy, and academic integrity, aimed at leveraging AI's capabilities to support academic success without undermining foundational skills. The discussion extends to the implications of AI in the South African educational context, addressing the digital divide and advocating for equitable access to technology. This chapter encapsulates the essence of the proposed proactive framework for navigating AI's impact on academia, focusing on adaptation, critical engagement, and the cultivation of an advanced form of academic literacy that integrates AI technologies responsibly.

Chapter 3

Charles Wiggill, Stadio Higher Education, South Africa & University of Johannesburg, South Africa
Jacqueline Batchelor, University of Johannesburg, South Africa

This chapter explores the integration of artificial intelligence (AI) in South African K-12 education and its influence on literacy, especially as students progress to higher education. It addresses the varying levels of school development in South Africa and the challenges teachers face, including infrastructure issues and differing attitudes towards AI. Using Rogers' diffusion of innovations model, teachers are categorised into five groups, from innovators to laggards, to assess their openness to AI in education. The study emphasises the crucial role of early adopters in successfully implementing AI technologies. It suggests that by supporting innovators and early adopters, significant improvements in literacy levels in schools could be achieved, potentially elevating literacy in higher education. The chapter discusses AI's potential to transform traditional educational models and its role in literacy enhancement within South Africa's K-12 sector.

Chapter 4

Dickson Kanakulya, Makerere University, Uganda

There is high potential for AI in education, but the technology also presents creative learning challenges. Educationists are experimenting with AI which is re-configuring creativity learning. Reports indicate a creativity crisis in contemporary education, and this chapter investigates whether the adoption of AI will enhance or diminish human creativity. The chapter posits that due to AI's focus on artificial efficiency, the reductionism decreases human literary creative freedom and risks creating automated brains. AI's LLMs focus on reductive artificial linguistic efficiency which narrows literary variation, eroding the spell power of human language. Artificial intelligence can reconfigure but could not replace human creativity. Since creativity undergirds human inventions, business, social development, and progress, it needs to be protected and enhanced. There is need for research into enhancing authentic human literary and philosophical creativity in the time of AI.

Chapter 5

    Veronika Makarova, University of Saskatchewan, Canada
    Zhi Li, University of Saskatchewan, Canada
    Zhengxiang Wang, Stony Brook University, USA

This chapter reports the results of a pilot study investigating the potential of ChatGPT to assess (or grade) texts produced by international graduate students whose mother tongue is other than English (IGS). The chapter overviews some suggested applications of ChatGPT to academic writing (AW) and particularly, for English as an additional language (EAL) contexts. Most works up to date consider ChatGPT applications for literacy and writing skills development. The authors compare evaluations of texts by ChatGPT vis-à-vis human experts. The texts employed for the study are short literature reviews written by IGS in Canadian universities. The results demonstrate some potential of ChatGPT for assessment. However, while ChatGPT provides mostly relevant scores and comments related to the assessment rubrics provided, the comments are not diversified and individualized enough. ChatGPT queries for assessment should be modified and the tool trained in diversifying comments to achieve better results.

Chapter 6

    Mirna Ibrahim, Ain Shams University, Egypt

Literacy education aims to develop students' reading, writing, speaking, and listening skills. Collaborative learning and peer feedback can enhance literacy development, but effectively facilitating these in the classroom presents challenges. This chapter explores how artificial intelligence (AI)-driven tools can be leveraged to augment collaboration and peer feedback in literacy tasks. AI features such as machine learning, natural language processing, and sentiment analysis are examined for their potential to make collaborative literacy learning more engaging, equitable, and productive. Examples of existing implementations demonstrate the feasibility of these approaches. Risks such as over-reliance on automation and bias in algorithms are also discussed, emphasizing the importance of human oversight when integrating AI into education.

Chapter 7

Aulia Puspaning Galih, Eötvös Loránd University, Budapest, Hungary
Ágnes Hajdu Barát, Eötvös Loránd University, Budapest, Hungary

In the big data era, we generate, use, and share data from many sources. Quantitative survey or experiment results are no longer the only data in academia. Data collection using artificial intelligence is common in academic and research settings, especially in meta-analysis. Data literacy involves understanding, analyzing, and communicating data. Everyone in higher education needs data literacy. Students must understand statistics to correctly interpret data, communicate research findings, and build evidence-based arguments. Artificial intelligence could help solve complex practical and academic problems in sustainable development research. Data literacy must be taught to stakeholders to help them analyze research data for sustainable higher education research. Additionally, higher education institutions must teach artificial intelligence to sustain their research. Transliteracy is another data literacy and AI education future concept. Transliteracy offers a new perspective on how higher education stakeholders with knowledge of education and academic communication can collaborate to better serve future generations.

Chapter 8

Kelly Burmeister Long, University of North Georgia, USA
Katherine Rose Adams, University of North Georgia, USA

This collaborative autoethnographic study explores the integration of AI tools in doctoral education, focusing on instructional methods, program planning, and curriculum development. Drawing on faculty experiences, strengths such as content speed and organization are identified alongside weaknesses like trustworthiness issues and limited critical thinking abilities. Implications highlight the need for quality assurance, AI literacy training, and clear policies. Recommendations include establishing guidelines, proper AI tool attribution, and continued research to understand AI's impact. The study underscores the importance of thoughtful integration of AI to maximize benefits while addressing limitations effectively.

Chapter 9

Oscar Oliver Eybers, University of Pretoria, South Africa

In the ever-evolving higher education landscape, the integration of AI, particularly Generative AI (GenAI), is causing a profound shift. This chapter explores how GenAI is reshaping teaching, learning, and academic literacies. Academic literacies facilitators now navigate a diverse terrain, bridging traditional materials, digital resources, and AI-enhanced texts. They cultivate scholars' proficiency in GenAI tools and pioneer innovative teaching methods. This chapter introduces a GenAI ontology to support this transformative journey. It equips facilitators and students to use GenAI effectively, fostering tailored teaching methods and personalised literacies assessments. In summary, this chapter presents GenAI's potential to innovate, enhance accessibility, and elevate academic prowess in higher education.

Preface

In recent years, the integration of artificial intelligence (AI) into various domains has sparked transformative advancements, and education is no exception. As editors, we are excited to present this edited reference book, *AI Approaches to Literacy in Higher Education*, which delves into the intersection of AI and literacy with a specific focus on higher education settings.

Our aim in compiling this volume is to explore the myriad ways in which AI can be harnessed to bolster literacy skills among students in higher education. Through an array of research studies, case analyses, and theoretical insights, we endeavor to illuminate the innovative methodologies, tools, and applications that hold promise in enhancing literacy development and improving learning outcomes.

This book serves as a platform to extend scholarly inquiry into the evolving landscape of academic literacy, while concurrently venturing into the burgeoning realm of AI. By offering fresh perspectives and practical insights, we aspire to contribute to the ongoing discourse surrounding AI's role in promoting literacy within higher education contexts.

Designed for educators, researchers, instructional designers, and practitioners alike, this volume is poised to offer valuable guidance and inspiration. Whether you are engaged in literacy instruction, educational technology, curriculum development, or pedagogical innovation, we believe that the diverse insights presented herein will prove invaluable to your professional endeavors.

We extend our gratitude to the contributors whose expertise and dedication have enriched this compilation. It is our hope that this book will serve as a catalyst for continued exploration, dialogue, and innovation at the nexus of AI and literacy in higher education.

ORGANIZATION OF THE BOOK

1.   **GenAI Policy for Academic Literacy in South African Higher Education**

Helena Kruger-Roux and Retha Alberts from the University of Pretoria delve into the realm of policy-making concerning academic literacy in South African higher education. Their chapter examines the implications of integrating AI into literacy policies, offering insights into how such initiatives can shape the educational landscape.

2.   **Ethical AI Integration in Academia: Developing a Literacy-Driven Framework for LLMs in South African Higher Education**

Zander Janse van Rensburg and Sonja van der Westhuizen, affiliated with North-West University, explore the ethical dimensions of AI integration in academia, focusing specifically on the development of a literacy-driven framework for LLMs (Masters of Laws) in South African higher education. Their chapter emphasizes the importance of ethical considerations in leveraging AI for literacy enhancement.

3.   **The Impact of AI Requires Integration Across K-12 and Tertiary Learning**

Charles Wiggill and Jaqueline Batchelor, representing Stadio School of Education and University of Johannesburg respectively, discuss the necessity of integrating AI across the educational continuum, from K-12 to tertiary learning. Their chapter underscores the significance of holistic AI integration to maximize its impact on literacy development.

4.   **From Automated Arms to Automated Brains: Robotic Human Learning and the Future of Literary and Philosophical Creativity**

Dickson Kanakulya from Makerere University, Uganda, explores the intersection of robotics, human learning, and creativity. His chapter investigates how advancements in AI and robotics may influence literary and philosophical creativity, offering a thought-provoking glimpse into the future of education.

5.   **Can ChatGPT Grade Non-native Academic English Writing?**

Veronika Makarova, Zhi Li, and Zhengxiang Wang, affiliated with the University of Saskatchewan and Stony Brook University, delve into the capabilities of ChatGPT in grading non-native academic English writing. Their chapter critically evaluates the potential of AI in assessing language proficiency, particularly in academic contexts.

6.   **AI as a Collaborative Partner: Fostering Peer Feedback and Cooperation for Higher Education Literacy**

Mirna Ibrahim, from Ain Shams University, Egypt, explores the collaborative potential of AI in fostering peer feedback and cooperation for higher education literacy. Her chapter highlights innovative approaches to leveraging AI as a supportive tool in literacy instruction.

7.   **Data Literacy and Artificial Intelligence in Higher Education**

Aulia Galih and Ágnes Hajdu Barát, associated with Eötvös Loránd University, Hungary, investigate the intersection of data literacy and artificial intelligence in higher education. Their chapter explores the role of AI in enhancing data literacy skills among students, addressing the evolving needs of the digital age.

8.   **Application of ChatGPT in Doctoral Education and Programming: A Collaborative Autoethnography**

Katherine Rose Adams and Kelly Burmeister Long, representing the University of North Georgia, USA, present a collaborative autoethnography on the application of ChatGPT in doctoral education and programming. Their chapter offers a reflective exploration of AI integration in academia, providing insights from both practitioner and researcher perspectives.

9.   **A GenAI Ontology for Academic Literacies Teaching and Learning Practices**

Oscar Eybers, from the University of Pretoria, South Africa, presents a GenAI ontology for academic literacies teaching and learning practices. His chapter introduces a conceptual framework that harnesses AI to enhance academic literacy instruction, providing a foundation for innovative pedagogical approaches.

CONCLUSION

As editors, we are delighted to present this comprehensive exploration of AI approaches to literacy in higher education. Through the diverse perspectives offered by our esteemed contributors, this edited reference book sheds light on the multifaceted intersections of AI and literacy, offering insights into its potential to revolutionize teaching and learning practices.

From the development of ethical frameworks to the practical applications of AI in grading and peer feedback, each chapter contributes to a nuanced understanding of how AI can be leveraged to promote literacy skills among students. Moreover, the discussions on data literacy, robotic human learning, and collaborative autoethnography showcase the breadth of possibilities that AI presents for reshaping educational paradigms.

As we conclude this volume, it is evident that the integration of AI into higher education holds immense promise for advancing literacy instruction. However, it is essential to navigate this terrain with careful consideration of ethical implications, pedagogical best practices, and the diverse needs of learners. By fostering collaboration, innovation, and critical inquiry, we can harness the transformative potential of AI to cultivate a more literate and empowered generation of students.

Oscar Oliver Eybers
University of Pretoria, South Africa

Alan Muller
University of Pretoria, South Africa

Introduction

Since humanity's earliest days on Earth, we have applied education, or academics, as well as diverse forms of literacies to interact with each other, with the natural environment and to interpret the broader universe of which we are a part. In these spheres, humans used various technologies to advance, modify and disseminate knowledge. Whether - as in Africa, knowledge was embodied through dance, dramatic enactments, or architecture and wearing masks to communicate connections with powers and entities greater than ourselves - there has always been an extra-human, yet humane mode of utilizing literacies to convey knowledge, academically.

After tens of thousands of years, when humans employed embodied and oral literacies, there was a gradual shift to utilizing material records, including signs with semantic meaning. For example, the first material records humanity used for recorded semiotics and signs emerged when cultural groups including Khoi and San of southern Africa utilized rock beds, mountain walls, animal bones, skins and other natural materials to inscribe epistemologies, histories and knowledge systems. As early humans shifted from purely oral and embodied modes of academics and literacies, to what some disciplines name visual and graphical art, they enabled the solidification of knowledge outside of the human body through extra-human semiotics.

It may be difficult for present-day scholars, researchers and academic literacy facilitators to construe humanity's first, ancient embodied and subsequently material and semiotic mediums as the first academic literacies. Additionally, it might be equally tasking to link these ancient mediums with the emergence of GenAI technologies. This chronological disjuncture is partially as a result of the passage of tens of thousands of years since humans, some in Africa, practiced ancient academic literacies in oral and embodied modes. Nonetheless, consciousness of the continuum of embodied, oral, graphic to systemic, alphabetical literacies through GenAI technologies is vital. By bearing in mind key transitions in academic knowledge preservation and dissemination, scholars may further probe the impacts of new literacies, including those emerging from GenAI technologies.

The transition from centralized, embodied and oral modes to material, systemic scripts in ancient societies, metaphorically, reflects the recent birth and effects of Large Language Models in the current academic dispensation. For example, during ancient literary revolutions, such as those observed amidst the start of extended, alphabetical systems in Ethiopia and ancient Egypt, humans can be argued to have initiated the first Large Language Models. Initially in Africa, manuscripts emerged on papyrus leaves and on the walls of deceased monarchs' tombs, as well as those of esteemed priests and scribes. These practices, unlike previous literary, oral dispensations, allowed humans to record knowledge for longer periods of time, in a systematic manner. Congruently, the establishment of the original systemic semiotics, alphabets and language models academic literacies were irrevocably altered.

In much the same way that ancient humans who initiated the first Large Language Models, academic literacy facilitators in the present age face similar challenges. For example, the genesis of writing introduced new ways of knowing and understanding in disciplines. Hence, writing led to new demands related to teacher training, blending of written and oral, embodied mediums through alphabetical codes, standardization of disciplinary communication. Further, the introduction of writing as a Large Language Model necessitated new teachers' methods of integrating written and oral literacies, including dramatic enactments in vocational contexts, as well as riddles, proverbs and other forms of prose.

In a similar fashion to ancient Africans who facilitated some of humanity's earliest transitions from embodied, oral to systemic records and scripts, present-day higher education practitioners and academic literacy facilitators are at the precipice of an epistemological revolution through Generative Artificial Intelligence that is altering how knowledge is recorded, argued, modified and represented. Like the ancient priests, scribes and elite members of Ethiopian and Kemetian cloisters who concurrently improved the ways in which knowledge is preserved, yet who also enabled hierarchical societal relations as a result of the emergence of scripted, Large Language Models, contemporary academic literacy facilitators are faced with comparable prospects of ushering knowledge into the future.

In ancient societies, from Africa, to Mesopotamia and as far East as India and China, writing developments reflecting the advent of GenAI altered societal organization and structures. Specifically, as humans across the globe transitioned from hunter, gatherer and pastoral modes to sedentary lifestyles, existing language models evolved to incorporate systemic, material records into embodied and oral expressions of knowledge. Yet, what is vital for present-day academic literacy facilitators who encounter new GenAI technologies – as related to humanity's shift to systemic scripts and records – is the power and influence of philosophies and literacies in shaping societal structures. As during pre-B.C. shifts from embodied and oral to systemic records, GenAI is revolutionizing contemporary educators' capabilities in knowledge development that can generate equitable social structures.

The matter of social equity, justice, hierarchies, whether in higher education or greater society, is a critical consideration for present-day academic literacy facilitators. This is because it was the original global scribes, priests and philosophers, in all regions of the globe, who facilitated their community's shifts from oral and embodied to systemic scripts, writing and Large Language Models. Globally, the original writing processes were organized by small, elite clusters of individuals. Likely, in present-day higher education systems, academic literacies facilitators working at the intersection of disciplinary epistemologies and new GenAI technologies could occupy elite social standings. Complicating this reality is that in South Africa, possibly reflecting other economically developing nations. According to the Organization for Economic Co-operation and Development (2019), approximately 6% of inhabitants in South Africa attend higher education. So, there is a global risk that if utilized unethically, or in ways that elaborate ideological and conceptual frameworks that breed unequal societal hierarchies, GenAI can replicate and broaden already existing epistemic and ontological inequalities active in global higher education systems.

New and emerging technologies, including Large Language Models such as ChatGPT, Gemini and CoPilot are currently transforming discourses around teaching, learning and assessing in universities. This indicates that scholars, researchers and academic literacy developers are at the precipice of a pedagogical revolution, poised to alter knowledge production in greater society. There are three pathways, according to observations in the chapters of this book, that GenAI is transforming knowledge generation in university disciplines. Firstly, GenAI is transforming policies that frame how educational experiences are designed. Secondly, authors of this manuscript are concerned about pedagogical impacts of GenAI applications among novice scholars. Thirdly, as conduits of knowledge, this manuscript narrows its focus on the interplay of academic literacy practices and knowledge production.

As with the evolving nature of embodied to oral and then systemic, material scripts in ancient, international societies - the emergence of GenAI Large Language Models is propelling governments and higher educational institutions to critically undergo re-assessment of their policies concerning the impacts of disciplinary knowledge on- and off-campus. Therefore, due to the massive impact of GenAI technologies in universities, there has been a move to updating teaching and learning, language and ethics policies that govern knowledge production in evolving ways. As is to be expected, any change in institutional policies around teaching, learning and assessments that draw on GenAI technology is bound to impact academic literacy development. Academic literacies are the discursive conduits of disciplinary epistemes, and any policy adjustment will affect teachers' and learners' development.

Academic literacy facilitators in higher education require consciousness of global, national and institutional policies surrounding GenAI technologies. As developers and facilitators of the conduits of knowledge in disciplines, academic literacy facilitators need to contribute to emerging discourses that are shaping the parameters and ethical frameworks that are determined acceptable for knowledge production. To illustrate, in developing and developed nations' contexts, such contributions necessitate academic literacy agents' inclusion of indigenous knowledge systems and languages in academic fields. Through academic literacy facilitators contribution to policy discourses around GenAI and ethics, the assurance that integration of students' multilingual skills with academic literacy outcomes can be secured.

Subsequent to policy formation, novel GenAI technologies require academic literacies facilitators inputs into the designing of new teaching, learning and assessment methods that incorporate or are developed by GenAI tools. As a case in point, similar to ancient writers' facilitation of the transition to and adoption of systemic literacies and records, academic literacy facilitators in universities' disciplines are essential agents for forging new GenAI frontiers and modes of cultivating disciplinary identities. Congruently, methodologies of activating disciplinary knowledge through diverse GenAI textual and contextual modes is the responsibility of academic literacy facilitators. In this vein, and as manifested throughout the chapters of this manuscript, contributing authors explore new and emerging policy and pedagogical frameworks that incorporate GenAI capabilities.

GenAI and the Future of Academic Literacies

As you, the reader, navigate the forthcoming chapters it is essential to bear in mind the historical continuum of academics and literacies. Your contextualization will be shaped by your geographic, epistemic and ontological affiliations. It is for this reason that earlier, repeated mention was made of the transition of embodied, to oral and subsequently, graphic and visual to systemic scripts and literacies. By starting with the various global origins of humanity's literacies and working our way through thousands of years of history that bring us to the present, academic literacy facilitators can theoretically and practically situate GenAI in local disciplines and domains of practice. Diverse nations, communities and educational institutions cater to the needs of their geographies. Hence, it is crucial that academic literacy facilitators and disciplinary practitioners draw on the needs, hopes and aspirations of local communities to further their social and economic development with the needed capabilities of GenAI.

One of the primary motivations for academic literacy facilitators to be at the forefront of GenAI technologies in disciplinary spheres, with a retrospective view on global, societal stratification that emerged partially as a result of systemic, alphabetical semiotics in ancient societies, is that similarly, GenAI Large Language Models can enhance democratization processes in and outside universities. Recall that in ancient Ethiopia and Kemet, it was the writing of priests, philosopher-scribes as in other ancient civilizations, which sustained the legal, governance orders of their day. However, as asserted above, these individuals constituted a minute percentage of the greater society.

At the same time, unequal access to GenAI tools in the present age stands to elaborate social, economic, epistemological and economic inequalities facing humanity and with which university disciplines grapple. In accord, it is essential that acknowledgement, from the classroom to institutional and societal governance structures - of a cohesive social ontology, specifically as related to conventions framing academic literacies is articulated. In so doing, new university entrants, especially first-year students, may be introduced to GenAI knowledge generation literacies that are ethical, non-harmful and which value the equitable and just development of humanity in the various cultural ecologies in which we live.

To understand academic literacy facilitators' roles in facilitating interactions between scholars, local communities, expert industries and GenAI technologies, it is necessary for disciplinary members and researchers to develop new technology philosophies. Afterall, GenAI is an extension of previous computer and literacies technologies. An emerging GenAI technological philosophy, as previously framed by scholars including Sellars (1962) and Mitcham (1994) necessitates critical dialogues regarding practical applications of GenAI tools themselves, as well as underlying humane objectives for incorporating new technologies, such as Large Language Models, into and to improve various spheres of human existence.

In this manner, innovative technologies in the GenAI domain can be harnessed to eradicate poverty, societal tensions and inequalities, hierarchical imbalances between nations, cultural communities, as well as war and conflict. From these perspectives, academic literacy facilitators and disciplinary members wielding GenAI technologies enhance their capacities to unify and divide humanity. In historical frameworks, as in ancient Ethiopia, Kemet, Mesopotamia as well as the near and far East, facilitators of GenAI educational applications can cultivate exclusive, elite disciplinary archives; alternatively, we can harness our knowledge and expertise and distribute it equitably, ethically and epistemically inclusively through Large Language Models.

One of the strategies academic literacy facilitators, and on a broader scale – institutions of higher education – can employ to utilize GenAI tools for purposes of social justice is centralizing the principle of epistemic inclusivity. Epistemic inclusivity displays when the academic literacy curriculum, teaching, learning and assessment experiences enable and motivate students to display their full range of intelligences and technological aptitudes. Inclusivity equally involves allowing students to draw on their multilingual and pre-epistemic knowledge traditions. In this respect, GenAI technologies have unleashed an array of new mediums through which students' creativity, knowledge interpretation and production can be facilitated through personalized instruction, methods that were previously constrained as a result of university's financial and digital barriers.

Although there are multiple ways that GenAI technologies are transforming teaching, learning and assessment in institutions of higher learning, four features stand out. The first is the capability of Large Language Models (LLMs) to generate personalized instruction to novice scholars. The second innovative pathway is the capacity of LLMs to interact with academic literacy students by tapping into their in-built, and trained databases. The third revolutionary feature of GenAI tools in pedagogic and academic literacy arenas is their ability to allow academic literacy facilitators to tailor teaching and learning to students' areas of strength and weakness. Lastly, when deployed as chatbots, LLMs possess pedagogic agency that, if effectively primed, can supplement face-to-face human tuition in accord with academic literacy learning outcomes. Let us explore the enabling and pedagogic capacities of GenAI tools.

With the advent of massification in higher education as well as the increasing time that has lapsed since global educational communities have systemically incorporated ancestral epistemes into disciplinary instruction, personalized educational practices are rare. To demonstrate, university lecturers, including academic literacy staff, are often overwhelmed with large student numbers in lecture halls, tutorials and practical sessions. This status quo is different from ancestral pedagogic traditions where families, gendered age-grades and expert disciplinary clusters were responsible for ensuring all the youth received personalized education for the benefit of the entire community. In the present age, however, new GenAI applications allow academic literacy facilitators and disciplinary instructors to personalize teaching, learning and assessments in ways that not long before were difficult to implement.

Globally, within hunter-gather and pastoral cultures, community elders recognized that each child possessed unique talents, skills, needs and disciplinary preferences. In such a way, the gradual education and integration of children into vocational practices was facilitated to ensure that on the one hand, youth acquired essential knowledge and skills to care for themselves and their families. On the other hand, education and ancient academic literacies were also cultivated to secure holistic needs of the community, clan and extended village networks. To achieve the aforementioned pedagogic goals, individualized teaching and student feedback was vital. In this context, individualized education involved personalized feedback on tasks, along with consistent progress reports. In a comparable manner, GenAI teaching and learning tools allow present-day academic literacy facilitators to implement personalized education.

If global governments and institutions of higher education invest in Large Language Models it is feasible to reintroduce humanity's original, personalized modes of education. That is, as a result of GenAI technologies it is now within the reach of academic literacy facilitators to overcome epistemic, disciplinary, linguistic and agential hurdles to design new teaching, learning and assessment modes that adapt to the peculiar skills and aptitudes of each student. One beneficial offshoot of Large Language Models, as analyzed in this manuscript, is chatbots. Through the capabilities of chatbots, which can be trained to converse with humans according to module specific and disciplinary data, personalized methods are implementable. GenAI now allows new university entrants to interact with the curriculum without pressures of large lecture halls, linguistic insecurities that may emerge from dominant institutional tongues and longstanding, unimodal assessment practices.

Personalized modes of academic literacy facilitation, as practiced in ancient Africa and other global hunter-gatherer, pastoral and indigenous educational modes, transpire when the pace of learning and students' agency are central in their navigations of the curriculum (Kucirkova, Gerard & Lynn, 2021). (Personalized, or individualized methods of instruction, allows contemporary educators and academic literacy facilitators to overcome experiences of epistemic rigidity as encountered through unimodal and multiple choice assessments. The rigidity of these evaluative mechanisms prevent students from displaying their creativity, diverse multilingual and multimodal literacies when interacting with domain-specific theories and vocabularies of disciplines. GenAI technologies, in contrast, when primed to cultivate critical thinking, argumentative reasoning and graphic visualizations of disciplines' focal areas - are capable of overcoming the unbending borders of monolingual, multiple choice tests by requiring students' multimodal and critical discourses.

Academic literacy facilitators are suitably positioned, not only in institutions of higher learning, but also throughout greater society to bring transformation, social justice through GenAI technologies, in the same way that the emergence of systemic, material scripts and records in ancient Africa and throughout the globe forever altered social structures, governance modes, interactions with the land as well as humans' ontologies. The paradox facing academic literacy facilitators, though, is that in a similar fashion to the ancient scribes who had to make a choice to write on behalf of hierarchical societal visions, or according to more egalitarian precepts and principles – in the present day and age decisions also need to be made around matters of social justice. That is: Do academic literacy facilitators and disciplinary educators utilize new GenAI technologies for further entrenchments of societal inequalities, or do we harness these tools to cultivate more egalitarian and sustainable social ecologies?

These are questions that you, the reader, will have to navigate as you navigate through the insights generated, and propositions advanced in the ensuing chapters.

For now, whether our interactions with academic literacies and new, emerging GenAI technologies are from the perspectives of policymakers and researchers, teachers, curriculum and instructional designers or students, there are shared imperatives that we can consider.

This Book in the Age of GenAI

Compiling a book under any circumstance, we think any editor will agree, is a challenge of tremendous proportions. It requires an editor to have a clear vision of a large project, dedication to the finished artifact, dedication to potential contributors and their work, and perhaps most importantly a discerning eye when it comes to potential contributions. This last aspect, the critical eye, has been tested to new degrees in this age of GenAI. While many chapters contained in this volume consider the potential benefits of GenAI in the field of higher education, we must take some time here to reflect on the role of GenAI in putting this book together.

When the publishers and editors circulated the initial call for papers, we, the editors, assumed perhaps naively that potential contributors to our project would share our enthusiasm and insight into the new world of GenAI and the precarious position that this new technology occupies on the landscape of higher education and research. It was not long, however, before we began receiving abstracts that were clearly generated by GenAI tools. Anyone with even a passing familiarity with GenAI platforms like ChatGPT know that they tend to have strong authorial voices when untrained. Characteristically, we were pitched many projects that aimed to 'delve into' new territories and to 'seamlessly integrate' GenAI tools into unspecific educational contexts. The irony of GenAI stymying attempts by editors to compile a book on it was not lost on us, and so we proceeded to sift through proposals in favor of those that showed both clarity of thought and clarity of authorial voice.

Going forward, we corresponded with potential authors, approved abstracts, and set deadlines for final chapter submissions. And that was that... or so we thought. However, as chapters began coming in, we realized that GenAI was not done with us yet. We began reading final submissions and noticed in several cases that the 'scholarship' lacked any real real scholarship. The most frequent telltale sign that a chapter was generated by AI was that there was the lack of a literature review that the piece of writing was not situated in an existing body of cited works. This has been a hallmark of GenAI writing up to this point.

We also identified GenAI writing in the number of chapters that existed as a litany of vague pros and cons of GenAI in higher education or as a list of unspecific ways of implementing GenAI into uncontextualized university teaching and learning. These are, we believe, things that academic editors will see more and more of in times to come.

It is in light of these challenges that we extend to the contributors here our sincerest thanks for taking seriously both our project and your work and for your dedication to scholarship and academic ethics. Without your sincere and meaningful contributions, this book would not exist in its current form.

The Scope and Structure of this Book

We have spent a great deal of time (re)arranging the chapters of this volume so that the reader follows some kind of journey in thinking through GenAI in literacy in higher education. The book opens with a focus on policy and frameworks for AI in higher education, then thinks through actioned and actionable integration of AI in teaching and learning various literacies. The book concludes with two chapters that think through how AI can be used in training future academics and then how academics might apply reconsidered ontologies in the age of AI. In gathering contributions to this volume, we, the editors, and the publishers cast our nets wide so that the collected chapters present as far as possible global perspectives. With authors from Canada, Egypt, Hungary, South Africa, Uganda, and the USA, we believe that we have a volume that has views from both the Global North and Global South. We must, however, acknowledge that there is a noticeable absence of contributors from South Asia and the Far East. It is our feeling that research from these global regions is indeed both extant and forthcoming but did not reach us for inclusion in this volume.

Oscar Oliver Eybers
University of Pretoria, South Africa

Alan Muller
University of Pretoria, South Africa

REFERENCES

Kucirkova, N., Gerard, L., & Linn, M. C. (2021). Designing personalised instruction: A research and design framework. *British Journal of Educational Technology, 52*(5), 1839–1861. doi:10.1111/bjet.13119

Mitcham, C. (1994). *Thinking Through Technology: The Path Between Engineering and Philosophy*. University of Chicago Press. doi:10.7208/chicago/9780226825397.001.0001

Organisation for Economic Co-operation and Development. (2019). Country note: Education at a glance. Retrieved April 7, 2024, from https://www.oecd.org/education/education-at-a-glance/EAG2019_CN_ZAF.pdf

Sellars, W. (1962). Philosophy and the Scientific Image of Man. In R. Colodny (Ed.), *Frontiers of Science and Philosophy* (pp. 35–78). University of Pittsburgh Press.

Chapter 1

Generative Artificial Intelligence Policy for Academic Literacy in South African Higher Education

Helena Kruger-Roux
University of Pretoria, South Africa

Retha Alberts
University of Pretoria, South Africa

ABSTRACT

As artificial intelligence (AI) models become widespread, South African universities need policies that balance access and uphold standards. Literature shows generative AI offers opportunities like personalised support, but risks like plagiarism require addressing. Current university guidance focuses narrowly on misconduct, not innovation. Principles proposed for policies include recognising AI's value if governed well; developing inclusive policies through participation; regular updating as AI advances rapidly; effectively communicating policies; anticipating AI's impact across teaching, learning, research, and assessment; and partnering between universities and AI companies. Case studies show involving stakeholders is vital. Comprehensive policies outlining ethical use across contexts are lacking. Guidance tends to emphasise constraints, not possibilities. However, responsible leveraging can expand access without compromising literacy development. This needs evidence-based governance upholding enduring educational values amid emerging tools.

DOI: 10.4018/979-8-3693-1054-0.ch001

INTRODUCTION

As innovative generative artificial intelligence (GenAI) models like ChatGPT become widely available, South African higher education (HE) institutions face complex governance decisions across teaching, assessment, learning and research. While GenAI offers potential benefits such as enhanced personalized learning support and increased research productivity, overreliance on machine-generated content without prudent policies can undermine the development of foundational competencies like academic literacy and threaten academic integrity. Recent research by Duah and McGivern (2024) has highlighted the differing perspectives of students and educators:

Students showed a more open engagement with GenAI, considering it a tool for overcoming obstacles rather than a means to plagiarize. Educators were generally more cautious and less optimistic about the academic role of GenAI. Lack of clear institutional policies surrounding such tools also contributed to ethical ambiguities.

To integrate GenAI into the fabric of HE effectively, inclusive multi-stakeholder decision-making frameworks are needed to engage staff, students, and administrators in steering our common digital futures transparently and responsibly. Co-designing context-appropriate policies requires balancing the opportunities for pedagogical innovation and research efficiency with the imperative to avoid uncritical adoption of technological solutionism while addressing the varying perspectives and concerns of different stakeholders.

By harmonizing emerging GenAI tools with enduring educational values, HE institutions can embed integrity safeguards throughout instructional systems to expand access and personalisation without diminishing the rigorous analytical and communication skills at the heart of higher learning. If evidence-based governance judiciously scaffolds human-AI complementarity across the diverse functions of HE, South Africa's universities can progressively transform teaching, assessment, learning and research by leveraging AI's capacity to serve the aspirations of all stakeholders. This chapter explores the policy considerations necessary to unlock the potential of GenAI to enhance the core missions of HE institutions whilst mitigating risks to academic literacy development and navigating the ethical ambiguities that arise from the lack of clear institutional guidelines.

Early Responses to GenAI by HE

Since its launch in late 2022, ChatGPT has been heralded as a revolutionary force across many fields. However, nowhere has its impact been more evident and controversial than in education. A highly cited opinion paper by 43 scholars from diverse areas predicted that "education will experience some of this technology's 'most disruptive effects'" (Dwivedi et al., 2023, p. 53). Soon after ChatGPT's was unveiled, Microsoft incorporated its large language model into the Bing search engine, with GenAI competitors like Google's Bard and Claude swiftly emerging.

Initial HE reactions to GenAI ranged from describing it as a "bullshit spewer" that signals "the end of traditional assessments" (Rudolph et al., 2023, p. 1) to a generator of "artificial hallucinations" (Alkaissi & McFarlane, 2023, p. 1) to it being framed as a "guardian angel" that is also a devil (Tlili et al., 2023, p. 1) or a "powerful tool in education" (Tlili et al., 2023, p. 22). Eminent linguists and artificial intelligence experts also weighed in on the debate, pointing to its astonishing machine-learning capacity to search vast data for statistically probable language predictions that can seem "humanlike" while at the same time cautioning that it is far from reasoning or using language like a human (Chomsky et al., 2023):

The human mind is not, like ChatGPT and its ilk, a lumbering statistical engine for pattern matching, gorging on hundreds of terabytes of data and extrapolating the most likely conversational response or most probable answer to a scientific question. On the contrary, the human mind is a surprisingly efficient and elegant system that operates with small amounts of information; it seeks not to infer brute correlations among data points but to create explanations.

In short, ChatGPT and its brethren are constitutionally unable to balance creativity with constraint. They either overgenerate (producing both truths and falsehoods, endorsing ethical and unethical decisions alike) or undergenerate (exhibiting noncommitment to any decisions and indifference to consequences). Given the amorality, faux science and linguistic incompetence of these systems, we can only laugh or cry at their popularity.

In practice, GenAI gained many early adopters in HE, from students using the new "homework machine" (Newell, 2023), hoping it can boost academic achievement (Strzelecki, 2023, p. 3) to lecturers attempting to stay ahead of students to uphold academic integrity (Fazackerly, 2023) to postdocs leveraging it to refine their writing, coding, or organizing literature (Nordling, 2023, p. 655). A September 2023 *Nature* global survey of postdocs revealed that this group most commonly used AI chatbots for polishing writing, especially in engineering (44%) and social sciences (41%), while the uptake was lower for biomedical and clinical research (29%) (Nordling, 2023, p. 656).

With teaching, learning and research representing the core knowledge-building activities in HE, the following sections examine GenAI's impact on each domain.

GenAI and Teaching and Assessment in HE

GenAI elicits divergent perspectives regarding its potential effects on HE, especially since it can generate seemingly cogent essays within seconds (Dwivedi et al., 2023, p. 8). This capability disrupts traditional assessment methods like essay writing (Dwivedi et al., 2023, p. 4; King, 2023, p. 6), which aim to cultivate academic literacies in analysis, synthesis, structure, conventions, and time management. Consequently, GenAI enables students to cheat on assignments while avoiding plagiarism detection, potentially jeopardizing assessment integrity (Dwivedi et al., 2023, p. 3). Overreliance may also undermine motivation, innovation, and critical thinking (Thorp, 2023, p. 2). Moreover, GenAI sometimes provides inaccurate or biased outputs that require verification (Thorp, 2023, p. 6).

However, GenAI offers valuable educational applications, such as providing model answers or assisting curriculum development (Thorp, 2023, p. 2). It can also save teachers time on administrative tasks and facilitate personalized, flipped classrooms (King, 2023, p. 8). Indeed, GenAI can potentially transform education profoundly (Imran & Almusharraf, 2023, pp. 3–4).

Considering GenAI's capacity to generate exam responses swiftly, it seems set to disrupt conventional educational assessment, necessitating new evaluation methods that emphasize process over product (Tlili et al., 2023, p. 4). As AI capabilities advance, HE must grapple with GenAI's potential benefits and drawbacks to preserve academic integrity while realizing emerging opportunities.

GenAI and Learning in HE

Views differ on whether GenAI will revolutionize or severely damage learning – analysis is needed to shape policies (Strzelecki, 2023, p. 2).

GenAI's ability to provide instant, custom answers presents opportunities to facilitate student learning, like having an automated tutor (Dwivedi et al., 2023, p. 4). The technology can enhance learning by giving sample answers and explanations that improve student comprehension (Thorp, 2023, p. 2). It also enables new personalized, student-centered teaching methods to improve engagement and outcomes (King, 2023, p. 8).

While promising to innovate education, GenAI may enable shortcutting some learning processes (Imran & Almusharraf, 2023, pp. 3–4). GenAI allows students to quickly generate content like essays, which may undermine actual learning as students bypass meaningful learning processes such as effortful reading, writing and critical thinking (Dwivedi et al., 2023, p. 7; King, 2023, p. 6). Dependence on GenAI may reduce students' motivation and engagement in analyzing content (Thorp, 2023, p. 2). Some scholars believe that GenAI threatens traditional learning goals in HE, like writing competence and critical thinking, requiring the rethinking of learning objectives (Tlili et al., 2023, p. 4).

GenAI and Research in HE

With its ability to generate written texts rapidly, GenAI could significantly increase research productivity by freeing up time (Dwivedi et al., 2023, p. 4). About 30% of scientists surveyed by *Nature* reported using these tools to help write manuscripts (Prillaman, 2024, p. 3). Benefits of GenAI in research include editing and translating the writing of non-native English speakers, taking on repetitive tasks like literature reviews, and promoting productivity by helping researchers write papers faster (King, 2023, p.8; Prillaman, 2024, p. 3). Given that it is useful for polishing text, GenAI may benefit researchers from non-English speaking backgrounds.

The virtual tutor/assistant capabilities of GenAI provide opportunities to enhance scholarship and collaboration (Thorp, 2023, p.2). Other possibilities include using GenAI to find literature faster or for collaborative technology-enhanced scholarship (King, 2023, p.8). However, diverging opinions exist about whether GenAI spells revolution or danger for research priorities.

GenAI can help researchers cheat and plagiarize in writing research papers, threatening research integrity and necessitating new detection methods (Dwivedi et al., p. 3). Downsides also include the potential for language mistakes, hallucinations (fabricated information), and low-quality papers. Increasing the volume of published papers could further strain editors and peer reviewers (Prillaman, 2024, p. 4). GenAI threatens the conventional aims of competence development and idea ownership by automating research tasks (Tlili et al., 2023, p.4). Exceptional essay generation from GenAI fosters concerns about appropriating research contributions, and protection is necessary (Alkaissi & McFarlane, 2023, p. 6).

Most publishers allow some disclosed use of large language models in manuscript preparation but prohibit their use in peer review to protect confidentiality and ensure reviewers devote their full attention to the manuscript (Prillaman, 2024, pp. 4–5). Views differ regarding the acceptability of using GenAI to prepare grant proposals, with some funders prohibiting it and others allowing it with proper disclosure (Prillaman, 2024, p. 5). While useful for polishing text, dependence on GenAI may undermine the novelty, rigor, and integrity of human-led scholarship, necessitating safeguards. Regardless of evolving policies, researchers will likely continue using GenAI tools, and there is no practical way to police their use fully (Prillaman, 2024, p. 6).

Policy and the Use of GenAI in Global HE

Significant policy development about the ethical usage, impacts, and emerging issues related to AI technologies like GenAI appears necessary across HE. Needs exist concerning teaching and assessment, learning, and research.

Regarding teaching and assessment, guidelines are required on permissible GenAI assistance in student work to uphold academic standards (Thorp, 2023, p. 2). Policies may prevent misconduct enabled by GenAI tools while allowing appropriate applications to ensure positive impacts (Dwivedi et al., 2023, pp. 3–4). University policies also need updating to cover GenAI use in assignments while upholding conduct standards (Imran & Almusharraf, 2023, pp. 3–4). A recent study by Luo (2024) analyzed GenAI policies from 20 world-leading universities and found that the primary problem represented in these policies is that students may not submit original work for assessment when using GenAI. The study highlights that universities have prescribed rules such as requiring teacher approval for GenAI use, proper attribution of AI contributions, and redesigning assessments to verify students' independent work (Luo, 2024, pp. 3, 7, 9). However, Luo argues that the policies fail to acknowledge the evolving notion of originality in the digital age, as knowledge production becomes increasingly distributed, collaborative, and mediated by technology (2024, p. 1).

As far as learning is concerned, analysis is urgently required to shape policies and guidelines on the role of GenAI in achieving HE priorities (Strzelecki, 2023, p. 2). Policies can mitigate threats of GenAI to established goals like writing skills and critical thinking (Tlili et al., 2023, p. 4). Luo's study suggests that the current framing of originality in GenAI policies may stigmatize students who use the technology and discourage them from leveraging it even for legitimate learning purposes (2024, p. 10). The study calls for more nuanced and situated conceptualizations of originality in policies, recognizing the disciplinary context, learning goals, and different degrees of human-AI collaboration (Luo, 2024, p. 11).

Australian universities seem at the forefront of reflecting and reporting on updated policies for using GenAI. Fowler, Korolkiewicz and Marrone examined Australian university and media discussions in the first 100 days after ChatGPT's release (2023, p. 2). They found that 36% of universities had updated policies to address AI-enabled cheating, but none had policies guiding AI's use for learning (Fowler et al., 2023, p. 3). Recommendations include developing an AI strategy aligned with institutional goals and establishing ethical GenAI use guidelines (Fowler et al., 2023, p. 5).

De Maio (2024, p. 2) analyzed four Australian universities' academic integrity policies against a framework of an exemplary policy. It found that the policies lacked key elements like currency in addressing GenAI issues, outlining support for stakeholders, and flexibility regarding emerging misconduct enabled by AI (De

Maio, 2024, p. 6). Recommendations include regular university policy updates, clear definitions of appropriate GenAI use, and timely communication with stakeholders (De Maio, 2024, pp. 6–7). Luo's study also emphasizes the importance of open communication, student consultation, and fostering a culture of trust in developing and implementing GenAI policies (2024).

Based on the above, initial Australian university policies narrowly focused on preventing GenAI cheating rather than harnessing opportunities. Recommendations include developing a considered AI strategy, updating policies regularly, establishing GenAI use guidelines, improving communication, and investing in infrastructure and staff training. Luo's study further highlights the need for policies to take a more inclusive approach beyond the narrow lens of surveillance, reframing originality from a collaborative perspective and emphasizing support for students in producing meaningful original work (2024).

For research, policies, structures and guidelines are essential regarding proper GenAI usage and citation to address issues like plagiarism and research quality (Naidu & Sevnarayan, 2023, p. 2). Warnings have also been sounded that careless use of GenAI in research may lead to substandard papers (Nordling, 2023, p. 656) and ethical and legal issues (Dwivedi et al., 2023, p. 41). China recently published *Guidelines for Responsible Research Conduct,* ruling out the use of AI as co-authors, requiring researchers to explicitly disclose any use of AI technology in their work and banning them from using GenAI for funding applications (Bela & Peng, 2023).

In conclusion, the rapid emergence of GenAI technologies has necessitated significant policy development across global HE to address the ethical usage, impacts, and challenges related to AI in teaching, learning, and research. While Australian and leading world universities have taken proactive steps to update their policies, there is still a need for more comprehensive and inclusive approaches that go beyond merely preventing misconduct.

Unique Approaches to the Use of GenAI in Global HE

Hibernia College, Ireland, and Arizona State University (ASU), US, have adopted very different but equally innovative approaches to GenAI in HE, with Hibernia proposing an academic integrity community of practice for inclusive policy development (Casey, 2023) and ASU proactively partnering directly with an AI company to explore applications in HE responsibly (Davis, 2024).

Hibernia College proposes a novel and possibly long-term solution, namely the establishment of an academic integrity community of practice (CoP) in the tradition of inclusive policy formulation (p. 38). After the introduction of ChatGPT/GenAI, Hibernia College established a college-wide Community of Practice (CoP) on academic integrity (Casey, 2023, p. 1). Though initially focused on addressing misconduct risks from AI, discussions redirected the CoP towards improving support and co-creating resources to help students develop their own integrity practices (Casey, 2023, p. 2). Guided by conceptual frameworks on value creation and policy analysis (Casey, 2023, p. 3), the CoP conducted a collaborative review of academic integrity policies, held student focus groups, and conducted interviews to inform the development of student supports and updated policies (Casey, 2023, pp. 4–5). Through this participatory approach of situated learning and stakeholder engagement, the CoP aims to move away from punitive outcomes towards a more holistic academic integrity culture and strategy with improved accessibility and authentic student participation (Casey, 2023, pp. 2, 5). The process provides a model for deconstructing ambiguous policies into accessible resources through a CoP approach (Casey, 2023, p. 2).

ASU is unique in the degree to which they are proactive. In January 2024, ASU partnered with OpenAI to collaborate on researching and deploying conversational AI tools in HE (Davis, 2024). ASU views these advanced AI capabilities as providing personalized, optimized learning opportunities that augment human abilities rather than replacing them. The collaboration aims to enhance student success, research, innovation, creativity, and administrative efficiency (Davis, 2024).

Specific plans include staff and students submitting proposals for AI projects focused on improving learning, boosting research productivity, streamlining processes, and revolutionary educational technologies (Davis, 2024). ASU prioritizes the ethical use of data and security in implementing these tools (Davis, 2024).

The partnership builds on ASU's commitment to pioneering AI exploration for social good. For instance, ASU's Knowledge Enterprise Center leads university research on AI (Davis, 2024). ASU also recently launched an AI Accelerator program to develop new AI technologies (Davis, 2024).

Overall, ASU stresses responsibly leveraging the power of AI to chart an innovative future for HE (Davis, 2024). The goal is AI-driven transformation that aids scholarship and expands access to personalized, thorough learning at scale while upholding academic standards. Careful oversight is vital to integrating advanced systems that augment capabilities under human guidance. Continual reassessment will occur as technology rapidly evolves (Davis, 2024).

GenAI in South African HE

While the community of practice model adopted by Hibernia College and the proactive partnership approach of Arizona State University provide examples of innovative global responses to harnessing AI, we now turn to examining recent literature documenting perspectives on GenAI technologies within South African universities.

Whereas recent scholarly publications analyze the use of GenAI in the South African HE context, highlighting associated opportunities and risks, university policies reveal varied governance approaches attempting to balance academic integrity with innovation.

Scholarly Views of GenAI in South African HE

In South Africa, questions arise around authorship designation and standards where AI, like GenAI, contributes to academic writing, which may necessitate policy changes (Chaka, 2023, p. 2). As artificial intelligence proliferates in HE, associated hopes and fears emerge, requiring nuanced analysis (Tarisayi, 2024, p. 1). Experiments show that ChatGPT can generate seemingly credible responses across question types (Chaka, 2023, p. 75; Cronje, 2023, p. 100). However, human content curation and interaction best facilitate learning (Singh, 2023, p. 209). Recommendations from South African researchers include redeveloping assessments using unfamiliar contexts (Chaka, 2023, p. 101; Stack, 2023, p. 75), training staff in manually detecting AI content (Chaka, 2023, p. 101; Stack, 2023, p. 75), upgrading integrity policies (Twinomurinzi & Gumbo, 2023, p. 213), developing proper AI tool use and integrating accurate AI detection where possible (Stack, 2023, p. 75; Twinomurinzi & Gumbo, 2023, p. 207), and improving critical thinking and writing instruction beginning at school level (Twinomurinzi & Gumbo, 2023, p. 217).

Several South African authors concur that AI threatens academic integrity, assessment quality, and writing standards in HE (Chaka, 2023, p. 95; Stack, 2023, p. 65; Twinomurinzi & Gumbo, 2023, p. 212). However, Twinomurinzi and Gumbo (2023, p. 218) propose that AI can assist language and writing development under human guidance. Responsibility for addressing AI impacts is organization-wide, targeting leadership, policy, infrastructure and culture alongside student education on AI limitations (Chaka, 2023, p. 96; Stack, 2023, p. 65; Twinomurinzi & Gumbo, 2023, p. 214). Progress requires collaboration among IT, staff and executives (Twinomurinzi & Gumbo, 2023, p. 218).

A recent socio-technical study (Tarisayi, 2024) applies systems theory in analyzing staff responses to ChatGPT. The paper argues that ChatGPT should not be dismissed as a threat but viewed as expanding capabilities if adequately governed. While risks like declining integrity and critical thinking are noted, benefits like efficiency and personalisation emerge if used transparently in defined contexts to complement humans. The study advocates updating policies, assessments, and training to assimilate AI responsibly rather than resisting or hastily adopting it. Similarly, the paper emphasizes a balanced approach, aligning innovation with academic purposes through flexible governance. This entails conceptualizing AI as expanding capabilities under human oversight, not as a threat (Tarisayi, 2024).

From the above, it is clear that appropriate integration strategies are imperative to transform teaching and learning positively (Stack, 2023, p. 75; Twinomurinzi & Gumbo, 2023, p. 218; Tarisayi, 2024). Nevertheless, continual reassessment remains vital amid rapid technological change (Chaka, 2023, p. 102). Evolving AI requires ongoing staff engagement through development programs and unions to uphold educational standards (Twinomurinzi & Gumbo, 2023, p. 217). Further research on evolving impacts and best practices for transparent, effective AI use is warranted. With responsible subsystem alignment, AI can play a complementary role in improving scholarship and learning (Tarisayi, 2024).

In light of these scholarly perspectives, the following section examines how South African universities have begun responding to the challenges and opportunities presented by GenAI through developing guidelines and policies.

Existing GenAI Policies and Guidelines in South African HE

In response to the rapid emergence and growing prominence of generative AI (GenAI) technologies, South African universities have begun developing policies and guidelines to govern their use in various aspects of HE. While these efforts are still in the early stages, several institutions have taken proactive steps to address the challenges and opportunities presented by GenAI, particularly in teaching, learning, academic integrity, and research. The following section provides an overview of the existing GenAI policies and guidelines implemented by some of the leading universities in South Africa, highlighting their key features, strengths, and limitations.

The University of Cape Town stands out with its comprehensive internal guides encouraging critical, ethical usage of AI tools like generative text models (UCT, 2023). Although it has no overarching AI policy yet, extensive resources from its Senate Ethics Committee guide staff and students to employ these technologies responsibly in research, considering factors like privacy, bias, and proper attribution. However, integration into pedagogical contexts appears limited currently beyond such advice.

The University of Johannesburg (2023) published a practice note for the university community outlining principles for the responsible and ethical use of GenAI technology. These principles include taking responsibility, being informed about GenAI's capabilities and limitations, exercising transparency when using GenAI, and adhering to ethical standards. The remainder of the UJ publication highlights the benefits of using GenAI in areas like teaching, learning, research and assessments but also emphasizes the importance of maintaining academic integrity as these AI tools continue to grow. In addition, the university published a guide for staff with principles and considerations for using AI tools responsibly in teaching, learning, assessment and research. It aims to promote informed, critical adoption while addressing academic integrity concerns (University of Johannesburg, n.d.).

The university publisher, UJPress, was also the first to issue guidelines for using GenAI in publishing (UJPress, 2023).

The University of the Witwatersrand similarly lacks a broad official policy but recognizes that widely available AI writing assistants raise pressing questions about academic misconduct and integrity (University of the Witwatersrand, 2023). Thus, updated student codes now help mitigate concerns like plagiarism. Simultaneously, its teaching center formulates guidance to aid lecturers in leveraging these GenAI tools to enhance learning outcomes constructively. Workshops will also promote digital literacy on modern AI capabilities and ethical implications across the university community.

The University of Pretoria issued basic guidance on ChatGPT for staff and students, focusing on security, attribution, and transparency (University of Pretoria, 2023a). However, comprehensive policies appear lacking. The university's Department for Education Innovations also compiled a student's guide which addresses academic integrity and suggests ways of leveraging GenAI in teaching and learning (University of Pretoria, 2023b).

While South African universities have started providing basic guidance on the responsible use of generative AI tools like ChatGPT, comprehensive official policies are still lacking in this emerging area. Much of the existing guidance has focused narrowly on academic integrity risks, mitigating concerns like plagiarism and misconduct.

While these initiatives demonstrate a growing awareness of the need to address the implications of GenAI in HE, they also highlight the current limitations and narrow focus of existing policies and guidelines. As GenAI technologies continue advancing and becoming more widely adopted, South African universities must develop more comprehensive and forward-looking policies beyond academic integrity concerns. These policies should provide a framework for the ethical, responsible, and effective integration of GenAI across various contexts, including teaching, learning, research, and institutional operations. The following section explores key principles that should guide the development of such policies to ensure that South African HE institutions are well-positioned to harness the potential of GenAI while navigating its challenges.

Principles for the Development of GenAI Policy in South African HE

The development of successful GenAI policies in South African HE should be guided by several fundamental principles. These include recognizing the value and importance of GenAI in writing and other academic activities, developing inclusive policies that involve all stakeholders, effectively disseminating policies to ensure awareness and understanding, acknowledging the wide-ranging impact of GenAI on university functions, maintaining flexibility and regularly updating policies to keep pace with technological advancements, and fostering collaboration between academia and the GenAI industry. By adhering to these principles, universities can create policies that harness the benefits of GenAI while mitigating potential risks and promoting responsible use.

Recognizing the Value and Significance of GenAI in HE

As GenAI models become more widely accepted internationally, their integration into South African HE is a crucial topic of discussion. These technologies offer unique opportunities to enhance access to teaching and learning, particularly in a multilingual society where students often study in a language other than their home language. Therefore, balanced governance is essential to promote digital literacy and navigate potential risks.

Given the public accessibility of GenAI, restricting student use is exceptionally challenging, and current AI detection tools have limited accuracy. Experts suggest that managed incorporation using carefully designed prompts is more feasible and beneficial than outright bans. This approach allows GenAI to strengthen student competencies through iterative refinement, nurturing critical thinking and creativity by directly confronting misconceptions in AI-generated outputs.

By providing translations, grammar corrections, and vocabulary expansions, GenAI's language support applications are particularly valuable in assisting students studying in non-native languages. These functionalities can dramatically improve access to knowledge by overcoming linguistic barriers faced by minority groups in English-dominated academic settings. Properly guided use of GenAI may thus help to democratize learning within diverse student populations.

Addressing risks related to plagiarism, security, and bias requires the development of digital academic literacy. Hybrid human-AI approaches enable generative models to enhance personalized pedagogy by leveraging strengths while cultivating an understanding of the technology's inherent limitations.

Developing Inclusive GenAI Policies

Involving all stakeholders, including students, staff, and administrators, in the policy-making process is crucial for effectively navigating the opportunities and challenges presented by GenAI. Studies have shown that different stakeholders may have varying perspectives on the role of GenAI in HE (Luo, 2024), underscoring the importance of inclusive policy development.

Inclusive policy development can bridge the gap between policy knowledge and practical application by engaging stakeholders in a collaborative process. Involving students and staff in co-creating policies through communities of practice ensures that guidelines are accessible, actionable, and responsive to on-the-ground realities. This approach also fosters a culture of academic integrity that emphasizes preemptive resources and transparent procedures rather than punitive reactions to misconduct.

Moreover, inclusive policy development enables universities to harness the democratizing potential of GenAI while responsibly navigating risks such as plagiarism and overreliance on machine-generated content. Consulting with diverse stakeholders, including those from multilingual and multicultural backgrounds, allows universities to develop contextually resonant policies adaptable to their communities' complex needs.

Developing inclusive GenAI policies is essential for South African universities to effectively integrate these technologies into teaching, learning, and research while upholding academic integrity and promoting equitable access. By engaging all stakeholders in a collaborative and participatory process, universities can proactively harness the strengths of GenAI while navigating its challenges responsibly and progressively.

Effective Dissemination of GenAI Policies

The effective dissemination of GenAI policies is closely linked to inclusive policy development. A recent study found that over half of Swedish students were unaware of their universities' policies on GenAI models (Nordling, 2023), highlighting the importance of policy dissemination. Opaque procedures that are not widely accessed fail to actualize ethical priorities, leading to a policy-practice gap that threatens South African HE as institutions address the proliferation of AI capabilities.

Effective policy dissemination ensures enacted values through accessible pedagogical resources, transparency procedures, and accountability mechanisms woven throughout academic activities. Without broad awareness and legibility, GenAI policies lose meaning, enabling circumvention and straining enforcement capacities. Ambiguity can lead to misconduct through uncertainty, while reactive approaches damage integrity cultures amidst distrust.

To promote effective dissemination, policies should be developed collaboratively, receiving mainstream prominence across university ecosystems. Participatory drafting promotes accessibility using non-legalistic language, examples, and multimodal formats that resonate across diverse learning contexts. Multi-channel outreach, including orientation and digital literacy education, should be used to embed institutional awareness of appropriate ethical use, limitations, attribution protocols, and support access.

Learning management systems can integrate modular tools explaining key provisions, while dedicated email updates alert campus residents to new procedures and training opportunities. Classroom activities should foster proactive policy application through collaborative dilemma analysis, and embedded metrics can help track usage data, user awareness, and effectiveness indicators.

Multifaceted outreach procedures transform passive policy spectatorship into participatory codetermination. South African universities can nurture collective responsibility for equitably directing disruptive generative technologies towards democratizing social goods by prioritizing accessibility design, co-development channels, and transparency ecosystems that adaptively nourish ethical AI cultures.

Anticipate Changes Across All HE Activities

Governance addressing the multifaceted impacts of GenAI on tertiary teaching, assessments, learning, and research is critical for institutions adopting policies amidst this technological transformation. Current policies often emphasize constraints over opportunities, imposing restrictive rules that fail to accommodate ground realities across interwoven academic activities increasingly dependent on AI assistants.

Teaching protocols deserve foregrounding, as proliferating generative tools offer both promise and peril. Guidelines help lecturers balance efficiencies, customization, and critical thinking development across subjects using well-crafted prompts aligned with course outcomes. However, dependence risks under developing analytical abilities, requiring monitoring indicators to assess appropriateness against benchmarks. Training also builds digital literacy, addressing limitations around accuracy, biases, and referencing through collaborative testing.

Assessments prove contentious terrain amidst generative capacities continually synthesizing information, requiring updated policies addressing appropriate supplementary use. Open-ended creative or exploratory tasks better evaluate integrative skills than rote replication through AI-generated drafts. Formulaic high-stakes testing risks undermining human competencies and mandating evaluation reforms centered on participation, collaboration, and unstructured demonstrations. Plagiarism policies warrant reconsideration, given AI attribution through reference cultures rather than mere text ownership. Revised academic codes reject punitive assumptions valuing process deficiencies over outcomes, with scaffolded competency development replacing sanctioning disengagement.

For learning assistance, guided AI incorporation as reference tools enables personalized and proactive multilingual support, clarifying concepts or summarizing texts to strengthen understanding, especially for non-native speakers. However, dependency risks inhibit independent analytical abilities, necessitating monitoring while emphasizing metacognition. Critical reflection replaces unquestioning appropriation of generativity produced content by verifying provenance, evaluating logical coherence, and considering biases or perspectives absent within homogeneous training data. Custom recommendations facilitate self-directed exploration, though human tutoring remains essential in developing reasoning capacities.

Research utilizations also mandate governance, given that data analysis and writing automation capacities transform methodologies with risks and opportunities. Generative probing of literature corpora offers bibliographic assistance, while formulaic article drafting may constrain originality or introduce errors without review. Literature reviews and pre-registration reports increase transparency over selective reporting but still require expert validation, ensuring scholarly rigor rather than inflated productivity alone. Data privacy, consent, and vulnerable community protections must be upheld, given the potential marginalizing impacts of aggregated datasets lacking representation. Nevertheless, increased access also bears democratizing possibilities for open participation. Oversight committees grounded in practice must establish reasonable review procedures, avoiding reactionary rejection of generative technologies but sustaining deliberative scholarship values and balancing trade-offs.

Overall, HE policies addressing proliferating generative tools require embedding support, transparency, and participation mechanisms engaging multi-stakeholder communities to negotiate AI integration into complexities across interconnected domains ethically rather than just restricting unfettered usage reactively. Participative policy-making and pedagogical advancement can steer emerging assistance technologies equitably if governance sustains accessible resources and regular multilateral exchange upholding academic values amidst accelerating innovation.

The Need for Flexibility and Regular Updates of GenAI Policy

The rapid advancement of GenAI technologies necessitates HE policies that embrace flexibility and continuous revision to remain responsive. Most South African universities currently lack formal GenAI-focused policies, and efforts to address basic access and integrity concerns are still catching up. Prolonged policy development cycles often fail to pivot from broad principles towards implementation plans attuned to ground realities, and ambiguous rules enable circumventive student behaviors.

Institutions can embed flexibility by acknowledging the necessity of recurring updates in governance based on monitoring impact and gathering user feedback. Iterative roadmaps allow evidence-based review of strengths, limitations, and ethical complexities revealed through practical GenAI integration across diverse learning activities. Tracking evolving usage patterns that balance productivity, critical thinking, and attribution provides vital data to refine policies.

Annual surveys and focus groups offer mechanisms to regularly re-align procedures with user needs. Participatory processes foster cultures celebrating innovation within reasoned constraints, with students and lecturers collectively shaping priorities instead of top-down strictures dictating conduct rigidly. Recurring engagement convenes stakeholders in cycles of collaborative meaning-making around GenAI's role, enabling policies to be written accessibly rather than in ambiguous legalese.

Through iterative learning, policies avoid prescriptive narrowness. Integrating monitoring mechanisms and campus input channels fosters evidence-based, socially legitimate governance vigilant to emerging realities. Such institutional reflexivity offers promise for participatory principles to constrain unaccountable systems' harms while enabling collective possibility. The accelerating pace of generative innovation mandates proactive, permeable, and flexible policies centered on human dignity over technology alone.

Industry Partnerships

The ASU-OpenAI partnership demonstrates the importance of academia and industry working together to guide the social impacts of emerging technologies. As AI models rapidly transform possibility landscapes across knowledge areas, proactive alliances that responsibly balance needs can shape beneficial trajectories rather than leave regulation reactive against private interests. Amid funding constraints, partnerships give South African institutions vital means to sustain equitable access and direct innovation priorities for better pedagogical futures.

ASU's Center for Digital Technology in Education models aligned principles through technical architecture. OpenAI's infrastructure and resources securely expand staff and student AI explorations under ethical oversight accountable to public stakeholders over profits. Platforms enable customized, marginalized group accessibility while mandating transparency via dataset documentation and algorithmic explainability to correct biases against homogenizing standardizations. User testing feedback loops further enhance localization responsively (Davis, 2024).

Such collaborations actualize participative policy-making to meet campus needs contextually through shared breakthroughs. Joint review boards guide the development of specialized prompting methodologies and personalized recommendations for learning enhancement using up-to-date cognitive science. The documentation explains complex system behaviors and trade-offs for scholar appropriation. Partners co-publish pilot results and convene conferences to evaluate successes and challenges while community advisory boards continuously inform universal public good improvements beyond financial motives.

Partnerships offer institutions facing economic constraints vital support to sustain leading-edge student and researcher access amid increasingly computationally intensive next-generation models. Multilateral collaboration gathers high-quality usage data under university oversight to demonstrate improvements using participatory benchmarks, shifting accountability to learning communities over investors. Regional expertise tailors global tools locally.

Joint institutes also employ talented graduates as in-house ethicists, designers, and architects crafting internal codebase governance guardrails beyond external policies alone. Funding enables classroom efficiency trials, augmented course projects, and writing tools to shape evidence-guided integration. Instead of restrictive rules barely containing underground usage reactively, partnerships proactively scaffold engagement via participative infrastructure and academic resources, upholding rights protections.

CONCLUSION

In conclusion, the rapid emergence of AI models is transforming HE across the spectrum of teaching, assessment, learning, and research activities. As discussed in the introduction, these technologies bring both opportunities and risks, potentially enhancing personalized learning support and research productivity and undermining foundational competencies like academic literacy if not governed prudently.

As outlined in the first section, HE institutions' early responses to GenAI often focused narrowly on threats to academic integrity and rushing to update plagiarism policies. However, the second section on GenAI in South African HE highlights that if governed responsibly, GenAI also provides capabilities to enhance personalized, inclusive learning. For South African universities, balanced leveraging is vital to democratizing quality education amidst diversity while upholding standards.

The principles for developing GenAI in South African HE, presented in the third section, emphasize that policy-making should transparently engage stakeholders to utilize AI affordances contextually while navigating trade-offs. Partnerships can help embed safeguards within the AI infrastructure itself. With judicious integration embracing participation and flexibility, AI progression can expand human capabilities to advance scholarship rather than undermine human roles.

Progress in directing our digital futures equitably lies in continual collaborative reassessment amidst multiplying uncertainties and the collective cross-sector cooperation for public good over individual gain. This key moment calls on universities worldwide to convene multi-sector dialogues on accelerating innovation, upholding diversity, and shaping our common horizons wisely through cooperation. Hopefully, the principles outlined here provide constructive guidance for praxis as we collectively navigate the ethical ambiguities arising from the lack of clear institutional guidelines surrounding GenAI in HE.

REFERENCES

Alkaissi, H., & McFarlane, S. I. (2023). *Artificial Hallucinations in ChatGPT: Implications in Scientific Writing*. doi:10.7759/cureus.35179

Bela, V., & Peng, D. (2024, January 5). China unveils new artificial intelligence guidelines for scientists and bans use in funding applications. *South China Morning Post*. https://www.scmp.com/news/china/science/article/3206531/china-unveils-new-artificial-intelligence-guidelines-scientists-and-bans-use-funding-applications

Casey, E. (2023). Pathways to Academic Integrity: Supporting Students through a Community of Practice Approach. *European Conference on Ethics and Integrity in Academia 2023*. https://hiberniacollege.com/news/a-community-of-practice-on-academic-integrity/

Chaka, C. (2023). Detecting AI content in responses generated by ChatGPT, YouChat, and Chatsonic: The case of five AI content detection tools. *Journal of Applied Learning and Teaching*, 6(2). Advance online publication. doi:10.37074/jalt.2023.6.2.12

Chomsky, N., Roberts, I., & Watumull, J. (2023, March 8). Noam Chomsky: The False Promise of ChatGPT. *New York Times*. https://www.nytimes.com/2023/03/08/opinion/noam-chomsky-chatgpt-ai.html

Cronje, J. (2023). Exploring the Role of ChatGPT as a Peer Coach for Developing Research Proposals: Feedback Quality, Prompts, and Student Reflection. *Electronic Journal of e-Learning*. Advance online publication. doi:10.34190/ejel.21.5.3042

Davis, A. (2024, January 24). A new collaboration with OpenAI charts the future of AI in higher education. *ASU News*. https://news.asu.edu/20240118-university-news-new-collaboration-openai-charts-future-ai-higher-education

De Maio, C. (2024). Institutional responses to ChatGPT. *Journal of Academic Language and Learning*, 18(1), T1–T8. https://journal.aall.org.au/index.php/jall/article/view/917

Duah, J. E., & McGivern, P. (2024). How generative artificial intelligence has blurred notions of authorial identity and academic norms in higher education, necessitating clear university usage policies. *The International Journal of Information and Learning Technology*. doi:10.1108/IJILT-11-2023-0213

Dwivedi, Y. K., Kshetri, N., Hughes, L., Slade, E. L., Jeyaraj, A., Kar, A. K., Baabdullah, A. M., Koohang, A., Raghavan, V., Ahuja, M., Albanna, H., Albashrawi, M. A., Al-Busaidi, A. S., Balakrishnan, J., Barlette, Y., Basu, S., Bose, I., Brooks, L., Buhalis, D., ... Wright, R. (2023). Opinion Paper: "So what if ChatGPT wrote it?" Multidisciplinary perspectives on opportunities, challenges and implications of generative conversational AI for research, practice and policy. *International Journal of Information Management*, *71*, 102642. doi:10.1016/j.ijinfomgt.2023.102642

Fazackerly, A. (2023, March 19). AI makes plagiarism harder to detect, argue academics – in paper written by chatbot. *The Guardian*. https://www.theguardian.com/technology/2023/mar/19/ai-makes-plagiarism-harder-to-detect-argue-academics-in-paper-written-by-chatbot

Fowler, S., Korolkiewicz, M., & Marrone, R. (2023). First 100 days of ChatGPT at Australian universities: An analysis of policy landscape and media discussions about the role of AI in higher education. *Learning Letters*, *1*, 1–1. doi:10.59453/JMTN6001

Imran, M., & Almusharraf, N. (2023). Analyzing the role of ChatGPT as a writing assistant at higher education level: A systematic review of the literature. *Contemporary Educational Technology*, *15*(4), ep464. doi:10.30935/cedtech/13605

King, M. R. (2023). A Conversation on Artificial Intelligence, Chatbots, and Plagiarism in Higher Education. [A conversation on artificial intelligence, chatbots, and plagiarism in higher education]. *Cellular and Molecular Bioengineering*, *16*(1), 1–2. doi:10.1007/s12195-022-00754-8 PMID:36660590

Luo, J. (2024). A critical review of GenAI policies in higher education assessment: A call to reconsider the "originality" of students' work. *Assessment & Evaluation in Higher Education*, 1–14. https://www.tandfonline.com/doi/full/10.1080/02602938.2024.2309963

Naidu, K., & Sevnarayan, K. (2023). ChatGPT: An ever-increasing encroachment of artificial intelligence in online assessment in distance education. *Online Journal of Communication and Media Technologies*, *13*(3), e202336. Advance online publication. doi:10.30935/ojcmt/13291

Newell, S. (2023). ChatGPT the homework machine. *HERDSA Connect*, 26–26.

Nordling, L. (2023). How ChatGPT is transforming the postdoc experience. *Nature*, *622*(7983), 655–657. doi:10.1038/d41586-023-03235-8 PMID:37845528

Prillaman, M. (2024, February 28). Is ChatGPT making scientists hyper-productive? The highs and lows of using AI. *Nature, 627*(8002), 16–17. Advance online publication. doi:10.1038/d41586-024-00592-w PMID:38418736

Rudolph, J., Tan, S., & Teaching, S. T.-J. (2023). ChatGPT: Bullshit spewer or the end of traditional assessments in higher education? *Journal of Applied Learning and Teaching, 6*(1). Advance online publication. doi:10.37074/jalt.2023.6.1.9

Singh, M. (2023). Maintaining the integrity of the South African university: The impact of ChatGPT on plagiarism and scholarly writing. *South African Journal of Higher Education, 37*(5). Advance online publication. doi:10.20853/37-5-5941

Stack, M. (2023). *E-Journal of Humanities, Arts and Social Sciences (EHASS) Investigating an Assessment Design that Prevents Students from Using ChatGPT as the Sole Basis to Pass Assessment at the Tertiary Level.* doi:10.38159/ehass.20234127

Strzelecki, A. (2023). To use or not to use ChatGPT in higher education? A study of students' acceptance and use of technology. *Interactive Learning Environments,* 1–14. Advance online publication. doi:10.1080/10494820.2023.2209881

Tarisayi, K. S. (2024). ChatGPT use in universities in South Africa through a socio-technical lens. *Cogent Education, 11*(1), 2295654. Advance online publication. doi:10.1080/2331186X.2023.2295654

Thorp, H. H. (2023). ChatGPT is fun, but not an author. *Science, 379*(6630), 313. doi:10.1126/science.adg7879 PMID:36701446

Tlili, A., Shehata, B., Adarkwah, M. A., Bozkurt, A., Hickey, D. T., Huang, R., & Agyemang, B. (2023). What if the devil is my guardian angel: ChatGPT as a case study of using chatbots in education. *Smart Learning Environments, 10*(1), 1–24. https://link.springer.com/article/10.1186/s40561-023-00237-x

Twinomurinzi, H., & Gumbo, S. (2023). ChatGPT in Scholarly Discourse: Sentiments and an Inflection Point. *Communications in Computer and Information Science, 1878 CCIS,* 258–272. https://link.springer.com/chapter/10.1007/978-3-031-39652-6_17

UCT. (2023). *Senate Ethics in Research Committee (EiRc) Guidelines and recommendations for the use of generative artificial intelligence (AI) tools in research.* https://uct.ac.za/sites/default/files/media/documents/uct_ac_za/87/EiRC_GenerativeAI_guideline_Oct2023_final.pdf

UJPress. (2023). *Artificial Intelligence and Generative AI Policy.* https://ujonlinepress.uj.ac.za/index.php/ujp/AI

University of Johannesburg. (2023). *UJ practice note: Generative artificial intelligence in teaching, learning and research.* https://www.uj.ac.za/wp-content/uploads/2023/08/uj-ai-practice-guide-2023.pdf

University of Johannesburg. (n.d.). *Staff guide: Generative artificial intelligence in teaching, learning and research.* https://www.uj.ac.za/wp-content/uploads/2023/08/uj-ai-guidelines-staff.pdf

University of Pretoria. (2023a). *Guide for ChatGPT usage in teaching and learning.* https://www.up.ac.za/media/shared/391/pdfs/up-guide-for-chatgtp-for-teaching-and-learning.zp233629.pdf

University of Pretoria. (2023b). *Leveraging Generative Artificial Intelligence for Teaching and Learning Enhancement at the University of Pretoria.* https://www.up.ac.za/media/shared/391/pdfs/up-student-guide_-leveraging-generative-artificial-intelligence-for-learning.zp242396.pdf

University of the Witwatersrand. (2023). *Approach to the use of AI in teaching and learning at Wits – Jan 2023.* https://www.wits.ac.za/media/wits-university/learning-and-teaching/cltd/documents/AI-in-teaching-and-learning-at-Wits.pdf

KEY TERMS AND DEFINITIONS:

Academic Integrity: The commitment to upholding ethical principles and values in academic settings, such as honesty, trust, fairness, respect, and responsibility.

Academic Literacy: The set of skills, knowledge, and competencies required for students to engage with and produce academic discourse in higher education effectively. It encompasses the ability to read, write, think critically, and communicate in a manner that adheres to the conventions and expectations of various academic disciplines.

Digital Literacy: The ability to effectively use, understand, and navigate digital technologies and platforms for communication, learning, and problem-solving. Digital literacy forms part of academic literacy.

Flexibility: The ability to adapt and respond to changing circumstances, needs, or requirements in a timely and effective manner.

Generative Artificial Intelligence (GenAI): Advanced AI systems capable of creating new content, such as text, images, or code, based on learned patterns from vast datasets.

Inclusive Policy Development: The process of creating policies that involve and consider the perspectives of all stakeholders, ensuring that the needs and concerns of diverse groups are addressed.

Industry Partnerships: Collaborative relationships between HE institutions and private sector companies or organisations to promote knowledge exchange, innovation, and mutual benefits.

Learning: The process of acquiring new knowledge, skills, and understanding through study, experience, or instruction.

Multi-Stakeholder Engagement: The practice of involving and consulting with various groups or individuals who have an interest in or are affected by a particular decision, policy, or initiative.

Personalised Learning: An educational approach that tailors learning experiences to individual students' needs, interests, and abilities, often leveraging technology to provide customised content and support.

Plagiarism: The act of presenting someone else's work or ideas as one's own without proper attribution or acknowledgement of the original source.

Research: The systematic investigation and inquiry into a specific subject or problem to expand knowledge and understanding in a particular field.

Responsible Use: The ethical and appropriate application of technology, taking into account its potential impacts on individuals, society, and the environment.

South African Higher Education (HE): The tertiary education sector in South Africa, aimed at providing advanced learning and research opportunities.

Teaching And Assessment: The core activities in HE that involve imparting knowledge and skills to students and evaluating their understanding and application of the learned material.

Chapter 2
Ethical AI Integration in Academia:
Developing a Literacy–Driven Framework for LLMs in South African Higher Education

Zander Janse van Rensburg
ⓘD https://orcid.org/0000-0001-9822-8860
North-West University, South Africa

Sonja van der Westhuizen
North-West University, South Africa

ABSTRACT

The chapter explores the transformative potential and challenges of integrating large language models (LLMs) into higher education. It highlights the opportunities AI presents for enhancing academic literacy, writing, and pedagogy, while also acknowledging the risks to traditional educational values and practices. It proposes a framework, developed with the guidance of academic literacy, information literacy, digital literacy, and academic integrity, aimed at leveraging AI's capabilities to support academic success without undermining foundational skills. The discussion extends to the implications of AI in the South African educational context, addressing the digital divide and advocating for equitable access to technology. This chapter encapsulates the essence of the proposed proactive framework for navigating AI's impact on academia, focusing on adaptation, critical engagement, and the cultivation of an advanced form of academic literacy that integrates AI technologies responsibly.

DOI: 10.4018/979-8-3693-1054-0.ch002

INTRODUCTION

With the emergence of artificial intelligence (AI) technologies, particularly Large Language Models (LLMs), in late 2022, academic literacy as a practice and pedagogy is on the cusp of transforming (Grassini, 2023). In the face of these advancements, higher education institutions (HEIs) are confronted with what Gimpel et al. (2023: 28) describe as the "educator's dilemma" where decisions need to be made on either banning such tools or fostering their responsible usage. The core of contention is the rapid content generation capability of LLMs (Elkhatat et al., 2023; Chen et al., 2024), which presents a contrast to traditional research and education practices of HEIs. This situation necessitates careful consideration and strategic planning for the integration and adaptation of AI technologies, especially within a South African context.

This chapter, therefore, proposes an integrative framework designed to harness AI's potential while anchoring educational values in the relevant digital, academic, and information literacies. Simultaneously, it emphasizes alignment with the bedrock principle of academic integrity. Our aim is not merely to equip learners with the tools of the future but to ensure these tools amplify, rather than eclipse, the functional and foundational academic skills requisite for success in higher education. It is, however, important to underscore the progressive and anticipatory nature of our endeavor. This chapter does not claim to provide conclusive research outcomes; instead, it aims to offer a proactive framework for navigating the burgeoning AI revolution in academia, particularly within the distinct South African literacy context. In doing so, our aim is not just to keep pace with rapid developments but also to develop a constructive critique that influences the trajectory of educational development, ensuring that our institutions remain adaptable, critical, relevant, and forward-thinking. Our approach, therefore, is more than conceptual; it's a commitment to cultivating an advanced form of existing literacies that leverages the positive aspects of LLMs. We provide educators with actionable insights for integrating these technologies into assessment design and curriculum development, thereby enriching the academic experience, and preparing students for a future intertwined with AI advancements.

The Integration of Large language Models Into Higher Education

Generative AI and Large Language Models (LLMs) represent yet another step in the evolution of academic technologies. Earlier steps in this evolution include tools such as Microsoft Word's grammar support, Google and Wikipedia. Initially received with skepticism, due, largely, to concerns about a "plagiarism epidemic," these technologies have, over time, proven to be enriching for both teaching and learning

(Gimple et al., 2023, pp. 10, 35). However, LLMs provoke mixed reactions in the academic community. While their potential in enhancing educational experiences is acknowledged, they also face scrutiny over issues like source traceability and occasional nonsensical outputs (Gimple et al., 2023, p.10), as well as concerns about academic integrity (Dempere et al., 2023; Neuman & Schön, 2023, p. 29).

The presence of LLMs has initiated a paradigmatic shift in how information is processed. In the evolution of how humanity organizes information, it is logical that data previously stored and accessed in a static form should now be accessed and processed more dynamically. With regard to the internet the user is required to do the "heavy lifting" of finding and processing information. By contrast, AI offers the ability to search and process information and relay it to the user according to specific preferences. In other words, the information is presented and readily processed without the considerable effort previously involved. Gimpel et al. (2023:13-14) define AI as the macrocosm of intelligent machinery that deciphers patterns and predictive outcomes from copious data. Thus, generative AI, a subset of AI, stands as the harbinger of new data outputs in the form of text, images, music, etc. With these new developments, higher education must come to terms with a profound shift in how knowledge is acquired and disseminated.

Drawing on the capabilities of ChatGPT and the technology behind it, naturally, has consequences – both positive and negative. With ChatGPT and similar tools poised to redefine the academic landscape, higher education stands at a crossroads. On the one hand, LLMs promise innovative pedagogical avenues, but on the other, they present challenges that institutions must address with vigilance and foresight. As noted by Creelman (2023), the rapid evolution of generative AI surpasses the trajectories of previous technological marvels like PCs or the internet. Consequently, as universities witness the ubiquity of AI technologies, there is a call for adaptation in teaching and learning paradigms to harness the value of tools like ChatGPT while upholding the sanctity of academic values (Eager & Brunton, 2023:2-3). What is of concern here is higher education's ability to define a balanced approach to the AI revolution in order to remain relevant to future generations. For a start, we need to understand AI's basic capabilities and how to define its advantages and shortcomings. More importantly, on a cognitive level, we need to shift from traditional modes of information processing (i.e., search engine orientated) and define what constitutes the new way of information processing (i.e., conversational models), whilst upholding the longstanding (and sometimes uncontested) values of scholarly work.

Opportunities of Integrating LLMs in Higher Education

An inherent capability of LLMs, specifically through their language-oriented design, is to offer students assistance in scientific writing. They could, for instance, assist in the development of arguments, formulation of hypotheses, and the composition of research papers, thereby improving the overall writing process (Utami et al., 2023, p. 2; Marzuki et al., 2023). It is particularly through their user-friendly design and real-time access that they aid students with their writing assignments (Fecher et al., 2023). Assistance includes providing grammatical feedback, enhancing clarity, assisting with brainstorming, transforming notes into structured texts, aiding in translations, and fostering critical thinking skills (Gimpel et al., 2023). In addition, Eager and Brunton (2023, pp. 3-9) highlight its capabilities to assist educators in developing assessments that align with learning objectives and cater to various question formats that reflect course content, encourage critical thinking and tailor content to suit the diverse needs of a varied student body. From this point of view, we liken LLMs to personalized academic aids that offer specialized educational support and design (Neuman et al., 2023, pp. 29-32). Specialized educational support involves enhanced engagement, individualized learning paths, and advice in critical thinking; however, it is crucial to recognize areas where students may feel less prepared for integrating LLMs into their academic practices, such as that of writing effectively.

While the integration of ChatGPT into higher education unlocks considerable opportunities for improving academic practices and pedagogy, it simultaneously presents a range of challenges that HEIs should address, such as writing effectively and maintaining academic integrity (Perkins, 2023), ensuring equitable access (Anis & French, 2023, p. 1140), and navigating the complexities of AI-assisted education.

Challenges of Integrating ChatGPT in Higher Education

While the integration of LLMs such as ChatGPT into higher education holds vast potential, it comes with a range of challenges. This implies the necessity for a proactive and well-informed approach regarding their integration. One primary concern is the issue of academic integrity (Neuman & Schön, 2023; Eager & Brunton, 2023). LLMs ability to generate content, oftentimes undetectable by traditional plagiarism detectors, raises concerns about originality and authenticity (Neuman et al., 2023, pp. 29-32; Perkins, 2023; Weber-Wulff et al., 2023). Additionally, there's the risk of "hallucination" and fabrication of facts or information (Smith et al., 2023; Azamfirei et al., 2023:1; Agrawal et al., 2023). Another significant challenge stems from the inherent biases in the data used to train these models (Southworth et al., 2023). Gimple et al. (2023, p. 16) point out that LLM may inadvertently reproduce and perpetuate these biases, potentially leading to skewed or prejudiced outputs. This issue is compounded by the possibility of over-reliance on AI tools by students, which could diminish critical thinking and independent research skills. Given the sophistication of models like ChatGPT, educators also face the administrative challenge of differentiating AI-generated content from student work. In addition to these issues there is the question of equal access to AI Technologies and LLMs. The potential social inequalities stemming from fee-based tools like ChatGPT therefore may necessitate HEIs to consider supporting the use of these tools by students financially to promote an inclusive educational environment.

How LLMs (Like ChatGPT) Function

At the core of LLMs lies their revolutionary language-driven nature. These models, exemplified by ChatGPT, represent applications meticulously trained on predefined corpora that encompass extensive language data. To demystify the inner workings of LLMs and elucidate how they forge coherent and meaningful responses we shall explore ChatGPT as an example by examining what is involved in the acronym 'Generative Pre-trained Transformer' (GPT). Exploring the operations of ChatGPT not only demystifies its response generation process but also underscores the critical role of varied literacies in navigating and leveraging the full potential of LLMs. This understanding equips users with the insight to effectively employ these models, fostering a more informed and skillful interaction with advanced AI technologies.

The term "Generative" refers to the model's ability to generate coherent and contextually relevant text based on input prompts. These models have been trained to predict and generate text that appears as if it has been written by a human, making them capable of producing text that can be creative, informative, and contextually appropriate. When provided with input prompts, LLMs wield their predictive prowess to craft text-tailoring responses to suit the given context and purpose. In other words, the user needs to take advantage of its conversational design by crafting critical questions in an attempt to generate contextually appropriate responses. "Pre-trained" refers to the notion that these models have undergone a significant initial phase of training on a vast corpora of text data before any specific fine-tuning for tasks or domains. During this pre-training phase, the model learns the structure, grammar, and vast knowledge base of language from the provided text data. Essentially, LLMs learn the relations between concepts by way of linguistic and statistical analysis. This pre-trained knowledge is then fine-tuned for specific tasks or domains, making the model adaptable to a wide range of applications. GPT-1 was trained on the BooksCorpus data set, which at that time contained 7000 unpublished books (Radford et al., 2018). GPT-2 was trained on a dataset called WebText, which consists of 8 million web pages scraped from the internet (Radford, Wu, Child, Luan, Amodei & Sutskever, 2019). The data on which GPT-3 was trained is proprietary, however, it is estimated that it contains 175 billion parameters (Brown, et al., 2020). What is important to note here is that the data sources are not fully disclosed or vetted by the scholarly community, which raises questions about the transparency, accountability, comprehensiveness, and biases of the data on which models are trained on.

The effectiveness of this pre-training and fine-tuning is exemplified in the implementation of Transformer architectures in models like ChatGPT. LLMs, including ChatGPT, are constructed upon Transformer architectures, which are exceptionally adept at processing sequential data, especially text (Vaswani et al., 2017). Transformers act like attention mechanisms that focus the model on different parts of the input data to make predictions. These attention mechanisms are driven by the prompts (questions) the user directs to the system, or "trains" it to focus on. The system analyzes the range of words of the prompts and finds a critical mass of these terms within its database, by means of which it calculates the most probable response. This understanding of Transformer architectures and attention mechanisms in models like ChatGPT points to the notion that literacy teachers will need to refocus their attention on fostering strategic questioning and prompt-construction skills among students, enhancing their ability to effectively interact with and constructively use AI for learning.

Interacting with LLMs like ChatGPT can be likened to having a conversation with a highly intelligent individual. This analogy is apt because these models are trained on vast banks of example text, equipping them with an extensive range of information and linguistic structures. This training enables them to determine, in a probabilistic sense, the most likely words, sentence structures, topics, and evidence to use in response to almost any given question (Committee on Publication Ethics, 2024). Just as in a dialogue with a knowledgeable person where the quality of the conversation often hinges on the thoughtfulness of the questions posed, the efficacy of LLMs similarly escalates with the precision and relevance of the prompts provided (and understanding the limitations of training data). This symbiotic relationship between the quality of input (prompts) and output (responses) underscores the importance of formulating the best possible questions to harness the full potential of these advanced linguistic systems. Hence, these models do not merely provide information; they engage in a dynamic interaction, mirroring the depth and adaptability of a conversation with a well-informed and articulate individual.

The South African Higher Education Context

Given the opportunities, challenges, and foundational functions of LLMs within South Africa's distinctive educational context, it is essential to not only seize these opportunities but also to actively address challenges. This approach will enhance the efficacy of the adoption of AI and LLMs, such as ChatGPT, into South African higher education institutions (HEIs), and ensure this adoption is executed efficiently and equitably, aligning with the nation's unique socio-economic and educational needs.

The Digital Divide

Developing nations, like South Africa, face a significant challenge with regard to technological access. This technological inequity is more than just a matter of hardware; it's deeply rooted in systemic discrepancies that affect information access. The digital divide, as defined by Naidoo and Raju (2012, p. 34), represents the disparity between those with convenient access to information and communication technology (ICT) tools and those lacking such access or the skills to utilize them. The United Nations Educational, Scientific and Cultural Organization (UNESCO) (2002, p. 7) highlights the paradoxical situation where individuals and communities in greatest need, such as disadvantaged groups, people in rural areas, and illiterate populations, lack the tools required for meaningful participation in the knowledge society. Jantjies (cited in Moonasamy & Naidoo, 2022, p. 77) breaks down South Africa's digital divide into three areas: access to hardware, understanding digital communication, and internet affordability. The real-world implications of this divide are stark, especially when observing the South African landscape. With scarce computer ownership (10%), limited electricity access (16%), and costly data, a glaring digital gap persists among a populace where 70% live below the "living wage standard" (Sokolow, 2020).

These disparities impact the South African higher education sector as reflected in the South African Department of Education concerns in 2020 over students' inability to access learning materials and participate in online classes due to inadequate energy and limited broadband strengths (Kativhu, 2021, p. 291). A historical perspective offers insight into the current challenges experienced by the South African HEIs. Post-Apartheid, the South African government aimed to redress the imbalances from the apartheid era by creating an inclusive HE system. However, the role of technology in HE was somewhat overlooked until the National Plan on HE in 2001. Between 2001 and 2005, the government took steps to mitigate the digital divide while the period from 2006 to 2010 saw a renewed focus on digital literacies, flexible learning, and the growing role of social media in education (Kativhu, 2021, p. 292). These intentions were good, but gaps persisted, especially in the rural areas, creating a disparity that echoed previous societal imbalances. Looking back, the roots of these struggles can be traced to foundational issues in the schooling system (Drennan, 2017:63). While there have been strides to transform education post-Apartheid, challenges persist, including limited access for marginalized students and deeply entrenched institutional cultures (Jacobs, 2013, p. 128; Mawere et al., 2021, p. 47).

The implication of this divide extends beyond a barrier to technology access. It sets the stage for examining how these technological inequities directly impact student literacy, particularly in a South African higher education setting. The integration of LLMs is at the forefront of student literacy challenges, particularly in the socio-linguistically and digitally diverse South African context. These challenges are compounded by a differentiated schooling system and the nation's intricate linguistic and socio-economic makeup, rooted in Bourdieu's theory of cultural capital, where linguistic proficiency plays a critical role in academic success (Hurst, 2015, p. 80). Therefore, in confronting these technological and linguistic disparities, South Africa's higher education institutions will need to navigate a complex web of socio-economic and educational challenges to ensure that the benefits of LLM integration truly democratize academic access, reflecting a commitment to equitable education for all.

Factors Surrounding the Literacy of South African Students

South African students, often studying in languages other than their native tongues, face challenges in meeting the literacy expectations of higher education institutions (Hurst, 2015, pp. 79, 83). This is reiterated by Bacha's (2002, p. 161) observation that "Students studying in institutions of higher learning in the medium English, which may not be their native language, have been found to face problems mainly in writing, making them unable to cope with the institution's literacy expectations". With the emphasis on the mass enrolment of South African students, the challenge of students struggling to meet the established academic writing standards (that are deemed a requisite within the context of higher education), becomes more prevalent (Pineteh, 2014, p. 12). Proficiency in this context is not just about linguistic competency; it encompasses a myriad of academic literacies in digital spaces, from reading and writing to engaging with subject-specific discourses (Wollscheid et al., 2021). It is disconcerting (to say the least) that the 2021 Progress in International Reading Literacy Study (PIRLS) concluded that "81% of Grade 4 learners [learners turning 10 years of age] in South Africa cannot read for meaning in any language, including their home languages" (Equal Education Law Centre [EELC], 2023).

In the light of these observations, the need for an intersection between linguistic competency and the effective utilization of LLMs in educational settings becomes apparent (Ou et al., 2024); effective reading, writing, and access (for a start) are crucial if these models are to be used effectively. Most South African students face significant challenges in engaging with LLMs, which predominantly operate in English and require linguistic fluency. However, again, the proficiency needed to use LLMs extends beyond linguistic ability—it encompasses various literacies, including the ability to critically engage with subject matter and technology. Statistics reported by PIRLS indicate systemic educational deficiencies that may hinder students' capacities to interact with advanced technologies like LLMs. Therefore, a paradigm shift is required—one that fosters comprehensive linguistic and literacy development to ensure equitable and effective use of LLMs. In this regard, Hurst (2015, p. 78) advises moving away from viewing students through a "deficit" lens and instead advocates universally supporting them, highlighting the need to introduce literacies effectively (Jacobs, 2013, p. 131). South African students furthermore hold different perceptions of academic honesty compared to traditional standards (Thomas & Van Zyl, 2012, p. 150). According to Thomas & Van Zyl (2012, p. 152), this necessitates a re-evaluation of ethical standards in academia, especially in the context of rapidly advancing digital technologies. The literacy spectrum, therefore, involves not only traditional skills of reading and writing, but also the nuanced discipline-specific literacies (information, digital and academic integrity literacy) essential in a in increasingly digital world (Elton, 2010, pp. 154, 157; Baker et al., 2019, p. 142).

The multifaceted challenges faced by South African students, particularly in navigating the complexities of academic writing and language barriers, underline the necessity for a more holistic approach to literacy. In other words, an approach is needed that augments traditional aspects of academic, information, and digital literacy by integrating these with AI literacy. A new framework should therefore consider the unique socio-linguistic and digital landscapes of South Africa, ensuring that the integration of AI in higher education is both equitable and effective.

Pillars of the Integrated Framework

The following framework's objective is to emphasize and refocus existing literacy skills to strengthen AI literacy within the context of South African HEIs. AI literacy "refers to the knowledge and understanding of AI that is necessary for individuals to participate in the broader discourse around AI and make informed decisions about its use and implications. It seeks to empower educators and students with the essential competencies for navigating and ethically utilizing AI technologies" (Southworth, 2023, citing Laupichler et al., 2022). Going beyond a technical understanding of AI, this approach acknowledges broader socio-cultural, political, ethical, and practical dimensions (Crabtree, 2023). In alignment with the real-world challenges and applications highlighted by Ng, Leung, Chu, and Qiao (2021), it extends AI literacy to include academic, information, digital, and academic integrity literacies (Kreinsen & Schulz, 2023). Collectively, these literacies develop a critical, multifaceted approach to engaging with AI technology, ensuring a responsible and enriched academic experience in the digital age – which is reflected in the framework we propose.

It is therefore essential to recognize that its success in the South African educational context is intrinsically linked to addressing access and the linguistic, cultural and literacy capabilities of the users. The true potential of LLMs is unlocked by those who have access, solid foundation of knowledge in the relevant domain, and relevant literacy capabilities and competencies (Markauskaite et al., 2022). These literacies include understanding how to formulate meaningful queries (prompt engineering), interpret results, and critically assess the outputs of AI systems. As a starting point the following elements need to be considered when attempting to integrate LLMs in literacy education:

Critical thinking skills and adequate subject knowledge to design prompts that will elicit relevant and appropriate responses;

- analysis and validation of LLMs responses, which requires education on information literacy;
- knowledge of genres and text formulation within academic discourse;
- well-grounded understanding of academic conduct (i.e., academic integrity) in a broader sense; and,
- access to and training on AI-technology.

LLMs serve as a powerful complement to human intelligence (Jarrahi et al., 2022), but require a knowledgeable and skillful user who guides their applications towards ethical, beneficial and insightful outcomes. Institutions must adapt to these needs, moving away from a "deficit" lens and towards universally supporting students in developing these comprehensive literacies, as pointed out above (Hurst, 2015, p. 78; Jacobs, 2013, p. 131).

Academic Literacy

Academic literacy prepares students to grasp and produce discipline-specific texts, to understand, challenge, and apply conventions of academic discourse, and navigate academic contexts. At a foundational level, academic literacy involves the ability to read and write while engaging in critical thinking (Beekman et al., 2019, p. 6). The academically literate student is not only able to comprehend subject-specific content but can also analyze and apply said content to the needs of their specific assignments. From a historical context, the interpretation of academic literacy has significantly evolved. While academic literacies were once seen as merely skills-based and cognitive, devoid of deep sociocultural underpinnings (Gee, 1990, p. 67), their significance is now seen to extend much further, profoundly influencing student learning outcomes (Jacobs, 2013, pp. 128-129). These literacies, encompassing both reading and writing skills, as well as basic disciplinary and academic working skills, play a vital role in a student's transition into higher education. The transition from high school to university, fraught with academic, cultural, and ethical challenges, is emphasized by the disparity between a student's ethical views and the academic institution's ethos. This is particularly true for the millennial generation, requiring them not only to adapt to new academic systems but also to align with institutional ethical standards (Thomas & Van Zyl, 2012, p. 146). Redefining their learner identities and developing autonomous working skills becomes a necessity during this phase (Wollscheid et al., 2021). Academic literacy is, therefore, crucial in the academic acculturation process, specifically initiating students into the way that knowledge is communicated, its dissemination, and, ideally, guiding critical thinking about prevailing ideologies.

When we consider the basic assumption of teaching academic literacy, i.e., to promote a functional understanding of the language of various disciplines, LLMs can be power tools to help interpret academic texts. However, though they are supremely effective tools for novice students or readers in the clarification and disambiguation of complex language or concepts, questions inevitably arise during the use and 'testing of these platforms; for instance: "When we read language that is difficult to understand and we revert to, say ChatGPT, we get satisfactory responses which do adequately frame and simplify complexity, but how does this initiate deep thinking about the function of words, phrases, and concepts, especially how these are taken together to create meaning?". Though ChatGPT can help us to process content more quickly and effectively, what is to say that the seemingly "neutral" interpretation by such a model does not contain biases or perpetuate bias in the inner world of the reader? The words themselves carry meaning, yes; but meaning is actualized in the context where the text is interpreted. Moving away from the theoretical to the practical, we wonder whether an LLM should rather be used intermittently, because when difficult texts are continually interpreted for the user how much deep or critical thinking is occurring?

To use LLMs effectively and ethically by way of academic literacy, educators might adopt a multifaceted approach. Drawing on outlines by Lea and Street (2006) and Li (2019) regarding the aims of academic literacy, we emphasize the following key areas: (1) cultivation of critical analysis skills; (2) effective scholarly communication; (3) knowledge synthesis; (4) disciplinary engagement; (5) information navigation; (6) ethical scholarship; (7) and adaptability to innovation within higher education. These areas function together to help equip students not only with skills but with a critical awareness of the world around them. It is, therefore, the role of literacy experts to develop a balanced approach when developing strategies to integrate (or not integrate) LLMs in curricula. In what follows we propose initial practical approaches that harness the seven principles from the academic literacy framework above:

(1) Cultivating students' critical awareness by way of evaluating LLM-generated versus human-produced texts to understand potential biases and the intricacies of language use.
(2) Developing workshops on prompt-writing skills, with a focus on clarity and conciseness in LLM interactions.

(3)   Promoting knowledge synthesis by integrating AI tools (especially literature review tools) with traditional research methodologies, allowing students to corroborate AI-generated information against established sources.

(4)   Encouraging disciplinary engagement by utilizing LLMs for subject-specific content creation, followed by critical peer reviews to refine understanding and application;

(5)   Advancing information-navigation skills by training students to effectively examine and verify AI-provided data.

(6)   Upholding ethical scholarship by incorporating discussions and practical demonstrations on the ethical use of AI in academic work.

(7)   Fostering adaptability to innovation by keeping curricula responsive to the latest AI advancements, preparing students to stay abreast with rapid developments and how they influence academic and literacy practices.

Thus, to summarize, the focus of academic literacy should extend beyond just understanding and mastering the language of academic discourse and producing discipline-specific texts, to adapting to the digital nature of contemporary education. This shift signifies a transformation where the proficiency in digital tools and platforms becomes as integral as traditional academic skills. This signifies the need for students and educators to develop comprehensive literacy skills that encompasses both academic and digital competencies to ensure they remain adept practitioners and effective in an AI-enhanced educational environment.

Digital Literacy

Given the increasing digital nature of education, we emphasize the importance of digital literacy to harness the capabilities of AI technologies and LLMs. In an era where AI technologies like ChatGPT are becoming integral to academic writing and literacy, understanding and utilizing these digital tools effectively becomes essential. JISC (2014) breaks down digital literacy into seven elements: ICT literacy, communication and collaboration, media literacy, information literacy, learning skills, digital scholarship, and career and identity management. Gilster (1997, pp. 1-2) describes digital literacy as the ability to understand and use information from various sources presented via computers. As education shifts towards LLMs, digital literacy becomes central, empowering students to extract, engage, integrate, and employ information from diverse digital repositories.

With respect to digital literacy in the context of LLMs we propose the following four key skills, following the 'Digital Literacy Framework' designed by Eshet (2012: (1) photo-visual thinking (understanding and using visual information); (2) real-time thinking (simultaneously processing a variety of stimuli); (3) information thinking (evaluating and combining information from multiple digital sources); (4) reproduction thinking (creating outcomes using technological tools by designing new content or remixing existing digital content). In what follows we suggest initial practical approaches that harness these four skills:

(1) Developing student's ability to navigate LLM graphical user interfaces, i.e., skills to interpret and utilize diverse visual data, by initiating step-by-step practical demonstrations of LLMs.

(2) Facilitating abilities to process multiple stimuli (i.e., the simultaneous use of multiple LLM applications), by demonstrating to students how various applications can be utilized.

(3) Critical evaluation and synthesis of information from various digital sources, by evaluating different AI-generated sources and demonstrating effective synthesis. This could perhaps include information on how LLM algorithms work and their potential shortcomings.

(4) Cultivating the ability to create new content or remix existing digital materials using technological tools, to help empower learners to contribute actively and creatively in digital spaces.

South African HEIs have a significant role to play in nurturing holistic digital literacy. This includes not only providing access to digital tools but also ensuring that students are equipped with the necessary skills and knowledge to navigate the digital world ethically and effectively. HEIs will benefit from investing in comprehensive digital literacy education to ensure that students utilize these technologies effectively and that their use thereof aligns with the ethical and educational standards of the academic community.

Information Literacy

According to the American Library Association (ALA, 1989), information literacy is defined as a set of abilities requiring individuals to "recognize when information is needed and have the ability to locate, evaluate, and use effectively the needed information." This definition underscores the importance of not only identifying and articulating the requirement for information but also the skills involved in searching for, assessing the relevance and credibility of the information sources (i.e., implementing effective search strategies), and the ethical and appropriate use of the information for a given purpose. According to the Association of College & Research Libraries (ACRL) (cited in Ottonicar et al., 2021, pp. 184) information literacy therefore involves a deep reflection on how information is produced, valued, and used to create new knowledge and ethically participate in learning communities.

These foundational elements of information literacy have traditionally played a significant role in safeguarding the scientific process.

The principles of information literacy hold the potential to guide students in harnessing the power of LLMs in educational settings. Students can adapt the information literacy skills required to navigate traditional information sources to LLMs. In doing so, students will be empowered to clearly define their queries, refine search strategies, evaluate responses critically, and effectively apply AI-generated insights (Heck et al. 2021, p. 129). By incorporating AI literacy alongside traditional information literacy, HEIs can play a central role in shaping informed, ethical, and empowered users in the digital age (Wheatly & Hervieux, 2022, p. 61). The development of protocols on how LLMs can be integrated into the higher education setting will furthermore ensure that students navigate the complex landscape of information with integrity, discernment, and responsibility (Ottonicar et al., 2021, p. 191). In what follows we propose initial practical approaches:

1. Education on various types of AI literature review applications and practical exercises to demonstrate the way in which these applications retrieve information.
2. Detailed step-by-step guidance, and real-world examples on how to formulate queries.
3. Practical demonstrations on how to evaluate sources.

It is evident that the journey towards enhanced information literacy in the digital age is not only about accessing information but about discerning its quality, relevance, and credibility, ensuring that students remain adept, ethical, and informed practitioners in an era of misleading narratives and rapidly evolving technologies. Hossain (2022) therefore surmises that "academic integrity is an essential part of information literacy", and should be rooted in, according to the International Centre for Academic Integrity (ICAI), six key values, namely, "honesty, trust, fairness, respect, responsibility, and courage" (cited by Hossain, 2022).

Academic Integrity Literacy

Academic Integrity Literacy (AIL) has become a critical skill in the 21st century that is comparable to other literacies such as information and digital literacy. According to Hossain (2022) AIL is a blend of values, behaviors, ethical decision-making, and skills vital for academic achievement – all the knowledge, skills, and actions necessary for the ethical use of information in academia. Incorporating AI and LLMs into academic settings necessitates a robust framework for maintaining a culture of academic integrity.

Academic integrity culture is the foundational commitment widely understood as involving a collective effort, i.e., all relevant stakeholders at every level of the institution are considered responsible for fostering a culture of integrity (Bretag & Mahmud, 2016). This culture is underpinned by the fundamental values indicated in the previous section: honesty, trust, fairness, respect, responsibility, and courage (International Center for Academic Integrity [ICAI], 2021). Thus, a collective effort must be mounted at "every layer of an institution…[to] embrace the strengthening process" involved in academic integrity culture development, according to Hendershott et al. (2000, p. 596). McCabe (cited in Robinson & Glanzer, 2017, p. 209) reiterates that an "ethical culture can be understood as a complex interplay among various formal and informal cultural systems that can promote either ethical or unethical behavior". Formal systems are developed by Institutions as a means of assuring compliance and quality, whereas informal systems are often a response to the formal ones, for instance, hosting non-mandatory academic integrity seminars, forming communities of practice, etc. An academic integrity culture, whether formal or informal, is essential for academic integrity development. In what follows we propose initial practical approaches:

1. Integrate AIL values, ethical decision-making, and behaviors into the curriculum, emphasizing them as a skill on par with academic, information and digital literacy.
2. Incorporate AI and LLMs into academic settings with guidelines ensuring academic integrity, thereby maintaining the credibility of scholarly work.
3. Engage all stakeholders in fostering an academic integrity culture, leveraging both formal (compliance and quality assurance processes) and informal (community practices, seminars) systems.
4. Offer specific training on the ethical use of AI and LLMs, including critical thinking and authorship, to navigate their impact on traditional academic values.
5. Facilitate discussions and experiences sharing on AI ethics, guiding students and staff through the complexities of digital tools in academia.
6. Document practical experiences with AI tools to inform relevant policy development, fostering a responsive educational environment.

Considering the fact that LLMs challenge traditional notions of authorship and originality, academic staff will need to investigate and understand how tools are used by students, to determine the point at which guiding interventions need to take place. Educators and institutions must navigate these advancements by fostering an environment that emphasizes the ethical use of AI, ensures students' work remains self-generated, and integrates critical thinking skills. This would require education regarding ethical conduct and safe environments which facilitate discussions on the ethics of LLMs in assessment. During these discussions participants might experiment and share their experience. These interactions could lead to fruitful discussions and training on the ethical use of LLMs. To return to the interplay between formal and informal systems, literacy experts need to document these experiences to inform policy developers in defining policies that are relevant to this "new" environment. As a consequence, informal structures could lead to special interest groups, communities of practice, and frequent non-mandatory training.

The exploration of academic, digital, and information literacies, along with the critical aspect of academic integrity, provides a foundation for understanding the multifaceted requirements of modern higher education. These literacies form the cornerstone of a well-rounded academic experience, especially in an era increasingly dominated by AI and digital technologies. In the following section, we integrate these essential literacies within an overarching framework that not only addresses academic integrity but also leverages the capabilities and potential of LLMs.

An Integrative Literacy-Driven Framework for LLMs in South African Higher Education

In the following section we propose a three-phase approach informed by the four pillars of the framework (i.e., academic literacy, information literacy, digital literacy, academic integrity) to initiate a holistic integration of LLMs into South African HEIs.

Phase 1: Stakeholder analysis
1. Determine the university's official position on AI in the teaching and learning context, assessing its readiness and openness to integrate AI technologies.
2. Initiate or assess faculty/department positions on AI use and understanding within various academic disciplines, faculties and subject-groups.
3. Gather academic staff perspectives on the role of AI and its impact on the education environment, focusing on potential benefits and challenges.
4. Evaluate how academic staff currently use or plan to use AI in their teaching and learning environments.
5. Include professional development assessments to determine the training needs of educators in integrating AI into their pedagogy effectively.
6. Determine stakeholders' (staff and students) perspectives and proficiency regarding academic literacy and information literacy, and identify the academic literacy model followed. Such an exercise will enable an evidence-based approach in formulating fit-for-purpose training.
7. Assess stakeholders' digital literacy and means of accessibility, to help ensure equitable access to AI technologies.

8. Measure stakeholders' perspectives on academic integrity, focusing on the understanding of originality, intellectual property rights, and plagiarism in the context of AI usage.
9. Evaluate the need for ethical AI usage policies within the university, focusing on data privacy, consent, and responsible AI usage.

Phase 2: Establish shared educational goals, objectives and outcomes

1. *Academic literacy:* Create a shared understanding of the value of academic literacy, its central components and how it contributes to the effective and ethical use of LLMs whilst ensuring that authentic learning is taking place. Emphasize the role of AI in supplementing traditional academic skills rather than replacing them.
2. *Digital literacy:* Develop guidelines emphasizing equitable access, responsible digital citizenship, and ethical use of AI, with a focus on how students and educators can utilize AI tools like LLMs effectively. This will raise students' and educators' awareness of the implications of AI-generated content and its appropriate use.
3. Inclusivity*: Emphasize* the importance of inclusivity and accessibility in AI integration, ensuring all students, including those with disabilities, have equitable access to AI tools.
4. *Information literacy:* Implement standards for the ethical and effective use of information, especially AI-generated content, focusing on plagiarism, misinformation, and data privacy.
5. *Transparency in education:* Promote collaboration among students, educators, and technology experts to make best use of AI in enhancing learning and teaching.
6. *Partnership:* Develop partnerships with AI developers and companies to stay updated with the latest AI advancements and best practices.
7. *Integration of cross-discipline perspectives:* Encourage cross-disciplinary collaboration to understand the impact of AI on various academic fields. This can foster a holistic understanding of AI's role in diverse academic contexts and promote the sharing of best practices.
8. *Infrastructure:* Address infrastructure and development needs for effective digital support for AI integration, including reliable internet access and appropriate hardware and software.

Phase 3: Design student-centric learning experiences

1. *Digital literacy:* Guide students on the use of LLMs and demonstrate that AI can support diverse learning styles and provide personalized educational experiences.
2. *Academic literacy:* Integrate AI tools into curriculum and assessment practices to enhance skills like critical thinking and research. Highlight

the importance of AI in aiding students' engagement (research, reading and writing) with complex academic texts and concepts, encouraging critical analysis and independent thought.

3. *Assessing outcomes:* Incorporate evaluation and research components to systematically assess the effectiveness and impact of AI integration on learning outcomes and student engagement.

4. *Information literacy:* Teach students to critically assess AI-generated information and use it to augment their academic work.

5. *Cultural inclusivity:* Highlight the importance of cultural and contextual relevance in AI utilization, ensuring the technology aligns with local languages and educational challenges specific to South Africa.

6. *Integration with industry and real-world scenarios:* Connect academic learning with real-world applications of AI, involving industry partners and real-world scenarios in the curriculum.

7. *Career and skills development:* Prepare students for AI-augmented workplaces by equipping them with relevant skills.

8. *Interdisciplinary development:* Foster an interdisciplinary approach in AI education, integrating insights from various fields to understand the broader societal implications of AI.

9. *Student agency in learning:* Encourage and empower active student involvement in using AI, promoting responsibility and ownership.

10. *Feedback loops for improvement:* Establish feedback mechanisms to continuously assess and improve the integration of AI in teaching and learning practices.

By considering the three-phases literacy-orientated approach, focusing on academic, information, digital, and academic integrity literacies, HEIs would be enabled to establish a shared vision for the effective and ethical integration of AI technologies while also taking into consideration socio-cultural, political, and ethical issues.

CONCLUSION

The advent of AI in the academic realm presents a challenge to the traditional pillars of higher education. At its core, the goals of higher education have always been the authentic acquisition of knowledge along with skills development. With AI's remarkable capabilities, these foundational goals are put to the test. In the evolving landscape of literacy studies, the central challenge is not merely to remain updated but to preserve the essence of genuine skill acquisition that serves as the bedrock for knowledge assimilation. It is no longer incumbent upon the learner to simply absorb information or master a skill manually; the need now is also to learn how to effectively unite human capabilities with AI's strengths.

In this chapter, we have presented an integrative framework for the ethical integration of AI technologies and LLMs into South African higher education. This framework emphasizes balancing the transformative capabilities of AI with the essential values of academic integrity and literacy development, where AI augments rather than replaces traditional learning methods.

In South Africa, addressing the digital divide and linguistic barriers is crucial for equitable AI access. The framework proposes strategies for stakeholder analysis, shared educational goals, and student-centered learning, ensuring that AI's integration benefits all learners and upholds academic integrity. The authors argue for literacy development in academic, information, digital, and AI areas, to prepare students and faculty for an AI-augmented academic and professional world.

This integrative approach aims to create an adaptive academic environment. By equipping stakeholders in academia with the necessary skills and knowledge, the framework envisions a future where AI enriches the academic experience while aligning technological advancements with the core educational values of originality, critical thinking, and ethical scholarly practice.

REFERENCES

American Library Association. (1989). ALA Presidential Committee on Information Literacy: Final Report, released January 10, 1989. https://www.ala.org/acrl/publications/whitepapers/presidential

Anis, S., & French, J. A. (2023). Efficient, Explicatory, and Equitable: Why Qualitative Researchers Should Embrace AI, but Cautiously. *Business & Society*, *62*(6), 1139–1144. doi:10.1177/00076503231163286

Anunobi, C., & Udem, O. K. (2014). Information literacy competencies: A conceptual analysis. *Journal of Applied Information Science and Technology*, *7*(2), 64–80.

Association of College & Research Libraries. (2000). Information Literacy Competency Standards for Higher Education. https://alair.ala.org/ handle/11213/7668

Azamfirei, R., Kudchadkar, S. R., & Fackler, J. (2023). Large language models and the perils of their hallucinations. *Critical Care*, *27*(1), 1–2. doi:10.1186/s13054-023-04393-x PMID:36945051

Bacha, N. N. (2002). Developing Learners' Academic Writing Skills in Higher Education: A Study for *Educational Reform. Language and Education, 16*(3), 161–177. doi:10.1080/09500780208666826

Baker, S., Bangeni, B., Burke, R., & Hunma, A. (2019). The invisibility of academic reading as social practice and its implications for equity in higher education: A scoping study. *Higher Education Research & Development, 38*(1), 142–156. doi:1 0.1080/07294360.2018.1540554

Bates, T., Cobo, C., Mariño, O., & Wheeler, S. (2020). Can artificial intelligence transform higher education? *International Journal of Educational Technology in Higher Education, 17*(42), 42. Advance online publication. doi:10.1186/s41239-020-00218-x

Bretag, T., & Mahmud, S. (2016). A conceptual framework for implementing exemplary academic integrity policy in Australian higher education. In T. Bretag (Ed.), *Handbook of Academic Integrity* (pp. 463–480). Springer. doi:10.1007/978-981-287-098-8_24

Brown, T., Mann, B., Ryder, N., Subbiah, M., Kaplan, J. D., Dhariwal, P., Neelakantan, A., Shyam, P., Sastry, G., Askell, A., & Agarwal, S. (2020). Language models are few-shot learners. *Advances in Neural Information Processing Systems, 33*, 1877–1901.

Centre for Teaching and Learning. (2023a). *Beginning University Survey of Student Engagement: North-West University* [Unpublished report]. University of the Free State.

Centre for Teaching and Learning. (2023b). *South African Survey of Student Engagement: North-West University Institutional Report* [Unpublished report]. University of the Free State.

Chen, K., Shao, A., Burapacheep, J., & Li, X. (2024). Conversational AI and equity through assessing GPT-3's communication with diverse social groups on contentious topics. *Scientific Reports, 14*(1561), 1561. Advance online publication. doi:10.1038/s41598-024-51969-w PMID:38238474

Committee on Publication Ethics. (n.d.). Artificial Intelligence and Authorship. https://publicationethics.org/news/artificial-intelligence-and-authorship

Crabtree, M. (2023). What is AI Literacy? A Comprehensive Guide for Beginners. https://www.datacamp.com/blog/what-is-ai-literacy-a-comprehensive-guide-for-beginners

Creelman, D. (2023). Embrace generative AI. *HR Future, 5*, 54. doi:10.10520/ejc-om_hrf_v2023_n5_a19

Dempere, J., Modugu, K., Hesham, A., & Ramasamy, L. K. (2023). The impact of ChatGPT on higher education. *Frontiers in Education*, *8*, 1206936. Advance online publication. doi:10.3389/feduc.2023.1206936

Drennan, L. M. (2017). Engaging Students through Writing: A Collaborative Journey. *South African Journal of Higher Education*, *31*(3), 63–81. doi:10.20853/31-3-1041

Eager, B., & Brunton, R. (2023). Prompting Higher Education Towards AI-Augmented Teaching and Learning Practice. *Journal of University Teaching & Learning Practice*, *20*(5), 1–19. doi:10.53761/1.20.5.02

Elkhatat, A. M., Elsaid, K., & Almeer, S. (2023). Evaluating the efficacy of AI content detection tools in differentiating between human and AI-generated text. *International Journal for Educational Integrity*, *19*(17), 17. Advance online publication. doi:10.1007/s40979-023-00140-5

Equal Education Law Centre. (2023). Joint statement: The 2021 Progress in International Reading Literacy Study (Pirls) results confirm a schooling system in crisis and the extent of learning losses created by COVID-19. https://equaleducation. org.za/2023/05/23/joint-statement-the-2021-progress-in-international-reading-literacy-study-pirls-results-confirm-a-schooling-system-in-crisis-and-the-extent-of-learning-losses-created-by-covid-19/#:~:text=On%20Tuesday%2016%20May%20 2023,language%2C%20including%20their%20home%20languages

Eshet, Y. (2012). Thinking in the digital era: A revised model for digital literacy. *Issues in Informing Science and Information Technology, 9*(2), 267-276.

Fecher, B., Hebing, M., Laufer, M., Pohle, J., & Sofsky, F. (2023). Friend or Foe? Exploring the Implications of Large Language Models on the Science System. *arXiv preprint arXiv:2306.09928.*

Gee, J. P. (2008). *Social Linguistics and literacies: Ideology in discourses* (3rd ed.). Routledge.

Gilster, P. (1997). *Digital literacy*. Wiley Computer Pub.

GimpelH.HallK.DeckerS.EymannT.LämmermannL.MädcheA.RöglingerM. RuinerC.SchochM.SchoopM.UrbachN.VandirkS. (2023). Unlocking the Power of Generative AI Models and Systems such as GPT-4 and ChatGPT for Higher Education: A Guide for Students and Lecturers. University of Hohenheim, March 20, 2023. doi:10.13140/RG.2.2.20710.09287/2

Grassini, S. (2023). Shaping the future of education: Exploring the potential and consequences of AI and ChatGPT in educational settings. *Education Sciences*, *13*(7), 692. Advance online publication. doi:10.3390/educsci13070692

Heck, T., Weisel, L., & Kullmann, S. (2021). Information literacy and its interplay with AI. In A. Botte, P. Libbrecht, & M. Rittberger (Eds.), *Learning Information Literacy across the Globe* (pp. 129–131). Leibniz-Institut für Bildungsforschung und Bildungsinformation. doi:10.25656/01:17891

Hendershott, A., Drinan, P., & Cross, M. (2000). Toward enhancing a culture of academic integrity. *NASPA Journal*, *37*(4), 587–598. doi:10.2202/1949-6605.1119

Hossain, Z. (2022). University freshmen recollect their academic integrity literacy experience during their K-12 years: Results of an empirical study. *International Journal for Educational Integrity*, *18*(4), 4. Advance online publication. doi:10.1007/s40979-021-00096-4

International Center for Academic Integrity. (2021). The fundamental values of academic integrity (3rd ed.). www.academicintegrity.org/the-fundamental-valuesof-academic-integrity

Jacobs, C. (2013). Academic literacies and the question of knowledge. *Tydskrif vir Taalonderrig*, *47*(2), 127–140. doi:10.4314/jlt.v47i2.7

Jarrahi, M. H., Lutz, C., & Newlands, G. (2022). Artificial intelligence, human intelligence and hybrid intelligence based on mutual augmentation. *Big Data & Society*, *9*(2). Advance online publication. doi:10.1177/20539517221142824

Joint Information Systems Committee. (2014). Developing digital literacies. https://www.jisc.ac.uk/guides/developing-digital-literacies

Kanarek, J. (2021). The tortoise and the hare: A new moral for an old fable. *The Intellectual Standard, 2*(1). https://digitalcommons.iwu.edu/tis/vol2/iss1/1

Kativhu, S. (2021). Covid-19 as a Catalyst for Digital Transformation in Higher Education: Insights for Rural-based Universities in South Africa. *African Renaissance*, *18*(4), 285–304.

KreinsenM.SchulzS. (2023). Towards the triad of digital literacy, data literacy and AI literacy in teacher education – A discussion in light of the accessibility of novel generative AI. doi:10.35542/osf.io/xguzk

Lea, M. R., & Street, B. V. (2006). The "Academic Literacies" Model: Theory and Applications. *Theory into Practice*, *45*(4), 368–377. doi:10.1207/s15430421tip4504_11

Li, D. (2022). A review of academic literacy research development: from 2002 to 2019. *Asian-Pacific Journal of Second and Foreign Language Education*, 7(1), 1–22. doi:10.1186/s40862-022-00130-z

Markauskaite, L., Rebecca Marrone, R., Poquet, O., Knight, S., Martinez-Maldonado, R., Howard, S., Tondeur, J., De Laat, M., Buckingham Shum, S., Gašević, D., & Siemens, G. (2022). Rethinking the entwinement between artificial intelligence and human learning: What capabilities do learners need for a world with AI? *Computers and Education: Artificial Intelligence*, 3(100056), 100056. Advance online publication. doi:10.1016/j.caeai.2022.100056

Marzuki, M., Widiati, U., Rusdin, D., & Indrawati, I. (2023). The impact of AI writing tools on the content and organization of students' writing: EFL teachers' perspective. *Cogent Education*, 10(2), 2236469. Advance online publication. doi: 10.1080/2331186X.2023.2236469

Masenya, T. M. (2021). Digital Literacy Skills As Prerequisite for Teaching and Learning in Higher Education Institutions. *Mousaion: South African Journal of Information Studies*, 39(2), 1–20. doi:10.25159/2663-659X/8428

Masenya, T. M. (2021). Digital Literacy Skills as Prerequisite for Teaching and Learning in Higher Education Institutions. *Mousaion: South African Journal of Information Studies*, 39(2), 1–20. doi:10.25159/2663-659X/8428

Mawere, J., Mukonza, R. M., & Kugara, S. L. (2021). Re-envisioning the Education System for 4IR: Exploring the Experiences Faced by First Entering Students from Rural-based Institutions on the Use of Digital Learning during the Coronavirus Pandemic in Limpopo province, South Africa. *Journal of African Education*, 2(2), 43–65. doi:10.31920/2633-2930/2021/v2n2a2

Moonasamy, A. R., & Naidoo, G. M. (2022). Digital Learning: Challenges experienced by South African university students' during the COVID-19 pandemic. *The Independent Journal of Teaching and Learning*, 17(2), 76-90.

Naidoo, S., & Raju, J. (2012). Impact of the digital divide on information literacy training in a higher education context. *South African Journal of Library and Information Science*, 78(1), 34–44. doi:10.7553/78-1-46

Neumann, M., Rauschenberger, M., & Schon, E.-M. (2023). *"We Need To Talk About ChatGPT": The Future of AI and Higher Education* [Paper Presentation]. IEEE/ACM 5th International Workshop on Software Engineering Education for the Next Generation (SEENG), Melbourne, Australia. https://doi-org.nwulib.idm.oclc.org/10.1109/SEENG59157.2023.00010

Ng, D. T. K., Leung, J. K. L., Chu, S. K. W., & Qiao, M. S. (2021). Conceptualizing AI Literacy: An Exploratory Review. *Computers and Education: Artificial Intelligence*, *2*(100041), 100041. Advance online publication. doi:10.1016/j.caeai.2021.100041

Nyamupangedengu, E. (2017). Investigating factors that impact the success of students in a Higher Education classroom: A case study. *Journal of Education*, *68*, 113–130.

Ottonicar, S., Manhique, I., & Mosconi, E. (2021). Ethical Aspects of Information Literacy in Artificial Intelligence. In B. Vassileva & M. Zwilling (Eds.), *Responsible AI and Ethical Issues for Businesses and Governments* (pp. 179–201). doi:10.4018/978-1-7998-4285-9.ch010

Ou, A. W., Stöhr, C., & Malmström, H. (2024). Academic communication with AI-powered language tools in higher education: From a post-humanist perspective. *System*, *121*(103225), 103225. Advance online publication. doi:10.1016/j.system.2024.103225

Perkins, M. (2023). Academic Integrity considerations of AI Large Language Models in the post-pandemic era: ChatGPT and beyond. *Journal of University Teaching & Learning Practice*, *20*(2). Advance online publication. doi:10.53761/1.20.02.07

Pineteh, E. M. (2014). The academic writing challenges of undergraduate students: A South African case study. *International Journal of Higher Education*, *3*(1), 12–22.

Radford, A., Wu, J., Child, R., Luan, D., Amodei, D., & Sutskever, I. (2019). Language models are unsupervised multitask learners. *OpenAI blog*, *1*(8), 9.

Robinson, J. A., & Glanzer, P. L. (2017). Building a culture of academic integrity: What students perceive and need. *College Student Journal*, *51*(2), 209–221.

Rudolph, J., Tan, S., & Tan, S. (2023). ChatGPT: Bullshit spewer or the end of traditional assessments in higher education? *Journal of Applied Learning and Teaching*, *6*(1).

Smith, A. L., Greaves, F., & Panch, T. (2023). Hallucination or confabulation? Neuroanatomy as metaphor in large language models. *PLOS Digital Health*, *2*(11), e0000388. doi:10.1371/journal.pdig.0000388 PMID:37910473

Sokolow, A. (2020). *South Africa's Fourth Industrial Revolution limited by lack of computer literacy, access*. https://news.medill.northwestern.edu/chicago/south-africas-fourth-industrial-revolution-limited-by-lack-of-computer-literacy-access/

Southworth, J., Migliaccio, K., Glover, J., Glover, J., Reed, D., McCarty, C., Brendemuhl, J., & Thomas, A. (2023). Developing a model for AI Across the curriculum: Transforming the higher education landscape via innovation in AI literacy. *Computers and Education: Artificial Intelligence*, *4*(100127), 100127. Advance online publication. doi:10.1016/j.caeai.2023.100127

Thomas, A., & Van Zyl, A. (2012). Understanding of and attitudes to academic ethics among first-year university students. *African Journal of Business Ethics*, *6*(2), 143–155. doi:10.4103/1817-7417.111028

United Nations Educational Scientific and Cultural Organisation. (2002). Open and distance learning: trends, policy and strategy considerations. Paris: UNESCO. https://unesdoc.unesco.org/ark:/48223/pf0000128463

Utami, S., Andayani, A., Winarni, R., & Sumarwati, S. (2023). Utilization of artificial intelligence technology in an academic writing class: How do Indonesian students perceive? *Contemporary Educational Technology*, *14*(4), ep450. Advance online publication. doi:10.30935/cedtech/13419

Vaswani, A., Shazeer, N., Parmar, N., Uszkoreit, J., Jones, L., Gomez, A. N., Kaiser, Ł., & Polosukhin, I. (2017). Attention is all you need. Advances in neural information processing systems [Paper Presentation]. *31st Conference on Neural Information Processing Systems*, Long Beach, CA, United States.

Weber-Wulff, D., Anohina-Naumeca, A., Bjelobaba, S., Foltýnek, T., Guerrero-Dib, J., Popoola, O., & Waddington, L. (2023). Testing of detection tools for AI-generated text. *International Journal for Educational Integrity*, *19*(1), 26. doi:10.1007/s40979-023-00146-z

Wheatley, A., & Hervieux, S. (2022). Separating artificial intelligence from science fiction: Creating an academic library workshop series on AI literacy. In S. Hervieux & A. Wheatley (Eds.), *The Rise of AI: Implications and Applications of Artificial Intelligence in Academic Libraries*. Association of College and Research Libraries.

Wollscheid, S., Lødding, B., & Aamodt, P. O. (2021). Prepared for higher education? Staff and student perceptions of academic literacy dimensions across disciplines. *Quality in Higher Education*, *27*(1), 20–39. doi:10.1080/13538322.2021.1830534

KEY TERMS AND DEFINITIONS

Academic Integrity: A commitment to five fundamental values of academic conduct: honesty, trust, fairness, respect, responsibility, and courage (International Center for Academic Integrity [ICAI], 2021).

Academic Integrity Literacy: Knowledge of academic integrity values, behaviours, and ethical decision; including, the skills and actions necessary for the ethical use and representation of information in academia.

Academic Literacy: The ability of students to comprehend, navigate, and apply conventions of academic discourse.

Artificial Intelligence Literacy: The knowledge and understanding of AI necessary for individuals to participate in the broader discourse around AI and make informed decisions about its use and implications.

Digital Divide: The disparity between those with convenient access to information and communication technology (ICT) tools and those lacking such access or the skills to utilise them.

Digital Literacy: The ability to understand and use information from various sources presented through digital devices, with specific emphasis on the skills to extract, engage, integrate, and employ information from digital platforms effectively.

Generative Pre-Trained Transformer (GPT): "Generative" is the capability of LLMs to generate text, which is contextually relevant to the inputs, "pre-trained" signifies that the model has undergone initial training on vast language datasets enabling it to produce human-like text, and "Transformer" is a type of model that weigh the significance of different words in the input data.

Hallucination (in AI Context): A phenomenon associated with LLMs whereby these models unintentionally fabricate information, posing challenges to the integrity of information.

Information Literacy: Skills required by individuals to recognise when information is needed, where to locate, evaluate, and use effectively in line with recognised standards.

Large Language Models (LLMs): Applications trained on extensive language data that predict and generate text based on input prompts in conversational manner.

Linguistic Capital: Rooted in Bourdieu's theory, where linguistic proficiency plays a critical role in academic success, especially in a socio-linguistically diverse context like South Africa.

Prompt Engineering: The skill of formulating queries to elicit relevant and appropriate responses from LLMs models.

Chapter 3
The Impact of AI Requires Integration Across K–12 and Tertiary Learning

Charles Wiggill
Stadio Higher Education, South Africa & University of Johannesburg, South Africa

Jacqueline Batchelor
University of Johannesburg, South Africa

ABSTRACT

This chapter explores the integration of artificial intelligence (AI) in South African K-12 education and its influence on literacy, especially as students progress to higher education. It addresses the varying levels of school development in South Africa and the challenges teachers face, including infrastructure issues and differing attitudes towards AI. Using Rogers' diffusion of innovations model, teachers are categorised into five groups, from innovators to laggards, to assess their openness to AI in education. The study emphasises the crucial role of early adopters in successfully implementing AI technologies. It suggests that by supporting innovators and early adopters, significant improvements in literacy levels in schools could be achieved, potentially elevating literacy in higher education. The chapter discusses AI's potential to transform traditional educational models and its role in literacy enhancement within South Africa's K-12 sector.

DOI: 10.4018/979-8-3693-1054-0.ch003

"Artificial intelligence is not a substitute for human intelligence; it is a tool to amplify human creativity and ingenuity." – Fei-Fei Li, Co-Director, Stanford Institute for Human-Centered Artificial Intelligence and IT Professor, Graduate School of Business

"I believe AI is going to change the world more than anything in the history of humanity. More than electricity." – Kai-Fu Lee, AI Expert, Chairman and CEO of Sinovation Ventures, Author of 'AI Superpowers' and 'AI 2041'

INTRODUCTION

South African education has a vast, divided past. While many institutions of learning are losing the literacy battle daily, others are flying ever higher and would rank highly in global metrics. However, in a contemporary world with increasingly digitized interconnectivity, one cannot merely consider literacy in its traditional milieu. Although the time-honored concept of the Three Rs (Reading, 'Riting and 'Rithmetic) is still vital (Ippolito, 2008), one must now consider several literacies when preparing young citizens for a happy, productive, successful, and rewarding future. So, according to Reddy et al. (2023), besides traditional literacy (as mentioned above), further important literacies to be considered and incorporated include communication literacy, computer literacy, information literacy, media literacy, technological literacy, and visual literacy.

Branson (2023) highlights the value of including New Literacies Studies at elementary schools, claiming that,

"Digital literacy goes beyond merely operating technology tools and devices. It includes the cognitive and social processes that take place when reading, writing, and communicating in digital spaces and with digital tools."

Furthermore, Lankshear & Knobel (2006) caution that the introduction of new technologies "widen the gap" between those with "insider status" who are comfortable with technology and those who are "outsiders", with minimal access to or experience of the digital world. Contemporary students also require academic literacy, digital literacy, and knowledge of how to work with artificial intelligence (AI literacy) to succeed in their studies.

Although this book is aimed at artificial intelligence and literacy in higher education, school-leavers enrolling at tertiary institutions need to be well-positioned in the aforesaid literacies to cope and excel in higher education. The better the literacy levels of school-leavers, the sounder the literacy levels of first year university students, with the concomitant likelihood of greater success in higher education.

Teachers in K-12 education prepare school-leavers for the shift from secondary to tertiary education. Should the teachers be well-placed with the requisite skills, expertise, and attitudes to facilitate the transfer of competencies required at the tertiary level, the chances of success are enhanced greatly. Therefore, this chapter is aimed at considering the various literacies required of a school leaver as well as the perceptions of South African K-12 teachers relating to the adoption of artificial intelligence in their classrooms.

Considering the issues facing South African education, could artificial intelligence help to bridge the gap between the haves and have-nots in K-12 schools, thereby improving literacy levels and also their chance of success in higher education?

An online portal asked, "Why are people talking about kids not being able to read anymore?" (PhenomenalPancake, n.d.). Venturing further, it asked whether teachers had experience of declining literacy rates in children and how severe the problem had become. Finally, it enquired whether there was real data to support the claims, or whether it was merely anecdotal. The responses from educators around the world indicated that, anecdotally at least, there is a concerning decline in literacy rates, that those who are ahead of the pack fly ever higher while the rest are left ever further behind, and that, in certain regions, there is a noticeable gender difference in literacy rates. So, what are teachers and lecturers to do about this conundrum?

Chan et al. (2018) reveal that digital storytelling significantly enhances higher education students' digital literacy by improving their digital competencies, engagement, and skills. The study advocates for incorporating digital storytelling into curricula as it fosters an authentic learning environment that boosts creativity, motivation, and reflective learning, proving effective for community college students' educational development.

The Arrival of Generative AI

Although artificial intelligence (AI) has formative roots in the 1940s and 1950s (Turing, 1950), for many years it was more of a theoretical construct housed and shrouded in academia and the technology space. Even when developments were taking place, these were largely in the back end and the general public did not have much knowledge of or contact with the concept or the technology itself. One needed advanced computer science training to gain any access. That all changed when the front-end emerged in a form with which it was easy to engage.

On 30 November 2022, a generative AI model became available and soon made headlines. The speed with which the public accepted ChatGPT was astounding (Pavlik, 2024; Haleem et al., 2022). GPT signifies a *generative pretrained transformer*, terms that primarily characterize the foundational neural network structure of the model.

Although there is now a plethora of generative AI tools of all types, ChatGPT was the first to catch the attention of the masses and acquired users at an unprecedented pace.

Where Netflix took 3.5 years to reach a million users, Twitter two years, Facebook 10 months and Instagram 5 months, with the average of the top ten fastest growing applications being 570 days, from the date it was launched, ChatGPT grew to a million users within just 5 days (Roth, 2023). Furthermore, in a mere two months, ChatGPT garnered 100 million users. By comparison, TikTok took nine months and Instagram 30 months to attract the same following (Tse, 2023). Investment followed, with Microsoft announcing an investment in ChatGPT maker OpenAI of $10 billion in January 2023 (Bass, 2023). The world was aflutter with headlines gripping not just the tech world, but the man in the street too, propelling artificial intelligence into the public consciousness. A surge of investment and recruitment across various sectors followed. Anders (2024) notes that, "Everything changed and exploded once we had ChatGPT because it democratized AI literacy" (00:01:32).

This emergence also ushered in a fresh period of "AI anxiety" (Nix, 2023), with coverage such as "Reaching 1 million users quicker than any other application, ChatGPT's rapid ascent has raised some fundamental questions about the nature of AI, and what it means for the broader economy" (ChatGPT: The Start of the AI Revolution, n.d.).

Verma (2023) reports that as technology rapidly advances, AI's integration into education is becoming more prevalent, with educators and researchers uncovering its transformative potential in learning. The AI education market is forecast to exceed $20 billion US by 2027.

Clearly, generative AI is here to stay and the range of generative AI tools spans far more than just text generation. There are tools for creating images, photographs, presentations, videos, lyrics, musical scores, coding and more.

In *The Artificial Intelligence Imperative: A Practical Roadmap for Business*, Lauterbach and Bonime-Blanc (2018), highlight the need for technology literacy and collaboration across sectors to ensure that AI is integrated responsibly into everyday business operations and monitored by governing bodies. AI's transformative effect on the global economy spans numerous fields, making tech proficiency essential for traditional companies, their leadership, policymakers, and governance experts (Lauterbach & Bonime-Blanc, 2018). These sectors need to draw skills from tertiary institutions able to provide AI-savvy graduates. These institutions, in turn, need to be able to draw from a pool of AI-literate school leavers who have been nurtured in K-12 classrooms.

Lauterbach and Bonime-Blanc (2018) explicitly mention the disruptive impact of AI on all sectors of the economy and education has certainly not been excluded from the disruption that ensued after the introduction of ChatGPT. The launch of ChatGPT raised questions among educators regarding the effectiveness and advantages of teaching essential writing and critical thinking skills, given the ease of access to AI-driven "cheating" tools.

The current status is that, while ChatGPT can produce persuasive student-like essays, it struggles with complex quantitative queries (Karaali, 2023). Educators and people in general have different experiences relating to AI. As a result, some are searching out AI solutions for issues in their environments while others are anxious and there are many who have legitimate concerns.

Concerns about plagiarism and ethics, students relying on AI tools to generate their writing assignments, students losing the critical skills required in an academic environment owing to a reliance on generative AI tools, and possibly concerns about job losses are not unfounded. However, societies have seen numerous innovative technological breakthroughs in the past, and we are still here, despite the challenges progress has brought. For instance, many thought the introduction of television would damage children's comprehension skills and that they may not learn to read (Buckingham, 2004) and some thought that the creation of the internet would prevent real learning (Carr, 2020).

I was at a high school in a rural South African town when television made its debut in local households in the late 1970s. It was reported anecdotally that teachers had concerns that children would never read again and that they would lose their skills of analysis and critical thought (Baron, 1985). There were also concerns about a future generation of passive television viewers being empty vessels awaiting the government propaganda that might fill the void. Luckily, there were also ardent teachers of English who believed in embracing the new technology while fervently teaching students to become judicious users of the innovation. They foreshadowed Baron (1985), who emphasizes the critical concern regarding the impact of television on children, particularly how they understand its content and structure, and notes the growing interest in enhancing children's awareness of the medium's conventions to mitigate its influence.

So, in much the same way, it falls on contemporary teachers and lecturers to prepare students for the world of generative AI and other innovations yet to come. Educators should teach students to use AI technologies judiciously to augment their skills and abilities and to be aware of the concomitant limitations and ethical issues.

As an example, Toncic (2020) completed an American study where teachers of English used an AI grammar checker in a writing program. The teachers recognized AI grammar checkers as potential private aides, possibly improving student writing, teaching grammar, and reducing educator workloads. The research indicates that online grammar checkers facilitate significant critical reflection regarding the assessment of Standard English in secondary schools. An observation of this study indicates how AI was actioned to augment the teachers' role, rather than supplant it. In fact, some AI researchers favor the term *augmented intelligence*, rather than or in addition to *artificial intelligence*, as they believe AI can enhance and support the role of the teacher (Sadiku & Musa, 2021).

A Brief Overview of the South African K-12 Education System

South African education transitioned from a fragmented system based on principles of Christian National Education (CNE) at the height of the Apartheid years, which comprised nineteen education departments based on race, to a single department for K-12 schools. The current system comprises provincial departments that fall under the unitary national department, all following the same curriculum. Nonetheless, the economic and social influences of the previous dispensation are still largely mirrored in schools across the country (*Apartheid Education - New Learning online*, n.d.).

South African schools fall into public (government) and independent (private) schools. The public schools are ranked in quintiles with quintile 1 schools being the least resourced and quintile 5 schools having the most resources. Independent schools are generally well resourced; however, they range from rural church schools with fewer resources to extremely well-resourced institutions that could challenge other institutions globally.

Although, by global standards, a substantial proportion of the national budget is allocated to education, citizens do not appear to be getting their money's worth. The system is hampered by inefficiencies and corruption, as well as the minimal standards expected of teachers in many areas across the country. Many schools have the bare minimum, and some are even without electricity, potable water, or water-borne sewerage. While most of these under-resourced schools are in deep rural areas, there are some in urban environments that are provisioned just as poorly. Literacy and numeracy rates are generally poor, and so are skills in educational technology. A dearth of libraries and media centers, a lack of computers and digital technology offerings (including poor connectivity and the cost of data) make a large contribution to this situation. So does the scarcity of skilled teachers and technologists. At present, the bulk of local K-12 schools do not have the necessary tools and resources to adequately address the benefits AI could offer.

AI in K-12 Education

In a study of the perceptions of local teachers to the adoption of AI in their classrooms, a range of attitudes was identified (Liu et al., 2019; Wiggill, 2024). While many teachers welcomed the advent of AI and excitedly looked forward to implementing aspects of AI in their learning ecosystems and practice, this was juxtaposed with feelings of skepticism and concern, largely as a result of concerns about the impact of

AI on student learning and the possibility of the role of the teacher in the classroom becoming redundant.

If AI is to aid the preparation of K-12 students for higher learning, K-12 teachers require sound AI knowledge and support, as well as positive perceptions of and perspectives on AI. If teachers feel threatened by AI, they are unlikely to introduce their charges to this technology in any meaningful way. This lack of enthusiasm for AI use and implementation in their practice will likely impact negatively on the learners in their teaching and learning ecosystems. In the absence of concerted efforts to harness the immense potential of AI in learning environments, the possible benefits of AI in this sphere will be forgotten and the country will fall behind global developments.

This calls for a conscious strategy to advance the adoption of AI in K-12 classrooms.

Rogers' Diffusion of Innovations Model Applied to AI Adoption

Research on the perceptions of South African teachers to the adoption of AI in their classrooms established that most participants were keen to dabble with AI while searching for benefits it might add to their practice (Wiggill, 2024). This local study used Rogers' Diffusion of Innovations (DOI) (Rogers, 1962) model to categorize teachers according to their perceptions of and acceptance of AI in their classrooms. Rogers' model categorizes personnel into five distinct cohorts, depending on their levels of acceptance and adoption of new technologies.

Figure 1. Technology adoption curve and lifecycle
(Bouchrika et al., 2018)

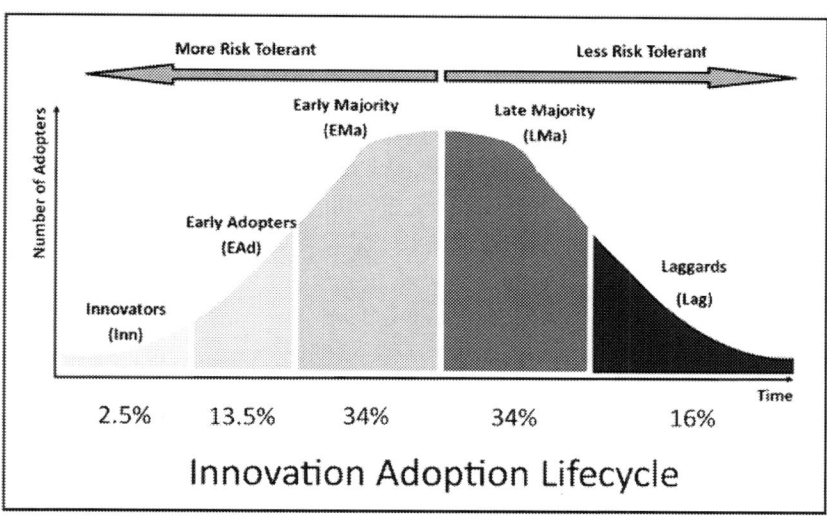

According to the model (above), the pioneers who experiment with, possibly create and transform or remodel the technology, are referred to as Innovators (Inn). They are followed by a second cohort identified as Early Adopters (EAd). This group are seen as leaders and influencers who hang back briefly while investigating a new technology to establish whether it is worth implementing. Once convinced, they do the missionary work of influencing and leading others to adopt the innovation. Innovators (Inn) and Early Adopters (EAd) are considered risk takers and are followed by the Early Majority (EMa) who are also not averse to taking risks, though they are more conservative and risk-aware than the first two adopter categories. The final two categories are less risk tolerant and less likely to adopt new technology in their classrooms. The Late Majority (LMa) are far more traditional in their beliefs and approaches to change. They do not alter their views easily and need convincing to change course. The final group is termed Laggards (Lagg). They are naysayers, stuck in their ways and do not wish to change. Regardless of compelling evidence to the contrary, they will dig in their heels, find every excuse to avoid the developments and change, and call out all progressives who do adopt the innovations.

A logical conclusion that can be drawn from Rogers' model is that educational managers and curriculum developers should focus on developing and supporting the top 16% of risk takers, Inn and EAd. These thought leaders can motivate others and facilitate the necessary change in attitudes and approaches towards AI. Their enthusiastic participation is likely to influence the thoughts and perceptions of the EMa and, with a potential 50% of personnel on board, the system will be on track to exploit the possible benefits of AI. By offering training and support to the Inn and EAd, which comprise 16% of the teaching corps (Bouchrika et al., 2018), senior education planners and managers could promote the positive effect of the availability of AI tools on all kinds of literacy in South African schools and enhance the literacy of students entering higher education.

To the average classroom practitioner, the concept of AI is new and novel. However, AI tools are available and accessible to anyone with a digital device and basic technology skill set, so the genie is out of the bottle. Teachers may still be trying to come to grips with it and mulling over its potential effects, but anecdotal evidence and Google trends suggest that their students are way ahead of them on the adoption curve. According to Google Trends (2023, December) interest in generative AI suddenly spiked in the latter parts of 2022, both worldwide and in South Africa, coinciding with the global launch of ChatGPT.

If teachers are to embrace AI, studies have shown they require professional learning and support, resources, and clear information to allay their skepticism and concerns (Liu et al., 2019). Therefore, by focusing the second stage of implementation on the EMa and LMa (68% of education personnel), education managers can harness the benefits of AI to enhance all kinds of future literacy levels.

AI's Influence on Literacy

As mentioned in the introduction, the term 'literacy' in its traditional sense primarily refers to the ability to read, write, and understand written text. Even by this narrow definition, K-12 students struggle. Reading comprehension and writing skills, as evidenced by South African scores in various global indices (PIRLS 2021 & TIMMS 2019), give cause for concern. However, the term *literacy* cannot merely be viewed in the traditional sense when the world is hurtling ever deeper into a technologically developing space. As mentioned earlier, various literacies must be considered side-by-side with traditional literacy and AI literacy for any real progress in a contemporary, digital world.

AI could be part of the literacy solution for basic education by making it possible to include more personalized learning, incorporating personalized reading programs, using AI tools for language learning, and including interactive writing workshops. In the higher education space, local students face challenges in academic writing and the critical analysis of texts. Remedies might include AI-assisted advanced writing courses, peer review groups, and academic literacy workshops. However, AI literacy is a requirement for any of this to work. Zhang, et al. (2023) appeal for the promotion of AI education at K-12 schools. They raise awareness of the complexities in producing AI-literate citizens from the pool of school children. They state that the elements of AI literacy are blurred and they are uncertain of the 'socio-political implications' for students learning about AI literacy as a 'sociotechnical system'. They posit that students should be taught three central components: technical concepts and processes, ethical and societal implications, and vocation prospects.

It must also be borne in mind that, although the concepts of AI literacy, computer literacy, digital literacy, information literacy, and technological literacy are closely related, they are distinct. Each of them focuses on a different aspect of how individuals interact with technology and information in the digital age. Computer literacy is about operating technology; digital literacy extends to navigating and communicating in a digital world; information literacy focuses on managing and critically evaluating information; and technological literacy encompasses a broader understanding and contextual awareness of technology's role in society. AI literacy pivots on comprehending AI's capabilities, limitations, and impacts on society, and on fostering critical thinking about its ethical and practical implications.

Impact of AI on Literacy Development in K-12

Luckin (2018) captures the vast power AI developments hold when she states:

"The transformative power of AI technologies in education is rapidly unfolding. They offer the potential for addressing some of the most pressing issues in education, including individualizing instruction, providing access to educational resources to more students, and enabling a lifelong learning trajectory for everyone. However, realizing the potential of AI in education requires that we engage in a broad-based dialogue that explores the risks, opportunities, and ethical considerations associated with their use in educational settings."

Hruby and Burns (2020) argue that scientific research confirms that the development of literacy is convoluted and extremely diverse and encompasses numerous "scales of process and context".

Wang & Lester (2023) appeal for the creation and implementation of K-12 AI literacy curricula that could provide students with the support required to prepare them for a working world that has changed greatly. The researchers acknowledge the complexities and challenges of designing and developing curricula that must be scaled for a range of students. They raise the point that, unlike for other subjects, no research foundation exists for K-12 AI education. Furthermore, they propose a comprehensive approach comprising research programs ranging across four spheres of AI education. These include elements for students, teachers and administrators, subject areas, and assessment.

Enhancing the Acquisition of Reading, Writing, and Comprehension Skills

AI has the potential to significantly enhance traditional literacy skills in K-12 education by various means. Many of these methods can be individualized and focused on each student in a class group, thereby creating greater student engagement and saving the teacher substantial time. Almusaed et al. (2023) highlight the interdisciplinary necessity of AI in education, particularly its potential to boost student engagement and learning quality in hybrid educational settings. The study emphasizes the importance of integrating AI technologies, like chatbots and virtual reality, to personalize and enhance learning experiences, while also acknowledging the need for sound pedagogical practices and ethical considerations, including data privacy and bias mitigation. It advocates for the exploration of AI's role in addressing educational challenges and innovating teaching, underscoring the balance between leveraging technological advancements and addressing associated risks and limitations.

AI could enhance traditional literacy skills by analyzing a student's learning style, strengths, and weaknesses to provide customized literacy instructions. For instance, it can adapt reading materials to suit the student's current reading level, helping them progress more effectively. AI-powered tools, such as educational games and interactive reading apps, can make learning more engaging. These tools often include features like voice recognition and text-to-speech, aiding in pronunciation and reading fluency. AI tools can also aid in improving writing skills by suggesting improvements in grammar, style, and coherence, thus enhancing students' writing abilities. AI-driven chatbots or virtual assistants can serve as reading companions, encouraging students to read more, and assisting with vocabulary and comprehension. AI can assist in curating and recommending a diverse range of reading materials tailored to students' interests and reading levels, keeping them engaged and motivated. AI can be used to teach students how to critically evaluate digital content, an essential skill in the modern, information-rich world. AI integrated with augmented reality (AR) and virtual reality (VR) can create immersive reading experiences, helping students visualize and understand complex texts and concepts.

For students with learning disabilities or those who are non-native speakers, AI tools can offer support through speech-to-text, text-to-speech, and language translation features, making literacy skills more accessible.

AI systems can also provide instant feedback on written assignments or reading comprehension exercises, allowing for quicker corrections, and understanding of mistakes. AI can help teachers by analyzing classroom data to identify trends, such as common areas where students struggle, enabling targeted interventions and support.

By leveraging AI in these ways, K-12 schools can significantly enrich traditional literacy education, making it more effective, engaging, and tailored to the individual needs of students.

Fostering Digital, Information, and Technological Literacy

While mathematics and languages are important, AI can also foster digital creativity by assisting students in creating their own digital content, such as blogs, videos, and presentations, and by providing feedback on their creations. By integrating AI into the curriculum, K-12 schools can significantly enhance digital and information literacy, preparing students to navigate and succeed in an increasingly digital world.

AI can play a significant role in fostering digital and information literacy in K-12 schools. From teaching online research skills and offering personalized learning paths, to developing critical thinking for media consumption and creating interactive learning environments. In addition, AI can help to make students aware of the ethical use of information, provide real-time cybersecurity education and enhance processes such as information verification. AI can assist in teaching data literacy by helping students understand how to collect, analyze, and interpret data, an increasingly important skill in the digital age. Students should be exposed to emerging technologies that would set them up for a future where digital and AI literacy will be paramount.

Nikou and Aavakare (2021) integrated the Unified Theory of Acceptance and Use of Technology (UTAUT) framework developed by Venkatesh et al. (2003) with information and digital literacy to investigate higher education staff and students' intentions to use digital technologies. This revealed a complex relationship between literacy and technology usage in higher education, finding that information literacy significantly influences the intention to use digital technology. This finding underscores the need for enhanced literacy skills to effectively employ educational technologies, whereas digital literacy's impact is mediated by performance and effort expectations. Highlighting the critical role of selecting appropriate digital technologies that align with teaching and learning strategies, the research suggests that fostering literacy skills is essential for integrating digital tools into higher education and advocates for policies and strategies that support the development of these skills to fully leverage the benefits of digital advancements in education.

Preparing K-12 Students for the Demands of Higher Education

AI can be a powerful tool in preparing K-12 students for the academic and skill-based demands of higher education. AI can provide tailored tutoring in core subjects, ensuring students have a strong foundation in skills like reading, writing, and mathematics, which are critical for success in higher education. AI can also teach students effective research methods, including how to find, evaluate, and use information, which is essential for the independent study required in higher education. Moreover, time management and organization are critical for tertiary studies. AI-powered tools can help students develop skills in these areas by supplying personalized planners and study schedules.

AI can also assist the development of fundamental skills. Critical thinking and analysis can be facilitated by AI by providing interactive problem-solving scenarios and exercises. AI-driven writing tools can assist students in improving their writing skills, offering feedback on grammar, style, and structure, which are crucial for the numerous writing assignments in higher education. AI can enhance digital literacy, teaching students how to effectively use digital tools and platforms that are commonly used in higher education settings.

Otero et al. (2023) examined the integration of AI literacy into K-12 education, identifying two primary approaches: hands-on learning experiences and theoretical frameworks. Their findings suggest that, while schools have primarily focused on domain-specific technical skills without extensive evaluation of learning outcomes, countries like the US and China are pioneering more comprehensive AI literacy programs that demand further assessment of their effectiveness. The study advocates for an interdisciplinary and competency-based AI literacy integration within existing curricular subjects, emphasizing the importance of project-based learning and the critical role of teacher competency in developing and implementing AI education strategies. This approach encourages breaking traditional disciplinary boundaries and enhancing overall learning through the application of AI literacy.

AI can simulate collaborative environments and facilitate online group projects, helping students to develop teamwork and communication skills that are essential in higher education. AI can also introduce students to advanced topics and subjects, sparking interest, and providing foundational knowledge in fields they may pursue in higher education.

Exposure to AI in learning helps students become comfortable and adaptable with evolving educational technologies, a skill increasingly important in tech-integrated higher education environments.

Finally, AI can provide career guidance and advice for university preparedness, helping students make informed decisions about their higher education paths and future careers. Incorporating AI into K-12 education can better equip students with the necessary skills, knowledge, and adaptability to succeed in the demanding environment of higher education.

Some Examples of AI Use in Education

Currently available AI tools already show potential to expedite mundane tasks, although users should always view their output with a critical eye and adapt, adjust and correct where necessary.

Teachers and learners could be supported by AI-driven Chatbots, also known as conversational agents or CAs (Bozkurt, 2023). Although a live human appears to be the desired form of support for many, should this not be available, a voice-generated or text-to-text chatbot could be a solution. Consider situations where 24/7-support could be useful: The chatbots would not necessarily replace education specialists but could fill in the gaps for continuity after hours or when the specialist educator is unavailable. Huddleston (2023) reports Bill Gates saying, "A.I. chatbots will teach kids to read within 18 months."

Ramandanis and Xinogalos (2023) note that chatbots mimic human-software conversations to support specific services, and their use, especially as educational teaching assistants providing content, has grown significantly in the past five years. Cunningham-Nelson (2024) completed a review on the use of chatbots to help students with content and queries. Chatbots offer potential in education by streamlining and personalizing learning, with early examples suggesting they can enhance student learning and content delivery through FAQs (Frequently Asked Questions) and short response applications. A study by Aleedy et al. (2022) examines the linguistic challenges in deploying chatbots across English, Arabic, and other languages, illustrating their educational benefits through a case study of the use of Hubert.ai in evaluating student feedback on a machine learning course.

Annamalai et al. (2023) indicate that chatbots boost English learners' skills, autonomy, and engagement and advocate for their use in supportive practice environments. They argue for the strategic incorporation of chatbots into language programs because of their potential to improve confidence and proficiency and underscore the importance of further research on their educational benefits. Reynolds and Wiggill (2022) created a cheerful blue goat named Landy, who became the iconic figure for helping students find support to various queries they posed. Landy exists as an example of how AI can be leveraged in a South African context.

Generative AI tools can create significant planning and scheduling documents in a matter of seconds. Think of this as automated mind maps and other graphic organizers. One needs to view the output with a critical eye, correcting and adjusting where this might be necessary. However, one should not discount its possible value.

In a similar vein, teachers and lecturers can use generative AI tools to create rubrics and marking guidelines for various assessments. AI tools can create valuable gradations in responses, from highlighting excellence in a particular descriptor to providing a nuanced suggestion for improvement within the marking guidelines. Of course, the critical eye of the teacher is required to correct any misaligned or inappropriate descriptors. Teachers and lecturers in South Africa have reported using generative AI tools to create individualized academic report comments, tailormade comments for individuals for their formative assessments and for other feedback. The tools are still new to most and practitioners are still learning about the possibilities. At present, comments abound about remaining aware of the limitations and ensuring all outputs are checked thoroughly.

South African educators have also mentioned using AI to create letters for students and parents. These include pro forma correspondence covering generalities as well as individual letters commending students, informing them, or correcting and disciplining them. Once one can produce a robust prompt, the tool can deliver a viable offering (Korzyński et al., 2023).

I am also aware of a few drama specialists at secondary schools and in higher education who have tried a novel concept using generative AI. Students were tasked with using AI to produce a script for their term/semester project. This was merely the starting point and required careful planning from the students.

Students had to think carefully about the prompts they used to inform the AI tool, considering aspects such as the setting, plot, main themes, number of characters, characterization and so on. Once the prompts had been submitted to the generative AI tool, a script was automatically generated. The assessor then posed questions to students about the success of the automated script. Without exception, students pointed out that the tool did not appear to understand much about humor and various aspects regarding nuances, emotional context, and weighting of words. Teachers then tasked students with editing these scripts to bolster the product, using the observations made during their analysis of the scripts initially generated. The final mark for the assessment was calculated on the difference the student made to the initial creation. Students soon observed and commented on the inherent weaknesses of the AI tools they used and were motivated by the realization that they, as people, held intrinsic value because of their critical and analytical skills.

Challenges and Lessons Learned

Unfortunately, before one even considers the benefits or challenges of AI itself, one must confront the issues faced by a developing nation. Practical challenges in the local context regarding any technological or digital developments include basic infrastructural challenges such as the provision of electricity, the impact of load shedding and power failures even when electricity is connected, the provision of computer hardware and software licensing, internet connectivity at sites, the security of equipment and its maintenance.

It also needs to be borne in mind that skills, time and financial resources are in limited supply. This is exacerbated by a lack of training and support of teachers and technicians as well as an already busy curriculum cluttered with many learning areas and subjects that are often separated from one another.

As of January 2024, 98.7% of South Africans accessed the internet using a mobile phone (Statista, 2024). Many of these devices can access AI software and tools, offering a window into the world of AI. Under the subtitle 'Augmented Working', Shripad (2021) says:

"By 2023, most humans will be working alongside robots and intelligent machines that were created to assist them in performing their tasks more effectively. This may come from smartphones that provide workers immediate access to data and analytics tools since these devices are increasingly utilized in industrial and retail industries".

While immobile desktop computers are available in many South African homes and schools, laptops are not as plentiful. Nevertheless, 81% of users access the internet with a laptop or desktop computer (Statista, 2024). However, mobile phones are available and used widely. Focusing on the use of these mobile devices while introducing local students to AI might foster a greater understanding and use of the AI tools available. By focusing on the personalized learning capabilities of AI coupled with the student's personal device, great strides could be made in restricting the limitations of overcrowded classrooms and overworked teachers.

STRATEGIES FOR EFFECTIVE AI INTEGRATION IN K-12 EDUCATION

Teachers and Student Teachers

In the rapidly evolving field of AI, it is critical for both current educators and those in training to stay informed about the latest developments. Teachers and student teachers must gain a foundational understanding of AI technologies and their potential effects on education. This includes not only theoretical knowledge but also practical experience with AI tools, preparing them for the technological demands of the future workplace. Integrating AI into teaching practices requires a hands-on approach, emphasizing the importance of data analytics for personalized learning and enhancing teaching strategies. Additionally, ethical considerations, such as privacy and data security, must be addressed, ensuring responsible AI use in classrooms (Zhao, Wu & Luo, 2022).

Pedagogical adaptation is essential, with a focus on combining traditional methods with AI to provide a comprehensive educational experience. Continuous professional development is necessary to keep up with new technologies and methodologies. Collaboration skills are also crucial, as they enable educators to work alongside AI experts to effectively implement AI solutions in educational settings. Moreover, fostering critical thinking and problem-solving skills is imperative, allowing teachers to critically evaluate AI tools and integrate them thoughtfully into their classrooms. Educators must maintain a balance between leveraging AI and nurturing human-centric skills like empathy and creativity, which AI cannot replicate.

Preparing for a diverse classroom environment, where AI can address various learning needs, is paramount. Training should empower educators to use AI to support an inclusive learning atmosphere, catering to students with different styles and abilities. By equipping current and future teachers with these competencies, they can confidently navigate the intersection of AI and education, ensuring they are prepared to leverage technology ethically and effectively in their teaching practices. This approach will ensure that educators are not only knowledgeable about AI but are also capable of integrating it into their classrooms in a way that enriches the learning experience for all students.

Classroom Teaching

Introducing K-12 students to AI necessitates a deliberate, age-appropriate approach, starting with basic explanations of AI's nature, operations, and its prevalence in daily life. This foundational step demystifies AI and paves the way for integrating AI-driven educational tools into core subjects, enhancing personalized learning experiences. Such early exposure ensures students build a solid understanding of AI, preparing them for more advanced interactions with technology. Beyond mere familiarity, the aim is to foster an environment where technology enhances the learning journey, tailored to each student's pace and style.

As the educational landscape evolves, teachers are tasked with equipping students with the digital literacy necessary for navigating and critically assessing online information and AI outputs. This includes teaching safe internet use, understanding digital etiquette, and developing problem-solving skills through technology-enhanced activities. Emphasizing these aspects of digital literacy ensures students not only become proficient in using technology but also develop the critical thinking skills needed to question and understand the technology that permeates their lives (Wang & Lester, 2023).

The ethical implications of AI technology also play a crucial role in education. Teachers are responsible for introducing students to the ethical dimensions of AI, such as privacy, data security, and the biases inherent in AI systems. This education is vital for shaping responsible digital citizens. Moreover, engaging students with AI through creative applications like AI-driven art or music programs encourages creativity while highlighting the importance of ethical considerations, such as copyright laws and the avoidance of plagiarism.

Ultimately, hands-on experiences with AI, through classroom projects and experiments, are instrumental in preparing students for future careers in AI-enabled fields. Such experiences not only cultivate technical skills and creativity but also emphasize the importance of inclusivity and accessibility in technology use. By involving parents and the broader community in the conversation about AI in education, teachers can foster a supportive ecosystem for technology-enhanced learning. The goal is to equip students with the technological fluency necessary to navigate a future where AI is an integral part of life and work, ensuring they are ready to contribute to and thrive in a technologically advanced society.

Curriculum Development

Makala, Schmitt & Caballero (2021) highlight global statistics of 750 million adults being "functionally illiterate", with two-thirds being women and half of these originating in Africa and South Asia. In this regard, AI emerges as a transformative force, challenging the traditional educational frameworks that have withstood numerous technological advancements, including the internet. The ever-increasing availability of mobile devices among children heralds AI's growing influence, signaling a shift away from conventional classroom settings. In South Africa, educators are tasked with revising the K-12 curriculum to incorporate AI literacy alongside traditional learning objectives. This endeavor necessitates a collaborative effort with educational and technological experts to develop a curriculum that is both academically sound and technologically forward-thinking. AI's integration extends beyond computer science, with its applications enriching a variety of subjects, from problem-solving in mathematics to language acquisition, illustrating AI's versatility in enhancing educational experiences across disciplines. Wang and Lester (2023) recommend AI literacy programs across all phases and grades.

The successful integration of AI into education relies heavily on teacher readiness, underscored by targeted training and professional development programs. Such initiatives aim to equip educators with the competencies required to incorporate AI tools into their pedagogy effectively. Partnerships with higher education and research institutions further enrich these efforts, offering access to cutting-edge AI applications and research, thereby bridging the gap between theoretical knowledge and practical application. This comprehensive approach not only prepares teachers to navigate the complexities of AI but also enriches students' learning experiences, fostering a deeper engagement with the technology.

Moreover, the curriculum must emphasize digital literacy, ensuring students are adept in both the use and ethical considerations of AI and digital tools. Project-based learning that incorporates AI can stimulate interest and enhance understanding of this technology, promoting critical thinking and problem-solving abilities. It is imperative that AI education in South Africa is culturally relevant and accessible to all students, reflecting the diverse needs and contexts of its learners. Continual reassessment of AI integration strategies is necessary to adapt to the rapidly evolving tech landscape, positioning South African education to meet the demands of the future. By addressing these considerations, South Africa can cultivate a generation well-prepared for the challenges and opportunities presented by the increasing prevalence of AI in various aspects of life and work.

Policy Recommendations

Addressing the digital divide and ensuring equitable access to AI education is paramount for fostering an inclusive learning environment. Policies must focus on making AI tools accessible to every student, including those from under-resourced schools and communities, and those with disabilities. Enhancing technological infrastructure, such as providing reliable internet access and adequate computing devices in schools, especially in rural and underprivileged areas, is crucial. This approach aims to level the playing field, ensuring all students can engage with and benefit from AI technologies in their education. However, to achieve these lofty aims, one must first conceptualize exactly what AI literacy is (Ng et al., 2021).

The critique by Hruby and Burns (2020) on the conventional policy-making approach in education, which overly relies on abstract averages and speculative benchmarks, calls for a re-evaluation of how educational goals are set and assessed. Similarly, the Reading Research Quarterly editorial team (2023) encourages a departure from outdated methodologies and an embrace of new technologies like AI, algorithmic logic, and data literacies (Ridley & Pawlick-Potts, 2021). This shift demands that future policies incorporate AI applications, recognizing them as tools to enhance rather than disrupt the educational status quo. The concept of prompt engineering emerges as a critical skill, underlining the importance of teaching students to formulate queries that effectively leverage AI capabilities, thereby promoting AI literacy.

The implementation of AI in South African K-12 education necessitates a comprehensive national strategy that includes curriculum development, teacher training, and infrastructure improvement tailored to AI integration. This strategy should guide the uniform adoption of AI across the educational spectrum, supported by significant investments in technological infrastructure and teacher training programs. These initiatives aim to prepare educators to integrate AI into various subjects and adopt innovative teaching methods, enhancing the educational experience and outcomes for students across disciplines.

To maximize the benefits of AI in education, it is essential to foster ethical practices and safe technology use within schools, focusing on data privacy and security. Establishing partnerships with technology companies and academic institutions can provide valuable support, resources, and opportunities for innovation in AI education. Moreover, ongoing evaluation of AI programs and community engagement will be crucial for refining strategies and ensuring broad-based support for these initiatives. By embracing these recommendations, South Africa can position itself to leverage AI effectively in education, equipping students with the skills and knowledge necessary for success in an increasingly AI-driven world.

Long-Term Impact on Higher Education Literacy

The adoption of AI in South African higher education institutions heralds a significant transformation in the landscape of higher education literacy, generating a wave of long-term changes. Foremost among these is the shift towards personalized learning (Fariani et al., 2023), which aligns educational content with the unique learning styles, speeds, and preferences of individual students. This approach is expected to markedly boost students' comprehension, retention, and academic outcomes. Concurrently, the definition of literacy is evolving beyond traditional confines to include digital, data, and AI literacy, requiring students to master the interpretation of digital content, comprehend AI-generated materials, and adeptly employ AI tools in their learning.

This evolution in higher education literacy is characterized by increased access to a broad array of learning resources and a stronger focus on critical thinking and analytical skills. As AI assumes responsibility for routine tasks and data analysis, there is a growing emphasis on nurturing students' ability to critically assess AI-generated content and make well-informed decisions. Kong et al (2023) suggest that exactly what to include in literacy programs in higher education has not yet been fully realized. However, the future envisions a synergistic collaboration between humans and AI, enhancing human capabilities in learning and problem-solving, which is essential for advancing higher education literacy. Furthermore, the ethical and responsible application of AI, addressing potential biases, privacy, and security issues, will become increasingly important in the educational discourse. Makala, Schmitt & Caballero (2021) refer to the dire need for programs preparing people for "rapid technological change" for the developing world to keep pace with the developed nations.

The long-term impact of AI on higher education in South Africa underscores a shift towards a more inclusive and skill-diverse educational framework, prioritizing personalized learning and readiness for an AI-integrated workforce. This transition not only involves teaching AI-centric skills but also emphasizes the development of inherent human qualities such as creativity, emotional intelligence, and interpersonal skills. With AI-driven analytics reshaping assessment methods to provide more tailored and constructive feedback, and the potential for AI to democratize education, the sector is poised for a future where continuous learning and adaptability are crucial for academic and professional success. This paradigm shift anticipates a future where AI significantly enhances educational practices, fundamentally altering the fabric of higher education literacy in the region.

Closing the Gap Between K-12 and Higher Education Literacy

Bridging the gap between K-12 and higher education literacy requires a comprehensive and interconnected approach that spans the full educational continuum. Ensuring curriculum alignment is crucial, as it allows for a smooth transition by making certain that skills developed during K-12, such as critical thinking and problem-solving, meet the expectations of higher education. Early intervention programs play a key role in identifying students with literacy challenges at an early stage, preventing the gap from widening as they progress in their education. Moreover, significant emphasis must be placed on professional development for educators, enabling them to recognize and cater to diverse literacy needs and modify their teaching strategies accordingly.

The creation of bridging programs is vital in easing the shift from K-12 to higher education by providing preparatory courses and tutoring, which clarify the demands of higher education and prepare students for its challenges. Advocacy for literacy across the curriculum is also fundamental, as integrating literacy skills into various subjects offers a more comprehensive educational experience. Leveraging technology, particularly AI tools, can transform education by offering personalized learning paths and pinpointing specific areas of need. Additionally, the impact of parental and community engagement in enhancing literacy outcomes and attitudes towards learning cannot be underestimated.

Emphasizing the development of critical reading and writing skills is essential due to their significant role in academic success and value in higher education. Implementing continuous assessment and feedback mechanisms is crucial for the ongoing monitoring and support of literacy development, facilitating timely and efficient interventions. Encouraging collaboration between K-12 and higher education institutions through shared resources and joint programs could further support a unified literacy education strategy. Addressing these facets will facilitate a smoother transition from K-12 to higher education, ensuring students are equipped with the necessary literacy competencies for academic achievement.

CONCLUSION

The potential transformative role of AI in South African K-12 education is immense, with far-reaching implications for the higher education sector. AI presents an opportunity to revolutionize learning experiences, catering to individual student needs through personalized learning. This approach is not only beneficial for addressing diverse learning styles and abilities but also crucial in reducing achievement gaps, thereby equipping students more effectively for the challenges of higher education.

AI-driven tools and resources enhance student engagement and interaction, which is pivotal in maintaining motivation and interest (Otero et al., 2023; Almusaed et al., 2023). Such an enriched learning environment fosters a deeper understanding of subjects, laying a solid foundation for academic success in higher education. Moreover, the data-driven insights provided by AI are invaluable for educators. These insights allow for the optimization of teaching strategies in K-12 education, setting the stage for a seamless transition to higher education.

In a country marked by educational inequalities, AI holds the promise of bridging educational gaps. By offering high-quality educational resources in under-resourced areas, AI can make the journey to higher education more equitable. Furthermore, the integration of AI in K-12 education prepares students with future-ready skills like digital literacy, problem-solving, and critical thinking, which are essential in the modern workforce and higher education.

AI also acts as a catalyst for curriculum reform, pushing for an education system that aligns with the demands of the 21st century and higher education requirements. Teacher empowerment is another critical aspect: AI can aid teachers with marking, grading, resources, and professional development, thereby enhancing their ability to prepare students for higher education.

The continuous learning model promoted by AI encourages students to develop skills in learning and adaptation, traits that are invaluable in higher education contexts. This approach also aids in closing the readiness gap for students entering higher education, particularly in key academic areas such as STEM subjects.

The adoption of AI in K-12 education heralds a long-term educational transformation. Higher education institutions will need to adapt to a new generation of students who are more tech-savvy and accustomed to AI-enhanced learning environments. The cascading effect of AI in South African K-12 education could, therefore, redefine the entire educational landscape, from foundational learning to advanced academic research and application.

Finally, the integration of AI into South African K-12 education holds the potential not only to enhance the learning experience at that level but also to fundamentally transform the expectations and methodologies employed in higher education, resulting in a more dynamic, inclusive, and effective educational system.

REFERENCES

Aleedy, M., Atwell, E., & Meshoul, S. (2022). Using AI chatbots in education: recent advances challenges and use case. In Algorithms for intelligent systems (pp. 661–675). doi:10.1007/978-981-19-1653-3_50

Almusaed, A., Almssad, A., Yitmen, İ., & Homod, R. Z. (2023). Enhancing Student Engagement: Harnessing "AIED"'s Power in Hybrid Education—A Review analysis. *Education Sciences*, *13*(7), 632. doi:10.3390/educsci13070632

Anders, B. A. (2024, March 4). The AI Literacy Imperative: Empowering Instructors & Students. TeachOnline.CA. Contact North/Contact Nord. https://bit.ly/4a2hzqO

Annamalai, N., Eltahir, M. E., Zyoud, S. H., Soundrarajan, D., Zakarneh, B., & Alsalhi, N. R. (2023). Exploring English language learning via Chabot: A case study from a self-determination theory perspective. Computers & Education. *Artificial Intelligence*, *5*, 100148. doi:10.1016/j.caeai.2023.100148

Apartheid Education - New Learning online. (n.d.). https://newlearningonline.com/new-learning/chapter-5/supproting-materials/apartheid-education

Baron, L. J. (1985). Television Literacy Curriculum in Action: A long-term study. *Journal of Educational Television, 11*(1), 49–55. doi:10.1080/0260741850110107

Bass, D. (2023). Microsoft Invests $10 Billion in ChatGPT Maker OpenAI. Retrieved from Bloomberg: https://www.bloomberg.com/news/articles/2023-01-23/microsoft-makes-multibillion-dollar-investment-in-openai#xj4y7vzkg

Bouchrika, I., Harrati, N., Mahfouf, Z., & Gasmallah, N. (2018). Evaluating the Acceptance of e-Learning Systems via Subjective and Objective Data Analysis. In S. Caballé & J. Conesa (Eds.), *Software Data Engineering for Network eLearning Environments: Analytics and Awareness Learning Services* (pp. 199–219). Springer International Publishing. doi:10.1007/978-3-319-68318-8_10

Bozkurt, A. (2023). Unleashing the potential of generative AI, conversational agents and chatbots in educational praxis: A systematic review and bibliometric analysis of GenAI in education. http://hdl.handle.net/20.500.12424/4299873

Branson, S. M. (2023). Chasing a Moving Target: Examining Shifts in Elementary Teachers' Language and Conceptions of Digital Literacy During Professional Learning. Academic Press.

Buckingham, D. (2004). Children Talking Television: The Making of Television Literacy. Taylor & Francis. https://books.google.co.za/books?id=kKBlAgAAQBAJ

Carr, N. G. (2010). *The Shallows: What the Internet Is Doing to Our Brains.* W.W. Norton & Co.

Casal-Otero, L., Catala, A., Fernández-Morante, C., Taboada, M., Cebreiro, B., & Barro, S. (2023). AI literacy in K-12: A systematic literature review. *International Journal of STEM Education, 10*(1), 29. doi:10.1186/s40594-023-00418-7

Chan, B. S. K., Churchill, D., & Chiu, T. K. F. (2017). Digital Literacy Learning in Higher Education Through Digital Storytelling Approach. *Journal of International Education Research, 13*(1), 1–16. https://files.eric.ed.gov/fulltext/EJ1144564.pdf. doi:10.19030/jier.v13i1.9907

Cunningham-Nelson, S. (2024, February 12). A review of chatbots in education: Practical steps forward. QUT ePrints. https://eprints.qut.edu.au/134323/

Fariani, R. I., Junus, K., & Santoso, H. B. (2023). A Systematic Literature Review on Personalised Learning in the Higher Education Context. *Tech Know Learn, 28*(2), 449–476. doi:10.1007/s10758-022-09628-4

Gilmore, D., Crain Soudien, C., & Donald, D. (1999). Post-Apartheid Policy and Practice: Educational Reform in South Africa. In M. Kas, M. Winzer, & C. Majorek (Eds.), *Education in a Global Society: A Comparative Perspective* (pp. 341–350). Allyn and Bacon.

Haleem, A., Javaid, M., & Singh, R. P. (2022). An era of ChatGPT as a significant futuristic support tool: A study on features, abilities, and challenges. BenchCouncil Transactions on Benchmarks. *Standards and Evaluations*, *2*(4), 100089. doi:10.1016/j.tbench.2023.100089

Hruby, G., & Burns, L. D. (2020). The Science of Adolescent Literacy. *Journal of Adolescent & Adult Literacy*, *63*(6), 693–696. doi:10.1002/jaal.1054

Huddleston, T., Jr. (2023, April 22). Bill Gates says A.I. chatbots will teach kids to read within 18 months: You'll be "stunned by how it helps." CNBC. https://www.cnbc.com/2023/04/22/bill-gates-ai-chatbots-will-teach-kids-how-to-read-within-18-months.html

Ippolito, J., Steele, J. L., & Samson, J. F. (2008). Introduction: Why adolescent literacy matters now. *Harvard Educational Review*, *78*(1), 1–6.

Karaali, G. (2023). Artificial Intelligence, Basic Skills, and Quantitative Literacy. Numeracy: Advancing Education in Quantitative Literacy, 16(1).

Kong, S. C., Cheung, W. M. Y., & Zhang, G. (2023). Evaluating an artificial intelligence literacy programme for developing university students' conceptual understanding, literacy, empowerment and ethical awareness. *Journal of Educational Technology & Society*, *26*(1), 16–30.

Korzyński, P., Mazurek, G., Krzypkowska, P., & Kurasinski, A. (2023). Artificial intelligence prompt engineering as a new digital competence: Analysis of generative AI technologies such as ChatGPT. *Entrepreneurial Business and Economics Review*, *11*(3), 25–37. doi:10.15678/EBER.2023.110302

Lankshear, C., & Knobel, M. (2006). *New literacies: Everyday practices and classroom learning*. Open University Press.

Lauterbach, A., & Bonime-Blanc, A. (2018). *The Artificial Intelligence Imperative: A Practical Roadmap for Business*. Praeger. doi:10.5040/9798400614835

Liu, L., Liu, Q., Li, Y., Li, J., Li, H., & Zhao, H. (2019). Teacher perceptions and attitudes towards artificial intelligence in education: A survey study. *Educational Technology Research and Development*, *67*(3), 9–20.

Luckin, R. (2018). The AI revolution: The road to superintelligence. https://www.researchgate.net/publication/324319843_The_AI_Revolution_The_Road_to_Superintelligence

Makala, B., Schmitt, M., & Caballero, A. (2021). How Artificial Intelligence Can Help Advance Post-Secondary Learning in Emerging Markets. Academic Press.

Morrow, W. E. (1990). Aims of Education in South Africa. International Review of Education/Internationale Zeitschrift fur Erziehunswissenschaft/Revue Internationale de l'Education 36, 171–181. doi:10.1007/BF01874882

Ng, D. T. K., Leung, J. K. L., Chu, S. K. W., & Qiao, M. S. (2021). Conceptualizing AI literacy: An exploratory review. *Computers and Education: Artificial Intelligence*, 2, 100041.

Nikou, S., & Aavakare, M. (2021). An assessment of the interplay between literacy and digital Technology in Higher Education. *Education and Information Technologies*, 26(4), 3893–3915. Advance online publication. doi:10.1007/s10639-021-10451-0

Nix, J. (2023, November 30). The year ChatGPT changed almost everything. Bloomberg.com. https://www.bloomberg.com/news/articles/2023-11-30/the-year-chatgpt-changed-almost-everything

Otero, L. C., Catalá, A., Morante, M. C. F., Taboada, M., López, B. C., & Barro, S. (2023). AI literacy in K-12: A systematic literature review. *International Journal of STEM Education*, 10(1), 29. Advance online publication. doi:10.1186/s40594-023-00418-7

Pavlik, G. (2024, January 16). What is generative AI? How does it work? https://www.oracle.com/za/artificial-intelligence/generative-ai/what-is-generative-ai/ doi:10.1007/978-3-030-77584-1_15

PhenomenalPancake. (n.d.). Why are people talking about kids not being able to read anymore? r/OutOfTheLoop. https://www.reddit.com/r/OutOfTheLoop/comments/18igdho/why_are_people_talking_about_kids_not_being_able/?rdt=59203

Ramandanis, D., & Xinogalos, S. (2023). Investigating the support provided by chatbots to educational institutions and their students: A systematic literature review. *Multimodal Technologies and Interaction*, 7(11), 103. doi:10.3390/mti7110103

Reynolds, A., & Wiggill, C. (2022). LandyBot: Learner support. https://chats.landbot.io/v3/H-1050800-XBXSFK7IKLM0J5NT/index.html

Ridley, M., & Pawlick-Potts, D. (2021). Algorithmic literacy and the role for libraries. *Information Technology and Libraries*, *40*(2). Advance online publication. doi:10.6017/ital.v40i2.12963

Roth, S., & de la Sota, B. (2023, April 26). ChatGPT: The start of the AI revolution. https://privatebank.jpmorgan.com/nam/en/insights/markets-and-investing/chatgpt-the-start-of-the-ai-revolution

Shripad, D. S. (2023, July 3). Top Artificial Intelligence (AI) Trends to Watch in 2023—MarkTechPost. Marktechpost. https://www.marktechpost.com/2023/01/07/top-artificial-intelligence-ai-trends-to-watch-in-2023/

Statista. (2024, February 26). Internet access by device in South Africa 2024. https://www.statista.com/statistics/1312851/internet-access-by-device-in-south-africa/

Toncic, J. (2020). Teachers, AI Grammar Checkers, and the Newest Literacies: Emending Writing Pedagogy and Assessment. Digital Culture &amp. *Education*, *12*(1), 26–51. https://doaj.org/toc/1836-8301

Tse, C. (2023, August 7). An AI on the Future. Goldman Sachs Asset Management. https://www.gsam.com/content/gsam/us/en/individual/market-insights/gsam-insights/perspectives/2023/artificial-intelligence-future.html

Turing, A. M. (1950). Computing Machinery and Intelligence. *Mind. New Series*, *59*(236), 433–460. doi:10.1093/mind/LIX.236.433

Venkatesh, V., Morris, M. G., Davis, G. B. D. F. D., & Davis. (2003). User acceptance of information Technology: Toward a unified view. *Management Information Systems Quarterly*, *27*(3), 425–478. . doi:10.2307/30036540

Verma, N. (2023, February 9). How Effective is AI in Education? 10 Case Studies and Examples. Axon Park. https://axonpark.com/how-effective-is-ai-in-education-10-case-studies-and-examples/Volume doi:10.1002/rrq.494

Wang, N., & Lester, J. (2023, June). K-12 Education in the Age of AI: A Call to Action for K-12 AI Literacy. International Journal of Artificial Intelligence in Education, 33(2), 228-232.

Wiggill, C. (2024). *South African Teachers' Perceptions of the Adoption of Artificial Intelligence in the Classroom. Submission of research report for part-fulfillment of MEd ICT*. University of Johannesburg.

Zhang, H., Lee, I., & Safinah, A. (2023, June). Integrating Ethics and Career Futures with Technical Learning to Promote AI Literacy for Middle School Students: An Exploratory Study. International Journal of Artificial Intelligence in Education, 33(2), 290-324.

Zhao, L., Wu, X., & Luo, H. (2022). Developing AI Literacy for Primary and Middle School Teachers in China: Based on a Structural Equation Modeling Analysis. *Sustainability (Basel)*, *14*(21), 14549. doi:10.3390/su142114549

Chapter 4

From Automated Arms
to Automated Brains:
Robotic Human Learning and the Future
of Literary and Philosophical Creativity

Dickson Kanakulya

 https://orcid.org/0000-0002-9676-2813
Makerere University, Uganda

ABSTRACT

There is high potential for AI in education, but the technology also presents creative learning challenges. Educationists are experimenting with AI which is re-configuring creativity learning. Reports indicate a creativity crisis in contemporary education, and this chapter investigates whether the adoption of AI will enhance or diminish human creativity. The chapter posits that due to AI's focus on artificial efficiency, the reductionism decreases human literary creative freedom and risks creating automated brains. AI's LLMs focus on reductive artificial linguistic efficiency which narrows literary variation, eroding the spell power of human language. Artificial intelligence can reconfigure but could not replace human creativity. Since creativity undergirds human inventions, business, social development, and progress, it needs to be protected and enhanced. There is need for research into enhancing authentic human literary and philosophical creativity in the time of AI.

DOI: 10.4018/979-8-3693-1054-0.ch004

INTRODUCTION

While walking in Makerere University in 2022, I talked with two students studying Bachelor of Fine Art. Jessica (real name withheld) mentioned recent news about Huawei offering artificial intelligence training to students (see: Kagolo, 2021). She opined that, 'we need to learn AI but it must help us to realize the dream of our department, 'to develop the intrinsic talents of the students'. Another student, John (real name withheld), commented that 'we use ChatGPT to do our course work but some responses we get are not so helpful'. This conversation implied to me that students are concerned about the impact of artificial intelligence on their creative learning. Universities and institutions are experimenting with advanced technology-based learning, which is reconfiguring creativity learning. Makerere University is experimenting with innovative education and rapid adoption of technology-assisted teaching methods and blended learning (BL) models (Kyakuwa, 2022). Makerere has partnered with Huawei to develop research and learning in artificial intelligence. The future of literary and philosophical creativity depends on developments and achievements in industrial technology. Just like how early industrial revolution technologies squeezed out the creative impulses of assembly workers, contemporary AI based algorithms are squeezing out human creativity by standardizing labor and language. Human literary creativity is at the core of human intellectual development and social progress, but there is the question of whether artificial intelligence-based learning enhances learners' creativity or limits it. Technological automation has been applied for labor control and enhancing industrialization. However, the 'automation of human arms' may be progressing in the 'automation of the human brain' which potentially negatively affects human education for good.

The potential of 'automated human brains' poses a profound challenge for human freedom and creativity. This paper philosophically interrogates the impact of adoption of artificial intelligence and augmented reality on literary learning and creativity. It examines the re-configuration impact of AI on the meaning of learning and creativity. It explores promises of efficient learning and easy access to learning materials vis-à-vis creativity in learning. It uses online-based self-learning that has been experimentally adopted by some universities in the East African region. The paper concludes that the future of literary creativity in an environment of robotic learning may be precarious thus calling on higher institutions to find ways to promote authentic human creativity amidst the adoption of AI.

CREATIVITY CRISIS

In a seminal article, "America's looming creativity crisis", Richard Florida (2004) examines the 'crisis of creativity' that is bedeviling America's education and industry. He posited that, "To stay innovative, America must continue to attract the world's sharpest minds. And to do that, it needs to invest in the further development of its creative sector." (Richard, 2004). He underscores the centrality of creativity in business, social development and humanity's progress. Creativity and innovative thinking have traditionally been considered a desired output of modern education because they push human society and industry forward. Artificial intelligence is disrupting conventional modern education as we know it. Conventional education systems and structures have been the avenues for shaping the human resources that sustain human society.

In 2023 the Department of Library and Information Science at the University of Nairobi organized a symposium on artificial intelligence, noting that 'the big question is how we can take advantage of the AI affordances while limiting its control on human society as we know it'. Researchers at the University of Nairobi are experimenting with developing AI Chatbots that may be applied to improving efficiency in handling student queries. Some reports are raising concerns that AI chatbots are compromising students' learning and work integrity (Mohammed, 2023). The growth of machine learning powered by artificial intelligence has been premised on the 'efficiency argument', in making human resources more cost effective. Big technological corporations like Alphabet (Google), Microsoft, Facebook, Apple, Amazon, Cisco Systems and ChatGPT, among others, are in the race to generate advanced software to achieve efficiency and speed of production. This has an unusual disruptive effect on training in human creativity. But the key question to raise concerning these developments is whether the growth of this software is for purposes enhancing profits from machine learning or for human creativity.

Marketers and promoters of artificial intelligence tools and products speak with a lot of prophetic confidence about the "future" that they are building. With more effective marketing technologies, AI products are pushed onto the public as making life better. It is becoming increasingly apparent that the last avenue for the fight for human freedom is the area of the creatives. The creative power of humanity is what has been determinant for social and human development over the centuries. Artificial intelligence corporations are using the marketable buzz words of innovation, efficiency, sustainability, etc. This paper is not against technological growth, but it aims at making those building the artificial intelligence tools think about the "future" of human creativity that they are selling to the education industry to ensure that it is not harmful to genuine organic human creativity.

Contemporary technological changes have been accepted to be disruptive; the disruption occasioned by technological advancement is taken as a given. The first line of disruption is the philosophy of creativity; there is a growing view that creativity is not uniquely human but can also be done by computers. This view is disrupting not only the creativity in education but the industry as a whole. Artificial intelligence is considered disruptive technology (see: Păvăloaia & Necula, 2023); the disruptive effects of AI technology are changing how people interact and they will revolutionize the creative landscape. It can also be argued that, although humans are superior in terms of creativity and imagination, AI can enhance human's abilities by assisting them in processes that involve data analytics and the use of precise and advanced algorithms. This emphasis on data analytics-based creativity education and reliance on precision algorithms in learning is disrupting the understanding of human creativity. Human creativity education ought not to be mainly predicated on precision and data analytics but on bringing out the human creative spirit from within. But when students' research and grading of their work is AI based, they increasingly resort to AI tools such as chatbots to do their education assignments, and this disrupts their creative growth.

As indicated earlier, universities in Africa are experimenting with cutting edge technologies such as AI in creative education. Makerere University is a leading higher education institution on the continent and is experimenting with innovative education models (Kyakuwa, 2022). Makerere has partnered with Huawei to develop research and learning in artificial intelligence; currently it is being applied in health studies and e-learning but has been rolled out in other areas such as air pollution monitoring.

AI IN AFRICAN CREATIVES AND HIGHER EDUCATION

The 2023 *State of AI in Africa Report* indicates that the adoption of AI may lead to 'democratization' of the creative industries which have for long been considered exclusive clubs that lock out Africans. According to the Report, the advent of AI has increased participation of individuals in the creative fields with AI offering essential support in artistic visions in areas such as AI image generation which assists designers to discover novel ideas (CIPIT, 2023:18). The question is whether the discovery of AI generated 'novel ideas' enhances human creativity or not. Forbes reported that AI has lowered the barrier to entry for creative fields like graphic design and music production (Hironde, 2023). The report focuses on four key thematic areas: AI and Data; AI and Innovation; AI Use and Impact in Health; Agriculture, Legal and Creative Fields; and Responsible AI. It highlights the challenges faced in AI adoption in Africa, including ill-equipped policy frameworks, ethics, skills and capacity, and a need for a structured data ecosystem. The absence of robust policy frameworks leaves AI deployment largely unregulated, and ethical concerns such as accountability, data bias, transparency, and socio-economic implications arise (ibid).

The Inter-University Council of East Africa (IUCEA) has recommended that institutions of higher learning in the region need to adopt AI in their teaching. The Council observes that East African students were already using AI in their classwork and assignments; therefore, lecturers and students need guidance in how to use AI effectively and critically. It warns that it is important to explore AI carefully and critically, considering both its promises and its potential risks (IUCEA, 2023). The Council observes that AI poses risks to higher education, but it should be framed as an opportunity. Learners are already acquiring knowledge and will be quick to integrate it into their studying. Many universities in the East African region still struggle to apply ICT to improve learning and teaching; the rapid adaptation of AI may pose yet further challenges. AI could be positively used to support the core functions of universities – teaching, research and innovation. In the report titled: "Exploring the Potential of AI for Teaching and Learning in East Africa" (2023), the Council noted that ChatGPT can be used on smartphones, enabling students to access learning support. While ChatGPT could be misused for plagiarism or shortcuts, intentional use by facilitators could promote student learning and creativity. This could encourage students to use AI as a tool for learning, not just exam preparation.

The adoption of AI in higher education is rapidly advancing in East African institutions, with Makerere establishing the Makerere AI Lab, which is adapting AI in learning. In 2023, Google invested 1.5M USD in an AI system called 'Mak-Ocular' (Nabatte, 2023). This was additional funding after the 'AirQo' project, which uses AI to monitor air pollution through the generation and quantification of data collected in designated areas in Uganda. The Mak-Ocular project is an AI automated mobile microscopic diagnosis of malaria, cancer & tuberculosis. Makerere has also implemented the Makerere University E-learning Environment (MUELE) which is the official online learning platform for the university. It is designed as an intuitional learning management system.

It is increasingly being argued that AI enables students to improve their learning experience and writing skills and enables them to grasp subject matter better. But there is a need to explore how advanced AI technologies like ChatGPT are reconfiguring education across disciplines. The Times Higher Education reports that students urgently need to develop their AI literacy skills if they are to gain graduate-level jobs and help society tame the perils of the technology (Xianghan, 2023). They observe that while higher education institutions recognize the need for digital literacy, there is no dedicated AI literacy framework nor is there agreement on what AI literacy entails. This could partly account for the skills gap in generative AI tools among the current generation of graduates.

Southworth and others (2023) can be credited for trying to meet the need for developing AI curriculum for higher education. They have argued education institutions need to transform higher education using AI powered innovation models (Southworth, et. al, 2023). Their research focuses on the University of Florida and its plan to develop the 'AI Across the Curriculum program'. The university needed to focus on developing a highly innovative approach to a campus-wide AI Across the Curriculum program to provide an opportunity for every undergraduate student to engage and learn about AI, both within their discipline and more importantly, in an interdisciplinary manner often more reflective of the real-world workplace environment. (Southworth, 2023:8). They propose an AI curriculum that covers five aspects: i) enabling AI, ii) know & understand AI, iii) use & apply AI, iv) evaluate & create AI, and v) AI ethics. It is, however, notable in this model that there is no specific focus on the enhancement of human creativity within the AI curriculum ecosystem, a probable indicator to the lack of thinking about how AI may affect the creativity of learners.

Matthias Laupichler and others (2022) have recommended that more research should be carried out on AI literacy training and validated assessment scales (Laupichler, et. al, 2022). The focus of most higher education institutions is on being 'AI literate', i.e., the ability to understand, use, monitor, and critically reflect on AI applications. But the focus on the basic level of producing 'AI literates' may be limiting to the learners. The incorporation of AI in higher education requires AI instructional designers and curriculum developers to design learning parameters that enhance human linguistic and philosophical creativity rather than diminish it because language and philosophy provide the basis for other forms of human creativity. AI pedagogy refers to the methods and strategies used to teach artificial intelligence encompassing technical skills such as programming, robotics, algorithms, coding, etc., but should also include creative skilling.

Algorithmic Workplaces

One of the enduring legacies of the first industrial revolution was the automation of manufacturing. In the 19th Century, factory work was increasingly automated, and the focus of managers was on making human labor as efficient as possible in the production chain. Human beings were pushed to perform functions of automated arms that simply stand in the production line to efficiently add small components to the finished product. This led to the ascendance of creativity i.e., the process by which creative thinking and adjustment to products is left to fewer individuals and curated by higher officers in a production chain. There was less and less need for workers to be creative in their work since creative decisions were being made by other offices. The education systems were also adjusted to respond to the changes that had taken place in the early industrialized production.

The focus of the factory owner is on mass production and efficiency of factory work led to minute subdivision of tasks among workers, hierarchization of work supervision; and the resulting complexity decreased the drive for creative thinking among workers. The managers preferred automated arms rather than creative minds. Beatrice Gonzalez (2021) has referred to this as 'labor control'; she observes that since the late 19th Century the challenge of labor autonomy has been a constant feature of the sociology of work. Technologies of labor control have emerged over time which limit workers' scope of action and decision (Gonzalez, 2021:88). This is resulting in less creativity among the workers of today. Investigating the question of the future of creativity is in a sense an inquiry into the freedom of humans; their ability to be themselves and create what they want. Just like early industrial revolution technologies squeezed out the creative impulses of workers, contemporary AI based algorithms are squeezing out human creativity by standardizing labor and language at the microwork level.

Herr (2021) has argued that today's work algorithms are consciously constructed and implemented in the capitalist labor process to discipline and control labor (Herr, 2021:41). In his paper he investigates the implication of algorithmic application used to automate food delivery dispatches on contemporary conditions of labor. The new artificial intelligence-based algorithms are creating more micro minuted labor tasks that are too detailedly disaggregated which disempowers workers the most. Phil Jones (2021), has reported that technological companies are pushing for automation online in the form of 'microwork' but this automated microwork is very exploitative and lacks creative room (Jones, 2021). Andrew Kersley (2022) refers to it as digital 'clickwork' which has become the new type of labor exploitation in the digital economy (Kersley, 2022). Alex Press (2021), has reported that microworkers are disempowered to a degree previously unseen in capitalist history (Alex, 2021). The disempowerment is a result of working on very small tasks of the overall work which makes the workers lack any impulse to be creative while doing the work.

The education system also responds to this emphasis on mere production by removing creative learning from the classroom to produce workers fit for the labor market. Duli Pllana (2019), has discussed the response education systems to controlled labor and automated arms in production chains in modern times. For example, he observed that in Latino education systems, the reorganization of teaching and learning was marked by less cognitive competency and non-application of creativity in their schools because they were more focused on other basic educational concerns (pg.138). The focus on basic skills in education leads to less creativity. He observes that cognitive processes and the development of creativity is confined to arts and language, which implies that language is very important in human creativity. Julian

Astle (2018) argues that true creativity is based on knowledge which in turn is based on literacy foundations young people need to be properly creative.

Our concern with human creativity is actually at the deeper level a concern over authentic human freedom. Technological advancements and artificial intelligence in particular; since the human creative power expresses itself better in the continuum of freedom. Puaschunder (2020) has observed that AI poses historically unique challenges for humankind; generative intelligence, robotics and big data derivatives hold novel and unprecedentedly-described challenges to freedom in our contemporary world (pg.75). Michael Bader (2016) has demonstrated the 'incapacitating effect' on society. Robotic autonomy is not the same as human autonomy; likewise, human creativity is predicated on human freedom. However, artificial intelligence is an extension of ontological and naturalistic explanatory reductionism. The creative space is weaved together using linguistic power which spells new things into existence and creates rituals on which the creations thrive.

Generative Disruption

Artificial intelligence is disrupting and re-inventing education as we know it. AI is publicly defined as machine theory and computer systems that are developed to perform tasks normally done by humans, such as visual perception, speech recognition, decision-making, and translation between languages. There are many researchers and engineers who are building AI search algorithms to be self-propelled in accurately identifying and determining data queries and commands. Computers are increasingly becoming autonomous in carrying out these tasks on their own. The major branches of research in artificial intelligence are: a) Machine learning (ML), b) Deep learning (DL), c) Natural language processing (NLP), d) Robotics (R), and e) expert systems (ES). Machine learning is developing algorithms that can learn from data and used to make applications that perform tasks like image recognition. Deep learning research uses artificial neural networks to make knowledge out of data to solve problems in language and speech. Natural language processing researches the interaction between computers and human language to process tasks like translation. Robotics research engineers and designs robots for automated jobs in industries such as transport. Expert systems is the design of computer programs that mimic advanced human reasoning and decision-making.

Artificial intelligence is classified according to capabilities and functionalities. Capabilities are in levels of power which include: Artificial Narrow Intelligence (ANI), Artificial General Intelligence (AGI); and Artificial Super Intelligence (ASI). ANI does narrow tasks with limitations; AGI is being built to simulate the human brain for autonomous decisions, and ASI is envisioned to be capable of higher complex tasks and activities better than a human. According to AI functionalities these include: Reactive machines, Limited memory machines, Theory of mind machines, and Self-awareness machines. The specific focus in artificial intelligence today include: a) machine perception, b) deep learning; c) reinforcement learning, and d) stable diffusion. Machine perception is the ability of computers to use input data from sensors to learn about the world. In this case the computer has the ability to capture sensory information and process in terms of selection, organization and interpretation.

Deep learning is where the computer imitates the human brain. Artificial intelligence teaches computers to process data in near similarity to the human brain, modeling combinations of complex data including pictures, text, sounds, and others. Reinforcement learning is where AI teaches computers to learn to reward desired behaviors and punish the undesired. The computer learns through trial and error using feedback from its actions. AI uses a trial-and-error approach to train each computer which can perceive its environment, take autonomous action, and learn from trial-based processes. Stable diffusion is one of the most recent developments in AI which does text-to-image modeling; it is known as generative AI which produces images from text and image prompts.

Artificial intelligence depends on language modeling. This means that language is central to the development of AI, which seems to have been the holy grail of machine learning for decades. With the improved and faster capacity to work through language, AI is able to do tasks such as data collection, social events labeling, data categorization, among others. AI designers labor to make the machines process language as naturally as possible. This is known as Natural Language Processing (NLP), which is an important field in AI that is focused on enabling computers to understand human language. NLP is divided into: Natural Language Understanding (NLU) and Natural Language Generation (NLG). These two concepts of 'understanding' and 'generation' are key to our discussion of AI creativity in contrast with human creativity.

Hyperautomation

The threat to teaching authentic human creativity in education is now coming from hyperautomation. The apologetics for AI inspired hyperautomation are using the same argument for efficiency to market the application of these technologies. Bellhorn (2023) argues that, by automating time-consuming manual processes such as data entry and payment processing, corporations become more efficient; and by 2028 the hyperautomation market is predicted to grow to around $26.5 billion (Bellhorn, 2023). Robotic Process Automation (RPA) is increasingly transforming the labor landscape into turning workers into automated brains who are simply hired to perform micro tasks that are a result of hyperautomation. Stephanie Overby (2020), has argued that RPA will enable corporations to get benefits such as cost reduction, operations optimization, improved customer experience, fewer errors, easier management and control, and quick implementation and ROI (Overby, 2020).

The creativity that is being marketed as artificial intelligence using advanced targeted marketing technology is inherently inferior to authentic human creativity and our education should not abandon the genuine thing. It is necessary to differentiate between these two types of creativity and encourage the preservation of the authentic; and the naturally authentic is the inspiration for the artificial. Artificial intelligence is regarded as the miracle of automation; it is being argued that automation using AI will improve company human resource practices using advanced technologies. Forbes (2022) argues that artificial intelligence and automation are reshaping the way we live and work. These advancements hold incredible potential, promising to simplify tasks, enhance accuracy and redefine our experiences (Vamsi, 2023). Some experts in new technologies are calling for the creation of a 'digital workforce with robotic process automation' (Jim, 2019).

Robotic process automation (RPA) is the integration of RPA software, tools and bots into business production and management. It is a natural progression from earlier industrial revolution automation of the manual conveyor belt that required human arms to perform tasks faster to improve the production at the assembly lines in manufacturing plants. Today hyperautomation seeks to make humans perform micro tasks that may render the human brain automated. AI hyperautomation seeks to address increasing productivity through ever-increasing levels of intelligent automation. The most common areas to start with in regard to RPA are manual tasks or replacing process steps with rules or bots. By studying human decisions and actions on business processes, those processes can be improved to new levels of automation (Jim, 2019). The drive in AI is to transform the human mind into augmented reality using cloud software to give the human brain superhuman abilities like a cyborg ('robot human being') that can automatically communicate with computers. If this succeeds, it may give AI access to one of the innermost aspects of human life – the mind. The technology businessman, Elon Musk has started the process of monetizing this AI neuroscience with a business called, 'Neuralink'. Musk has demonstrated that there is technology designed to insert a computer chip inside the human head to control the brain. The Neuralink team said they also would like to see the technology permitting the uploading of memories for later use (Bryan, 2020). Musk and others who think like him believe that humans are the ones to catch up with AI. They are marketing AI brain chips as software that could be used to improve intelligence and help humans keep up with supercomputers and artificial intelligence technology (Bryan, ibid.).

AI hyperautomation is based on AI Natural Language Processing which uses artificial intelligence to teach computers to understand and generate human language.

The implication is that language is central in both human and artificial intelligence creativity. Understanding how language creates enables us to understand literary creativity and its centrality in the future of human creativity. One of the precursors of contemporary computer-based language processing was the philosopher Bertrand Russell. Russell philosophically wanted to create an ideal language for analysis that is free from the ambiguities of natural language (Russell, 1905; Russell, 1940). Bertrand Russell aimed to anchor language into the understanding of reality. Ulf Persson (2012) asks the question: What relation does language have to reality? To the naive man in the street, there is no real problem, but to a philosopher there is a major one. In fact, the closer he scrutinizes the relationship the more likely he is to conclude that there is language and that we cannot go beyond language, and reality is something that is ultimately defined by language (Ulf, 2012:2).

Analysis of the creativity behind words and language can enable us to differentiate between authentic human creativity and AI creativity. The power of AI lies in the technological ability to process language faster and more efficiently; AI is an advancement that has emerged due to economic and capitalistic desire to minimize costs of production while maximizing profit. Faster and more efficient does not necessarily equate to creativity. The capacities within NLP technology include tasks such as: information retrieval, summarization, word or language classification, machine translation, spam detection, grammatical error correction, text generation (i.e., auto-completion and chatbots), among others. These tasks are indeed biomimicry of the human brain but with faster speed and more efficiency, which can easily be confused with creative power.

In AI NLP the more recent developments are taking place in the area of Deep Learning (DL). In deep learning there are multiple networks which can surpass human performance in language and image data processing. Each level of the network is programmed to independently learn to transform the input data into more abstract and composite representation. The generative linguistic software in deep learning is built on earlier systems such as the Markov model developed by Claude Shannon. The Markov model of natural language is based on orders that are predictive. This is improved by introducing choice probability for successive letters, but this probability is also dependent on the preceding letter or letters. For example, a Markov model of order 'k' can predict the occurrence of a letter(s) with a fixed probability, but this probability also depends on the previous 'k' consecutive letters (Sedgewick & Wayne, 2004). The resultant outcome of the application of predictability and probability in modeling natural language in a classical model like the Markov is what I call a linguistic tautological loop.

A similar challenge may exist in the more recent and popular language processing model which are generative in nature such as the Generative Pre-trained Transformer 4 (GPT-4). GPT models fall under the category of Large Language

Models (LLM), which are far more improved in functionality and speed. LLMs are deep learning algorithms that depend on massive datasets to perform multiple natural language processing (NLP) tasks. LLMs are general-purpose language algorithms for understanding and generative tasks such as recognition, summarizing, translation, predicting, and generating content. These models are far more powerful in comparison with the foundational classical ones like Markov; they process far more data and faster language capabilities. GPT-4, as one the most recent models, has been advertised to have potential to attain higher level interaction with humans and even artificial consciousness. Michal Kosinski presented research results which suggest the possibility that GPT artificial intelligence could attain theory of mind (ToM) capability and far more improved language skills that may reach sentient levels of the human mind (Kosinski, 2023). Kosinski and his team think that GPT AI may attain "theory of mind" (ToM) i.e., the ability to have social interactions, empathy, self-consciousness, moral judgment, and even religious beliefs (ibid.). If this is attainable, then AI could be getting close to human creativity because these are some of the abilities that enable human creativity.

However, some scholars like Kaddour and his research group have observed that there are several challenges with LLMs in aspects ranging from tokenization to reasoning and creative capacities (Kaddour, et al, 2023). Their main observation about the creativity of LLMs in terms of script writing (or content creation) is that LLMs can only generate short scripts without long nuanced and interesting storylines such as those the human mind can create. To apply LLMs to long-form story generation, the task is broken down into a series of short-form sub-tasks. The current creative capabilities of LLMs are limited and require a human-in-the-loop for co-writing (pg.40). For visual creative tasks, LLMs use image generation models that are based on a text-based user prompt. Even diffusion image generation models perform strongly on text-to-image generation and indoor scene synthesis (ibid.). This implies that human infused language is at the core of AI creativity and that authentic human literary creativity is vital for LLM creativity to function in a satisfactory fashion. The human ability to create is not only being sentient; neither is it only possessing theory of mind but it also involves the capability to create words or a language that can spell and result in rituals that move society. The need for the 'human-in-the-loop' for co-writing and co-creation of LLMs implies that there is a continuum of human creativity that exists within which AI functions, and we need to understand this continuum and train our learners appropriately for future creative tasks.

CONTINUUM OF HUMAN CREATIVITY

There are four main observations about the continuum of human creativity: cultural interaction, intelligence, natural environment, and language. Lundvall (2008) has argued that the root of the creativity and innovation crisis in Europe can be solved by learning from the USA's approach of relying on social diversity. He argues that individual creativity reflects a criticism of the existing state of affairs – be it technology or society. According to him, creative people are not always highly appreciated. Lundvall's observation posits that human creativity is strongly linked to *social diversity and interaction* of humans. In discussing how to reboot creativity in post COVID-19 pandemic Australia, Alison Pennington and Ben Eltham (2001) observed that a major health pandemic of global scale like COVID-19 had resulted in a creativity crisis. This resulted from disrupting human cultural interaction; according to them, culture is an inescapable part of what it means to be human. The implication is that *culture is the continuum of human creativity*; human creativity does not take place or is extremely limited in a cultural interaction vacuum. Ronald Carter (2015) cautions us against making the assumption that creativity is a product of a single individual (Carter, 2015:39).

Bronson and Ashley (2010) examined the creativity crisis and observed a certain inverse phenomenon when it comes to analyzing intelligence and creativity quotient scores. They observed the phenomenon called the Flynn Effect whereby each successive generation of children scores 10 points higher on the intelligent quotient (IQ) than the previous one. But when it comes to the creativity quotient (CQ), there is a reverse trend whereby CQ scores of American children have steadily fallen since 1990. Their article brings out a unique observation that *intelligence is not the same as creativity*; increase in intelligence is not necessarily followed by increase in creativity. Intelligence and creativity are almost always understood to be interchangeable. This synonymous view of intelligence and creativity lies at the bottom of the creative crisis in not only human resource departments but also in literary studies.

In their recent study on the effects of different natural environments on attention restoration and creativity, Yeh, Hung and Chang (2022) found that interaction with natural environments improves creativity in humans. Their research found that viewing natural environments stimulates curiosity and fosters flexibility and imagination. Highly natural environments distract our minds from work, and the benefits of attention restoration can improve the uniqueness and diversity of creative ideas. This means that the natural environment is crucial to human creativity. Nature is crucial in human technological creativity. Researchers in the field of biomimicry hold that engineers make technological breakthroughs when they uncover and copy nature's hidden marvels. According to them, technology mirrors nature and this enlarges human powers. Janine Benyus (1997) argues that inventors need to explore nature's masterpieces and copy these designs and processes to solve human problems (Benyus, 1997).

Writing on the relationship between artificial intelligence and literary creativity, Selmer Bringsjord and David Ferrucci (1999) observed that "…literary creativity will be the hardest kind of creativity to crack…" (pg.7). Their discussions on literary creativity are unique and provide human and AI creativity; they observed that if creativity was inducible, then it would be viewed as a matter of solving problems by adapting known solutions to solutions that can crack new problems (p.152). Creativity is not understood on a shallow level of simply adapting, but it is a deeper level of linguistic transcendence of what exists to create more. From the discussion of creativity by Ronald Carter (2015), we learn that to be creative requires *linguistic transcendence*, to use language as a tool to go against what is considered the norm. Human creativity is the formation of desire to go beyond what already exists, and language becomes the vehicle by which the ideas and images of those who go against the existing norm are expressed as a form of contrast.

Discussing the difference between AI based and human creativity, Guido Sirna (2022), has what I consider a contentious view that, "creativity no longer seems to be a resource reserved for human genius." (Guido, 2022). In my view this is a shallow conclusion due to the inability to fathom the actual nature of human creativity. Guido references what is increasingly getting to be known as "algorithmic creativity". Algorithmic creativity 'learns from large sets of input data' and what is referred as machine experience is actually processing large sets of data. It can never equate to human experience because human genius does not emanate from having gathered large sets of data from history and all geographical locations as

Figure 1. AI-art creative process
(Mazzone & Elgammal, 2019)

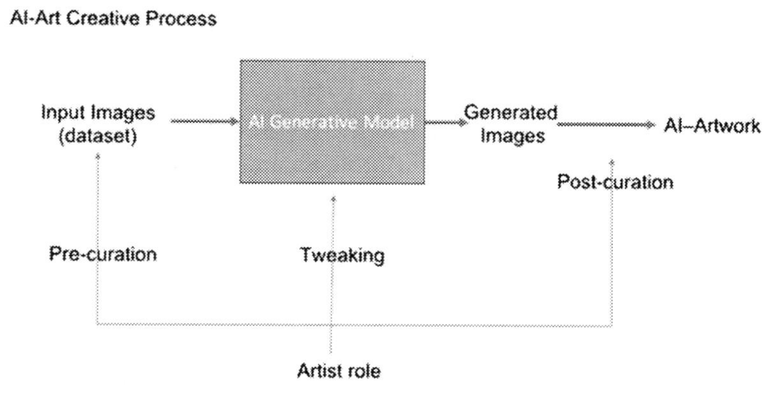

AI-Art Creative Process

Input Images (dataset) → AI Generative Model → Generated Images → AI–Artwork

Pre-curation   Tweaking   Post-curation

Artist role

AI powered computers and machines do. Human genius is not merely intellectual prowess but also transcendent mental superiority. Human creativity includes supra-computer abilities such as accurate prophetic insight into the future; computers can only do prediction and simulations using huge volumes of data collected from the past with human curation. This is exemplified in the diagram generated by Mazzone & Elgammal, (2019) as cited by Sirna:

It is obvious that generative AI creativity needs human curation or 'tweaking' as Mazzone and Elgammal illustrated in the above model. The human artist plays a pivotal role in the artist output of generative AI. The question then is: what is the true source or inspiration of human creativity which can transcend history and physical realms? AI based creativity can only work with input data, yet humans are born innately creative.

Limited as the above rendering of AI creativity may be, it is even more difficult to map human creativity. The author consulted several sources that have tried to map or model human creativity, but the differences are as vast as the number of authors consulted. We can illustrate the complexity of human creativity in the image below:

Realms of Human Creativity

The author's survey of several studies and renderings of human creativity fall under a number of domains. My categorization of the many models of human creativity falls into three categories: i) Transcendental creativity; ii) Emotional / pleasure creativity; and iii) Physical creativity. Humans create from a higher transcendental realm whereby we find abilities like prophetic creatives that go far into the future of time. Such creativity is not based on gathering vast amounts of data (historical); this goes beyond computer aided prediction or simulation and intersects into the spiritual. The second realm of human creative energy is emotional or pleasurable, which implies creativity occasioned by emotional state or for the pleasure of humans. Human emotions empower creativity which can be spontaneous or otherwise; this kind is in the realm of the emotional energy and the psychological. The third aspect is physical creativity which humans carry out using their physical organs such as hands, feet, etc.; even though it is coordinated by the mind, it is manifested physically. Understanding how these three realms of human creativity is complicated and many aspects are not replicable by computers or artificial intelligence.

Spells and 'Derivee' Words

The exponential advancements in artificial intelligence has caused upheavals in humanity's assumptions about the philosophy of creativity, but AI may never be able to perceive the human creative continuum. Questions like 'what is creativity?'

Figure 2. Realms of human creativity

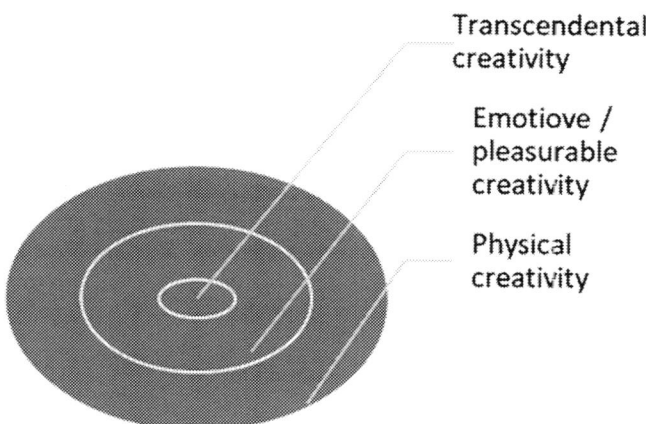

Transcendental
creativity

Emotiove /
pleasurable
creativity

Physical
creativity

are being reexamined in the light of artificial intelligence. Is human creativity the same as computer creativity? Jack Copeland (1993) concluded that in a sense the human mind is a computer because, according to him, there is no difference between how the human mind and the computer processes symbols and language. John von Neumann and Ray Kurzweil (2012), posit that understanding human intelligence enables us to build computer formulations; artificial intelligence is therefore the 'reverse engineering' of the human brain (pg. ix). It is on this basis that they generated the principles of the 'universality of computation' and the 'essential equivalence of the human brain and a computer'. The foundation on which artificial intelligence is based is the human brain; to trace the future of AI enabled literary and philosophical creativity, we must examine these roots.

This raises the question of whether it is possible to reverse engineer the human brain. In discussing this matter, Copeland examines the philosophical question: Is thought a biological phenomenon [like] every other biology-dependent process? (pg.1). In the late 1950s, Paul Torrance laid the ground for creativity research that culminated into the standardized Creativity Quotient (CQs) scales that we see today. In his seminal book, *Why Fly? A Philosophy of Creativity* (1995), Torrance argues that create thinking among learners has to be rewarded as one of the ways to encourage creativity to flourish. He also lays emphasis on using problem solving learning as a model of teaching creativity.

Authentic human creativity comes from intrinsic motivation (Mekonnen, 2023) that artificial intelligence cannot possess. The power of human literary creativity comes from the power of spell and ritual and computers may never attain that capacity.

Bertrand Russell who laid the philosophical foundations of computational language sought to realize 'definite' description in human language. He sought to create an ideal language that is free from the ambiguities of natural language to anchor language into the definite understanding of reality. By so doing he centralized language in human understanding and the re-shaping of reality. But, at the same time, his pursuit of 'definite' language devoid of 'ambiguities' strips human language of the power of conjuring spells that result in creating. Tambiah (2010) discussed the 'magical theory of language' drawing it from the 'ethnographic theory of language' by which he concludes that words have magical power (Tambiah, 2010). Göran Malmstedt (2021) has argued that certain words have innate power that creates connections with supernatural forces (Malmstedt, 2021).

In Russellian terms, language that is indefinable is primitive; word phrases have no meaning apart from that which is assigned to them. The Russellian argument, when applied to computational language, strips words of spell power because, according to him, linguistic meaning should be separated from the 'sense' of the word. Spell power comes from the ambiguous meaning that is conjured up in the mind of the hearer or reader, which is the authentic generative and creative power of human words. But, based on the famous argument that 'a phrase may be denoting and yet not denote anything', some thinkers have criticized Russell for not recognizing both the attributive and referential employment of definite descriptions (see: Donnellan, 1966). I think that Russell missed another dimension of word description i.e., the generative power of words. They create by giving rise to what is not in the mind of the hearer and reader in the form of referring to something that may not be as something that actually exists. This can be considered to be spelling the human world. This capacity to spell using words is intimately human art founded on the continuum of human creativity as discussed above, and it is doubtable that language processing models of artificial intelligence will be able to develop it.

It is this capacity of the human mind to conjure up new words and phrases that provides a key pillar in authentic human literary and philosophical creativity. This explains the creation of portmanteau words that are a result of blending other words. Portmanteau word combinations and derivations are a higher art of harnessing the spell power in each original word into the 'derivee word'. In generative grammar derivation of a word has to consider its etymological roots and more so the creative power within. The 'derivee word' being created by the portmanteau artist or creator has to be determined to conjure the right emotional, spiritual and intellectual power in the hearer or reader. Based on this observation, it is not enough for LLMs to potentially attain theory of mind; this is because literary creation requires not only spelling power but also the capacity to create portmanteau words. Nicholas Webber (2011) has tried to capture this observation as the complex, liminal dynamics which underpin moments of creativity (Webber, 2011).

CONCLUSION

Educationists are experimenting with advanced technology-based learning, which is reconfiguring creativity learning. But there is a creativity crisis in contemporary education, yet creativity undergirds human business, social development and progress. Artificial intelligence can either enhance human creativity or reconfigure it permanently. However, reductive artificial efficiency narrows literary variation and erodes the expressive power of human language, thus affecting literary creativity. The Language Processing software in AI is devoid of the spell power; over reliance on it may reverse authentic human creativity. There is a need for research and education policy to enhance authentic human literary and philosophical creativity in education.

REFERENCES

Alex Press. (2021). Microworkers are disempowered to a degree previously unseen in capitalist history. *Jacobin, Science and Technology, 22.*

Alison & Eltham. (2001). *Creativity in Crisis: Rebooting Australia's Arts and Entertainment Sector After COVID*. The Centre for Future Work at the Australia Institute. https://apo.org.au/sites/default/files/resource-files/2021-07/apo-nid313299.pdf

Astle, J. (2018). Do schools really 'kill creativity'? *RSA Journal*. https://www.thersa.org/blog/2018/04/do-schools-kill-creativity

Bader, M. W. (2016). Reign of the Algorithms: How 'artificial intelligence' is threatening our freedom. *Herrschaft der Algorithmen, 8*(22). https://stiftung-media.de/web/wp-content/uploads/2016/06/Herrschaft_der_Algorithmen_V08_22_06_16_EN-mb04.pdf

Bengt-Åke, L. (2008). Innovation and creativity - the crisis as opportunity for change. https://www.researchgate.net/publication/237833821_Innovation_and_creativity_-_the_crisis_as_opportunity_for_change

Benjamin. (2021). Delivering food on bikes: Between machine subordination and autonomy in the algorithmic workplace. In *Augmented Exploitation: Artificial Intelligence, Automation and Work*. Pluto Press.

Bertrand, R. (1905). On Denoting. *Mind, 14*(56), 479–493.

Bertrand, R. (1940). *An Inquiry into Meaning and Truth*. George Allen and Unwen Ltd. https://archive.org/details/in.ernet.dli.2015.458710

Betty, K. (2022). Research shows need for training of staff and students on online learning. https://news.mak.ac.ug/2022/09/research-shows-need-for-training-of-staff-and-students-on-online-learning/

Bob, S., & Wayne, K. (2004). Markov Model of Natural Language. https://www.cs.princeton.edu/courses/archive/spring05/cos126/assignments/markov.html

Brian, B. (2023). How Hyperautomation and AI in Accounts Payable Can Increase Profits. https://www.kofax.com/learn/blog/how-hyperautomation-and-ai-in-accounts-payable-can-increase-profits

Bringsjord, S., & Ferrucci, D. (1999). *Artificial Intelligence and Literary Creativity: Inside the Mind of Brutus, A Storytelling Machine.* Psychology Press. doi:10.4324/9781410602398

CIPIT. (2023). *The State of AI in Africa Report – 2023.* Strathmore University.

Donnellan, K.S. (1966). Reference and Definite Descriptions. *The Philosophical Review*, 75(3), 281–304.

Fall, J. (2019). Create a digital workforce with robotic process automation. https://www.linkedin.com/pulse/create-digital-workforce-robotic-process-automation-jason-miracle

Florida, R. (2004, October). America's looming creativity crisis. *Harvard Business Review*. PMID:15559581

Francis. (2021). Huawei Uganda offers free artificial intelligence training. *The New Vision*.

Gonzalez, B. (2021). Automated and Autonomous? Technologies mediating the exertion and perception of labour control. In *Augmented Exploitation: Artificial Intelligence, Automation and Work.* Pluto Press. doi:10.2307/j.ctv1h0nv3d.13

Gosu, V. K. (2023, October). Navigating ethical AI and the future of automation. *Forbes*, 13.

Inter-University Council of East Africa (IUCEA). (2023). *Exploring the Potential of AI for Teaching and Learning in East Africa - TESCEA Phase 2.* IUCEA. https://www.inasp.info/sites/default/files/2023-08/AI%20event%20summary%20July%202023.pdf

Jack, C. (1993). *Artificial Intelligence: A Philosophical Introduction.* John Wiley & Sons.

Janine, B. (1997). *Biomimicry: Innovation Inspired by Nature*. Reed Business Information, Inc.

Jones, P. (2021, Oct. 27). Big tech's push for automation hides the grim reality of 'microwork'. *The Guardian*.

KaddourJ.JoshuaH.MaximilianM.BradleyγH.RaileanuR.McHardyR. (2023). Challenges and applications of Large Language Models. arXiv:2307.10169v1 [cs. CL]. https://arxiv.org/pdf/2307.10169.pdf

Kersley, A. (2022, October 5). Clickwork and labour exploitation in the digital economy. *Computer Weekly*.

Laupichler, M. C., Aster, A., Schirch, J., & Raupach, T. (2022). Artificial intelligence literacy in higher and adult education: A scoping literature review. *Computers and Education: Artificial Intelligence*, *3*, 100101. doi:10.1016/j.caeai.2022.100101

Lynn, B. (2020). Elon Musk demonstrates technology linking computer to brain. *VOA News*. https://learningenglish.voanews.com/a/elon-musk-demonstrates-technology-linking-computer-to-brain/5565332.html

Malmstedt, G. (2021). Spells and Charms. In Premodern Beliefs and Witch Trials in a Swedish Province. Palgrave Macmillan. doi:10.1007/978-3-030-76120-2_8

Mazzone, M., & Elgammal, A. (2019). Art, Creativity, and the Potential of Artificial Intelligence. *Arts*, *8*(1), 26. doi:10.3390/arts8010026

Michal, K. (2023). Theory of Mind might have spontaneously emerged in Large Language Models. arXiv preprint arXiv: 2302.02083. https://arxiv.org/ftp/arxiv/papers/2302/2302.02083.pdf

Neumann & Kurzweil. (2012), *The Computer and the Brain*. Yale University Press.

Nicholas, W. (2011, Fall). Within language, through language, beyond language: The portmanteau-word neologism as agent and emblem of contingent change. *Journal of South Texas English Studies*, *3*(1), 1–28.

O'Dea, X. (2023). Teaching AI literacy: how to begin. *Times Higher Education*. https://www.timeshighereducation.com/campus/teaching-ai-literacy-how-begin

Paul, T. E. (1995). *Why Fly? A Philosophy of Creativity*. Bloomsbury Academic.

Pllana, D. (2019). Creativity in modern education. *World Journal of Education*, *9*(2), 136–140. doi:10.5430/wje.v9n2p136

Po, B., & Merryman, A. (2010). The Creativity Crisis. *Newsweek Education*. https://www.newsweek.com/2010/07/10/the-creativity-crisis.html

Proscovia. (2023). Google invests US$1.5M in Mak Ocular: An AI Automated Mobile Microscopic Diagnosis of Malaria, Cancer & Tuberculosis. *Mak News*. bit.ly/3ZWQb9K

Puaschunder, J. M. (2020). On Freedom in the Artificial Age. *RAIS Conference Proceedings*, 75-80.

Ronald, C. (2015). *Language and Creativity: The Art of Common Talk*. Routledge.

Sirna, G. (2022). Can Artificial Intelligence replace human creativity? An essay on Borges, Artificial Intelligence, DALL-E 2.0 and the future of work. https://medium.com/@guidosirna/can-artificial-intelligence-replace-human-creativity-b5e96ccd356a

Southworth, Migliaccio, Glover, Glover, Reed, McCarty, Brendemuhl, & Thomas. (2023). Developing a model for AI Across the curriculum: Transforming the higher education landscape via innovation in AI literacy. *Computers and Education: Artificial Intelligence*, *4*, 1-10.

Tambiah, S. J. (2017). The magical power of words. In Ritual. Routledge. doi:10.4324/9781315244099-20

Vasile-Daniel, P., & Sabina-Cristiana, N. (2023). Artificial Intelligence as a Disruptive Technology - A Systematic Literature Review. *Electronics (Basel)*, *12*(5), 1102. doi:10.3390/electronics12051102

Yeh, C.-W., Hung, S.-H., & Chang, C.-Y. (2022). The influence of natural environments on creativity. *Frontier Psychiatry*, *13*. https://www.frontiersin.org/articles/10.3389/fpsyt.2022.895213/full

Yohannes, M. Y., Demis, A. G., & Asemamaw, T. D. (2023). Factors affecting "employees' creativity": The mediating role of intrinsic motivation. *Journal of Innovation and Entrepreneurship*, *12*(31).

Yusuf. (2023). AI poses new threat to integrity of Kenyan university students' work. *Voice of America*.

Chapter 5
Can ChatGPT Grade Non–Native Academic English Writing?

Veronika Makarova
University of Saskatchewan, Canada

Zhi Li
University of Saskatchewan, Canada

Zhengxiang Wang
Stony Brook University, USA

ABSTRACT

This chapter reports the results of a pilot study investigating the potential of ChatGPT to assess (or grade) texts produced by international graduate students whose mother tongue is other than English (IGS). The chapter overviews some suggested applications of ChatGPT to academic writing (AW) and particularly, for English as an additional language (EAL) contexts. Most works up to date consider ChatGPT applications for literacy and writing skills development. The authors compare evaluations of texts by ChatGPT vis-à-vis human experts. The texts employed for the study are short literature reviews written by IGS in Canadian universities. The results demonstrate some potential of ChatGPT for assessment. However, while ChatGPT provides mostly relevant scores and comments related to the assessment rubrics provided, the comments are not diversified and individualized enough. ChatGPT queries for assessment should be modified and the tool trained in diversifying comments to achieve better results.

DOI: 10.4018/979-8-3693-1054-0.ch005

INTRODUCTION

ChatGPT has been called "the best artificial intelligence chatbot ever released to the general public" (Roose, 2022, nPg). It is the fastest-growing technology application in history (and caused an avalanche of discussions and research studies Ciampa et al., 2023, p. 186). A considerable amount of debate surrounding ChatGPT revolves around its use in academic writing (e.g., Guo et al, 2023). The proponents of ChatGPT note its multiple applications in diverse areas, such as in creating dictionaries (Lew, 2023), in healthcare (Salam, 2023), in medical education (Lee, 2024), in producing research papers from scratch (Conroy, 2023) supporting the writing of medical articles (Benichou & ChatGPT, 2023), etc. Anecdotally, some individuals even tried to make ChatGPT write new recipes, but it did not go so well (Roose, 2022). Some scholars point out ChatGPT's potentially negative effect on society including fake news, false information, unlawful use, stereotyping, plagiarism, social security breaches, reduced human interaction, ethical concerns about privacy, and the potential for bias (Ciampa et al., 2023; Dempere et al., 2023; Guo et al, 2023). The fears of ChatGPT have even caused some countries, such as Italy, to temporarily ban its use (Shidarta & Martinelli, 2023). To alleviate potential negative effects, 'responsible' use of ChatGPT has been suggested (e.g., Yang, 2023) along with training students how to use it ethically and responsibly (e.g., Ciampa et al, 2023).

Multiple earlier studies have provided accounts of ChatGPT's role in developing literacy and writing skills (e.g., Ciampa et al., 2023; Creely et al., 2023). Writing skills development is a concern shared by many instructors in North American universities especially when it comes to writing by international students who are non-native speakers of English (e.g., Okuda & Anderson, 2018; Li et al., 2023). The authors of this article have also been concerned with the quality of academic writing produced by international graduate students whose mother tongue is other than English (IGS) in their graduate programs of studies. Therefore, the focus of this paper is graduate level English as an Additional language (EAL) writing. For simplicity, we understand EAL here as being composed of English as a Foreign (EFL) or as a Second (ESL) language (the differences between the terms that we ignore here are described in Nayar, 2021). EAL writers are known to experience "the triple disadvantage of having to read, do research and write in another language" (Van Dijk, 1994, p. 276).

In the study reported in this chapter we address the capability of ChatGPT to provide adequate evaluations of EAL students' writing at a graduate level (international graduate students' short Literature Reviews). The writing samples were produced by IGS participants in an online free open Literature Review Writing (LRW) Tutorial developed by the authors (Authors 2022, 2023). The idea of the Tutorial came in response to the local Canadian context and was inspired by Genre analysis (Halliday, 1978; Halliday & Matthiessen, 2014) and Computer Assisted Language Learning (CALL) approaches (Hegelheimer & Lee, 2013; Yeh, 2015) to writing skills development.

In Canada, not many universities have adequate resources for providing Academic writing courses to IGS in general and in their disciplines in particular. In an attempt to remedy the above issues, the authors developed an extracurricular free Academic Writing Tutorials set for graduate students in Linguistics and Social Sciences with a focus on the genre of Literature Review. The choice of the genre was determined by its high frequency among the different types of assignments at graduate level in Canadian universities across different programs of studies (Shi & Dong, 2015). The purpose of the tutorial was to provide additional online Academic Writing support resources for IGS to enhance their academic writing skills and to release the EFL/ESL grading problem off the instructors through cost-efficient e-learning. The writing samples analyzed in our paper come from this online tutorial.

LITERATURE REVIEW

This section introduces difficulties in academic writing for AEL students at university level and for their instructors. We will also look at earlier recorded attempts to address these difficulties with the help of ChatGPT.

Challenges With Academic Writing for AEL Students

Academic writing provides a formidable challenge for international graduate students (IGS) who are not native speakers of English, particularly when they enroll in programs in universities with English as a language of instruction (e.g., Badenhorst, 2018). As earlier studies have shown, graduate students in Social Sciences and other programs have difficulties with the universal features of AEW (such as grammar, vocabulary, logic and structure), they are also concerned with the logic of presentation and putting ideas together (Li et al., 2023).

However, there is very little research available on the writing by international graduate students' whose mother tongue is other than English (Storch & Tapper, 2009). Difficulties with academic writing have a negative impact on these students' programs of studies and thesis completion (Hyland, 1999; Li et al., 2023).

Challenges With Academic Writing Evaluation and Feedback Faced by Instructors

Grading and providing meaningful feedback on students' written assignments is one of the major challenges for university instructors (Ciampa et al, 2023). Evaluating written assignments of non-native English speakers poses an extra burden on university instructors in content courses, since they may face a number of additional challenges with it (Douglas & Landry, 2021). These may include:

Time constraints: providing comments on writing errors (in addition to the assignment rubrics related to content-matter) is time-consuming, particularly in large classes.

Training constraints: content instructors typically do not have an adequate background in EAL writing for an effective evaluation, assessment and feedback on non-native writing.

Bias in Attitudes: instructors may give lower grades to non-native English essays based on an impression of lower English writing skills (Baffour, 2023; Douglas & Landry, 2021).

Ways to Resolve These Difficulties Through Automated Grading

A solution to resolve the instructors' burden of evaluating and scoring EAL students' texts has been sought in automated text analysis systems, such as Automatic essay scoring (AES) (e.g., Vajjala, 2018). Multiple forms and systems for automated text analysis and scoring have been suggested, for example, Intelligent Essay Grader (Landauer et al., 2003), Project Essay Grade (Page, 2003) or E-rater (Attali and Burstein 2006), a lexical network approach that allows grading of written texts produced by Chinese language learners according to proficiency levels (Chen, 2023). Real-time automatic writing analysis is incorporated into multiple tools, such as grammarly.com, turnitin.com, e-rater® and WriteToLearn™ (Vajjala, 2018).

The problems with the use of automated text evaluation systems include their unavailability in free formats and lack of relevant computer skills and knowledge from instructors. By contrast, ChatGPT-3.5 is free, available to anyone with internet access, and its use does not require any computer or programming skills.

However, it should be noted that ChatGPT would 'inherit' some unresolved issues in automated writing assessment, such as lack of clarity on standards, linguistics features, semantic and discourse features and rubrics along which the assessment should be conducted (Nedungadi & Raj, 2014; Vajjala, 2017).

ChatGPT Use in Academic Writing

Since its launch in November 2022, ChatGPT (generative pretrained transformer) launched by OpenAI has become the most widely used generative AI model and has been identified as either a friend or a foe of academic writing across multiple disciplines (e.g., Dergaa et al., 2023; Herbold et al., 2023). Some research works compared human-written and ChatGPT-generated essays. For example, Herbold et al. (2023) found that human experts (teachers) scored argumentative essays generated by ChatGPT higher than essays written by high school students. The same study also showed that ChatGPT uses higher sentence complexity, whereas high school students engage in more attitude expression. Guo et al (2023) observed that ChatGPT uses linguistic devices in a slightly different way than humans and based on those, developed an algorithm for detecting ChatGPT-generated texts.

Thus, most research work addresses the use of ChatGPT for composing texts (Bhatia, 2023; Culp, 2023), but so far, to the best of our knowledge, no works have focused on its potential use for evaluating students' writing, and especially non-native English writing. It is not clear whether ChatGPT could be up to this challenge, as earlier research shows that it has some issues with comprehending low-frequency grammar constructions (Dentella et al, 2023). ChatGPT has also been 'caught' fabricating references, making errors in references, and not being able to produce a required number of references (Walters & Wilder, 2023; Ciampa et al, 2023). These shortcomings question its ability to judge the quality of referencing in graduate students' work. To fill in the gap with ChatGPT applications to scoring human writing, we designed a study comparing ChatGPT's vs. human expert raters' evaluations of non-native writing at a relatively high level (international graduate students' mini-Literature Review writing).

The purpose of the proposed chapter is to compare the assessment of the participants' writing by human assessors and by ChatGPT. The primary research goal is to conduct a pilot study that would shed light on the scoring capabilities of ChatGPT applied to a high level of non-native academic writing. More specifically, we were interested to find out whether ChatGPT could provide an assessment of IGS' writing that would be comparable to human assessment along the eight rubrics developed by the authors for human rating of the quality of short Literature reviews. Thus, the following two questions were posed in this pilot study:

Research Question 1: Is ChatGPT quantitative (numeric) evaluation of writing quality along nine rubrics of analysis similar or different from assessments provided by human graders?

Research Question 2: Is ChatGPT qualitative evaluation (comments) of writing quality along nine rubrics similar or different from assessments provided by human graders?

MATERIALS AND METHODS

Materials and Methods section outlines the structure of the tutorial series (from which the writing samples were extracted) and methods employed in the analysis.

Materials

The materials for the investigation (56 short Literature Reviews between 800-1200 words each) came from an online five-unit Academic Writing Tutorial Series designed by the authors for IGS whose native language is other than English. Three of these tutorials (T1, T3, T5) involved individual writing tasks (the writings produced by participants constitute the data for the current study), and two tutorials included collaborative writing (the latter are not included in the data analysis here). The theoretical frameworks behind the tutorial series were Genre analysis of academic writing and corpus linguistics. The tutorial units included themes that were identified as problematic for IGS in earlier research: Genre requirements, logic and structure in literature review, sentence structures, academic vocabulary, and grammar of reported speech (Swales & Feak, 2012).

The materials presented in an interactive e-book employing H5P (HTML5 Package) were supplemented with practices and writing tasks and mounted on MoodleCloud learning platform. The individual writing tasks produced by participants in three tutorials (T1, T3, T5) with three individual writing tasks were originally evaluated by human assessors and later by querying ChatGPT. Most of the participants were master's students (52) and a few doctoral students (4), average age of 29 years. The programs of the participants included 9 different specialties, and, in total, the respondents identified 19 languages as their mother tongues. The English proficiency levels were at 'upper intermediate' to 'advanced' levels as identified in their self-reported standard English proficiency tests results.

Methods

We selected ChatGPT-3.5 for our study, since it is free and openly available for everyone online. For the ChatGPT-3.5 generated outputs, we employed eight scoring categories: citation/referencing, materials integration, overall structure, logic, content clarity, coherence/cohesion, use of connectors and grammar/vocabulary. These categories were available in all the outputs we analyzed.

The prompt employed in the study used an assessment form guide developed for the tutorial by the second author following the above eight assessment rubrics. The prompt was an essay text written by an IGS participant plus a query: "Please assess the writing above using the following assessment guides. The output format should be json." The outputs were manually examined by the researchers to identify whether they were successful depending on whether ChatGPT at least superficially answered all the evaluation questions asked (score + comment) in a specified format ("json"). The outputs that were not satisfying the above criteria, i.e., if ChatGPT failed to answer all the evaluation questions, were identified as "other" group and discarded. The major reason for discarding the 'other' group outputs was first, because they could not be converted automatically into a csv file for analysis due to their inconsistencies. Discarding failed outputs is a procedure often employed in AI language output studies (Ciampa et al., 2023).

The above ChatGPT outputs were compared with numeric evaluations of the same mini-Literature Reviews done by three expert human assessors (all with ESL background) using an analytic scoring scale (Li et al., 2023). We also compared the qualitative comments on the writing samples produced by human raters and ChatGPT using word frequencies on word cloud.

RESULTS

Based on consistency of formats and texts matching scoring rubrics, ChatGPT-3.5 outputs with its automated assessments of IGS' writing samples were manually split by the researchers into three major categories 'good' (both scoring and comments are done and appear acceptable), 'OK' (both scoring and comments are done) and 'other' (incomplete outputs). In our analysis, we focused only on the 'good' and 'OK' output categories (56 assessment files generated by ChatGPT) to compare them to human raters' assessments.

It should be noted, that out of a total of 63 writings rated by ChatGPT, only 7 (11%) were failed outputs, which constitutes a positive result for ChatGPT performance.

Ratings Comparison Between ChatGPT and Human Ratings of Writing Samples

A summary of the descriptive statistics of the ChatGPT ratings of 56 writing samples is provided in Table 1 below, and of human ratings- in Table 2.

Table 1. Ratings of 56 writing samples by ChatGPT

	Materials Citation (S1)	Integration (S2)	Overall Structure (S3)	Logical Structure (S4)	Content Clarity (S5)	Coherence Cohesion (S6)	Connectors (S7)	Grammar Vocabulary (S8/9)
mean	7.96	7.32	7.63	7.39	8.36	7.25	6.34	7.75
std	0.19	0.81	0.56	0.82	0.72	0.69	0.58	0.61
Min, max	7, 8	6, 9	6, 9	6, 9	7, 9	6, 8	5, 7	6, 9

Table 2. Ratings of 56 writing samples by three human assessors (averaged scores)

	S1	S2	S3	S4	S5	S6	S7	S8	S9
Mean	7.57	7.11	7.61	7.80	7.91	7.84	7.82	7.63	7.86
Std	0.60	0.78	0.71	0.70	0.64	0.63	0.72	0.68	0.84
Min, max	6, 9	6, 8	6, 9	6, 9	6, 9	6, 9	6, 9	6, 9	6, 10

The descriptive statistics suggest that the scores from ChatGPT and human raters (averaged scores) are comparable. However, the inter-rater reliability (Cohen's Kappa and correlation coefficients) show that some score categories have low agreements (see the Table 3 below). Some score pairs (ChatGPT vs. human raters) show moderate correlations (e.g., S2, S4, S5, S6, and S7, S8/9-S9), only S5 shows fair agreement between ChatGPT and human raters (averaged scores) and S2, S4, and S8/9-S9 show slight agreement.

Comments on Writing Samples by ChatGPT and Human Raters

Since each essay was rated by three raters, there are more comments written by them than provided by ChatGPT. Therefore, we sampled 56 comments on the same group of essays and formed a target corpus to conduct comparative analysis of the comments from ChatGPT and human raters.

Overall, the comments from ChatGPT are usually short, with a total of 13945 tokens and an average of 31 words in a comment. Furthermore, those comments

Table 3. Inter-rater reliability between ChatGPT and human scores

	S1 -S1	S2-S2	S3-S3	S4-S4	S5-S5	S6-S6	S7-S7	S8/9-S8	S8/9-S9
Cohen's Kappa	0.007	0.082	0.080	0.104	0.095	-0.009	0.036	0.052	0.140
Correlation	0.023	0.319	0.266	0.263	0.266	0.220	0.061	0.386	0.496

Table 4. The top-ten words used in the comments from ChatGPT and human raters

Rank	ChatGPT Comments		Human Rater Comments	
	Word	Normalized Frequency (per 1000 Words)	Word	Normalized Frequency (per 1000 Words)
1	could	24	you	17
2	review	20	use	10
3	there	20	this	10
4	literature	19	that	8
5	ideas	19	your	7
6	more	16	as	7
7	where	12	would	6
8	generally	12	cannabis	6
9	author	11	some	6
10	materials	10	sentence	5

Note: common functional words such as 'the' and 'of' are not included in this table.

are highly repetitive as shown by the low type-token ratio (496/13945 = 0.036). By contrast, human raters' comments are much longer (25268 tokens in human raters' comments, with an average of 50 words per comment) and more diverse in terms of type-token ratio (2985/25268 = 0.118). This strong contrast in word frequencies is also observed, as demonstrated in Table 4 below reporting the most commonly used words in comments by ChatGTP and by human raters.

The content of the comments also differs greatly as captured in the word clouds below (see Figures 1 and 2). To further analyze the difference, we conducted a keyness analysis on the two subcorpora, one target corpus of human rater comments and a reference corpus of ChatGPT comments. Based on the likelihood measures

Figure 1. Word cloud for ChatGPT comments on all categories (S1-S8/9) from 56 essays

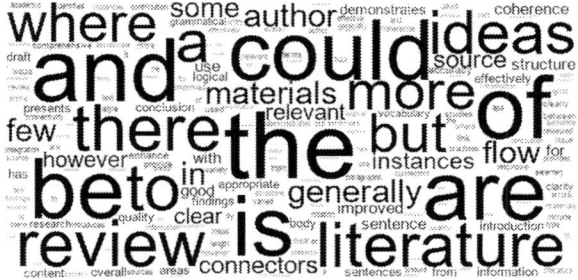

Figure 2. Word cloud for human rater comments on all categories (S1-S9) from 56 essays

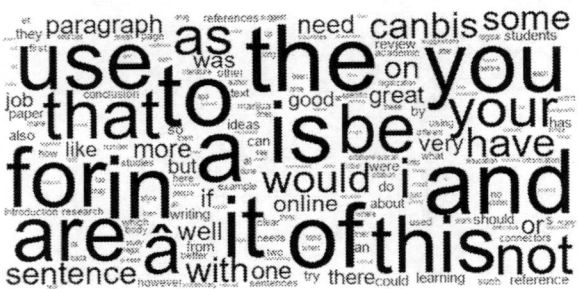

provided in AntConc 4.2 (Anthony, 2023), the top keywords or the words that are more frequently used in the human rater comments (target corpus) include 'you', 'this', 'your', 'I', 'have', 'Cannabis', 'not', 'it', 'as', and 'in'. The words such as 'you' and 'I' reflect how human raters positioned themselves in giving feedback to the writers and thus maintain interpersonal relationships with the participants. Other words such as 'Cannabis' are prompt-specific, showing how human raters referred to the content of the submitted essays in which 'legalized marijuana' was the topic.

Some examples of comments on assessment rubrics by ChatGPT and human raters are provided below.

Example 1. ChatGPT-3.5 Assessment of One Essay

"*Selection of materials & citation practices*":
"score": 8,
"comment": "The author has selected relevant and appropriate source materials for the literature review. The quantity of materials is sufficient, but it could be improved by including more recent studies to ensure the information is up to date."
"*Integration of source materials & citation practices*":
"score": 7,
"comment": "The integration of source materials is generally clear, but there are some instances where the information could be presented more clearly. The citation practices follow APA style, but there are a few minor errors that need to be corrected."
"*Overall structure*":
"score": 8,
"comment": "The overall structure of the literature review is effective. The introduction clearly introduces the research area and identifies the significance of the issue. The body presents relevant ideas and findings from the reviewed studies. The conclusion highlights the contribution of the literature review."

"*Logical structure*":

"score": 8,

"comment": "The logical structure of the literature review is well-developed. The ideas flow logically and are supported by evidence from the reviewed studies. There is a clear progression from the introduction to the body and the conclusion."

"*Content and clarity of ideas*":

"score": 9,

"comment": "The content of the literature review is comprehensive and addresses the social, behavioral, mental, and psychological effects of marijuana on young adults. The ideas are expressed clearly and effectively."

"*Coherence and cohesion*":

"score": 8,

"comment": "The literature review demonstrates good coherence. The flow of ideas is natural and the connectivity between sentences is generally effective. However, there are a few instances where the use of connectors could be improved to enhance the overall cohesion."

"*Grammar & vocabulary*":

"score": 7,

"comment": "The draft has some grammatical errors that need to be corrected. Sentence length and type variety are generally appropriate. The vocabulary quality is good, but there are a few instances where word choice could be improved for clarity and precision."

Example 2. Human Rater's Comments on the Same Mini-Literature Review

"*Selection of materials & citation practices*":

"score": 7

"comment": the selection was OK, but it was hard to tell without seeing the references in the end

"*Integration of source materials & citation practices*":

The hurricane must have blown away the Reference List in the end. Reference list is missing. Some of the in-text references are not in APA format: (Ben C Kuo, 2004)…(WeiNa Lee, 1994).. (Jeffrey G. Reitz, 2007). – should be only last name in the in-text ref: (Kuo, 2004), (Lee, 1994), (Reitz,2007). (Loulou Edelman). – no year, and Loulou is probably the first name?

"*Overall structure*":

"score": 7

"comment": The components were clearly identifiable and the writer understands the concept of LR structure. Introduction would be better off mentioning that we are dealing with Canada a bit earlier (because otherwise some things said in the intro paragraph are not clear). The conclusion is missing a connection with linguistic landscape. Speaking one's language is one thing, having signs in the streets in it or graffiti is another thing.

"*Logical structure*":

"score": 6

"comment": if we are talking about logical connections between paragraphs, then it is fine, there is logical connection, and one thought follows another quite admirably. One thought for you is connected with linguistic landscapes brought up in the beginning. If you want to talk about linguistic landscapes (which is representation of multilingualism in the streets and public spaces), then the body should have focused on this more, adding immigrant and acculturation topics as background information.

"*Content and clarity of ideas*":

"score": 7,

"comment": Content is interesting and exciting. I liked that you brought

linguistic landscapes idea, it is indeed, much fun! It is amazing how many signs in Saskatoon (e.g., in shopping malls, banks, etc.) are now in Mandarin Chinese, for example. Some ways of improving clarity and logic: This would only be true of countries where English is a dominant language, but there could be other dominant languages.

(Finnish in Finland, Russian in Russia, French in France, etc.) Also "includes the dominance of English, the minority languages…" – this is not clear: dominance of minority languages? >> includes English (as a dominant language),the minority languages …. It would be better to define we are talking about Canada and about its Anglophone population/provinces (not to mix in French and Indigenous). How can acculturation benefit diversity?

"*Coherence and cohesion*":

"score": 8,

"comment": the ideas flow well and sentences are connected.

"*Grammar & vocabulary*":

"score": 7,

"comment": Sentence structure and length are fine. Grammar on the whole is very good. A couple of suggestions: < to keep their own values and including speaking their own language.> >>> to keep their own values including the use of their own language. < For example, strong English skills increase the ability to acquire cultural knowledge in most of the Canadian provinces, have cross-cultural interaction, and avoid conflicts due to misunderstanding (Ben C Kuo, 2004).> For example, strong English skills increase the ability to acquire cultural knowledge in most of the Canadian provinces, to engage in cross-cultural interaction, and to avoid conflicts due to misunderstanding (Ben C Kuo, 2004).

Vocabulary use is appropriate and fits academic writing style. 'of the contracting groups'> of the contacting groups.

In sum, ChatGPT provides very 'uniform' comments on individual writing samples that do not differ much across the writers, whereas human raters provide more diverse and individualized comments, employing humor and metaphors and refer directly to the parts of text that need some improvement. The human rater is engaging and has their own stance on the subject of the Literature Review that they openly express and challenge the learner to reveal their opinions as well. In future, ChatGPT or other analogous AI applications would need to be trained to provide more diverse and individualized evaluations of writing and to identify the exact problem and the part of the text that the problem refers to.

DISCUSSION

ChatGPT in Writing Skills Development: Challenges and Perspectives

While according to The New York Times, the general public may see ChatGPT as a 'mixture of software and sorcery" (Roose, 2022), earlier research suggests wide applications for the use of ChatGPT "as a potentially powerful interactive tool for improving students' reading, writing, and critical thinking skills" (Ciampa et al., 2023, 186). In particular, a positive impact of ChatGPT has been noted on writing skills and literacy (Ciampa et al., 2023).

The problems with referencing identified for ChatGPT (Ciampa et al., 2023; Walters & Wilder, 2023) have caused a change in the programming of this AI. Since October 2023, ChatGPT-3.5 refuses to provide references and suggests that the users should be doing academic library and academic journal searches, which strongly devalues its applications for research articles, theses, coursework writing and academic writing training at university graduate level, in our opinion.

Ethics considerations have been brought forward in relation to the use of ChatGPT-generated texts highlighting that ChatGPT "should be used responsibly and ethically with human feedback and guidance to provide a comprehensive learning experience" (Ciampa et al, 2023). The same concerns need to be taken into account when using ChatGPT for human writing product evaluations. Researchers indicate that ChatGPT and other AI lack "empathy and understanding, such as coaching and providing emotional assistance" (Dempers et al, p. 5), nor do they possess "human judgment and discretion" (Murtarellia et al, 2021). AI has also been criticized for not being able to provide adequate learning experiences in regard to ethical norms and values, existential reflection, or a sense of self, history and society (Felix, 2020).

All these features make it questionable that ChatGPT can fully substitute a human instructor and grader.

On the other side, one can argue that ChatGPT treats everyone equally and has no bias or favoritism. In any case, to become a useful grader, ChatGPT would need much more training on writing assessment. While in near future, ChatGPT could hopefully be used as an editor, proofreader and a corrector of syntactic mishaps and vocabulary use, as well as other linguistic features of the produced text, there is likely to be still a place for more creative, supportive and individualized feedback from instructors identifying pathways for each student's growth as a thinker, disciplinary content expert, and a writer.

Beyond ChatGPT

ChatGPT or any other generative AI could hopefully assist with developing writing skills by providing a model of an essay, some ideas for development, and in future, hopefully, by grading writing products numerically and providing some comments on rubrics of writing quality. However, Academic English Writing (AEW) problems cannot be resolved just by any AI applications. We believe that only a combination of different approaches can help with AEW skills development at university graduate (and undergraduate) levels.

The first component of the solution is creating professional academic writing courses by joint efforts of ESL writing specialists and area content experts (Spiliotopoulos et al, 2022).

Instructor training in their new jobs along with course development and lesson outline could contain a few seminars on ESL writing and grading techniques. Such seminars could be provided by ESL specialists and university structures, such as writing centers.

Instructors of content courses also need training in multilingualism and multicultural sensitivity in order to broaden their minds and approaches when grading non-native English written assignments.

Assessment rubrics can be designed to exclude technical writing issues (such as grammar and minor vocabulary errors) for a more equitable grading of non-native English speakers. Even if not being graded, the vocabulary and grammar are still worth correcting to eliminate recurrent non-target forms.

Automated text assessment whether it is done by ChatGPT or another AI or software application could be widely introduced in the university practice to correct non-target forms and sentence structure of both native and non-native writers. They could address the grammar, vocabulary, referencing and punctuation issues allowing the instructors to devote more time on providing comments on content, logic and meaning construction.

Of course, any form of traditional or non-traditional instruction in academic English writing, such as a traditional course and a textbook have a room in writing skills development as well.

To summarize, ChatGPT can be seen as one (of many) educational and writing skills development tools. As suggested by Dempere et al, 2023, "Faculty should proactively embrace AI chatbots such as ChatGPT as powerful teaching, research, and service tools. By becoming informed and trained on AI, they can learn its capabilities and limitations, identify assessment strategies to reduce academic fraud and create innovative pedagogical solutions for future developments" (p. 10).

Limitations of the Study

The study is a pilot, and should be treated as such, with interpreting the results as preliminary observations rather than far-going conclusions. The limitations of the study include a small sample size. We only had 56 samples for the tutorial since it was voluntary and non-credited, and many participants dropped from the study which lasted for 3.5 months, without completing it. Drop-out rates in MOOC courses tend to be high (Kinash, 2013), and were even higher in our non-credited tutorial, as the participants had no commitment or obligation to finish it.

ChatGPT was not trained to rate essays, and this would be a promising direction for the future. We only conducted a limited quantitative analysis, and no qualitative analysis of the comments produced by human raters and ChatGPT, which is a direction for our future research.

CONCLUSION

As a pilot investigation, our conclusions are only very preliminary, and need confirmation in further research with larger samples of writing and the AI training to perform the task. Based on our pilot study, ChatGPT was not trained to rate essays, and yet most numeric evaluations were acceptable and somewhat similar to human raters' evaluations, which is a promising start. By contrast, the verbal comments of ChatGPT on learners' writing samples are uniform and not varied enough, so they cannot be relied upon for the time being.

Thus, ChatGPT has the potential to be employed for quantitative assessment of non-native academic English writing in the near future, whereas qualitative feedback still needs a strong improvement. Already at the current stage, ChatGPT can be successfully used for identifying citation and referencing errors as well as non-target grammar, vocabulary and punctuation. In this way, it is emerging as another tool that can effectively support literacy development and improve learning outcomes.

However, the comments provided by ChatGPT at the given point in this AI tool development are not yet sufficient to provide adequate general feedback as well as reliable and individualized comments on the logic of narrative development, content depth, and argumentation. Thus, ChatGPT can replace some, but not all functions of human assessors or instructors.

More work needs to be done in identifying the full scope of ChatGPT applications to evaluation of writing in general and more specifically, of non-native academic English writing by international students whose native language is other than English. This research direction warrants larger samples and training of ChatGPT to provide more diversified and relevant individualized comments on non-native writing.

As far as the learners' writing goes, the issue of assessing non-native academic English writing is not an easy one to resolve. The solutions could be found along multiple directions that relate not only to AI, assessment and feedback tools, but also to other measures, such as:

1) teacher training and professional development (multilingual and multicultural sensitivity, training on ESL writing assessment);
2) continued development of automated assessment tools;
3) developing professional writing courses by joined efforts of Applied Linguists and content instructors;
4) employing innovative applications of ChatGPT, especially higher versions, refining the wordings of queries and specifying output formats in more detail.

Understanding the challenges and possibilities in adapting ChatGPT to functioning as a free teaching assistant and a grader in an academic course is important for technology literacy as well as for teachers and learners of multiple subjects. The findings in this article are of relevance to e-learning and CALL scholars and practitioners, faculty, and administrators of universities with substantial intakes of international graduate students.

ACKNOWLEDGMENT

We thank Z. Wang for providing assistance with querying ChatGPT-3.5 and outputs compilation.

We are also grateful to SSHRC Canada for providing a research grant that enabled this study.

REFERENCES

Anthony, L. (2023). *AntConc (Version 4.2.4)* [Computer Software]. Waseda University. Available from https://www.laurenceanthony.net/software

Attali, Y., & Burstein, J. (2006). Automated essay scoring with e-rater®; V. 2. *The Journal of Technology, Learning, and Assessment, 4*(3).

Badenhorst, C. (2018). Citation practices of postgraduate students writing literature reviews. *London Review of Education, 16*(1), 121–135. doi:10.18546/LRE.16.1.11

Baffour, P. (2023, January 25). AI can strengthen student writing, not weaken it. *Language Magazine Improving Literacy & Communication.* https://www.languagemagazine.com/2023/01/25/ai-can-strengthen-student-writing-not-weaken-it/

Benichou, L. (2023). The role of using ChatGPT AI in writing medical scientific articles. *J Stomatol Oral Maxillofac Surg., 124*(5), 101456. doi:10.1016/j.jormas.2023.101456

Bhatia, P. (2023). ChatGPT for academic writing: A game changer or a disruptive tool? *Journal of Anaesthesiology, Clinical Pharmacology, 39*(1), 1–2. doi:10.4103/joacp.joacp_84_23 PMID:37250265

Chen, H. (2023). A lexical network approach to second language development. *Humanities & Social Sciences Communications, 10*(1), 735. doi:10.1057/s41599-023-02151-6

Ciampa, K., Wolfe, Z. M., & Bronstein, B. (2023). ChatGPT in education: Transforming digital literacy practices. *Journal of Adolescent & Adult Literacy, 67*(3), 186–195. doi:10.1002/jaal.1310

Conroy, G. (2023). Scientists used ChatGPT to generate an entire paper from scratch — But is it any good? Nature. *Nature, 619*(7970), 443–444. doi:10.1038/d41586-023-02218-z PMID:37419951

Creely, E., Apps, T., Beckman, K., & McKnight, L. (2023). Chat about ChatGPT. *Literacy Learning, 31*(2), 35–39.

Culp, W. C. (2023). Artificial Intelligence and ChatGPT: Bane or boon for academic writing? *The Journal of Education in Perioperative Medicine : JEPM, 25*(2), E702–E702. doi:10.46374/VolXXV_Issue2_Culp PMID:37377506

Dempere, J., Modugu, K., Hesham, A., & Ramasamy, L. K. (2023). The impact of ChatGPT on higher education. *Frontiers in Education*, *8*, 1206936. doi:10.3389/feduc.2023.1206936

DentellaV.MurphyE.MarcusG.LeivadaE. (2023) Testing ai performance on less frequent aspects of language reveals insensitivity to underlying meaning. arXiv:2302.12313.

Dergaa, I., Chamari, K., Zmijewski, P., & Ben Saad, H. (2023). From human writing to artificial intelligence generated text: Examining the prospects and potential threats of ChatGPT in academic writing. *Biology of Sport*, *40*(2), 615–622. doi:10.5114/biolsport.2023.125623 PMID:37077800

Douglas, R. S., & Landry, M. H. (2021). English for Academic Purposes Programs: Key trends across Canadian universities. *Comparative and International Education*, *50*(1), 49–73. doi:10.5206/cieeci.v50i1.10925

GuoB. (2023). How close is chatgpt to human experts? comparison corpus, evaluation, and detection. arXiv:2301.07597.

Halliday, M. A. K. (1994). *An Introduction to Functional Grammar*. Edward Arnold.

Halliday, M. A. K., & Matthiessen, C. M. I. M. (2004). *An Introduction to Functional Grammar* (3rd ed.). Hodder Arnold.

Hegelheimer, V., & Lee, J. (2013). The role of technology in teaching and researching writing. In M. Thomas, H. Reinders, & M. Warschauer (Eds.), *Contemporary Computer-Assisted Language Learning* (pp. 287–302). Bloomsbury Academic.

Herbold, S., Hautli-Janisz, A., Heuer, U., Kikteva, Z., & Trautsch, A. (2023). A large-scale comparison of human-written versus ChatGPT-generated essays. *Scientific Reports*, *13*(1), 18617. doi:10.1038/s41598-023-45644-9 PMID:37903836

Hyland, K. (1999). Academic attribution: Citation and the construction of disciplinary knowledge. *Applied Linguistics*, *20*(3), 341–367. doi:10.1093/applin/20.3.341

Kinash, S. (2013). MOOCing about MOOCs. *Education Technology Solutions*, *57*, 56–58.

Landauer, T. K., Laham, D., & Foltz, P. W. (2003). Automated scoring and annotation of essays with the intelligent essay assessor. Automated essay scoring: A cross-disciplinary perspective, 87–112.

Lax, J. (2002). Academic writing for international graduate students. 32nd ASEE/ IEEE Frontiers in Education Conference, November 6 – 9, 2002, Boston, MA. http://fie2012.fie-conference.org/sites/fie2012.fie-conference.org/history/fie2002/ papers/ 1301.pdf

Lee, H. (2023, March 14). The rise of ChatGPT: Exploring its potential in medical education. *Anatomical Sciences Education*, ase.2270. Advance online publication. doi:10.1002/ase.2270 PMID:36916887

Lew, R. (2023). ChatGPT as a COBUILD lexicographer. *Humanities & Social Sciences Communications*, *10*(1), 704. doi:10.1057/s41599-023-02119-6

Li, Z., Makarova, V., & Wang, Z. (2023). Developing literature review writing skills through an online writing tutorial series: Corpus-based evidence. *Frontiers in Communication*, *8*, 1035394. Advance online publication. doi:10.3389/ fcomm.2023.1035394

Murtarellia, G., Gregory, A., & Romentia, S. (2021). A conversation-based perspective for shaping ethical human–machine interactions: The particular challenge of chatbots. *Journal of Business Research*, *129*, 927–935. doi:10.1016/j.jbusres.2020.09.018

Nayar, P. B. (1997). ESL/EFL dichotomy today: Language politics or pragmatics. *TESOL Quarterly*, *31*(1), 9–37. doi:10.2307/3587973

Nedungadi, P., & Raj, H. (2014). Unsupervised word sense disambiguation for automatic essay scoring. *Advanced Computing Networking and Informatics*, *1*, 437–443.

Okuda, T., & Anderson, T. (2018). Second-language graduate students' experiences at the writing center: A language socialization perspective. *TESOL Quarterly*, *52*(2), 391–413. doi:10.1002/tesq.406

Page, E. B. (2003). Project essay grade: PEG. Automated essay scoring: A cross-disciplinary perspective, 43–54.

Roose, K. (2022). The brilliance and weirdness of ChatGPT. The New York Times. https://www.nytimes.com/2022/12/05/technology/chatgpt-ai-twitter.html

Rosmawati. (2014) Dynamic development of complexity and accuracy: A case study in second language academic writing. *Australian Review of Applied Linguistics*, *37*(2), 75–100. . doi:10.1075/aral.37.2.01ros

Shi, L., & Dong, Y. (2015). Graduate writing assignments across faculties in a Canadian university. *Canadian Journal of Higher Education*, *45*(4), 123–142. doi:10.47678/cjhe.v45i4.184723

Shidarta & Martinelli, I. (2023). Should Indonesia Block ChatGPT? E3S Web of Conferences, 426, 2046. doi:10.1051/e3sconf/202342602046

Spiliotopoulos, V., Wallace, A., & Ilieva, R. (2023). Diffusing Innovation to Support Faculty Engagement in the Integration of Language and Content across the Disciplines in an Internationalized Canadian University. *Higher Education Research & Development*, *42*(2), 453–467. doi:10.1080/07294360.2022.2052813

Storch, N., & Tapper, J. (2009). The impact of an EAP course on postgraduate writing. *Journal of English for Academic Purposes*, *8*(3), 207–223. doi:10.1016/j.jeap.2009.03.001

Swales, J., & Feak, C. (2012). *Academic writing for graduate students: Essential tasks and skills* (3rd ed.). University of Michigan Press. doi:10.3998/mpub.2173936

Vajjala, S. (2018). Automated Assessment of Non-Native Learner Essays: Investigating the Role of Linguistic Features. *International Journal of Artificial Intelligence in Education*, *28*(1), 79–105. doi:10.1007/s40593-017-0142-3

Van Dijk, T. A. (1994). Academic nationalism. *Discourse & Society*, *5*(3), 275–276. doi:10.1177/0957926594005003001

Walters, W. H., & Wilder, E. I. (2023). Fabrication and errors in the bibliographic citations generated by ChatGPT. *Scientific Reports*, *13*(1), 14045. doi:10.1038/s41598-023-41032-5 PMID:37679503

Yang, H. (2023). How I use ChatGPT responsibly in my teaching. *Nature*. Advance online publication. doi:10.1038/d41586-023-01026-9 PMID:37045954

Yeh, H.-C. (2015). Facilitating metacognitive processes of academic genre-based writing using an online writing system. *Computer Assisted Language Learning*, *28*(6), 479–498. doi:10.1080/09588221.2014.881384

Chapter 6
AI as a Collaborative Partner:
Fostering Peer Feedback and Cooperation for Higher Education Literacy

Mirna Ibrahim

https://orcid.org/0009-0005-3685-9866
Ain Shams University, Egypt

ABSTRACT

Literacy education aims to develop students' reading, writing, speaking, and listening skills. Collaborative learning and peer feedback can enhance literacy development, but effectively facilitating these in the classroom presents challenges. This chapter explores how artificial intelligence (AI)-driven tools can be leveraged to augment collaboration and peer feedback in literacy tasks. AI features such as machine learning, natural language processing, and sentiment analysis are examined for their potential to make collaborative literacy learning more engaging, equitable, and productive. Examples of existing implementations demonstrate the feasibility of these approaches. Risks such as over-reliance on automation and bias in algorithms are also discussed, emphasizing the importance of human oversight when integrating AI into education.

INTRODUCTION

Strong literacy skills in reading, writing, listening, and speaking are critical for students' academic achievement and career readiness (Graham & Perin, 2007). However, many students lack proficiency in key areas like reading comprehension,

DOI: 10.4018/979-8-3693-1054-0.ch006

writing quality, and oral communication. Collaborative learning and peer feedback are effective instructional strategies that allow students to develop literacy skills together with scaffolded support (Graham & Perin, 2007). However, implementing these strategies effectively requires substantial teacher time and expertise. Collaborative learning activities like peer review of writing can support literacy development by providing authentic feedback and encouraging reflection on language use (Gielen et al., 2010). However, implementing effective peer review is challenging, as students may lack the skills to provide high-quality feedback (Cho & MacArthur, 2010).

Literacy involves complex cognitive and social practices encompassing reading, writing, speaking, listening, and critical analysis across digital and print media (Leu et al., 2018). While foundational literacy skills were traditionally conceived as basic decoding and comprehension, contemporary definitions recognize literacy as an evolving multidimensional capacity essential for full civic and economic participation (Gee, 2000). As social practices, literacies entail crafting messages tailored to purpose, audience, and context, not just absorbing information. Developing literacy in modern society also requires appreciating diverse perspectives, fostering cultural awareness, determining credibility, and synthesizing across multimodal sources (Coiro et al., 2014).

However, typical teacher-centered literacy instruction focuses on individual repetition of isolated skills disconnected from authentic reading and writing experiences (Allington & Cunningham, 2002). Opportunities for meaningful collaboration, peer feedback, and project-based learning are limited (Applebee & Langer, 2009). This misses chances to situate literacy as social knowledge construction. Literacy development involves gradually participating in collaborative disciplinary discourses while building genre awareness and rhetorical flexibility guided by more experienced mentors (Cook-Sather, 2016).

Emerging applications of artificial intelligence (AI) offer new possibilities for promoting collaborative and socially supported literacy learning at scale. AI presents new opportunities to scaffold collaborative literacy tasks. Natural language processing (NLP) can analyze student work to enable personalized feedback and peer matching. Machine learning (ML) algorithms help guide collaborative writing and peer review sequenced to ability (Grimes & Warschauer, 2010). AI tutoring systems and virtual peers show potential for modeling good feedback practices and facilitating productive student interactions (Ezen-Can & Boyer, 2015). Automated writing evaluation (AWE) shows promise for efficient diagnostic assessment and drafting support (Shermis, 2014). Educational data mining reveals patterns informing differentiated instruction and predictive interventions (Gibson & de Freitas, 2016).

This paper reviews state-of-the-art AI techniques applied in collaborative literacy tasks and peer feedback scenarios. First, we discuss the nature of literacy learning, collaboration and feedback. Then, we outline key theoretical foundations related to collaborative learning, peer feedback and literacy skill development. Next, we analyze existing AI methods leveraged to facilitate collaboration and peer feedback. We then present innovative tools integrating these techniques to scaffold collaboration and feedback in literacy activities, discussing their benefits and limitations. Finally, we examine challenges and future research directions for responsible and ethical AI integration. Our analysis aims to provide insights into harnessing the potential of AI-driven innovations to augment human intelligence in advancing literacy education.

AI IN EDUCATION FOR COLLABORATIVE LITERACY LEARNING

Literacy encompasses the skills of reading, writing, speaking, listening, viewing, and visually representing. It is fundamental to academic success across disciplines and professional achievement. However, traditional literacy instruction often relies heavily on individual seatwork and teacher-centered pedagogies (Applebee & Langer, 2006). This can limit opportunities for peer collaboration, interactive feedback, and the development of 21st-century communication skills (Larson, 2009).

AI refers to computing systems that demonstrate human-like capabilities of sensing, comprehending, acting, and learning (Nilsson, 2009). AI includes techniques like ML algorithms, NLP, computer vision, intelligent agents, and data mining. Rapid advances in these techniques, along with ubiquitous computing power and data collection, have led to expanding real-world applications of AI. In education, AI offers new affordances through capabilities like capturing and analyzing complex student data, providing real-time feedback, personalizing content and activities, automating routine tasks, and responding conversationally like a human tutor or peer (Woolf et al., 2013).

Adaptive learning systems use AI to provide customized content, activities, and guidance tailored to each student's changing strengths and weaknesses. By analyzing fine-grained student learning data and performance patterns, adaptive systems model mastery of skills and misconceptions continuously to adapt instruction appropriately (VanLehn, 2011).

AI affords new possibilities for providing the benefits of one-on-one tutoring and peer interaction at scale, personalizing collaboration and feedback, and giving teachers real-time insights into group work. However, challenges remain around equitable access, privacy, and ethical design as AI becomes further enmeshed in education (Holmes et al., 2023).

Benefits of Collaborative Literacy Learning

Research shows collaborative learning improves literacy outcomes. Discussing texts promotes critical thinking as students articulate opinions and consider different viewpoints (Gillies, 2016). Co-writing builds communication skills and exposes students to diverse styles and techniques (Dale, 1994). Providing peer feedback develops perspective-taking, evaluative abilities and awareness of rhetorical conventions (Nicol, 2014). However, large class sizes and time constraints limit these activities. AI tools could automate parts of collaboration and feedback to make them more feasible.

Challenges in Teaching Literacy Skills

Multiple factors make it difficult to ensure all students gain proficiency in literacy skills. First, students enter school with varying levels of language development and background knowledge (Gee, 2008). These differences mean students have diverse literacy learning needs. Second, literacy requires mastering multiple interconnected competencies like fluent decoding, extensive vocabulary knowledge, comprehension strategies, and language conventions (Catts & Kamhi, 2005). Teachers must address this wide range of skills and abilities.

Third, effective literacy instruction requires considerable individual attention and feedback (Graham & Perin, 2007). Teachers often lack time to mentor each student's skills closely. Peer learning and feedback can help, but they also require monitoring and guidance to be productive. Fourth, literacy tasks like reading complex texts, writing long compositions, and presenting ideas orally require persistence and self-regulation, which many students lack (Gillespie & Graham, 2014). Providing ongoing motivation and metacognitive development presents an additional instructional demand. Given these challenges, AI technologies that can supplement human teaching with personalized and adaptive literacy instruction have great potential value.

Challenges of Facilitating Collaboration in Traditional Classrooms

Meaningful collaboration requires careful planning and monitoring. Teachers must intentionally group students, structure activities and set expectations. Without support, students may not participate equitably or stay on task (Cohen & Lotan, 2014). Providing timely teacher feedback on collaborative work is difficult. Peer feedback also needs oversight to ensure comments are constructive. Students need training on how to give relevant suggestions while maintaining sensitivity (Nicol, 2014). These human resource demands often exclude collaboration from literacy curricula.

Significant challenges arise in implementing high-quality collaborative learning and peer feedback in traditional classrooms. Teachers often lack time to design collaborative activities, provide adequate guidance, and monitor multiple groups simultaneously. Students may not have sufficient skills for collaborative work for providing constructive feedback, especially in early grades. Equitable collaborative participation among culturally diverse learners can be difficult to achieve (Webb et al., 2002). Peer relationships and group dynamics influence the quality of collaboration, making outcomes less consistent (Kirschner, et al., 2011). Logistical issues like scheduling and room layouts can constrain peer interaction opportunities. Without support, collaborative tasks often default to dividing work individually rather than meaningful joint effort (Dillenbourg, 1999).

Peer feedback also faces barriers like reluctance to criticize others, focusing only on surface features, attention to protecting self-esteem over improvement, and failure to utilize feedback to revise work (Nicol, et al., 2014). Online and distance courses add further challenges for collaboration and peer interaction. Teachers lack visibility into how well groups are functioning or if students are providing substantive peer feedback. As class sizes and diversity grow, the challenges multiply for teachers aiming to facilitate impactful collaboration and feedback among all students. Intelligent systems that provide scaffolding, guidance, and monitoring could help address these persistent challenges.

BENEFITS AND LIMITATIONS OF AI TECHNOLOGIES FOR SUPPORTING COLLABORATION IN LITERACY CLASSROOMS

AI can make collaborative literacy learning more engaging, equitable, and effective if thoughtfully integrated. However, further progress is needed in areas like discourse processing, meaning understanding, and transparent algorithmic bias mitigation to realize AI's full potential. Open challenges remain in coordinating peer and AI contributions in pedagogically sound ways. Tables 1 and 2 highlight both the benefits and limitations of existing AI technologies for supporting collaboration in literacy classrooms.

Key Principles for Human-AI Collaboration

Table 3 discusses the recommendations that can guide the effective design and use of AI for collaboration support in literacy classrooms. By considering these

Table 1. Benefits of AI technologies for supporting collaboration in literacy classrooms

Benefits	References
Personalized feedback adapted to learner needs and group functioning.	Biswas et al. (2016)
Direct instruction on discussion skills and literacy strategies is missing from peer talk.	Adamson et al. (2014)
Automated analysis to direct peer feedback toward key areas of need in writing.	Grimes & Warschauer (2010)
Multimodal analytics provides nuanced pictures of collaborative interactions.	Schneider & Pea (2017)
Automates tedious tasks, allowing educators to focus on high-value work.	Luckin & Holmes (2016)
Generates data for understanding collaboration dynamics.	Wise & Cui (2018)
Increases access to high-quality peer interactions.	Tegos et al. (2016)

Table 2. Limitations of AI technologies for supporting collaboration in literacy classrooms

Limitations	References
Difficulty interpreting unique learner expressions and inferring deeper meaning.	Spiro (2017)
Focus on surface features of texts rather than global coherence and meaning.	Roscoe et al. (2012)
Peer orientation diminished when collaborating with AI agents.	Adamson et al. (2014)
Potential to perpetuate biases in datasets used to train AI models.	Hutchinson et al. (2020)
Over-scripting collaboration in ways that limit natural discussion.	Roll & Wylie (2016)
Potential biases in automated evaluations and groupings.	O'neil (2017)
Difficult to ensure transparency, interpretability and fairness.	Mittelstadt (2019)
Risk of overreliance on AI without developing self-monitoring skills.	Selwyn (2019)
Limited pedagogical alignment and focus on long-term literacy growth.	Holmes et al. (2023)
Ethical concerns around data privacy, surveillance and student agency.	Selwyn (2019)

recommendations, developers and educators can work toward AI technologies that fluidly promote collaborative literacy learning.

There are eight proposed principles to guide the design of AI systems that effectively collaborate with humans in educational contexts, as highlighted in Table 4. These humanistic principles emphasize ethical, empowering partnerships. Technology is not an end in itself but rather a means to amplify human flourishing through knowledge exchange.

Table 3. Effective design and use of AI for collaboration support in literacy classrooms

Recommendations	References
AI should supplement but not replace peer interaction and teacher facilitation.	Roll & Wylie (2016)
AI scaffolds should be adaptive rather than scripted, responding to nuances in peer discussion.	Kim et al. (2022)
AI feedback should highlight patterns for peers to interpret rather than provide authoritative judgments.	Grimes & Warschauer (2010)
AI systems must be monitored for algorithmic biases and trained on diverse, equitable datasets.	Hutchinson et al. (2020)
Students should build metalinguistic awareness by critiquing AI limitations and contributions.	Vinall & Hellmich (2022)
Multimodal analytics should provide tools for student self-assessment rather than surveillance.	Schneider & Pea (2017)
Researchers, educators, and students should collaboratively design AI systems and learning activities.	Carvalho et al. (2022)

Table 4. Proposed principles to guide the design of AI systems

Principle	Discussion
Scaffold, do not automate	AI should enhance human learning, not replace it. Applications should aim to stretch skills like a supportive peer, not provide complete solutions.
Elevate agency and efficacy	AI collaborators should empower students' initiative and identity development, fostering growth mindsets.
Respect social context	AI should demonstrate awareness of classroom dynamics and social positioning among peers. Adaptive collaboration is key.
Facilitate dialogue	Technologies should spark meaningful exchanges and idea flow between peers. Listening and questioning are as important as commenting.
Promote coherence	AI contributions should build on students' ideas and connect topics into coherent narratives, not introduce randomness.
Assess sensitively	AI can provide feedback to learners but should avoid harsh criticality or judgment, especially related to personal qualities.
Ensure transparency	Students should understand an AI collaborator's capabilities and limitations clearly to support informed expectations and consent.
Champion equity	AI should scaffold diverse learning needs and styles. Mitigating bias must remain an ongoing priority.

THEORETICAL FOUNDATIONS

It is helpful to draw on seminal learning sciences theories in order to understand how AI could augment learning and literacy development in higher education. Vygotsky's (1978) social development theory emphasizes that cognitive growth emerges through social interaction. Vygotsky introduced the "zone of proximal development" to describe how a learner can achieve more with assistance from a "more knowledgeable other" than they could independently. Socio-constructivist learning theories posit that knowledge is co-constructed through social processes and dialogue (Vygotsky, 1978). In this light, AI systems have the potential to scaffold and extend human learning as semi-knowledgeable partners, although limitations exist.

Bandura's (1971) social learning theory further explicates how behaviors and attitudes are shaped through observation, imitation, and modeling. This suggests AI partners could demonstrate and reinforce productive academic practices. However, Bandura also highlights the importance of self-efficacy, intrinsic motivation, and reciprocal determination. Human agency and bidirectional collaboration are critical. Meanwhile, Papert's (2020) constructionism emphasizes learning through meaning making, discussing, and sharing creations with a community. This points to the value of project-based AI applications that spark dialogue and exchange of ideas.

Collaborative learning aligns with this viewpoint, with students jointly making meaning of texts and building knowledge through peer interaction. Integrating AI into collaborative literacy activities can provide scaffolds to enhance the quality of peer discourse and collaboration around texts (Woolf et al., 2013).

For decades, theories of collaborative and socio-cultural learning have recognized the benefits of dialogue, interaction, and cooperation with peers for cognitive development and knowledge construction (Dillenbourg, 1999; Vygotsky, 1978). Collaborative learning typically involves students working together in small groups or pairs to accomplish shared goals, while peer feedback or peer review provides a structured opportunity for students to offer critiques and suggestions on each other's work (Gielen et al., 2010). Both approaches allow students to articulate their thinking, engage in thoughtful discussion, provide and receive help, and practice perspective-taking as they communicate with peers. Collaborative dialogue builds shared understanding as students ask questions, explain concepts, identify problems, and negotiate solutions together (Roscoe & Chi, 2007). Giving and receiving constructive feedback pushes students to evaluate their own and others' work more deeply (Nicol, et al., 2014).

Extensive research highlights the benefits of collaborative learning and peer feedback for developing literacy skills. In reading, peer collaboration allows students to discuss texts, build comprehension, and learn new vocabulary and reading strategies (Palincsar & Brown, 1984). In writing, peer review helps students improve their drafts by getting constructive feedback before turning in finished work (Graham & Perin, 2007). Students also learn by critiquing others' writing and articulating suggestions for improvement. Oral peer feedback on speeches helps improve public speaking and communication skills. Across these literacy domains, peer interaction provides scaffolding, promotes reflection and awareness of one's learning, and enables practice articulating knowledge and giving elaborated responses – skills correlated with literacy achievement (Chi et al., 1989; Graham & Hebert, 2011).

Collaborative learning with AI support can be more effective than either human or AI instruction alone (Rummel & Spada, 2005). AI provides responsive, personalized support, while peer interaction supplies diverse perspectives and models thinking processes that AI cannot replicate. However, achieving this symbiotic relationship requires careful integration of AI capabilities with human collaboration. Just adding an AI system to a learning environment does not guarantee improved outcomes (Roll & Wylie, 2016). The system must be designed to fluidly support peer interaction and provide scaffolding adapted to group functioning and needs. Overall, major socio-cognitive theories recognize learning as an inherently social process fueled by collaboration. Thoughtfully designed AI partnerships could support this vision.

Collaborative Learning

Collaborative learning refers to instructional approaches where students work together in groups towards shared goals, interacting and exchanging ideas to construct knowledge (Dillenbourg 1999; Panitz 1999). Key elements include positive interdependence, individual accountability, interpersonal skills, and continuous monitoring and improvement (Johnson & Johnson 2009). Research shows collaboration improves learning outcomes, motivation and interpersonal competencies (Kyndt et al., 2013).

AI systems present new opportunities to address these challenges. Features like Natural Language Processing allow AIs to analyze text and provide automated feedback (Roscoe & McNamara, 2013). Intelligent tutoring systems (ITS) have been used to demonstrate effective feedback strategies to students. Virtual peers that simulate

Table 5. AI for collaboration

Theme	Discussion	References
Intelligent analysis of discussion posts	NLP techniques like sentence classification, topic modeling, sentiment analysis and semantic similarity measures can automatically analyze textual posts to generate collaboration metrics and study patterns.	Wise & Cui (2018); Wang et al. (2015)
Automated grouping	Clustering and classification algorithms help create balanced groups based on competence levels, learning styles, personalities etc., to improve team dynamics.	Ounnas et al. (2009)
Stimulating interaction	Chatbots and virtual agents powered by dialogue systems and affective computing can ask probing questions, summarize discussions, provide feedback and motivate team interactions.	Chou et al. (2003);Tegos et al. (2015)

student behaviors create opportunities for realistic collaborative practice (Ezen-Can & Boyer, 2015). Table 5 highlights the potential use of AI for collaboration.

Peer Feedback

Peer feedback entails students providing critiques on each other's work based on set criteria, enabling them to improve performance (Gielen et al. 2010). High-quality feedback should be specific, timely, constructive and aligned with goals (Hattie & Timperley, 2007). Providing and receiving feedback develops metacognitive skills crucial for self-regulated learning (Nicol 2014).

High-quality peer feedback can improve student writing by emphasizing areas for revision and encouraging critical reflection (Gielen et al., 2010). Through both giving and receiving feedback, students gain meta-cognitive skills for evaluating and improving their work. However, peer feedback interventions face challenges like students' reluctance to criticize peers' work or inability to provide helpful suggestions (Cho & MacArthur, 2010). Table 6 highlights the potential use of AI for peer feedback.

Literacy Development

Literacy development requires building skills in reading, writing, speaking and listening across subjects (Hanemann & Scarpino 2016). Active engagement in collaborative tasks and feedback processes promotes literacy by improving communication, critical thinking and learning strategies (Graham & Hebert 2010; Slater & Horstman 2002). Table 7 highlights the potential use of AI for literacy education.

Table 6. AI for peer feedback

Theme	Discussion	References
Automated essay scoring	NLP methods assessing semantic, syntactic and discourse features of texts can automatically evaluate writing quality and provide scoring and diagnostic feedback.	Shermis & Hamner (2013)
Feedback generation	Large language models can be fine-tuned on expert feedback corpora to generate personalized and elaborated feedback on literacy tasks.	Benharrak et al. (2023)
Nudging and notifications	Intelligent nudging systems can remind students to provide timely feedback, while similarity detection methods can encourage more personalized comments.	Xiao & Lucking (2008)

Table 7. AI-driven tools for literacy education

Theme	Discussion	References
WritingPal	Uses automated essay scoring, feedback generation, and nudging features to provide adaptive writing support and peer review scaffolding.	Butterfuss, et al. (2022)
PeerLens	Leverages automated analysis of forum posts and stimulating chatbots to orchestrate productive peer learning around literacy tasks.	Tegos et al. (2016)
MUSE	Employs neural methods to assess text, generate feedback, and create balanced groups for collaborative writing activities.	Patrickson (2019)

EMERGING AI INNOVATIONS

Recent advancements in AI are creating new opportunities to support collaboration and peer interaction, enhance peer learning in literacy classrooms and provide feedback at scale (Luckin, 2016). As defined by Woolf et al. (2013), AI comprises technologies that can engage in human-like processes such as reasoning, learning, and dialogue. In education, AI has been applied in a variety of ways to support teaching and learning across disciplines. Within literacy education specifically, AI tools show potential for enhancing collaborative learning activities like peer writing feedback, comprehension strategy discussion, and textual analysis.

Machine Learning Scaffolds for Collaborative Writing

Machine Learning and educational data mining techniques offer additional possibilities for designing adaptive collaborative literacy environments. Algorithms trained on previous collaborative patterns can help sequence reciprocal peer feedback and guide groups through complex composing tasks. Such intelligent collaboration support tools have a strong potential to amplify active learning and metacognitive development essential for literacy growth.

However, risks of bias, surveillance, and privacy erosion must be acknowledged as Machine Learning permeates educational settings. Equitable access and inclusion for culturally diverse learners remain imperative. Teacher involvement, ethical oversight, and learning sciences principles should guide appropriate AI integration. Further research measuring long-term literacy impacts using robust experimental designs is warranted.

NLP for Personalized Peer Feedback

Human one-to-one tutoring has proven highly effective for literacy skill development but remains resource-intensive (Cohen et al., 1982). AI could help approximate personalized literacy support by facilitating optimized peer feedback. Emerging Natural Language Processing applications show the potential to enhance collaborative writing and reading skills development at scale by matching learners and recommending feedback strategies tailored to their needs.

NLP could analyze students' written work and assign peer reviewers who are likely to provide meaningful feedback based on specific learning needs and strengths. It could also suggest personalized feedback guidance pegged to each writer's demonstrated proficiencies and areas for growth. This will improve the quality and specificity of peer feedback compared to default rubrics. Natural Language Processing also increases perceptions of feedback usefulness and equity among students. Similar NLP peer-matching approaches designed for massive open online courses (MOOCs) have also demonstrated learning gains and writing improvements at scale (Xiong et al., 2010).

Other collaborative literacy platforms also use NLP to offer sentence-level writing diagnosis. The Writing Pal tutoring system provides adaptive feedback on writing quality and style based on analyzing text features against a corpora of quality exemplars. Students who used Writing Pal showed statistically significant gains in writing and self-efficacy compared to those in the control group. Researchers suggest that Intelligent Tutoring Systems using NLP and automated scoring hold promise for enhancing revision and collaborative editing skills at a low, marginal cost.

However, possible barriers to efficacy and ethics merit attention. NLP approaches rely on training corpora that can perpetuate sociolinguistic biases (Sap et al., 2019). Feedback driven by static rubrics risks over-constraining divergent expression and creativity. Ongoing teacher guidance within collaborative systems remains essential to nurture voice and meaning-making. Equitable access to personalized digital tools also requires consideration to avoid widening achievement gaps.

Automated Writing Evaluation for Efficient Diagnosis

Augmented Writing Environments (AWE) use Natural Language Processing and Machine Learning to appraise writing proficiency based on structural, grammatical, and semantic features (Shermis, 2014). AWE software could provide efficient diagnostic information to strengthen literacy skills collaboratively. Though limitations exist, judicious applications show promise for complementing human feedback with consistent standards-based assessments.

E-rater, developed by Educational Testing Service, exemplifies a robust commercial AWE system using NLP trained on an extensive corpora of expert-scored writing samples (Attali, 2013). It generates holistic scores predicting human raters with moderate to high reliability while also providing formative feedback on dimensions like grammar, style, mechanics, and vocabulary usage. Teachers can leverage such automated assessments for rapid diagnostic insights to differentiate instruction. Students receive immediate feedback, enabling iterative drafting. Cost savings from AWE allow for the redistributing of teacher time from grading to rich coaching interactions.

However, AWE has downsides requiring mitigation. NLP models risk encoding sociolinguistic biases from flawed corpora. Constraining voice and style too narrowly risks formulaic writing. Research shows that the use of AWE in isolation limits creativity and metacognitive development; integration with collaborative project learning is advised (Warschauer & Grimes, 2008). Scores should always be interpreted cautiously, supplementing rather than replacing teacher judgment. Nonetheless, thoughtfully implemented AWE holds promise for amplifying collaborative literacy instruction.

AI-DRIVEN TOOLS FOR ENHANCING COLLABORATION AND PEER FEEDBACK IN LITERACY TASKS

These AI systems monitor learners' progress to provide personalized feedback and guidance. Intelligent tutors have been developed for writing, reading, and collaborative discussion activities. For example, Writing Pal uses NLP to analyze essays and provide personalized feedback (Roscoe et al., 2012). AutoTutor fosters collaborative knowledge construction through dialogue (Graesser et al., 2018).

Intelligent Tutoring Systems

Intelligent Tutoring Systems (ITS) are computer programs that aim to simulate human tutors and facilitate personalized learning experiences (Ma et al., 2014). They build models of students' knowledge and skills to adapt instruction, feedback, and practice to individual needs and abilities. ITS typically incorporates NLP to interpret student responses and speech recognition to enable conversational dialogue (Olney et al., 2012). ITS simulates human tutors with domain expertise and pedagogical strategies to provide hints, explanations, and problems of optimal difficulty, which has been shown to improve learning outcomes (Ma et al., 2014).

In literacy education, ITS have been used to provide personalized reading strategy instruction (Mostow & Aist, 2001), writing process scaffolding (Roscoe et al., 2014), and metacognitive feedback (McNamara et al., 2004). For example, AutoTutor helps students construct conceptual knowledge by holding mixed-initiative dialogues and responding continuously to their natural language explanations (Graesser, 2011). It uses computational linguistics to analyze semantic features of students' responses and provide hints or corrections as needed. ITS can significantly improve reading comprehension and summarize writing quality (McNamara et al., 2004; Mostow & Aist, 2001).

Intelligent Tutoring Systems use AI techniques like Machine Learning and Natural Language Processing to provide personalized instruction, feedback, and practice (Ma et al., 2014). For literacy skills, systems like iSTART and Writing Pal tutor reading strategies like summarization and comprehension monitoring. iSTART improved summarization skills in multiple trials with high school and college students (Jackson et al., 2009. Writing Pal studies found similar gains in middle school comprehension.

A key advantage of ITS is its ability to engage students in sustained practice with real-time feedback tailored to their zone of proximal development (Vygotsky, 1978). ITS reduces the cognitive load on teachers to continuously diagnose individuals' abilities and needs during instruction. They also enable opportunities for collaborative dialogue, question generation, and knowledge co-construction with an automated tutor. Limitations include difficulties handling ambiguous language, modeling motivation and affect, and integrating ITS data with classroom assessment systems (Olney et al., 2012).

Conversational Agent Tutors for Collaborative Literacy Tasks

One major challenge of collaboration is providing sufficient guidance and oversight when the teacher cannot monitor every group simultaneously. AI-driven conversational agents could be designed to play an intelligent tutoring role within student work groups. Each group could be assigned a virtual agent tutor with domain expertise in key literacy skills. The conversational agent would interact using natural language and provide personalized guidance tailored to the group's needs and goals.

Conversational agents that interact via dialogue offer another means of supporting literacy development. Virtual tutors have been shown to improve learning outcomes by providing ongoing scaffolding, probing questions, explanations, formative feedback, and adaptive questions as humans would (Graesser & McNamara, 2010). Conversational agents are advancing to handle increasingly sophisticated dialogue with appropriate affect, humor, and interpersonal dynamics (Zhao & Eskenazi, 2018). Conversational agents like human peers or tutors can engage students through natural dialogue. Chatbots and virtual assistants use NLP to comprehend student queries and respond conversationally (Jia, 2004). Such systems make personalized, conversational tutoring and feedback scalable across large classes.

For literacy tasks, the virtual tutoring agent would monitor the group discussion, highlight strong examples of target skills in action, offer hints and leading questions if the team gets stuck, and provide formative feedback on how to improve collaboration and the work product. For developing reading comprehension, the chatbot tutor could ask probing questions about the text, prompt students to summarize key points and encourage the building of conceptual connections. For writing, it could highlight exemplary elements in drafts, remind students of criteria for high-quality work, and reference graphic organizers or outlines. For public speaking practice, the agent could provide tips for improving eye contact, pacing, and projection based on automated speech and video analysis. Across all domains, the ultimate goal would be facilitating groups to have substantive dialogue, provide constructive peer critiques, and complete the literacy task skillfully with minimal direct teacher intervention needed.

Conversational agents that interact in natural language could guide students through collaborative literacy activities, providing instructions, prompts and resources (Tegos et al., 2015). These virtual facilitators could model constructive dialogue, rephrase statements neutrally, and intellectually challenge students. If conflicts arise, the agent can privately message suggestions to resolve interpersonal issues. This on-demand support system enhances collaboration quality (Gweon et al., 2017).

Conversational agents that simulate human discussion can participate in collaborative literacy tasks. For example, Betty's Brain guides students to teach a virtual agent by collaboratively constructing concept maps (Biswas et al., 2005). Other systems act as peer tutors or discussion facilitators focused on comprehension strategies or textual analysis.

Automated Writing Evaluation

Automated Writing Evaluation uses AI to assess written work instantly and provide feedback without teacher effort. AWE systems analyze linguistic features and semantics to evaluate writing quality and provide personalized suggestions for improvement. AWE programs use Natural Language Processing to provide feedback on writing tasks without human rating. They analyze linguistic features related to writing quality and generate scores and diagnostic reports for students. Some also compare students' word usage and grammar against a corpus database to detect plagiarism. Examples of Automated Writing Evaluation software include Intelligent Essay Assessor (IEA), Criterion, MY Access, and Turnitin. AWE tools like MI Write (formerly PEG writing) and WriteLab analyze linguistic features of student writing to provide scoring, diagnostic feedback, and revision support. AWE could assist peer writing feedback by providing an initial analysis for peers to discuss (Grimes & Warschauer, 2010).

Research suggests Automated Writing Evaluation tools can reliably score essays on dimensions like grammar, mechanics, style, and organization (Shermis, 2014). Students generally find the immediate feedback helpful and often incorporate AWE suggestions to improve their drafts. Teachers also value the time savings and consistent grading support provided by AWE tools. Using AWE in conjunction with targeted teacher feedback can enhance the revision process and improve writing outcomes (Warschauer & Grimes, 2008).

Automated Writing Evaluation tools use AI to analyze text features and provide feedback on writing quality. They offer efficiency advantages for teachers and recursive practice benefits for students (Wilson & Czik, 2016). Similar benefits of AWE tools have been found across academic levels from elementary to high school (Wilson & Czik, 2016). Automated scoring consistency and efficiency, along with support for revision through detailed feedback, contribute to these outcomes.

However, studies caution that over-reliance on automated scoring can neglect the rhetorical and audience aspects of writing. AWE feedback is usually limited to surface errors without any sense of interpersonal exchange or audience. There are also risks that may promote conformity over creativity or meaningful self-expression (Elbow, 2013). Researchers advocate balancing AWE with human rating and feedback focused on higher-order concerns like ideas, organization, and coherence. Overall, AWE shows promise for efficiently differentiating literacy instruction but should not fully replace responsive teacher guidance.

AI-Powered Social Platforms

Social networking technologies are becoming integrated platforms for collaborative learning, feedback, and assessment. For example, Flipgrid allows students to post short videos introducing themselves, respond to discussion prompts, or provide peer feedback on literacy projects. Comments and likes on the videos create positive community engagement. AI capabilities can analyze patterns in videos and discussion threads to alert teachers about potentially struggling students or positive trends.

Similarly, AI real-time translation features are being incorporated into collaborative literacy apps to make them more accessible for multilingual learners. TalkingPoints facilitates translated two-way communication between families and teachers via text and voice messages. Machine translation allows students to engage with texts, peers, and school staff in their home languages while also developing academic English proficiency.

However, there remain risks of marginalizing diverse voices if social platforms depend solely on dominant forms of communication or engagement (Kimmons & Veletsianos, 2016). Students from non-dominant cultures may be disadvantaged if AI analytics do not account for cultural differences in interaction styles. Researchers caution that algorithms can perpetuate biases and compromise privacy rights if not developed thoughtfully with community stakeholder input (Williamson et al., 2020). Overall, studies recommend a balanced approach that leverages AI to create more equitable access but retains nuanced human judgment of learning processes and goals.

Adaptive Process Dashboards for Teachers

Teachers need greater visibility into small group processes, engagement, and collaboration dynamics, which is challenging in traditional classrooms. AI-driven dashboards could compile data from learning activities and observational tools to summarize key indicators of collaboration quality for teachers to monitor. Adaptive notifications could flag where intervention is advisable.

Learning analytics applies AI techniques like neural networks and cluster analysis to model learners and interpret complex educational data sources (DiCerbo & Behrens, 2014). This enables phenomena like collaboration to be automatically detected, analyzed, and supported adaptively (Martinez-Maldonado et al., 2016). Dashboards are already being designed to visualize collaborative learning analytics for teachers. Data sources include conversation patterns, interactive tabletop actions, online discussion threads, document co-editing logs, and surveys. Algorithms analyze this multilayer data to model group participation, surface problems, and predict outcomes (Wise et al., 2014). The system can notify teachers of events like under-participation, overload, conflict, or lack of consensus. These insights allow timely pedagogical intervention to improve collaboration.

For literacy classes, the dashboard could highlight imbalanced contribution levels, lack of critical feedback, minimal revision between drafts, or disconnects between professed beliefs and peer comments. Teachers could quickly scan for groups needing guidance. Student-facing dashboards could show individuals their progress and areas for self-improvement. For those learning remotely, virtual observation tools would enable tracking engagement and participation. Intelligent analysis makes group literacy processes more visible so teachers can better support successful collaboration and peer learning.

AI OPPORTUNITIES TO ENHANCE COLLABORATIVE LITERACY LEARNING

Emerging AI capabilities could help implement collaborative literacy activities at scale. NLP allows software to evaluate written and spoken content (McNamara et al., 2017). ML algorithms can be trained on collaborative dialogues and effective peer feedback examples to gain skills for facilitating group work. Features like sentiment analysis allow the detection of problematic peer interactions.

AI-Assisted Group Formation

Artificial Intelligence could help teachers optimize the composition of groups for collaborative literacy projects based on student's skills, needs and compatibility. Algorithms can determine optimal group size, identify ideal roles for students based on their strengths, and suggest combinations of learning styles and personalities most conducive to cooperation (Woolf et al., 2013). This data-driven approach replaces arbitrary grouping with an evidence-based method. The tool ThoughtExchange has used AI to improve student group formation with promising results.

Automated Monitoring of Equitable Participation

Natural Language Processing can track the frequency and content of individual students' spoken contributions during collaborative discussions. Sentiment analysis can detect engagement levels through lexical clues. If dialogue patterns become imbalanced or disengaged, the system can privately prompt withdrawn students to increase participation and suggest dominant speakers allow others to contribute. This promotes inclusive collaboration dynamics. Simulearn's conversational agent, Jill Watson, monitors student participation and engagement in Georgia Tech course discussions (Goel & Polepeddi, 2016).

MULTIMODAL ANALYTICS

Artificial Intelligence can analyze patterns in students' speech, text, facial expressions, gestures, and more during collaborative learning. These technologies are emerging but offer the potential to provide adaptive scaffolds by recognizing collaborative patterns and discussion quality (Schneider & Pea, 2017).

AI Tools to Enhance Formative Feedback on Writing

Intelligent analysis provides ubiquitous feedback at each stage of the writing process, complementing teacher review. Such functionality could make collaborative work a systematically enriching component of literacy instruction. Certain design principles can guide the development of AI tools for peer review in literacy tasks, as discussed in Table 8.

Table 8. Principles for AI-supported peer feedback systems

Principles	References
Provide adaptive scaffolding based on individual student needs.	Ezen-Can & Boyer (2015)
Use Natural Language Processing to analyze text and highlight areas for specific feedback.	Roscoe & McNamara (2013)
Model effective feedback provision, including praise and constructive criticism.	Farrokhnia et al. (2023)
Simulate authentic student interaction patterns during peer review.	Ezen-Can & Boyer (2015)
Track student progress over time and adjust support accordingly.	Chen et al. (2020)
Present feedback multimodally (e.g., text, speech), accounting for different learning needs.	Cukurova et al. (2019)

AI-Supported Peer Feedback on Written Work

Automated literary analysis tools can evaluate written drafts based on dimensions like vocabulary sophistication, flow, and grammar (McNamara et al., 2017). Students get instant feedback for revision outside of class. For peer feedback, AI can monitor critique length and content to ensure high quality. Sentiment analysis prevents unconstructive criticism. Plagiarism checks maintain academic integrity. This monitoring supplements teacher feedback at scale. Turnitin provides an AI solution for Automated Writing Evaluation and plagiarism detection used by many K12 schools and universities.

INTELLIGENT VIRTUAL PEER REVIEW PARTNERS

Before sharing written drafts with classmates, students could get initial feedback from intelligent virtual peers trained in effective critique practices. The virtual partner provides examples and non-evaluative sentence starters to scaffold the peer review process. Students then provide feedback to each other, prepared with strategies for success. This staged approach develops feedback skills.

Automated Formative Feedback on Writing

In writing instruction, AWE tools already provide automated scoring and evaluation of final essay drafts to complement teacher grading. However, integrating formative AWE systems during the drafting process could be highly beneficial for peer review and collaboration. As students are writing collaboratively or providing peer feedback, they could consult the AWE tool for instant formative feedback on drafts. This would improve the quality of peer input, catch mistakes early, and develop students' metacognitive editing skills.

Automated Writing Evaluation can analyze writing on levels from surface grammar and spelling to coherence, organization, and semantics. Automated feedback can explain identified issues and reference instructional materials related to students' needs. AWE is customizable for genre, discourse style, and grading criteria without extensive technical knowledge, making it adaptable across literacy tasks and skill levels. Students get meaningful feedback instantly, allowing efficient revision during drafting. Receiving automated feedback first gives peers higher-quality drafts to review collaboratively. As such, AWE systems have been shown to help students improve their writing as a supplement to human instruction.

To implement this effectively, the interface must facilitate integration with the writing workflow and discussion of feedback during collaboration. Secure cloud-based access allows any-time writing with automated analysis in the background. Alerts can flag where peer input is needed most. Clickable links let peers discuss and resolve questions raised by the artificial tutor. For teachers, dashboards would summarize class and individual progress with automated feedback and revision. Overall, integrating continuous formative assessment via AWE can improve the depth of collaborative analysis of writing while building autonomous writing skills.

Intelligent Grouping for Peer Review Teams

Another common struggle is how to group students strategically for peer review teams. Random assignment is easy, but it often leads to imbalanced teams and missed learning opportunities. Teachers may manually form groups based on ability, personality, or goals, but this takes considerable effort and guesswork. AI-driven grouping algorithms could automate the strategic formation of peer review teams tailored to students' complementary skills, needs and learning objectives.

Researchers can also develop algorithms to model student characteristics and generate balanced groups using constraint optimization methods. Such group formation algorithms can analyze data like achievement scores, neuropsychological profiles, interests, and observational records to assign students strategically (Kardan & Conati, 2012). Moreover, ML techniques can infer strengths, weaknesses, knowledge gaps, and interpersonal traits from patterns in students' learning data. Then, optimal peer teams can be constructed automatically for differentiated activities and peer mentoring.

For literacy tasks specifically, the algorithm could assess students' current proficiency levels in key competencies like reading fluency, writing conventions and vocabulary size. Students needing practice giving quality feedback could be paired with strong, exemplary peers. Struggling writers could be matched with editors with strengths in grammar and mechanics. Mixed-ability groups could encourage modeling and knowledge sharing. The algorithm would adapt assignments iteratively based on updated formative performance data. Teachers can also vet and adjust groups as needed. Automated, data-driven peer grouping can provide better-balanced teams, exposing students to diverse perspectives and appropriate challenges to achieve collaborative literacy goals.

Ethical Perspectives and Future Research

Artificial Intelligence offers extensive opportunities to enhance education, but limitations persist. Thoughtful integration entails aligning applications with learning sciences while centering ethics and human agency. As AI becomes more integrated into education, significant ethical issues emerge that require careful consideration. Additional research and innovation must continue advancing pedagogical AI systems that enrich human development and connections through ethical partnership.

Ethical Perspectives of Using AI in Collaboration and Feedback

In addition to learning theories, ethical perspectives illuminate key opportunities and pitfalls to consider regarding AI in education. Buckingbam Shum & Luckin (2019) applies a social realist lens, cautioning that AI reflects the biases and values of its creators. Equitable access, transparency, and human agency must remain priorities, not technocratic efficiency alone. Selwyn (2019) echoes these concerns, warning of the risks of datafication and surveillance when AI is applied crudely or without consent. From a social justice perspective, AI should empower marginalized voices, not marginalize them further.

Alternatively, an existentialist lens emphasizes freedom and authenticity. AI should aim to expand human capabilities but not override human judgment and meaning-making. Phenomenology also highlights the primacy of lived experience, arguing knowledge emerges through embodied perception situated in the world. By complementing physical learning activities and exchanges, AI could enrich the human experience. Overall, critical perspectives emphasize the inherent subjectivities and asymmetries in any human-AI collaboration. A thoughtful, ethical approach must continually reinforce humanity, equity and justice within these relationships.

As AI becomes more integrated into education, significant ethical issues emerge that require careful consideration, as highlighted in Table 9. It is worth noting that these ethical pitfalls do not outweigh potential benefits but demand rigorous, human-centered design that prioritizes protecting student rights. Interdisciplinary teams, including ethicists, should audit systems regularly.

Table 9. Ethical considerations of using AI

Area	Discussion
Algorithmic Bias & Equity	AI systems can perpetuate human biases against marginalized groups if not designed thoughtfully. Representatives from diverse backgrounds must be involved in design and testing to identify and mitigate potential harms.
Student Privacy	Collecting student data is necessary to personalize AI systems, but practices must comply with privacy laws and norms. Only essential data should be collected, stored securely, never sold, and deleted when no longer necessary. Transparent data policies with opt-out options are crucial.
Human-AI Boundaries	Care must be taken not to overtly deceive or manipulate students with AI's growing ability to mimic human behavior. Intelligibility principles should be made clear when an AI agent is involved. Scaffolding should promote interdependence, not total automation dependence.
Accessibility	Universal design principles must guide inclusive AI that works equitably for diverse learners with disabilities or special needs. Testing with population groups can identify interaction barriers.

FUTURE RESEARCH DIRECTIONS

While promising, applying AI to support collaboration, peer feedback, and literacy learning has limitations. First, technical challenges remain in effectively analyzing messy natural language peer discussions, modeling interpersonal group dynamics, detecting conceptual understanding, and personalizing appropriately across diverse contexts. More multidisciplinary research is needed to improve AI's capabilities for the nuances of collaborative learning. Second, equitable access challenges must be proactively addressed, as biases can emerge from unrepresentative data and design choices. Steps should be taken to prevent the exclusion of non-native language speakers, students without home technology access, or learners with disabilities (Holmes et al., 2023).

Third, appropriate safeguards are needed to maintain positive human interaction alongside automation. Over-scripting peer discourse through AI could diminish open-ended creativity and relationship-building. The benefits of teacher presence, emotional connection, improvisation, and serendipity should not be lost. AI tools should aim to augment, not replace, human collaboration. Over-automation could undermine interpersonal exchanges that make collaboration meaningful. Students may become over-reliant on AI feedback rather than developing self-monitoring abilities. Biases encoded in algorithms could lead to unfair evaluations or grouping suggestions unless addressed through rigorous testing and oversight. Teachers play an important oversight role in using AI responsibly to meet pedagogical goals without introducing harmful biases.

Moreover, these studies provide evidence AI tools can supplement human teaching and peer collaboration during literacy activities, but important limitations remain. First, most studies were short-term trials in restricted domains like vocabulary, so expanded research on long-term impacts across the full span of literacy skills is needed. Second, developing AI systems' cultural competence to ensure tools work equally well for diverse student groups requires further effort (Ogan et al., 2015).

Further research is still required to develop best practices for balancing automation with human autonomy and oversight. The long-term impacts of extended exposure to AI tutors and peers remain unknown. More studies must track not just learning outcomes but changes in human behavior interdependencies within AI-mediated environments. Additional research should include learners in design iterations of AI collaborative learning tools to maximize educational and ethical value (Tegos et al., 2014). More research is needed to develop AI systems tailored for literacy education (Holmes et al. 2023) and adhere to ethical AI principles focused on beneficence (Floridi et al. 2021). Ongoing study of human-AI collaborative learning dynamics through these theoretical lenses is needed. Extra research should examine optimal NLP integrations supporting personalized literacy development while mitigating risks.

There is a need to ensure that AI literacy support is accessible for students with disabilities. AI technologies should enhance, not replace, opportunities for authentic literacy skill practice and human connection. With careful design and integration, AI tools show significant promise for advancing literacy instruction and peer learning. However, sustained research and development is essential to realize their full potential.

CONCLUSION

This analysis indicates that AI-driven tools show promising capabilities to enhance collaboration, feedback, and differentiated literacy instruction. Intelligent tutors and AWE can provide personalized scaffolding and practice opportunities that complement human teaching. Social platforms powered by machine translation and learning analytics may help make learning more accessible, inclusive, and engaging.

However, it is essential that AI is not implemented in isolation or adopted without critical examination. The unique affordances of human connection, creativity, and relationship-building in literacy education cannot be matched or replaced solely by algorithms. Instead, research suggests AI tools should be thoughtfully combined with evidence-based instructional strategies and equitable assessment practices (Williamson et al., 2020).

Future research also needs to better address issues of privacy, bias, and validity in literacy AI. Studies should involve participatory design with stakeholders and examine long-term impacts on learning outcomes. With responsible implementation,

AI technologies can help amplify student voices, provide responsive scaffolding, and promote literacy engagement. However, human teachers must remain at the pedagogical center guiding literacy development. AI-driven tools are not an end in themselves but rather a potentially promising means for enhancing collaboration, feedback, and communities of practice in literacy education.

REFERENCES

Adamson, D., Ashe, C., Jang, H., Yaron, D., & Rosé, C. P. (2014). Intensification of group knowledge exchange with academically productive talk agents. In *Proceedings of the 10th International Conference on Computer Supported Collaborative Learning* (pp. 10-17). Academic Press.

Allington, R. L., & Cunningham, P. M. (2002). *Schools that work: Where all children read and write*. Allyn & Bacon.

Applebee, A. N., & Langer, J. A. (2006). *The state of writing instruction in America's schools: What existing data tell us*. Center on English Learning and Achievement.

Applebee, A. N., & Langer, J. A. (2009). EJ extra: What is happening in the teaching of writing? *English Journal*, 98(5), 18–28. doi:10.58680/ej20097117

Attali, Y. (2013). Validity and reliability of automated essay scoring. In *Handbook of automated essay evaluation* (pp. 181–198). Routledge.

Bandura, A. (1971). *Social learning theory*. General Learning Press.

Benharrak, K., Zindulka, T., Lehmann, F., Heuer, H., & Buschek, D. (2023). Writer-defined AI personas for on-demand feedback generation. *arXiv preprint arXiv:2309.10433*.

Biswas, G., Segedy, J. R., & Bunchongchit, K. (2016). From design to implementation to practice a learning by teaching system: Betty's Brain. *International Journal of Artificial Intelligence in Education*, 26(1), 350–364. doi:10.1007/s40593-015-0057-9

Buckingham Shum, S. J., & Luckin, R. (2019). Learning analytics and AI: Politics, pedagogy and practices. *British Journal of Educational Technology*, 50(6), 2785–2793. doi:10.1111/bjet.12880

Butterfuss, R., Roscoe, R. D., Allen, L. K., McCarthy, K. S., & McNamara, D. S. (2022). Strategy uptake in writing pal: Adaptive feedback and instruction. *Journal of Educational Computing Research*, 60(3), 696–721. doi:10.1177/07356331211045304

Carvalho, L., Martinez-Maldonado, R., Tsai, Y. S., Markauskaite, L., & De Laat, M. (2022). How can we design for learning in an AI world? *Computers and Education: Artificial Intelligence*, *3*, 100053. doi:10.1016/j.caeai.2022.100053

Catts, H. W., & Kamhi, A. G. (Eds.). (2005). *The connections between language and reading disabilities*. Psychology Press. doi:10.4324/9781410612052

Chi, M. T., Bassok, M., Lewis, M. W., Reimann, P., & Glaser, R. (1989). Self-explanations: How students study and use examples in learning to solve problems. *Cognitive Science*, *13*(2), 145–182.

Cho, K., & MacArthur, C. (2010). Student revision with peer and expert reviewing. *Learning and Instruction*, *20*(4), 328–338. doi:10.1016/j.learninstruc.2009.08.006

Chou, C. Y., Chan, T. W., & Lin, C. J. (2003). Redefining the learning companion: The past, present, and future of educational agents. *Computers & Education*, *40*(3), 255–269. doi:10.1016/S0360-1315(02)00130-6

Cohen, E. G., & Lotan, R. A. (2014). *Designing groupwork: Strategies for the heterogeneous classroom* (3rd ed.). Teachers College Press.

Cohen, P. A., Kulik, J. A., & Kulik, C. L. C. (1982). Educational outcomes of tutoring: A meta-analysis of findings. *American Educational Research Journal*, *19*(2), 237–248. doi:10.3102/00028312019002237

Coiro, J., Knobel, M., Lankshear, C., & Leu, D. J. (2014). Central issues in new literacies and new literacies research. In *Handbook of research on new literacies* (pp. 1–22). Routledge. doi:10.4324/9781410618894-7

Cook-Sather, A. (2016). Creating brave spaces within and through student-faculty pedagogical partnerships. *Teaching and Learning Together in Higher Education*, *1*(18), 1.

Dale, H. (1994). Collaborative writing interactions in one ninth-grade classroom. *The Journal of Educational Research*, *87*(6), 334–344. doi:10.1080/00220671.19 94.9941264

DiCerbo, K. E., Behrens, J. T., & Barber, M. (2014). *Impacts of the digital ocean on education*. Pearson.

Dillenbourg, P. (1999). What do you mean by collaborative learning? Elbow, P. (2013). High stakes and low stakes in assigning and responding to writing. In *Dialogue on Writing* (pp. 289–298). Routledge.

Ezen-Can, A., Boyer, K. E., Kellogg, S., & Booth, S. (2015). Unsupervised modeling for understanding MOOC discussion forums: A learning analytics approach. *In Proceedings of the Fifth International Conference on Learning Analytics and Knowledge* (pp. 146-150). 10.1145/2723576.2723589

Floridi, L., Cowls, J., Beltrametti, M., Chatila, R., Chazerand, P., Dignum, V., ... Vayena, E. (2021). An ethical framework for a good AI society: Opportunities, risks, principles, and recommendations. *Ethics, Governance, and Policies in Artificial Intelligence,* 19-39.

Gee, J. P. (2000). Teenagers in new times: A new literacy studies perspective. *Journal of Adolescent & Adult Literacy*, *43*(5), 412–420.

Gee, J. P. (2008). A sociocultural perspective on opportunity to learn. *Assessment, Equity, and Opportunity to Learn,* 76-108.

Gibson, D., & de Freitas, S. (2016). Exploratory analysis in learning analytics. *Technology. Knowledge and Learning*, *21*(1), 5–19. doi:10.1007/s10758-015-9249-5

Gielen, S., Peeters, E., Dochy, F., Onghena, P., & Struyven, K. (2010). Improving the effectiveness of peer feedback for learning. *Learning and Instruction*, *20*(4), 304–315. doi:10.1016/j.learninstruc.2009.08.007

Gillespie, A., & Graham, S. (2014). A meta-analysis of writing interventions for students with learning disabilities. *Exceptional Children*, *80*(4), 454–473. doi:10.1177/0014402914527238

Gillies, R. M. (2016). Cooperative learning: Review of research and practice. *The Australian Journal of Teacher Education*, *41*(3), 39–54. doi:10.14221/ajte.2016v41n3.3

Goel, A. K., & Polepeddi, L. (2016). *Jill Watson: A virtual teaching assistant for online education*. Georgia Tech Library.

Graesser, A., & McNamara, D. (2010). Self-regulated learning in learning environments with pedagogical agents that interact in natural language. *Educational Psychologist*, *45*(4), 234–244. doi:10.1080/00461520.2010.515933

Graesser, A. C. (2011). Learning, thinking, and emoting with discourse technologies. *The American Psychologist*, *66*(8), 746–757. doi:10.1037/a0024974 PMID:22082403

Graesser, A. C., Hu, X., Nye, B. D., VanLehn, K., Kumar, R., Heffernan, C., Heffernan, N., Woolf, B., Olney, A. M., Rus, V., Andrasik, F., Pavlik, P., Cai, Z., Wetzel, J., Morgan, B., Hampton, A. J., Lippert, A. M., Wang, L., Cheng, Q., ... Baer, W. (2018). ElectronixTutor: An intelligent tutoring system with multiple learning resources for electronics. *International Journal of STEM Education*, *5*(1), 1–21. doi:10.1186/s40594-018-0110-y PMID:30631705

Graham, S., & Hebert, M. (2010). Writing to read: Evidence for how writing can improve reading. *A Report from Carnegie Corporation of New York*.

Graham, S., & Hebert, M. (2011). Writing to read: A meta-analysis of the impact of writing and writing instruction on reading. *Harvard Educational Review*, *81*(4), 710–744. doi:10.17763/haer.81.4.t2k0m13756113566

Graham, S., & Perin, D. (2007). Writing next-effective strategies to improve writing of adolescents in middle and high schools. Academic Press.

Grimes, D., & Warschauer, M. (2010). Utility in a fallible tool: A multi-site case study of automated writing evaluation. *The Journal of Technology, Learning, and Assessment*, *8*(6).

Gweon, G., Jun, S., Finger, S., & Rosé, C. P. (2017). Towards effective group work assessment: Even what you don't see can bias you. *International Journal of Technology and Design Education*, *27*(1), 165–180. doi:10.1007/s10798-015-9332-1

Hanemann, U., & Scarpino, C. (2016). *Literacy in multilingual and multicultural contexts: Effective approaches to adult learning and education*. UNESCO Institute for Lifelong Learning.

Hattie, J., & Timperley, H. (2007). The power of feedback. *Review of Educational Research*, *77*(1), 81–112. doi:10.3102/003465430298487

Holmes, W., Bialik, M., & Fadel, C. (2023). *Artificial intelligence in education*. Globethics Publications.

Hutchinson, B., Prabhakaran, V., Denton, E., Webster, K., Zhong, Y., & Denuyl, S. (2020). Social biases in NLP models as barriers for persons with disabilities. *arXiv preprint arXiv:2005.00813*. doi:10.18653/v1/2020.acl-main.487

Jackson, G. T., Boonthum, C., & McNamara, D. S. (2009). iSTART-ME: Situating extended learning within a game-based environment. In *Proceedings of the Workshop on Intelligent Educational Games at the 14th Annual Conference on Artificial Intelligence in Education* (pp. 59-68). Academic Press.

Jia, J. (2004). The study of the application of a web-based chatbot system on the teaching of foreign languages. In *Society for Information Technology & Teacher Education International Conference* (pp. 1201-1207). Association for the Advancement of Computing in Education (AACE).

Johnson, D. W., & Johnson, R. T. (2009). An educational psychology success story: Social interdependence theory and cooperative learning. *Educational Researcher*, *38*(5), 365–379. doi:10.3102/0013189X09339057

Kardan, S., & Conati, C. (2012). Exploring gaze data for determining user learning with an interactive simulation. *User Modeling, Adaptation, and Personalization: 20th International Conference, UMAP 2012, Montreal, Canada, July 16-20, 2012 Proceedings*, *20*, 126–138.

Kim, M. K., Kim, N. J., & Heidari, A. (2022). Learner experience in artificial intelligence-scaffolded argumentation. *Assessment & Evaluation in Higher Education*, *47*(8), 1301–1316. doi:10.1080/02602938.2022.2042792

Kimmons, R., & Veletsianos, G. (2016). Education scholars' evolving uses of twitter as a conference backchannel and social commentary platform. *British Journal of Educational Technology*, *47*(3), 445–464. doi:10.1111/bjet.12428

Kirschner, F., Paas, F., & Kirschner, P. A. (2011). Task complexity as a driver for collaborative learning efficiency: The collective working-memory effect. *Applied Cognitive Psychology*, *25*(4), 615–624. doi:10.1002/acp.1730

Kyndt, E., Raes, E., Lismont, B., Timmers, F., Cascallar, E., & Dochy, F. (2013). A meta-analysis of the effects of face-to-face cooperative learning. Do recent studies falsify or verify earlier findings? *Educational Research Review*, *10*, 133–149. doi:10.1016/j.edurev.2013.02.002

Larson, L. C. (2009). e-Reading and e-responding: New tools for the next generation of readers. *Journal of Adolescent & Adult Literacy*, *53*(3), 255–258. doi:10.1598/JAAL.53.3.7

Leu, D. J., Kinzer, C. K., Coiro, J., Castek, J., & Henry, L. A. (2018). New literacies: A dual-level theory of the changing nature of literacy, instruction, and assessment. In *Theoretical Models and Processes of Literacy* (pp. 319–346). Routledge. doi:10.4324/9781315110592-19

Luckin, R., & Holmes, W. (2016). Intelligence unleashed: An argument for AI in education. Academic Press.

Luckin, R., Holmes, W., Griffiths, M., & Forcier, L. B. (2016). Intelligence unleashed: An argument for AI in education. Academic Press.

Ma, W., Adesope, O. O., Nesbit, J. C., & Liu, Q. (2014). Intelligent tutoring systems and learning outcomes: A meta-analysis. *Journal of Educational Psychology, 106*(4), 901–918. doi:10.1037/a0037123

Martinez-Maldonado, R., Schneider, B., Charleer, S., Buckingham Shum, S., Klerkx, J., & Duval, E. (2016). Interactive surfaces and learning analytics: Data, orchestration aspects, pedagogical uses, and challenges. In *Proceedings of the Sixth International Conference on Learning Analytics & Knowledge* (pp. 124-133). 10.1145/2883851.2883873

McNamara, D. S., Allen, L., Crossley, S., Dascalu, M., & Perret, C. A. (2017). Natural language processing and learning analytics. In Handbook of Learning Analytics (pp. 93). doi:10.18608/hla17.008

McNamara, D. S., Levinstein, I. B., & Boonthum, C. (2004). iSTART: Interactive strategy training for active reading and thinking. *Behavior Research Methods, Instruments, & Computers, 36*(2), 222–233. doi:10.3758/BF03195567 PMID:15354687

Mittelstadt, B., Russell, C., & Wachter, S. (2019). Explaining explanations in AI. In *Proceedings of the Conference on Fairness, Accountability, and Transparency* (pp. 279-288). 10.1145/3287560.3287574

Mostow, J. (2001). Evaluating tutors that listen: An overview of Project LISTEN. Academic Press.

Nicol, D. (2014). Guiding principles for peer review: Unlocking learners' evaluative skills. In Advances and Innovations in University Assessment and Feedback (pp. 197-224). Academic Press.

Nicol, D., Thomson, A., & Breslin, C. (2014). Rethinking feedback practices in higher education: A peer review perspective. *Assessment & Evaluation in Higher Education, 39*(1), 102–122. doi:10.1080/02602938.2013.795518

Nilsson, N. J. (2009). *The Quest for Artificial Intelligence*. Cambridge University Press. doi:10.1017/CBO9780511819346

O'Neil, C. (2017). *Weapons of Math Destruction: How Big Data Increases Inequality and Threatens Democracy*. Crown.

Ogan, A., Walker, E., Baker, R., Rodrigo, M. M. T., Soriano, J. C., & Castro, M. J. (2015). Towards understanding how to assess help-seeking behavior across cultures. *International Journal of Artificial Intelligence in Education*, *25*(2), 229–248. doi:10.1007/s40593-014-0034-8

Olney, A. M., Graesser, A. C., & Person, N. K. (2012). Question generation from concept maps. *Dialogue & Discourse*, *3*(2), 75–99. doi:10.5087/dad.2012.204

Ounnas, A., Davis, H. C., & Millard, D. E. (2009). A framework for semantic group formation in education. *Journal of Educational Technology & Society*, *12*(4), 43–55.

Palinscar, A. S., & Brown, A. L. (1984). Reciprocal teaching of comprehension-fostering and comprehension-monitoring activities. *Cognition and Instruction*, *1*(2), 117–175. doi:10.1207/s1532690xci0102_1

Panitz, T. (1999). Collaborative versus cooperative learning: A comparison of the two concepts which will help us understand the underlying nature of interactive learning. Academic Press.

Papert, S. (2020). *Mindstorms: Children, computers, and powerful ideas*. Basic Books.

Patrickson, B. L. (2019). The reflective muse. *Student Engagement in Higher Education Journal*, *2*(3), 77–83.

Roll, I., & Wylie, R. (2016). Evolution and revolution in artificial intelligence in education. *International Journal of Artificial Intelligence in Education*, *26*(2), 582–599. doi:10.1007/s40593-016-0110-3

Roscoe, R. D., Allen, L. K., Weston, J. L., Crossley, S. A., & McNamara, D. S. (2014). The Writing Pal intelligent tutoring system: Usability testing and development. *Computers and Composition*, *34*, 39–59. doi:10.1016/j.compcom.2014.09.002

Roscoe, R. D., & Chi, M. T. (2007). Understanding tutor learning: Knowledge-building and knowledge-telling in peer tutors' explanations and questions. *Review of Educational Research*, *77*(4), 534–574. doi:10.3102/0034654307309920

Roscoe, R. D., Kugler, D., Crossley, S. A., Weston, J. L., & McNamara, D. S. (2012). Developing pedagogically-guided threshold algorithms for intelligent automated essay feedback. *International FLAIRS Conference*.

Roscoe, R. D., & McNamara, D. S. (2013). Writing Pal: Feasibility of an intelligent writing strategy tutor in the high school classroom. *Journal of Educational Psychology*, *105*(4), 1010–1025. doi:10.1037/a0032340

Rummel, N., & Spada, H. (2005). Learning to collaborate: An instructional approach to promoting collaborative problem solving in computer-mediated settings. *Journal of the Learning Sciences*, *14*(2), 201–241. doi:10.1207/s15327809jls1402_2

Sap, M., Gabriel, S., Qin, L., Jurafsky, D., Smith, N. A., & Choi, Y. (2019). Social bias frames: Reasoning about social and power implications of language. *arXiv preprint arXiv:1911.03891*.

Schneider, B., & Pea, R. (2017). Real-time mutual gaze perception enhances collaborative learning and collaboration quality. *Educational Media and Technology Yearbook*, *40*, 99–125. doi:10.1007/978-3-319-45001-8_7

Selwyn, N. (2019). *Should robots replace teachers?: AI and the future of education*. John Wiley & Sons.

Shermis, M. D. (2014). State-of-the-art automated essay scoring: Competition, results, and future directions from a United States demonstration. *Assessing Writing*, *20*, 53–76. doi:10.1016/j.asw.2013.04.001

Shermis, M. D., & Hamner, B. (2013). Contrasting state-of-the-art automated scoring of essays. In *Handbook of Automated Essay Evaluation* (pp. 313–346). Current Applications and New Directions.

Slater, W. H., & Horstman, F. R. (2002). Teaching reading and writing to struggling middle school and high school students: The case for reciprocal teaching. *Preventing School Failure*, *46*(4), 163–166. doi:10.1080/10459880209604416

Spiro, R. J., Bruce, B. C., & Brewer, W. F. (Eds.). (2017). *Theoretical issues in reading comprehension: Perspectives from cognitive psychology, linguistics, artificial intelligence, and education* (Vol. 11). Routledge. doi:10.4324/9781315107493

Tegos, S., Demetriadis, S., & Karakostas, A. (2015). Promoting academically productive talk with conversational agent interventions in collaborative learning settings. *Computers & Education*, *87*, 309–325. doi:10.1016/j.compedu.2015.07.014

Tegos, S., Demetriadis, S., Papadopoulos, P. M., & Weinberger, A. (2016). Conversational agents for academically productive talk: A comparison of directed and undirected agent interventions. *International Journal of Computer-Supported Collaborative Learning*, *11*(4), 417–440. doi:10.1007/s11412-016-9246-2

Tegos, S., Demetriadis, S., & Tsiatsos, T. (2014). A configurable conversational agent to trigger students' productive dialogue: A pilot study in the CALL domain. *International Journal of Artificial Intelligence in Education*, *24*(1), 62–91. doi:10.1007/s40593-013-0007-3

VanLehn, K. (2011). The relative effectiveness of human tutoring, intelligent tutoring systems, and other tutoring systems. *Educational Psychologist, 46*(4), 197–221. do i:10.1080/00461520.2011.611369

Vinall, K., & Hellmich, E. (2022). Do you speak translate?: Reflections on the nature and role of translation. *Journal of Linguistics and Language Teaching, 14*(1). Advance online publication. doi:10.5070/L214156150

Vygotsky, L. S., & Cole, M. (1978). *Mind in society: The development of higher psychological processes*. Harvard University Press.

Wang, X., Yang, D., Wen, M., Koedinger, K., & Rosé, C. P. (2015). *Investigating how students' cognitive behavior in MOOC discussion forums affect learning gains*. International Educational Data Mining Society.

Warschauer, M., & Grimes, D. (2008). Automated writing assessment in the classroom. *Pedagogies, 3*(1), 22–36. doi:10.1080/15544800701771580

Webb, N. M., Nemer, K. M., & Zuniga, S. (2002). Short circuits or superconductors? Effects of group composition on high-achieving students' science assessment performance. *American Educational Research Journal, 39*(4), 943–989. doi:10.3102/00028312039004943

Williamson, B., Eynon, R., & Potter, J. (2020). Pandemic politics, pedagogies, and practices: Digital technologies and distance education during the coronavirus emergency. *Learning, Media and Technology, 45*(2), 107–114. doi:10.1080/1743 9884.2020.1761641

Wilson, J., & Czik, A. (2016). Automated essay evaluation software in English Language Arts classrooms: Effects on teacher feedback, student motivation, and writing quality. *Computers & Education, 100*, 94–109. doi:10.1016/j.compedu.2016.05.004

Wise, A., Zhao, Y., & Hausknecht, S. (2014). Learning analytics for online discussions: Embedded and extracted approaches. *Journal of Learning Analytics, 1*(2), 48–71. doi:10.18608/jla.2014.12.4

Wise, A. F., & Cui, Y. (2018). Unpacking the relationship between discussion forum participation and learning in MOOCs: Content is key. In *Proceedings of the 8th International Conference on Learning Analytics and Knowledge* (pp. 330-339). 10.1145/3170358.3170403

Woolf, B. P., Lane, H. C., Chaudhri, V. K., & Kolodner, J. L. (2013). AI grand challenges for education. *AI Magazine, 34*(4), 66–84. doi:10.1609/aimag.v34i4.2490

Xiao, Y., & Lucking, R. (2008). The impact of two types of peer assessment on students' performance and satisfaction within a Wiki environment. *The Internet and Higher Education, 11*(3-4), 186–193. doi:10.1016/j.iheduc.2008.06.005

Xiong, W., Litman, D., & Schunn, C. (2010). Assessing reviewers' performance based on mining problem localization in peer-review data. In *Educational Data Mining 2010-3rd International Conference on Educational Data Mining* (pp. 211-220). Academic Press.

Zhao, T., & Eskenazi, M. (2018). Zero-shot dialog generation with cross-domain latent actions. *arXiv preprint arXiv:1805.04803*. doi:10.18653/v1/W18-5001

Chapter 7
Data Literacy and Artificial Intelligence in Higher Education

Aulia Puspaning Galih

https://orcid.org/0000-0003-0264-6916
Eötvös Loránd University, Budapest, Hungary

Ágnes Hajdu Barát

https://orcid.org/0000-0002-6774-5440
Eötvös Loránd University, Budapest, Hungary

ABSTRACT

In the big data era, we generate, use, and share data from many sources. Quantitative survey or experiment results are no longer the only data in academia. Data collection using artificial intelligence is common in academic and research settings, especially in meta-analysis. Data literacy involves understanding, analyzing, and communicating data. Everyone in higher education needs data literacy. Students must understand statistics to correctly interpret data, communicate research findings, and build evidence-based arguments. Artificial intelligence could help solve complex practical and academic problems in sustainable development research. Data literacy must be taught to stakeholders to help them analyze research data for sustainable higher education research. Additionally, higher education institutions must teach artificial intelligence to sustain their research. Transliteracy is another data literacy and AI education future concept. Transliteracy offers a new perspective on how higher education stakeholders with knowledge of education and academic communication can collaborate to better serve future generations.

DOI: 10.4018/979-8-3693-1054-0.ch007

INTRODUCTION

In today's modern society, data is an element that is present in every aspect of daily life. The amount of data that is produced by humanity every day is 2.5 quintillion bytes (Farrell, 2023). Data has a value that is inherently limited when taken alone. The process of providing value entails analyzing and making sense of one or more datasets concerning the particular circumstances currently being considered. Consequently, people frequently use data to assist them in making decisions regarding their lives (Hanegan, 2021). Data helps people create and enhance knowledge, evaluate and analyze development, estimate results, assist decision-making, and guide our actions and choices in the present and future. Efficient data collection and analysis assist decision-makers in confirming, comprehending, and measuring intricate issues that require logical and perceptive solutions (Farrell, 2023).

In the big data era, we constantly produce, utilize, and share data from and to various sources. The world we live in is referred to as a "datafied" society (Aradau, 2023) because almost everything is constantly converted into data, which is being measured and analyzed. It becomes increasingly crucial for individuals to comprehend the data presented in the reports, whether from the internet, government, academic publications, or other sources. Furthermore, data and technologies increasingly influence decisions made by businesses (Wei, 2023) and governments (Gu, 2023). Individuals lacking data literacy skills may be more likely to accept biased interpretations of data as truth, which can result in erroneous understandings or potentially harmful choices.

The significance of data development and interpretation has been elevated due to a more expansive definition of its meaning. There is a wealth of data available in the digital world in this age of the Fourth Industrial Revolution (4IR or Industry 4.0), including data from the Internet of Things (IoT), data from cybersecurity, data from mobile devices, data from businesses, data from social media, data from medical histories, etc. The understanding of artificial intelligence is an essential component for performing intelligent analysis of these data and developing innovative and automated applications that correspond to them (Sarker, 2021).

In the academic field, quantitative findings derived from surveys or experiments are no longer the sole domain of data (Wallwey & Kajfez, 2023). Through the utilization of meta-analysis techniques, which search through massive textual databases for recurring themes and trends, text can also be converted into data in digital settings. This is possible through the use of meta-analysis techniques. Because of the new ways that numerical results can be visually represented, researchers, students, and librarians need to modify their approaches to handling data to adapt to these new possibilities. In academic and research settings, artificial intelligence is not rarely used to collect data, especially in meta-analysis techniques. This shows that artificial intelligence relates to data.

DATA LITERACY

When it comes to achieving success in higher education, having a strong command of quantitative literacy is absolutely necessary. Most literacy skills are acquired in a roundabout way through the practices involved in various school subjects rather than being taught in a formal setting (Prince et al., 2021). A distinct aptitude for quantitative and statistical literacy is the ability to analyze, interpret, and evaluate quantitative and statistical evidence in a proficient manner. The ability to understand data and statistics is one of the essential components of information literacy. The findings of the statistics offer a condensed summary of the data. Data literacy is enhanced by the ability to search for statistics. This entails understanding both the objective and the research site (Sabbati, 2022). When selecting, converting, and manipulating the data that underlies a statistic, the methods utilized significantly impact the numerical value of the statistic. Having the ability to convert and manipulate data is a specialized skill that requires a significant amount of knowledge and practice. For this reason, data literacy should be an essential component of both information and statistical literacy.

Data literacy relies on critical thinking. It is in line with the definition of information literacy. Knowing how to collect, organize, evaluate, and use data in a thoughtful and critical manner is an essential component of data literacy (Downes, 2023). On the other hand, being data literate requires the skills to access, evaluate, manipulate, condense, and present data. The fact that the library community has long considered data literacy to be an extension of information literacy is proved by Dai (2020), which provides confirmation of this perspective. Information literacy is considered to be an extension of data literacy, along with its variants, such as data information literacy, research data literacy, and science data literacy.

Data literacy refers to the capacity to pose and resolve practical inquiries using extensive and limited data collections, employing an investigative approach while also considering the ethical utilization of data (Ghodoosi, Torrisi-Steele, et al., 2023). Data literacy is centered around fundamental practical and creative abilities, allowing for expanding expertise in specialized data management skills based on individual objectives. These skills encompass the capacity to choose, clean, examine, describe, evaluate, and comprehend data, as well as to convey narratives derived from data and incorporate data into a design strategy (Wolff et al., 2016). In other words, data literacy means understanding, interpreting, and conveying data in various contexts. The capacity to explain a particular application and the value produced is an integral part of this, as is knowledge of the sources and structures of data and analytical techniques and approaches. Data literacy is a concept that evolves over time as new technologies and data become available to the public (Ghodoosi, Torrisi-Steele, et al., 2023).

THE IMPORTANCE OF DATA LITERACY

Post-secondary education is the ideal starting point for students entering the workforce to build a strong foundation in data literacy. Community colleges, known for their diverse student bodies, have the opportunity to promote general data literacy among their undergraduate students (J. Kim et al., 2023). Not only is data literacy essential for students, but it is also essential for all of the stakeholders in today's higher education system. It is essential for individuals as well as organizations to take steps to improve their data literacy. Data will be the primary factor in decision-making across all sectors, regions, and functions of the organizations (Gu, 2023; Wei, 2023) and artificial intelligence programs will either support or replace human personnel in performing tasks. Humans will not be replaced by artificial intelligence, but humans with artificial intelligence will eventually replace humans without artificial intelligence (Lakhani, 2023). Having a solid foundation in data literacy from an early age is indispensable to cope with the rapid digitization and technology-driven nature of our global society. On the other hand, developing fundamental skills through prior education and work experience can provide valuable perspectives on the practical application of data science. Considering the profound connection that exists between data, digitization, and artificial intelligence in research (Leal Filho et al., 2023), academic, and higher education, it is essential for students to have a solid foundation in data literacy.

In the present day, despite the fact that the target audience for learning differs across different fields of study, the target audience for data literacy education in higher education is comprised of students eighty percent of the time, faculty members fourteen percent of the time, and librarians, seven percent of the time. Students at the undergraduate and graduate levels are the primary recipients of data literacy education in STEM fields (Ghodoosi, West, et al., 2023). Why is it so important for students to have a comprehensive understanding of data, and what are the reasons for this? In light of the fact that we are entering an era of big data, it is of the utmost importance to teach the next generation about data literacy and to encourage statistical thinking. It is crucial to keep this in mind as that era draws near. The significance of data literacy lies in the fact that it enables the expansion of access to, knowledge of, and utilization of microdata and statistics for research, scientific works, and educational purposes.

Data literacy should be a requirement for all students enrolled in higher education. They will finish their final assignment, which requires them to have a strong understanding of data and statistics. In order to reinforce the findings of their research, students are required to provide scientific arguments to back up their findings. Robust data and statistical analysis will support these arguments. Students absolutely need to have a solid understanding of statistics to analyze data effectively, accurately represent the results of their research, and construct arguments supported by scientific evidence (Lukman & Wahyudin, 2020). This is the reason why data literacy is becoming increasingly important.

The ability to perform data analysis is an essential skill for a wide range of individuals and organizations, not only students but also all stakeholders involved in higher education. In order to evaluate student progress and provide direction for instruction, teachers need to improve their data literacy skills by collecting a variety of data on student learning opportunities (M. S. Kim & Yu, 2023). On the other hand, Wayman and Jimerson (2014) stated that data literacy training for faculty members should be contextual, consistent, funded, and long-lasting. This is because data literacies are frequently treated primarily in terms of technical competencies, despite the fact that understanding data requires the development of a variety of skills. Therefore, the development of the curriculum for data literacy should be done with careful consideration. It is of the utmost importance to encourage the development of data literacy among educators to incorporate these skills into their pedagogical content knowledge and expertise in the curriculum (M. S. Kim & Yu, 2023). The purpose of a critical approach to data literacy should be to make it possible for students and teachers to collaborate as creators of new knowledge (Cronin, 2017).

In the unlikely circumstance, those committed to higher education do not acquire the skills necessary to comprehend, analyze, and evaluate data. The proliferation of student information systems and digital learning environments in educational institutions has made it possible to store and analyze a wide variety of distinct types of educational data. Additionally, digital formats come with an increased number of opportunities to store, process, and display data for the purpose of making pedagogical decisions (Michos et al., 2023). As a consequence of this, for the purpose of educating people on how to make effective use of data, it is essential to have a holistic perspective of data that extends beyond its technical and context components (Atenas et al., 2020).

DATA LITERACY SKILLS

The Data Literacy Charter emphasizes five guiding principles to characterize the importance and role of data literacy as a critical competence of the 21st century:

Table 1 Data Literacy Skills

Conceptual framework	Introduction to Data
Data collection	Choose Suitable Sensors for Gathering Data
	Data Discovery and Collection
	Evaluating and ensuring quality of Data and Sources
Data management	Organization
	Storage
	Prioritisation
	Examination
	Manipulation
	Conversion (from format to format)
	Metadata creation and use
	Curation, Security and Re-Use
	Preservation
Data evaluation	Tools
	Analysis
	Interpretation (Understanding Data)
	Identifying problems using data
	Visualization
	Presenting data (verbally)Communicating data
	Data-driven decision-making (DDDM)
Data application	Critical thinking
	Culture
	Ethics
	Citation
	Sharing
	Evaluating decisions based on data

Source: (Ghodoosi, West, et al., 2023)

data literacy should be accessible to all individuals, data literacy should be taught consistently across all levels of education, data literacy should be taught as a transdisciplinary and interdisciplinary skill, data literacy must comprehensively address all aspects of knowledge acquisition and decision-making using data, and data literacy must include understanding, abilities, and principles for the deliberate and ethically sound management of data (Schüller, 2022).

The concept of data literacy encompasses several different aspects that, when taken together, contribute to an individual's capability of managing, comprehending, and analyzing data. Data literacy involves gaining knowledge about the nature of data and its attributes (including types, sources, formats, and features), the various ways data is used (such as analysis, business intelligence, data science, decision support, artificial intelligence, automation, and analytics), the methods employed to work with data (such as pattern discovery, pattern recognition, and prediction), and the means of effectively conveying data (such as storytelling, evidence-based reasoning, decision support, and visualization) (Tableu, n.d.). Data literacy encompasses several processes in the academic and research field, including the following: identifying, scoping, planning, storing, protecting, evaluating, managing, and providing.

It is shown in Table 1 that the skills required for data literacy can be broken down into four distinct categories. Data collection skills, data management skills, data evaluation skills, and data application skills are the four competencies in question. The skills that are required to be mastered in the process of data collection are the ability to discover and evaluate the methods, as well as the quality of the data and its resources. The ability to organize, manage, convert, store, curate, and preserve data has been referred to as "data management skills." The skills necessary for data evaluation are primarily focused on the ability to use the tools as well as analyze, interpret, and communicate statistics. An increased emphasis is placed on data culture, ethics, sharing, and evaluating data decision-making when it comes to data application skills (Ghodoosi, West, et al., 2023).

ARTIFICIAL INTELLIGENCE AND DATA LITERACY

The current paradigm shift toward data-centric artificial intelligence, which calls for a more data-oriented approach to artificial intelligence methods, is well aligned with the coordination of artificial intelligence and data literacy (Abedjan, 2022). Data and artificial intelligence are becoming increasingly integral to every aspect of running an organization; a data-driven culture requires a foundational level of data literacy (Prolifics, 2023). Artificial intelligence refers to the ability of machines to learn from previous experiences, adjust to unconventional stimuli, and carry out activities comparable to those carried out by humans (Coursera, 2023). Using these technologies, computers can be taught to carry out specific tasks by analyzing vast amounts of data and recognizing patterns within the data. This can be accomplished by training the computers to perform the tasks. The ability to read and understand data will be in high demand as artificial intelligence continues to have an impact worldwide. However, implementing artificial intelligence requires a consistent supply of high-quality data because it relies on analyzing enormous datasets (Aldoseri et al., 2023). High-quality data can only be acquired if data literacy is mastered. Concerns regarding artificial intelligence and data literacy have been raised about the fairness of the data, respect for privacy and security, ethical considerations, and decision-making (Schmarzo, 2023).

One of the most significant obstacles that the field of artificial intelligence faces is the shortage of qualified experts. To address this issue, some potential solutions are expanding investments in education and training, fostering collaboration across subject areas, and designing learning resources based on artificial intelligence (Aldoseri et al., 2023). Data and artificial intelligence education data compete with one another to educate the coming generation of leaders. Given that data is an essential component of artificial intelligence, it is reasonable to assume that data literacy, which refers to the capacity to collect, process, and analyze data in order to arrive at conclusions based on that data, ought to be prioritized alongside artificial intelligence as a core competency. Hong and Kim (2020) conducted research on artificial intelligence data science education programs. Their research proved that students' data literacy improved significantly after participating in the artificial intelligence data science education program. This improvement was seen in a variety of areas, including understanding data, collecting data, analyzing it, and expressing their findings. Hong and Kim's research shows that data literacy is associated with artificial intelligence.

THE STRATEGIES OF DATA LITERACY AND ARTIFICIAL INTELLIGENCE EDUCATION IN HIGHER EDUCATION

For children to be successful in a society that is driven by data, researchers in the discipline of artificial intelligence education propose that children should be exposed to artificial intelligence at a young age and nurture competency in data and artificial intelligence literacy (Olari, 2023). Early education significantly influences students' knowledge, experience, and skills as they progress to higher education.

The first strategy to improve data literacy and artificial intelligence education in higher education is to include real case studies and artificial intelligence. Teachers can elaborate on real-world case studies involving applying artificial intelligence technology to address practical issues. Olari (2023) collaborated with experts and educators in the field of history to develop a practical case study for students on data lifecycles and machine learning. The results of her experiment were that students developed skills in data literacy, which included understanding the data lifecycle like modeling, collecting, and cleaning data, as well as artificial intelligence literacy, which involves requirements analysis, training, fine-tuning, and deploying classification models, through their work on the case study.

The second strategy involves the use of an artificial intelligence-based learning management system, such as Carnegie Learning's Platform (Michos et al., 2023).

This innovative education technology, developed by Carnegie Mellon University, leverages artificial intelligence and machine learning in its high school and higher education learning platforms (McFarland, 2024). Notably, this platform not only provides education but also serves as a data-driven tool to manage students' data and enhance their data literacy.

The third strategy is combining data literacy skills and artificial intelligence tools. There is a case study from Qatar (Usova & Laws, 2021). In the spring of 2020, two librarians from George University Qatar (GU-Q) worked together to determine whether or not a data visualization and data literacy course in one credit course would be suitable for students. In order to accomplish these objectives, it was helpful to give students the opportunity to acquire a theoretical understanding of data literacy while at the same time giving them practical experience with data and tools for data visualization. Artificial intelligence data visualization technologies utilize advanced algorithms to analyze datasets, detect patterns, and visually display the results (York, 2024). In order to ensure the excellence of the lessons, the librarians had to enhance their skills before teaching. Those librarians had acquired a high proficiency level in the software they had initially intended to utilize for the class. Concurrently, they conducted an extensive examination of relevant literature, carefully chose course textbooks, enrolled in numerous data visualization preparatory courses, and fostered strong connections with faculty members from other universities who were providing data visualization programs.

In the higher education field, the stakeholders are not only students and faculty members but also librarians. The position of librarians is crucial for the improvement of higher education because they provide information for all students, faculty members, and researchers in the university. They also need data literacy and artificial intelligence education.

THE CHALLENGES OF DATA LITERACY AND ARTIFICIAL INTELLIGENCE EDUCATION IN HIGHER EDUCATION

Following the undeniable fact that well-established learning theories and instructional strategies are unquestionably beneficial, it is abundantly clear that there is a requirement for developing novel approaches to the instruction of data literacy and artificial intelligence education. Educators, students, and even administrators need to have sufficient knowledge regarding the significance of data literacy and artificial intelligence in education. There is a knowledge gap regarding the skills (Tenopir et al., 2020) that the next generation of academia will need to fill this void. During the process of evaluating the data literacy education project, Tenopir discovered that there was a significant gap in the participants' skill levels. Furthermore, there were some students who needed help locating datasets that were relevant and comprehending numerical data (Usova & Laws, 2021). It means that they are not only lacking data literacy skills but also are lacking technological skills.

Another challenge is the lack of knowledge, workload, and time constraints of the teachers. Olari et al. (2023) conducted an experiment about a professional development program for in-service computer science teachers without prior knowledge of artificial intelligence and digital literacy. The participants highlighted several challenges regarding the perceived ability and willingness of teachers to incorporate artificial intelligence and digital literacy into their teaching. Their obstacles are a lack of knowledge, workload, and time constraints. Those are the primary obstacles that prevented computer science teachers from implementing artificial intelligence and digital literacy in their classrooms.

The problem in teaching data literacy and artificial intelligence is that the teachers frequently do not possess the knowledge, skills, and capabilities required to teach the subject. They must fulfill requirements for ongoing education and retraining throughout their lives. Because computer-based instruction is another essential aspect of teaching data literacy at the university level, more research needs to be conducted in this field. This is due to the fact that computer-based teaching is more important than other aspects of teaching data literacy. This is a result of the existing data literacy gap in higher education institutions as well as the rapidly shifting technological landscape, in this case, artificial intelligence..

Besides challenges in education, due to the growing utilization of technology for the purpose of gathering and analyzing educational data, there are growing concerns regarding the protection of student information from unauthorized access or breaches, as well as the confidentiality of student information (Evanick, 2023). These concerns are growing as a result of the fact that there is an increase in the utilization of technology.

Integrating data literacy and artificial intelligence education into the curriculum will be difficult due to the limitations that are currently in place, as well as the competing priorities. There was a scarcity of qualified information professionals to oversee scientific data and artificial intelligence. The higher education curriculum needs to be revised and able to accommodate the evolving landscape of education, research, and technology. The majority of the time, data literacy and artificial intelligence education are taught in various formats, and there is no connection to a more comprehensive framework of research methodology and research design applicable to real-life environments.

THE FUTURE OF DATA LITERACY AND ARTIFICIAL INTELLIGENCE EDUCATION IN HIGHER EDUCATION

Data literacy and artificial intelligence literacy are closely connected. Data and artificial intelligence literacy refer to the ability to generate, manage, analyze, and convey significant information derived from data. The skill set also includes the capacity to develop, use, and apply artificial intelligence and related algorithmic tools and strategies to enhance well-informed, optimized, and contextually relevant decision-making processes based on data. The ability to objectively assess data-driven artificial intelligence results is located at the boundary of these areas. Data literacy allows individuals to pose insightful inquiries regarding data gathering, analysis, and findings. Artificial intelligence literacy delves into the creators of algorithms, their functionality, inherent biases, and resulting consequences. Integrating artificial intelligence literacy into the curriculum does not imply that every student must become an artificial intelligence specialist. The emphasis should be on raising awareness, stimulating interest, and establishing a solid understanding (Hanegan, 2023).

In a world increasingly dominated by digital technology, the Data Literacy Charter is a preliminary outline of a road map that is urgently required. The standard establishes an operational framework and capabilities to coordinate worldwide endeavors in data and artificial intelligence literacy development. The standard will define a common set of terms, terminology, and understanding of data and artificial intelligence literacy, skills, and preparedness (Schüller, 2022). According to the State of Data Literacy Report 2023 published by DataCamp (Crabtree, 2023), an astounding ninety percent of individuals who participated in the survey agreed that educational institutions, including schools and universities, must immediately begin teaching classes on data literacy. Data literacy is not something that can be mastered in a way that is both permanent and effective because of the extremely rapid pace at which technological advancements are occurring. In its place, it emphasizes the necessity of continuous training and adaptation to consider the development of novel techniques for data collection and analysis. By highlighting the significance of data skills in enhancing resilience, adaptability, and competitiveness in the labor market, this perception brings to light the importance of data skills.

The introduction of data literacy skills at the beginning of undergraduate programs has the potential to encourage the development of effective strategies for working with data (Ghodoosi, West, et al., 2023). Data literacy is essential in education and research, and it ought to be regarded as a "second language" for all academics and researchers because of its importance. If these competencies and skills are not mastered, education and research will not be able to achieve a competitive advantage. The future of data literacy can be successfully attained through the collective support of all stakeholders in higher education by fostering lifelong learning. This entails acquiring the skills to effectively use data in both professional and personal settings, which is a direct consequence of utilizing data within the context of learning and practical application. Additionally, it is crucial to emphasize the relevance of coursework concerning data, as the learning environment significantly influences the outcomes related to data.

In higher education institutions, it is incumbent upon data librarians to seriously consider the possibility of incorporating statistical literacy into their data literacy curricula. It is not possible for a course in data literacy to be considered remedial for it to be recognized for college credit. Despite the fact that they are essential, the roles of information professionals, such as public and academic librarians, archivists, administrators of documents and data, content and data curators, and so on, cannot be broken down into separate categories. Instead, they ought to be put to work for the extensive networks of academics, researchers, technicians, and managers who are engaged in the process of constructing a society and an economy based on the utilization of data in a methodical manner (Pinto et al., 2023).

The acceleration of technology or cyberinfrastructure linkage could signify a significant change in the connections between humans and the services they use. It establishes the foundation for advancements in artificial intelligence (Chester & Allenby, 2020). The concept of cyberinfrastructure, which refers to a network of interconnected computer networks and software applications that are related to them, has evolved into an essential instrument in the management of modern information. The implementation of artificial intelligence in educational settings has the potential to revolutionize the standard of education entirely. The integration of data, artificial intelligence, the Internet of Things, and cloud computing technologies has been identified as advantageous for developing and innovating curricula in higher education. Data that is both structured and unstructured can be processed by artificial intelligence, which can reduce the amount of work management needs to do and speed up the decision-making process altogether (Slimi & Carballido, 2023). The use of artificial intelligence in creative instruction has had a positive impact on the academic reputation and citation index of universities and colleges, as well as on the preparation of students for the future (Vinichenko et al., 2020).

Artificial intelligence is being frequently used in sustainability development research and the United Nations Sustainable Development Goals (Vinuesa & Sirmacek, 2021) because of its analytical capabilities, especially in big data analyses, and its capacity to refine and predict outcomes. Artificial intelligence could assist in addressing the intricate challenges of practical and academic tasks in sustainable development research. Artificial intelligence-assisted research can analyse, execute, and communicate progress on Sustainable Development Goals (SDGs) and their targets (Leal Filho et al., 2023). For sustainable research in higher education, data literacy needs to be taught so stakeholders can proceed and analyze research data well. Besides that, artificial intelligence education needs to be conducted if higher education institutions want their research activities to be sustained.

Another concept that will be suitable for data literacy and artificial intelligence education in the future is called transliteracy. The concept of transliteracy creates challenges for the frameworks that have been established for information literacy as well as academic communication initiatives. Researchers have advocated for transliteracy, which involves the convergence of information, visual, digital, and other literacies, to assist students in locating and evaluating information (Cobourn et al., 2022). The concept of transliteracy provides a fresh perspective on the types of collaborations of higher education stakeholders who are knowledgeable in the fields of education and academic communication could establish in order to better cater to the requirements of future generations of higher education.

CONCLUSION

When viewed independently, data has a finite amount of value. When making decisions about their lives, people often use data as a tool. Information is crucial for many reasons, including but not limited to gaining a better understanding of the world, making informed decisions, gauging progress, estimating outcomes, and guiding our actions now and in the future. Data literacy entails comprehending, analyzing, and communicating data in different settings. Data literacy is crucial for everyone involved in today's higher education system, not just students.

Mastering statistics is not just an individual achievement, but a collaborative endeavor that enables students to correctly interpret data, convey research findings accurately, and build arguments backed by evidence. In the academic world, data literacy involves learning to identify, scope, plan, store, protect, evaluate, manage, and provide data. This collective understanding of data literacy, which should be prioritized as a core competency alongside artificial intelligence literacy, is crucial as data forms the backbone of artificial intelligence.

Methods and approaches that have proven to be effective in guiding data literacy education include educational institutions, organizations, and other entities forming a cooperative relationship to ensure that everyone's needs are being satisfied, using technology effectively while incorporating a variety of creative and modern teaching methods, learning is both a sequential and iterative process; it involves integrating skills that are complementary to one another, as in project-based learning, stressing the importance of both abstract ideas and concrete applications (such as learning by doing), increasing engagement by drawing on real-world data to strengthen connections to the content.

Among the many facets that make up the complex problem of data literacy and artificial intelligence in the classroom are educators, students, and administrators, who all need to understand the importance of data literacy in education. More knowledge about the skills is needed. Another area for improvement in teaching data literacy and artificial intelligence is that many instructors need to gain the necessary knowledge, skills, and capabilities. Data literacy and artificial intelligence education can also benefit from another idea known as transliteracy.

REFERENCES

Abedjan, Z. (2022). Enabling data-centric AI through data quality management and data literacy. *It - Information Technology, 64*(1–2), 67–70. doi:10.1515/itit-2021-0048

Aldoseri, A., Al-Khalifa, K. N., & Hamouda, A. M. (2023). Re-Thinking Data Strategy and Integration for Artificial Intelligence: Concepts, Opportunities, and Challenges. *Applied Sciences (Basel, Switzerland), 13*(12), 7082. doi:10.3390/app13127082

Aradau, C. (2023). Algorithmic Security and Conflict in a Datafied World. In C. Bjola & M. Kornprobst (Eds.), *Digital International Relations: Technology, Agency and Order* (1st ed.). Routledge. doi:10.4324/9781003437963-11

Atenas, J., Havemann, L., & Timmermann, C. (2020). Critical literacies for a datafied society: Academic development and curriculum design in higher education. *Research in Learning Technology, 28*(0). Advance online publication. doi:10.25304/rlt.v28.2468

Chester, M. V., & Allenby, B. R. (2020). Perspective: The Cyber Frontier and Infrastructure. *IEEE Access: Practical Innovations, Open Solutions, 8*, 28301–28310. doi:10.1109/ACCESS.2020.2971960

Cobourn, A. B., Brown, J. C., Warga, E., & Louis, L. (2022). Toward Metaliteracy and Transliteracy in the History Classroom: A Case Study Among Underserved Students. *The American Archivist, 85*(2), 587–608. doi:10.17723/2327-9702-85.2.587

Coursera. (2023, November 29). *What Is Artificial Intelligence? Definition, Uses, and Types.* Https://Www.Coursera.Org/Articles/What-Is-Artificial-Intelligence

Crabtree, M. (2023, May). *The Future of Data Literacy: A Fundamental Skill Shaping Society: Uncover the role of data literacy in the 21st century.* Https://Www.Datacamp.Com/Blog/the-Future-of-Data-Literacy-a-Fundamental-Skill-Shaping-Society

Cronin, C. (2017). Openness and Praxis: Exploring the Use of Open Educational Practices in Higher Education. *International Review of Research in Open and Distance Learning, 18*(5). Advance online publication. doi:10.19173/irrodl.v18i5.3096

Dai, Y. (2020). How many ways can we teach data literacy? *IASSIST Quarterly, 43*(4), 1–11. doi:10.29173/iq963

Downes, S. (2023, October 21). Three frameworks for data literacy. *20th International Conference on Cognition and Exploratory Learning in the Digital Age (CELDA 2023)*.

Evanick, J. (2023, November 4). *Ethical Dilemmas In Student Data Privacy: Navigating EdTech Safeguards.* Https://Elearningindustry.Com/Ethical-Dilemmas-in-Student-Data-Privacy-Navigating-Edtech-Safeguards

Farrell, M. (2023, January 6). *Data and Intuition: Good Decisions Need Both.* Harvard Business Publishing Corporate Learning.

Ghodoosi, B., Torrisi-Steele, G., West, T., & Li, Q. (2023). An Exploration of the Definition of Data Literacy in the Academic and Public Domains. *International Journal of Adult Education and Technology, 14*(1), 1–16. doi:10.4018/IJAET.325218

Ghodoosi, B., West, T., Li, Q., Torrisi-Steele, G., & Dey, S. (2023). A systematic literature review of data literacy education. *Journal of Business & Finance Librarianship, 28*(2), 112–127. doi:10.1080/08963568.2023.2171552

Gu, H. (2023). Data, Big Tech, and the New Concept of Sovereignty. *Journal of Chinese Political Science.* Advance online publication. doi:10.1007/s11366-023-09855-1 PMID:37359767

Hanegan, K. (2021). *Turning Data into Wisdom: How We Can Collaborate with Data to Change Ourselves.* Our Organizations, and Even the World.

Hanegan, K. (2023, November 1). *From Data Literacy to AI Literacy. The Evolution of Critical Thinking in the Digital Age.* Turning Data into Wisdom. https://www.turningdataintowisdom.com/from-data-literacy-to-ai-literacy/

Hong, J.-Y., & Kim, Y. (2020). Development of AI Data Science Education Program to Foster Data Literacy of Elementary School Students. *Journal of The Korean Association of Information Education, 24*(6), 633–641. doi:10.14352/jkaie.2020.24.6.633

Kim, J., Hong, L., Evans, S., Oyler-Rice, E., & Ali, I. (2023). Development and Validation of a Data Literacy Assessment Scale. *Proceedings of the Association for Information Science and Technology, 60*(1), 620–624. doi:10.1002/pra2.827

Kim, M. S., & Yu, F. (2023). 'Teacher data literacies practice' meets 'pedagogical documentation': A scoping review. *Review of Education, 11*(2), e3414. Advance online publication. doi:10.1002/rev3.3414

Lakhani, K. (2023, August 4). Humans will not be replaced by artificial intelligence, but humans with AI will eventually take the place of humans without AI. *Harvard Business Review*.

Leal Filho, W., Yang, P., Eustachio, J. H. P. P., Azul, A. M., Gellers, J. C., Gielczyk, A., Dinis, M. A. P., & Kozlova, V. (2023). Deploying digitalisation and artificial intelligence in sustainable development research. *Environment, Development and Sustainability, 25*(6), 4957–4988. doi:10.1007/s10668-022-02252-3 PMID:35313685

Lukman, & Wahyudin. (2020). Statistical literacy of undergraduate students in Indonesia: Survey studies. Journal of Physics: Conference Series, 1521(3). doi:10.1088/1742-6596/1521/3/032050

McFarland, A. (2024, February 28). *10 Best AI Tools for Education*. Unite.AI. https://www.unite.ai/10-best-ai-tools-for-education/

Michos, K., Schmitz, M.-L., & Petko, D. (2023). Teachers' data literacy for learning analytics: A central predictor for digital data use in upper secondary schools. *Education and Information Technologies, 28*(11), 14453–14471. doi:10.1007/s10639-023-11772-y PMID:37361815

Olari, V. (2023). Data Literacy as a Fundamental Component of Artificial Intelligence Education in Schools (Doctoral Consortium). *Proceedings of the 23rd Koli Calling International Conference on Computing Education Research*, 1–2. 10.1145/3631802.3631839

Olari, V., Zoppke, T., Reger, M., Samoilova, E., Kandlhofer, M., Dagiene, V., Romeike, R., Lieckfeld, A. S., & Lucke, U. (2023). Introduction of Artificial Intelligence Literacy and Data Literacy in Computer Science Teacher Education. *Proceedings of the 23rd Koli Calling International Conference on Computing Education Research*, 1–2. 10.1145/3631802.3631851

Pinto, M., Caballero-Mariscal, D., García-Marco, F.-J., & Gómez-Camarero, C. (2023). A strategic approach to information literacy: Data literacy. A systematic review. *El Profesional de la Información*, e320609. Advance online publication. doi:10.3145/epi.2023.nov.09

Prince, R. N., Frith, V., Steyn, S., & Cliff, A. F. (2021). Academic and quantitative literacy in higher education: Relationship with cognate school-leaving subjects. *South African Journal of Higher Education*, *35*(3). Advance online publication. doi:10.20853/35-3-3943

Prolifics. (2023, June 23). *Foster a culture of data literacy.* Prolifics. https://prolifics. com/us/stream-articles/category/data-analysis/6839209/02/25/2024/foster-a-culture-of-data-literacy

Sabbati, G. (2022). Statistical and Data Literacy, a practitioner's view for policy-making: How to provide independent, objective and authoritative data and information for policy-making. *Statistical Journal of the IAOS*, *38*(2), 463–469. doi:10.3233/SJI-220942

Sarker, I. H. (2021). Machine Learning: Algorithms, Real-World Applications and Research Directions. *SN Computer Science*, *2*(3), 160. doi:10.1007/s42979-021-00592-x PMID:33778771

Schmarzo, B. (2023). *AI & Data Literacy: Empowering Citizens of Data Science.* Packt Publishing.

Schüller, K. (2022). Data and AI literacy for everyone. *Statistical Journal of the IAOS*, *38*(2), 477–490. doi:10.3233/SJI-220941

Slimi Z. Carballido B. V. (2023). Systematic Review: AI's Impact on Higher Education - Learning, Teaching, and Career Opportunities. *TEM Journal*, 1627–1637. https:// doi.org/ doi:10.18421/TEM123-44

Tableu. (n.d.). *Top data literacy skills for becoming data literate.* Tableu.Com. https://www.tableau.com/data-insights/data-literacy/skills

Tenopir, C., Rice, N. M., Allard, S., Baird, L., Borycz, J., Christian, L., Grant, B., Olendorf, R., & Sandusky, R. J. (2020). Data sharing, management, use, and reuse: Practices and perceptions of scientists worldwide. *PLoS One*, *15*(3), e0229003. doi:10.1371/journal.pone.0229003 PMID:32160189

Usova, T., & Laws, R. (2021). Teaching a one-credit course on data literacy and data visualisation. *Journal of Information Literacy*, *15*(1). Advance online publication. doi:10.11645/15.1.2840

Vinichenko, M. V., Melnichuk, A. V., & Karácsony, P. (2020). Technologies of improving the university efficiency by using artificial intelligence: Motivational aspect. *Entrepreneurship and Sustainability Issues*, *7*(4), 2696–2714. doi:10.9770/jesi.2020.7.4(9)

Vinuesa, R., & Sirmacek, B. (2021). Interpretable deep-learning models to help achieve the Sustainable Development Goals. *Nature Machine Intelligence, 3*(11), 926–926. doi:10.1038/s42256-021-00414-y

Wallwey, C., & Kajfez, R. L. (2023). Quantitative research artifacts as qualitative data collection techniques in a mixed methods research study. *Methods in Psychology (Online), 8,* 100115. doi:10.1016/j.metip.2023.100115

Wayman, J. C., & Jimerson, J. B. (2014). Teacher needs for data-related professional learning. *Studies in Educational Evaluation, 42,* 25–34. doi:10.1016/j.stueduc.2013.11.001

Wei, X. (2023). Data-Driven Revolution: Advancing Scientific and Technological Innovation in Chinese A-Share Listed Companies. *Journal of the Knowledge Economy.* Advance online publication. doi:10.1007/s13132-023-01476-6

Wolff, A., Gooch, D., Cavero Montaner, J. J., Rashid, U., & Kortuem, G. (2016). Creating an Understanding of Data Literacy for a Data-driven Society. *The Journal of Community Informatics, 12*(3). Advance online publication. doi:10.15353/joci.v12i3.3275

York, A. (2024, February 14). *Make Informed Decisions: 10 First-Class AI Tools for Data Visualization.* ClickUp. https://clickup.com/blog/ai-tools-for-data-visualization/

KEY TERMS AND DEFINITIONS

Artificial Intelligence: Computer systems possess the ability to execute intricate tasks that were traditionally exclusive to humans, such as logical thinking, decision-making, and problem-solving.

Big Data: A massive and heterogeneous collection of structured: unstructured, and semi-structured data that exhibits exponential growth over time.

Critical Thinking: The process of intellectually systematically conceptualizing, applying, analyzing, synthesizing, and evaluating information obtained from, or generated by, observation, experience, reflection, reasoning, or communication serves as a guiding framework for individuals' beliefs and actions.

Data: Quantitative or qualitative data gathered for the purpose of analysis, evaluation, and utilization in facilitating decision-making processes.

Data Literacy: The capacity of an individual to comprehend, interpret, and employ data in diverse manners.

Data Management: The practice of acquiring, organizing, and retrieving data to enhance productivity, effectiveness, and the process of making sensible decisions.

Data Science: Knowledge obtained from structured and unstructured data is a multifaceted field that employs scientific methodologies, procedures, algorithms, and systems to derive knowledge and gain valuable insights.

Data Visualization: The visualization of data using prevalent visual aids, including charts, plots, infographics, and animations.

Data-Driven Culture: A setting in which the utilization of analytics, statistics, and factual insights serves as the foundation for enhancing processes and achieving organizational objectives.

Digital Literacy: The proficient and analytical utilization of a comprehensive array of digital technologies for the purposes of information retrieval, communication, and fundamental problem-solving across various fields.

Higher Education: Education offered by a college or university beyond the secondary level.

Literacy: The capacity to identify, comprehend, analyze, generate, convey, and calculate, utilizing printed and written materials linked to diverse contexts.

Sustainable Development Goals: A comprehensive campaign to eradicate poverty, protect the environment, and guarantee that by 2030, every individual will experience tranquillity and prosperity.

Transliteracy: Proficiency in reading, writing, and engaging with various platforms, tools, and media, including signing, oral communication, handwriting, print, television, radio, film, and digital social networks.

Chapter 8

Application of ChatGPT in Doctoral Education and Programming:
A Collaborative Autoethnography

Kelly Burmeister Long
https://orcid.org/0000-0002-2332-9955
University of North Georgia, USA

Katherine Rose Adams
University of North Georgia, USA

ABSTRACT

This collaborative autoethnographic study explores the integration of AI tools in doctoral education, focusing on instructional methods, program planning, and curriculum development. Drawing on faculty experiences, strengths such as content speed and organization are identified alongside weaknesses like trustworthiness issues and limited critical thinking abilities. Implications highlight the need for quality assurance, AI literacy training, and clear policies. Recommendations include establishing guidelines, proper AI tool attribution, and continued research to understand AI's impact. The study underscores the importance of thoughtful integration of AI to maximize benefits while addressing limitations effectively.

DOI: 10.4018/979-8-3693-1054-0.ch008

INTRODUCTION

Even as the field of higher education grapples with its strengths and limitations, artificial intelligence (AI) tools are actively in use in academia. Therefore, regardless of opinion, these tools should be acknowledged. As Farrelly and Baker (2023) contend, "if our aim is to equip our students with skills, knowledge, and competencies that will allow them to thrive in the 21st century, we need to rapidly adapt our programming to include AI literacy and competency" (p. 7). Developing writing skills is crucial for doctoral students (Calle-Arango & Ávila Reyes, 2023), and the field of AI, particularly natural language processing (NLP) technologies, is poised to become a powerful tool for supporting the education of doctoral students.

One popular NLP model is OpenAI's ChatGPT (Generative Pre-trained Transformer). There is a lively debate regarding the appropriate use of NLP technology in teaching and learning, especially around academic integrity (Sullivan et al., 2023). Small studies of scholars and students reveal a positive reception (Limna et al., 2023) and a recent study of the literature concluded that AI and ChatGPT are viewed as having the "potential to serve as a significant asset in education" (Grassini, 2023, p. 2). Overall, the perceived quality of AI systems like ChatGPT relate to an increased likelihood that students and educators view AI as relevant to their learning (Chen et al., 2023).

Amidst this literature is a debate on the paradigm and pedagogical shifts that come with the AI revolution. Early findings from Firat (2023) reflected on how student interactions with these tools may shift pedagogy from constructivism (i.e., forming an understanding) to constructionism (i.e., using critical thinking to build knowledge). Another purported paradigm shift was in student access to academic assistance (Wibowo et al., 2023). Furthermore, Firat's findings emphasized how using the tool, even for writing literacy, would rely on digital literacy skills to support effective use of the tool, which has been supported by other authors (Rudolph et al., 2023b). While there is much to understand about the impacts of AI on teaching paradigms and pedagogical approaches, students and educators are using these tools, thus underscoring the need for continued research on their strengths and weaknesses.

Scholars have been publishing on how ChatGPT and similar NLP tools are being used in education settings since their release. Many of these papers are literature reviews documenting the strengths and weaknesses of ChatGPT in supporting student writing. This chapter diverges from the existing literature to capture the ways that faculty are using this tool in practice, in light of the documented strengths and weaknesses. Furthermore, this chapter focuses on supporting research writing, through programming and curriculum development, for doctoral students studying in the field of higher education. Using a collaborative autoethnography methodology, this chapter aims to construct meaning through lived experiences in their practice

(Chang et al., 2013; Lapadat, 2017), providing stories of how ChatGPT was used to create writing-intensive courses and establish program procedures for AI use policy in academic writing. The discussion of findings examines strengths and weaknesses through the creation of future recommendations and implications gleaned through the structured narrative process.

LITERATURE REVIEW

There has been an explosion of literature documenting the strengths of AI and ChatGPT. In an analysis of the literature, Wibowo et al. (2023) concluded that ChatGPT was effective in enhancing "the quality of support provided" by faculty and allows students to "actively engage in their educational journey" (p. 134). As we are considering the inclusion and implementation of AI use within a doctoral program through the creation of policy and curriculum supporting academic writing, the purpose of this literature review was to focus on the current literature on the strengths and weaknesses related to using AI in scholarly writing.

Strengths

In terms of academic writing, AI has been described as a useful tool (Ifelebuegu et al. (2023), that is also capable of serving as a sort of tutor to students that can assist with their writing tasks (Rudolph et al., 2023a). Prior scholars have recommended AI be used as a writing support to generate ideas, gain feedback on writing, answer conceptual questions (Limna et al., 2023), and summarize research papers (Limna et al., 2023; Rudolph et al., 2023b). AI could also be used to brainstorm and plan research (Megawati et al., 2023) and may help overcome writers' block (Lauria, 2023, as cited by Raheem et al., 2023). ChatGPT can assist with the first four phases of research including "idea generation, prior literature synthesis, data identification and preparation, testing framework determination and implementation" (Xames & Shefa, 2023, p. 391). Some scholars have proposed that ChatGPT could be used to support the creation of survey questions or to conduct text categorization, though they noted the tool cannot effectively analyze output (Xames & Shefa, 2023). Furthermore, ChatGPT can assist in improving writing and addressing spelling or grammatical issues (Andrea, 2023, as cited by Raheem et al. 2023; Xames & Shefa, 2023). Literature has also discussed how AI tools can help students format references (Raheem, 2023).

Grassini (2023) reviewed literature that suggested AI might be used in grading essays or short answer responses, with the power to improve impartiality in grading. However, Grassini argued that there are currently limitations when applied to complex assignments. Moreover, ChatGPT may be useful in creating educational content (Atlas, 2023, as cited by Grassini, 2023). Little has been written relating to the application of these practices to doctoral education and specifically, supporting research writing.

Weakness

As much exists on the strengths of AI and ChatGPT, similar attention has been given to its weaknesses. In terms of weakness in its ability to support writing, some scholars have argued that ChatGPT is limited in its capacity to support critical thinking (Firat, 2023; Rasul et al., 2023; Rudolph et al., 2023). For example, while AI may help with certain steps of the research process as noted above, it is currently unable to identify gaps in the literature (Megawati et al., 2023).

A chief concern for AI is the inaccuracy and falsification of information produced by these models (Limna et al., 2023; Rasul et al., 2023). Little is known about the information used to train AI models, leaving room for subjectivity, bias, and persistent inaccuracies (Grassini, 2023). Moreover, the training materials may lack representation of diverse perspectives, resulting in limitations (Grassini, 2023), especially if there is an overreliance on the tool (Ifelebuegu et al., 2023).

In terms of plagiarism, at least one study showed that students engage in concerning behaviors more often when using ChatGPT (Bašic et al., 2023, as cited by Grassini, 2023). On the other hand, scholars have found that AI tools can be used to bolster plagiarism-checking (Raheem, 2023), though a literature review of this application revealed significant reliability concerns (Farrelly & Baker, 2023). Chief among these concerns was that "the most widely used AI detectors consistently misclassified non-native English writers' content as being generated by AI" (Liang et al., 2023, as cited by Farrelly & Baker, 2023, p. 5).

In terms of inequities, there are also concerns for disparities to arise between students who use AI and produce better quality work and students who avoid AI for ethical reasons (Cotton et al., 2023, as cited by Grassini, 2023). Other scholars viewed this tool as an improvement to accessibility in learning (Wibowo et al., 2023), for example, when the tool is used for translation (Raheem et al., 2023; Tran & Tran, 2023).

The use of AI might also mask student learning deficiencies (Grassini, 2023). However, future research is still needed regarding the impact of AI on the learning process (Wibowo et al., 2023). This is especially underscored as AI impacts human interaction in the learning process. Scholars have discussed how AI might negatively impact crucial points of human interaction in learning and empathy, which are critical to effective learning processes (Grassini, 2023; Wibowo et al. 2023). As Wibowo et al. (2023) contend, "Striking the right balance between technological solutions and human interaction becomes crucial in cultivating a comprehensive educational ecosystem" (p. 134).

PURPOSE AND RESEARCH QUESTIONS

The purpose of this study is to explore the practical applications of ChatGPT, an AI-driven natural language processing tool, in the context of doctoral education, specifically focusing on program development and academic curriculum writing within a higher education program. The research aims to move beyond existing literature reviews by delving into the lived experiences of faculty members who actively integrate ChatGPT into their professional and educational practices. By doing so, this study seeks to contribute valuable insights into how faculty members utilize AI tools in their instructional methods, program planning, and curriculum development within a doctoral program. This study addresses the following research questions:

RQ1) What are the strengths experienced by faculty using ChatGPT in supporting doctoral student programming and academic efforts?
RQ2) What are the weaknesses experienced by faculty using ChatGPT in supporting doctoral student programming and academic efforts?

METHODOLOGY

Autoethnography

Autoethnography is a qualitative approach or genre that utilizes the researcher as the tool of investigation by gathering self-data (Adams et al., 2015). Leavy (2023) stated that when researchers impart self-data they are "viewing themselves as a knowing subject and valuing their own experiences as worthy of the starting point for investigation into the larger culture" (p. 157).

Autoethnography creates a unique space as the researcher's voice is typically not included in the production of scholarship (Adams et al., 2015), as the researchers are working with 'insider status of insider knowledge' (Holman Jones et al., 2013 as cited in Leavy, 2013). Within autoethnography, "the researcher is at the center of the investigation as a 'subject' (the researcher who performs the investigation) and an 'object' (a/the participant who is investigated)" (Ngunjiri et al., 2010, p. 2).

Autoethnography incorporates personal accounts of the individual's narrative, and has been associated with autobiographies (Matechal, 2010), and as such the research employs techniques similar to the critical writing of an ethnography and autobiography (Ellis et al., 2011). Like ethnography, writing about the cultural phenomena of investigation is at focus, however, the personal experiences of the researcher are utilized to make a connection to the larger cultural context (Adams et al., 2015). And whereas an autobiography is written with the intention of the writing being the product, autoethnography rather seeks to reflect on past incidents or experiences that embody an epiphany (Ellis & Bochner, 1992) or designated topic of investigation that impacted one's current worldview. While epiphanies are self-claimed phenomena (Ellis et al., 2011), researchers in autoethnography are compelled to investigate issues or events that changed the trajectory of their personal or professional experiences.

Adams et al. (2017) suggested that autoethnography has two driving purposes. The first being that "autoethnographers speak against, or provide alternatives to, dominant, taken-for-granted, and harmful cultural scripts, stories, and stereotypes" (p. 3). Autoethnography researchers seek to bring about their topics of investigation to fill in gaps, highlight missing content or context, and provide an opening for new or lost voices (Adams et al., 2017; Ngunjiri et al., 2010). When emergent phenomena occur faster than the production of scholarly research on the topic, for example, the early periods of the Covid pandemic or the unprecedented acceleration of AI since November 2022, autoethnographers can unpack their own experiences of impact on personal culture within a dominant system.

The second purpose was to "articulate insider knowledge of cultural experience" (Adams et al., 2017, p. 3). The researcher represents an individual who has directly experienced the phenomena of investigation and also possesses the ability to find themselves within the broader story (Adams et al., 2015). Ellis (2004) suggested that the ability to present single participant data that constructs generalizability is done through engaging the readers and creating a story that elicits emotional responses that create future conversations and reflections.

Collaborative Autoethnography

With ethnography, one of the first steps is to identify the culture-sharing group and select the themes of investigation inherent to the group (Creswell & Poth, 2018). Through autoethnography, the individual narrative incorporates singular personal accounts into the investigation (Glesne, 2011), whereas collaborative autoethnography takes those individual narratives and re-incorporates the culture sharing dynamic into the shared analysis and critical reflection of the collaborative process (Blalock1 & Akehi, 2018). What Norris and Sawyer (2012) first identified as duoethnography when two researchers utilize individualized experiences which are co-communicated and analyzed to construct shared world understandings could be perceived as leveraging greater movement towards community autoethonography (Toyosaki et al., 2009) and collaborative autoethnography. Collaborative autoethnography is "characterized by two or more authors focused on a phenomenon of inquiry from the [perspective] of self through a concurrent or sequential systematic research approach that typically combines [...] perspectives, findings, and conclusions" (Throne, 2019, p.105). Collaborative autoethnography creates scholarship that encourages self and peer reflection and critical evaluation.

Chang et al. (2016) proposed, in alignment with autoethnography, that collaborative autoethnography as an approach was to be self-focused (researcher is instrument and data source), researcher-visible (transparent and vulnerable to the reader), context-conscious (aware of self within culture), and critically dialogic (reflecting that writing crates meaning and value). Lapadat (2017) summarized Chang et al.'s defined collaborative autoethnography as:

an autoethnographic qualitative research method that combines the autobiographic study of self with ethnographic analysis of the sociocultural milieu within which the researchers are situated, and in which the collaborating researchers interact dialogically to analyze and interpret the collection of autobiographic data (p. 598).

The methodological framework of collaborative autoethnography inherently facilitates a higher level of rigor compared to traditional autoethnography. Collaborative autoethnography involves the collaborative engagement of two or more researchers in the processes of data generation, analysis, and the subsequent stages of writing or performing. This collaborative endeavor enriches collaborative autoethnography with diverse and multidimensional perspectives on the research, as highlighted by Chang et al. The collective efforts of researchers, incorporating various disciplinary and experiential viewpoints, serve to enhance the analytical and interpretive facets of the research endeavor (Lapadat, 2017).

Narrative Inquiry as Method

The method of investigation for this study will be narrative inquiry, which can be used both as a methodological approach and a method (Savin-Baden & Niekerk, 2007). Narrative inquiry is a methodology that utilizes the narrative aspect of communication as a means of data creation (Chase, 2005; Clandinin, 2006). Narrative inquiry is an essential form of communication in which people ascribe meaning to their experiences (Seidman, 2013), then meaningfully construct, and reconstruct the analysis of an individual's lived experiences through structural storytelling (Clandinin, 2013). Narrative researchers seek to balance the voices, presentation, and audience of the stories being told (Clandinin & Caine, 2008).

Clandinin and Caine (2008) suggest that when employing narrative inquiry as a method there are two key components to consider when starting the process: hearing individuals narrate their experiences and being present alongside participants as they navigate through their stories. Clandinin and Caine (2008) stated that "narrative inquiries begin with inquiring into researchers' own stories of experience. Because narrative inquiry is an ongoing reflexive and reflective methodology, narrative inquirers need to inquire continually into their experiences before, during, and after each inquiry" (p. 543). As a feature of 'collecting stories' about individuals' lived and narrated experiences, the reflexivity of the process creates the co-construction of data between the researcher and participant (Creswell & Poth, 2018), and with collaborative autoethnography, those roles are one and the same to further collaborate the emerging story.

In alignment with our qualitative genres, narrative inquiry, along with a lived experiences approach, has a critical events approach where the research participants uncover, either intentionally or not, events that have led to changing, influencing, or reinforcing understood meaning (Webster & Mertova, 2007). Denzin (2014) also referred to the specific tensions that arose from recalling stories as 'turning points' from which one's worldview forever changes or is impacted, whereas Clandinin and Connolly (2000) used the term epiphanies to reflect such disruptions. Through evaluating critical events, researchers can adapt strategies and procedures to employ in new situations. As a method, in this chapter narrative inquiry includes detailed examples of how AI is being used by two faculty in a doctoral program in higher education. The primary goal will focus on utilizing AI tools to support program planning and curriculum development in doctoral-level research programs by providing stories of faculty experiences in reflection of the critical event of the emergence of popularized AI.

Data Collection

Collaborative autoethnography goes beyond mere storytelling; it encompasses meticulously structured research designs, questions oriented toward the process, and purposeful self-involvement (Chang, 2008; Chang et al., 2016; Glesne, 2011). The participants for this study are also the two researchers, both faculty of an online program for doctoral students. We each had a desire to utilize AI in the capacity of our work and with the current ambiguity of higher education's stances on the incorporation of AI in the classrooms and programming space, had intentionally decided to compose written narrations of our attempts at incorporating AI into our professional work. This research utilizes the document review of two 10- and 28-page narratives composed by each participant. Bogdan and Biklen (2006, as cited in Creswell & Poth, 2018) suggest there are three forms of documents used in qualitative research; personal documents, official documents, and popular culture documents (such as publicly facing audiovisual and social media documents).

The current study examines personal documents to analyze their reflective journal entries, and the process could be considered as incorporating popular culture documents through the use of ChatGPT. As such, what would be considered the research texts were also the field notes that portrayed the narration of the lived experiences in time (Clandinin & Caine, 2008), which because of the personal writing style we engaged in, presented in stories.

AI Stories

The first story composed was the reflection of trying the use ChatGPT to write a dissertation. The author teaches a dissertation writing course and the intent was to inquire if the AI tool would be able to complete the assignments that they teach in one course in the fall semester. By submitting a series of assignments through ChatGPT, the author was able to review the outputs. The author intentionally assessed the tool by crafting the assignment questions based on a topic that they are already an expert in, as such yielding a greater ability to assess the AI's outputs. Throughout the process, the author shared personal and individual perspectives of the content produced and the impact on potential student use.

In the second story, the author was seeking to compose a program-based policy on the use of AI in doctoral student assignments and the dissertation process and was inquisitive to see what AI would produce on the topic of itself. The author made the decision to enter the process blindly by not reviewing any peer or aspirational institutional policies and to start the process by submitting general questions on AI ethical issues and policy construction. The author utilized memoing, the process of bridging the gap between raw data and abstract concepts as a means to understand and explain research phenomena within its examined context (Creswell & Poth, 2018), during the initial reflection of the ChatGPT outputs as well as with the analysis. Unique to each story was also the inclusion of the text submitted to and received from ChatGPT, an almost artificial third participant to this research, which was also included in the analysis of this research.

Data Analysis

Dhungana (2021) suggested that dialogic narratives "concentrates on centrifugal processing [...] where plurality of experiences are transcribed as mutual consciousness of two speakers that has internally persuasive discourse as an essential element for analysis and research" (p. 29). The analysis of our collaborative autoethnography will be informed by the co-collaborators sharing their narratives, individually analyzing the shared narratives, and then coming back together for a cross analysis discussion of the emerging themes. Through content analysis, the method for systematically investigating texts, the researchers will seek to immerse into the content to fathom the bigger picture (Leavy, 2023). We sought to then identify and describe the story patterns amongst the objective set of experiences (Creswell & Poth, 2018). While conducting the initial coding and theme-ing process, we also stayed abreast of epiphanies within the collective stories. Then we sought to connect the findings through the goals of strengths, and weaknesses, to compare with the emerging literature on the topic, as well as implications and recommendations of the research questions to interpret and share the larger meaning of the stories.

FINDINGS

Strengths

Emerging research has started presenting the strengths of incorporating AI into supporting students in the creation (Atlas, 2023, as cited by Grassini, 2023) and evaluation of educational content (Grassini, 2023). Throughout our experiences using ChatGPT 3.5 to consider applying AI support to our designated use in the educational setting, we found many surprises and strengths of the content being produced by the AI program. The speed at which content was produced was noted by both collaborators and the ability to quickly synthesize basic content was discussed by both. As well, the tool garnered positive remarks from the collaborators for the ability to assist in organization and formatting.

Starting Point

In the narrative associated with the very first prompt one collaborator journaled, "I started just by asking what a policy on AI in higher education even is. The response was proactive and highly formal, highlighting important topical areas for the development, implementation, and ethical considerations of the use of AI." We discussed in the analysis phase that what appeared to be a major finding we identified in our narratives was that ChatGPT would be an excellent tool to assist students with their initial idea generation. As also supported in the literature (Megawati et al., 2023; Xames & Shefa, 2023), the early planning stages and initial idea generation that from our experience plague our doctoral students as they begin the deeper formulation of their proposed dissertation topics would greatly benefit students. One collaborator wrote that AI use could "serve as a jumping-off point." They expounded this idea by sharing an example:

I asked ChatGPT, "Write 500 words summarizing the primary gender theories used in social research from 2010 to 2020." The results included three theories: intersectionality theory, social constructionist theory, and queer theory. All three are indeed appropriate theories to consider when studying gender, so a student who is unfamiliar with research could use this list as a starting point.

There is also the consideration for engaging in new educational activities that are novel to students and educational professionals alike. "I never imagined five years ago when I became program director that I would need to be crafting a policy or statement on the use of AI within the doctoral program" stated one collaborator when reflecting on their starting point of using ChatGPT. Another stated their consideration for inclusion of use: "At least for now, when it comes to initiating research papers to tackling assignments that may be novel to students, such as creating an annotated bibliography, ChatGPT might offer several benefits." At the very least, as found in other studies (Megawati et al., 2023; Lauria, 2023, as cited by Raheem et al., 2023), when struggling with just getting pen to paper as you are tasked with something as significant as 'starting a dissertation,' we found the tool has significant benefits to help students overcome writer's block.

Organization

In alignment with how AI tools can assist doctoral students with creating a starting point was the identified finding of the strengths of AI's ability to organize content into outlines and discernible information. In reflection, participants observed: "First, I am impressed that the AI can organize information so well. On the face of it, AI is great at creating headers and an organization scheme that a student could use as a starting point." Xames and Shefa (2023) noted the strengths of AI in categorizing text into organizational chunks of data, which as one collaborator wrote, "what I found consistent and appropriate to the task requested was the use of strong outlining headers as a way to organize important content, such as ethics, privacy, and transparency." In one prompt given to ChatGPT, a set of bullet points, composed of previously ChatGPT-generated headers, was provided with a request to organize into one paragraph. Of which, a collaborator wrote, "the generated results were a more condensed, personal policy that would be more aligned with the style of organizing and presenting program policies."

Both collaborators wrote within their narratives, as well as discussed further in their collaborative analysis, that the ability to format references, as also highlighted positively by Raheem et al. (2023), into a requested formatting style, such as APA 7, was seen as a strength. However, while the formatting of the referencing was consistently correct, the results were often a fake citation of a source that does not exist, an issue discussed further in the weaknesses section. However, upon this reflection, we discussed how even this limitation could serve as an educational tool in teaching students accurate APA 7 reference formatting. As such, this follows the suggestions from Rudolph et al. (2023a) that AI programs can serve as "tutors" in student's educational writing experiences, and potentially improve academic writing quality and grammar (Andrea, 2023, as cited by Raheem et al., 2023; Xames & Shefa, 2023).

Synthesis of Broad Topics

Along with the speed of AI's ability to deliver content, its quickness associated with the ability to summarize and synthesize literature was discussed by the collaborators. Consistent with the previously uncovered strength of the tool in summarizing literature and research studies (Limna et al., 2023; Rudolph et al., 2023b; Xames & Shefa, 2023), we found that for basic applications of presenting traditional literature review content sections, ChatGPT generated a perfunctory response. One collaborator wrote:

When I asked ChatGPT to write a 500-word literature review on gender categories, it spit out a mostly coherent and organized review, including a general statement of the issue, and then subheadings of historical perspectives, cultural perspectives, biological perspectives, and psychological perspectives.

However, they did preface this with a warning, "there needs to be ample fact checking to the point that the student still reads all the literature, and searches for additional literature that ChatGPT did not include." In other words, while ChatGPT can model a possible organization and synthesis of literature, it did not replace the current process students would need to undertake to write a successful literature review, such as reading articles and summarizing/citing specifics. Instead, it offered a model of a synthesis, reinforcing the idea of ChatGPT as a tutor or a starting point for idea generation.

Pertaining to creating educational policies and procedures of novel concepts and eliciting that kicking-off point as previously noted, the ability to synthesize a topic is a notable strength specifically pertaining to content that already possesses a significant amount of data within AI's databases. Presenting broad questions or prompts to ChatGPT yielded the greatest return of broad responses, but which could often include content that was not known or considered by the collaborator. For the prompt, "suggest some guidelines for developing an AI policy," the resulting 15 header considerations included topics such as "compliance with regulations," "stakeholder involvement," "risk assessment and mitigation," and several other aspects that had not been under consideration when initially inquiring about areas of impact in utilizing AI. The access to a wide system of data permits the AI tool to produce well-condensed bits of large information.

Weaknesses

As highlighted in the literature, early responses from educational professionals have presented fears and anxiety around the use of AI in the classrooms as a threat to education resulting from the belief that students will be more likely to cheat on coursework (Mhlanga, 2023). Yet, emerging research out of Stanford University suggests that AI is not increasing the frequency of cheating, and even further provided student survey responses for why they would use AI in their course assignments such as "struggling to grasp subject material, not having enough time to do homework, and feeling pressured to perform well" (Spector, 2023, para. 12). However, in assessing the weaknesses of using AI in producing academic texts, we found that as a tool there were many issues that would prevent students from being able to produce quality dissertation writing relying solely on ChatGPT. From our findings, we found the major weaknesses of AI to be issues related to trustworthiness of the produced content, AI's limited ability to possess any critical thinking abilities, and the lack of diverse or cultural perspectives.

Trustworthiness

Potentially to those that have the greatest fears of the rapid emergence of AI and its impact on the educational system, an aggravation to that threat can simply be in the lack of reliable and trustworthy content that is being produced. As we will discuss in greater detail below, we both had experiences with content being produced by ChatGPT that was inaccurate and repetitive. One overall note from the authors was that while at times AI-produced content could be perceived as "appealing reference titles" or "well organized," the most commonly occurring term to describe any work produced by both authors was "generic." The most pressing issues related to trustworthiness were false content and direct lifting from other sources.

False Content. Previous research and articles on the use of AI in academic writing have expressed the abundance of persistent inaccuracy and falsification of created content (Grassini, 2023; Limna et al., 2023; Rasul et al., 2023). We had the same experiences of persistent falsified content, which most commonly occurred during the creation of citations that did not exist. One participant made a direct request to a "peer-reviewed research article" which resulted in an article that upon search, did not exist. The participants altered the wording of their search to inquire if a true article would be produced, however, yet another reference was produced that does not exist. The participant noted in their narrative that, "So, after a few minutes, I was seeing that ChatGPT was not going to make this particular assignment easy. In fact, because it fed me fake citations, it was a time waster." While content produced appeared plausible, the reality that can have significant implications for produced content is the lack of reliability and persistence of inaccuracy going unnoticed if the second action steps are not taken to verify the produced work.

Direct Lifts. One issue that occurred for both collaborators was that we found instances of content being taken directly from another public source. The generated results of one of the prompts to "create an AI policy for a higher education institution" offered a robust outline of 13 headers in which each area presented has direct information written in the style of a general program policy. However, upon inspection of one of the statements, in which the overall response included language like "The [Higher Education Institution Name]…," when deciding to copy the statement into a search engine resulted in finding the policy was on the public website of a comprehensive higher education institution in the Midwest of the United States. In the narration, after this incident occurred the collaborator recounted, "I've just had an intense feeling of having to walk away." The collaborator went on to explain their response by sharing, "I felt like I was using ChatGPT to inform myself and help with my own knowledge towards the creation of a policy, now I feel like I just did something wrong and that I've unintentionally stolen someone's content." Bašic et al. (2023, as cited by Grassini, 2023) found that when issues of trustworthiness, such as falsification and content being pulled from direct sources, that produced content may result in increased unintentional plagiarism. During our collaborative analysis stage, one person noted that the institution's policy could have itself been generated by AI going through the same process that we were seeking to develop as well.

LIMITED CRITICAL THINKING SKILLS

A significant weakness of using AI in the creation of scholarly work is the program's limited critical thinking abilities (Firat, 2023; Rasul et al., 2023; Rudolph et al., 2023). We also found this to be evident. One collaborator prompted ChatGPT to produce an annotated bibliography of an article and provided a direct citation. The AI program created an appropriately formatted annotated bibliography and short summary, however the collaborator wrote that, "it did not look as good, because it failed to mention some of the more interesting main points of the article." In another instance, the collaborator asked the AI program to summarize the results of a provided research study of which the collaborator wrote, "In terms of summarizing [the studies] results, ChatGPT offered high level and vague phrasing, to the point that it completely missed the most interesting results of the study."

For this particular instance, the culling of the information produced by the AI program resulted in a limited understanding of the article's intended results. For further explanation of the potential impact of this significant misinformation, the AI tool generated the following summation of Harper's (2012) study, Race Without Racism: How Higher Education Researchers Minimize Racist Institutional Norms, "Harper finds that researchers often overlook the ways in which institutional norms perpetuate racism in higher education. He argues that a more critical and nuanced approach is needed to understand the impact of racism on higher education institutions." While the summary was not wrong it was too generic as the collaborator, an expert in this topic, wrote of the AI-generated response:

What a student should have culled from the Harper results is that authors used the terms racism or racist in 21.6% of the publications mentioned, racism or racist 1-2 times, and only 16 of the 255 articles used either word 3+ times. The researchers of this study concluded that only a few authors suggested racism as a plausible interpretation for the differences seen in data split by race.

The lack of critical thinking skills currently being produced by AI programs, like ChatGPT, create deficits when produced content is unreliable, notably for topics and procedures that require active reflection and higher-level synthesis.

Repetition

Another weakness that was identified within the narrations that showcased the limited critical thinking skills of current AI programs was that when focusing on one specific topic, the content generated by ChatGPT was highly repetitive, especially when sought over a single period of inquiry. We found that when we reviewed the narrative and AI transcript for the creation of a program AI policy, which unlike the increased variations of prompts of the dissertation assignments, was focused on one task with multiple (11 overall) prompts, there was obvious repetition of content. The participant wrote in their narrative that the task of reviewing the created work was "seeing all of the same header titles over and over again" and "what felt like a death by synonyms." The repetition even existed when the focus of the topic's viewpoint made significant shifts in focus.

For the prompts "suggest some guidelines for developing an AI policy" and "how does culture play into issues of creating an AI policy," seven of the 12 guidelines had the exact same headers and the differences in the content under the proposed headers at times only newly incorporated the word culture. The same occurred when prompting to generate an outline for AI policies for online students and then a separate prompt for doctoral students. There was significant repetition with the notable changes between each being the word use of 'online' or 'doctoral' in sections. This was a shared issue faced by both collaborators as one member experienced using AI, inquiring of its use in academic writing assignments - shared that "the program repeated the vague statements" of the prompts they had posed ChatGPT. While we noted that consistency as an organizational tool was a strength for the AI program, the significant repetition of content was, and one participant noted, "a surprising disappointment."

Lack of Diverse Perspectives

Both narrative submissions wrote of the lack of diverse perspectives or ability to write from diverse perspectives, which has also been seen in the existing literature (Grassini, 2023; Ifelebuegu et al., 2023). For the task of creating an AI policy, one collaborator proposed a question of ChatGPT to incorporate culture as an aspect of a series of continuous prompts. The result was only the addition of the term into a previously generated response with the inclusion of variations of the term, different, for example, "cultures differ in…," "Different cultures…," or "cultural norms might differ for …" yet the remainder of the content followed the previous prompt of "guideline for developing an AI program."

As also seen as an issue with repetition, when diverse concepts such as online student compared to doctoral student are being used interchangeably, as one collaborator journaled:

I'm turned off by a program that is unable to create content that reflects the uniqueness of various populations within higher education, and as a personal value of institutional leadership feel discouraged in the inability to value student population distinctions for generated repetitive content.

A concern with the content generated by AI is that the AI systems generate content based on the patterns and trends that are being cycled through their data searches (Grassini, 2023), which creates, and potentially reinforces a homogeneity of information being composed. As one collaborator wrote of their assumptions, "with AI's database being reflective of decades of public scholarship primarily encompassing a historically singular perspective, I wonder what the implications for a possible resurgence of a lack of diverse voices if AI-generated data is not purposefully incorporating them." During the collaborators' discussion of analysis, the idea was proposed that we would need to continue to be diligent of this concept as we proceed in our journey of considering how to incorporate and partner with AI in supporting students while being mindful of the inclusion of diverse and cultural considerations and content.

IMPLICATIONS

This collaborative autoethnography sought to contribute insights into how faculty members utilize AI tools in their instructional methods, program planning, and curriculum development within a doctoral program. The results from this study offer interesting implications for practices using AI to support doctoral student programming. These findings suggest that while there were presented strengths and weaknesses that we experienced, the implications for using AI in the doctoral curriculum and programming space require a commitment to quality assurance and the continued engagement of human critical thinking skills.

Quality Assurance

A weakness identified in the study included issues related to the trustworthiness and limited critical thinking abilities of AI-generated content. Higher education institutions must exercise caution when relying on AI-generated content. There is a need for educators and students to verify the accuracy of information produced by AI, especially in areas where critical thinking and nuanced understanding are crucial. Regarding critically reflecting on the content being produced by AI in the assistance of academic writing, "I would suggest students resume the traditional research process and turn to the literature to confirm these statements (or refute them)" suggested one collaborator.

While AI presents opportunities for academic support, the integration of AI into educational settings should be approached with a thoughtful consideration of limitations and the need for ongoing human oversight and guidance (Chui, 2024; Rahman et al., 2023). As one collaborator journaled:

As a professor and researcher, I am hopeful about the ways Chat GPT might help us produce higher quality research faster. For example, imagine the day in which Chat GPT can cull a list of the research topics that could be most impactful, and the methods that are best to use, and then offer you a literature review of a paper. Then, it might analyze your data and write your results. Maybe it could even write a conclusion section of a paper. In that brave new world, researchers would provide oversight on quality.

Another finding of the study highlighted a strength of ChatGPT towards the process of effectively organizing content, such as creating headers and offering organizational alignment, suggesting that higher education institutions can partner with AI to constructively enhance students' learning of organizational and formatting skills. However, a dedication to quality assurance is still needed to ensure that the generated content is reliable and trustworthy.

Engaging Critical Thinking with AI

Our findings, in alignment with previous research (Firat, 2023; Rasul et al., 2023; Rudolph et al., 2023), found that a weakness in using AI in the creation of scholarly work is the program's limited capacity for critical thinking abilities. However, by incorporating AI into educational strategies, students can further develop their own critical thinking skills by questioning the limitations and gaps of AI-generated content. AI could in this fashion serve as the catalyst for advancing human critical thinking skills, such as inference and self-regulation (Ibna Seraj & Oteir, 2022) or fostering creativity (Guo & Lee, 2023). Students can be prompted to learn how to critically evaluate and fact-check AI-generated content to further their own abilities, to question and analyze data presented to them. As one collaborator suggested in their narrative, "I could imagine students not only using the suggested categories from the AI, but also using the language as a model. Still though, this does not mean that students could completely abandon the typical process for paper writing." As humans engage in problem-solving activities using AI systems, students are encouraged to assess innumerable perspectives and consider alternative solutions, fostering a broader and more nuanced understanding of topical areas. As our findings presented the AI's benefits of organization and speed, the utilization of programs like ChatGPT for student academic work, as one collaborator wrote, could be benefitted by "perhaps speeding it up for the folks who get stuck when it comes to ideas on how to organize their papers or what content to include when talking about a certain issue," whereas then the student can focus on the higher order challenges and scenarios that necessitate analytical thinking.

RECOMMENDATIONS AND DISCUSSION

While the literature documented and our research further supported the strengths and weaknesses through research, we sought to provide recommendations for future exploration. Our recommendations fall into three main groupings: creating policies and guidelines, opportunities for AI literacy training, and continued research.

Policies/Guidelines

As institutional use of AI becomes more prominent and incorporated, higher education leaders must establish clear and comprehensive policies and guidelines to govern the ethical and responsible use of AI in the classroom and with program planning (Chan, 2023; Tanveer et al., 2020). By establishing a framework that outlines the ethical principles and safeguards surrounding AI technologies, higher education institutions can ensure that AI tools are leveraged in a manner that aligns with their educational mission and values. Even within research investigating AI policy incorporation of national movements, higher education must also consider the role of culture when generating institutional policies, "One solution is by authoring ... policy that upholds cultural values and personal rights, ultimately reinforcing these values in their societies" (Robinson, 2020, p. 1). A holistic understanding of the ethical implications and practical applications of AI amongst various stakeholders should be incorporated into any policy planning.

Whereas higher education's AI policies should address institutional programming topics such as data privacy, transparency and accountability, and research standards, AI applications in curriculum need clear expectations of issues related to the potential impact of AI on academic integrity and cultural equity. For students, this includes a) using the service as a writing partner rather than a ghostwriter, b) encouraging students to read deeply to support their critical thinking skills (Rudolph et al., 2023b), and c) stating clear guidelines for academic integrity (Rasul et al. (2023). One main reason this task is essential is that differing faculty opinions on how the tool should be used has the potential to create confusion for students as they encounter different rules and expectations in each course.

A second but equally important consideration is an institution's policy on plagiarism. Our institutional policy defines plagiarism as the "use of another person or agency's (to include Artificial Intelligence) ideas or expressions without acknowledging the source" (University of North Georgia, 2023, para 44). If faculty endorse the use of AI, they may be encouraging plagiarism. In a preprint study on institutional policies on AI, Wang et al. found that the top 50 institutions in the U.S. were "open but cautious" when it came to using AI in the classroom (n.d., p. 1). Most institutions (58%) permitted faculty to decide on AI use in the classroom, with 35% revealing unclear/undecided positions (Wang et al., n.d.). When assessing the inclusion of AI tool use, higher education institutions could require students to acknowledge the tool and save the chat history.

Declarations of AI Use

Another central debate surrounds AI and academic integrity. One issue is that there are concerns about how AI should be credited in research (Xames & Shefa, 2023). However, there is a lack of recommendations on how students should acknowledge AI tools in research papers when it has helped improve writing, spelling/grammar, and explaining concepts from the literature. As Huang and Tan (2023) suggested for scholars:

Scientists should use AI tools to assist in writing their review article but should not rely solely on AI-generated text. It is important to review and edit the AI-generated text to ensure that it is accurate and appropriate for the context of the article. When using AI-generated text, scientists should properly attribute any sources used in the text. This includes properly citing any direct quotations or paraphrased information and avoiding copying and pasting large portions of text without attribution. (p. 1152).

There is still much discussion on how students and scholars can properly indicate which tools were used and how they were applied in academic writing. In April 2023, the American Psychological Association (APA) created a blog post entitled, How to Cite ChatGPT? (https://apastyle.apa.org/blog/how-to-cite-chatgpt). The APA formatting suggestion is that use is similar to citing personal communication yet does not include a distinction of the topic of inquiry, as such if multiple uses of different topics were employed in one paper, there would be little ability to replicate the generated response if needed for future research inquiry. Within our narratives, inquiry threads were used to continue to develop the previously generated content, which as stated by one collaborator, "how would I ever be able to cite the multiple prompts that it took for me to get to this content if I wanted to replicate this process in a different system?" Currently, there are still many limitations to the ability to professionally utilize AI in academic settings when there are still issues of transparent and ethical declarations of use.

AI Literacy Skills

Once established, policies and guidelines need to be supported by training in AI literacy (Ng et al., 2021; Rasul et al., 2023). As we both wrote in our narrations, we each participated in some form of learning about AI prior to starting our inquiries, and one collaborator shared, "I watched a twenty-minute YouTube tutorial covering some of the ways you can interact with the AI." Chui (2024) provided an implication in their systematic literature review of previous AI studies that "students that understand AI can work with GenAI while knowing its capabilities and risks (e.g., ethical and moral issues). They become more responsible and responsible GenAI users and learners" (p. 7). Even as we engaged in learning that would help us navigate effective prompt terms and thread modifications, we learned that there is still a greater need for increased literacy skills in AI use to be able to make the most out of the tool and to help protect against some of the encroaching issues around plagiarism and academic integrity.

AI literacy skills have been researched, but there is a lack of agreement on definitions for higher education (Laupichler et al., 2022). The most widely used definition describes AI literacy as "a set of competencies that enables individuals to critically evaluate AI technologies, communicate and collaborate effectively with AI, and use AI as a tool online, at home, and in the workplace" (Long & Magerko, 2020, p. 2, as cited by Laupichler et al., 2022). Chiu (2024) found that due to various forms of literacy not all being mutually exclusive and each possessing distinct definitions that "AI, media, data information, computational and algorithm literacies are more likely to be significant consequences for higher education" (p. 8). More studies are required in the area of AI literacy evaluation on the impact of increased AI literacy skills of doctoral students and educators.

Continued Research on AI in Doctoral Education

With the emergence of ChatGPT being less than 15 months old at the time of this study, continued empirical research on the topic of AI tools in the higher education landscape is still greatly needed. Scholars have recommended that future research examine AI's "effectiveness in promoting active collaborative learning, student engagement, and academic performance against traditional research methods" (Rasul et al., 2023, p. 46). However, as practitioners explore the uses of AI in their classrooms and given the rapidly developing application of AI in the classroom, it may be some time until faculty can formally measure the impacts. Chiu (2024) conducted 12 focus groups of undergraduate through postdoctoral students after they had received a three-hour training on AI in education, and an identified issue persisted of how to design effective assessment remained unclear, as well as the acceptance of new forms of assessment by both students and educators which they note also required additional research.

Particularly within doctoral education, continuing the inquiry of the impact of allowing doctoral students to be permitted and trained to use AI properly and ethically in their academic writing would be insightful, similar to studies conducted by Zou and Huang (2023). An additional area of investigation includes the effectiveness of AI programming in supporting doctoral students through various stages of their research, from content organization to literature review synthesis to data analysis, which can provide valuable insights, as well as investigating the role of AI on the mentor- doctoral student relationship in creating future leaders in higher education that are prepared to navigate and facilitate the emergence of AI into the higher education landscape.

AI Acknowledgement: This article was prepared utilizing Grammarly and ChatGPT to improve writing clarity, check spelling and grammar, and offer interpretations of information from the literature to aid in the author's ability to apply concepts to the present study context.

REFERENCES

Adams, T. E., Ellis, C., & Jones, S. H. (2017). Autoethnography. The International Encyclopedia of Communication Research Methods, 1-11.

Adams, T. E., Jones, S. L. H., & Ellis, C. (2015). *Autoethnography. Understanding qualitative research*. Oxford University Press.

Alhawiti, K. M. (2014). Natural language processing and its use in education. *International Journal of Advanced Computer Science and Applications*, 5(12), 72–76.

Blalock, A. E., & Akehi, M. (2018). Collaborative autoethnography as a pathway for transformative learning. *Journal of Transformative Education*, *16*(2), 89–107. doi:10.1177/1541344617715711

Calle-Arango, L., & Ávila Reyes, N. (2023). Obstacles, facilitators, and needs in doctoral writing: A systematic review. *Studies in Continuing Education*, *45*(2), 133–151. doi:10.1080/0158037X.2022.2026315

Chan, C. K. Y. (2023). A comprehensive AI policy education framework for university teaching and learning. *International Journal of Educational Technology in Higher Education*, *20*(1), 38. doi:10.1186/s41239-023-00408-3

Chang, H. (2008). *Autoethnography as method*. Left Coast.

Chang, H., Ngunjiri, F., & Hernandez, K. A. C. (2016). *Collaborative autoethnography* (Vol. 8). Routledge. doi:10.4324/9781315432137

Chase, S. (2005). Narrative inquiry. The Sage handbook of qualitative research, 651-679.

Chen, J., Zhuo, Z., & Lin, J. (2023). Does ChatGPT play a double-edged sword role in the field of higher education? An in-depth exploration of the factors affecting student performance. *Sustainability (Basel)*, *15*(24), 1–18. doi:10.3390/su152416928

Chiu, T. K. (2024). Future research recommendations for transforming higher education with generative AI. *Computers and Education: Artificial Intelligence*, *6*, 100197. doi:10.1016/j.caeai.2023.100197

Chiu, T. K., Xia, Q., Zhou, X., Chai, C. S., & Cheng, M. (2023). Systematic literature review on opportunities, challenges, and future research recommendations of artificial intelligence in education. *Computers and Education: Artificial Intelligence*, *4*, 100118. doi:10.1016/j.caeai.2022.100118

Clandinin, D., & Caine, V. (2008). Narrative inquiry. In L. M. Given (Ed.), *The Sage Encyclopedia of Qualitative Research Methods* (pp. 542–545). Sage Publications.

Clandinin, D. J. (Ed.). (2006). *Handbook of narrative inquiry: Mapping a methodology*. Sage Publications.

Clandinin, D. J. (2013). Living, telling, and retelling: Processes of narrative inquiry. In *Engaging in Narrative Inquiry* (pp. 9–31). Routledge.

Clandinin, D. J., & Caine, V. (2013). Narrative inquiry. In *Reviewing qualitative research in the social sciences* (pp. 166–179). Routledge.

Clandinin, D. J., & Connelly, F. M. (2000). *Narrative inquiry: Experience and story in qualitative research*. Jossey-Bass.

Creswell, J. W., & Poth, C. N. (2018). *Qualitative inquiry and research design: Choosing among five approaches* (4th ed.). Sage.

Denzin, N. K. (2014). *Interpretive autoethnography* (2nd ed.). Sage. doi:10.4135/9781506374697

Dhungana, S. (2022). Dialogic storying: A narrative research methodology in English language education. *Qualitative Research Journal*, *22*(2), 173–187. doi:10.1108/QRJ-05-2021-0057

Ellis, C. (2004). *The ethnographic I: A methodological novel about autoethnography* (Vol. 13). Rowman Altamira.

Ellis, C., Adams, T. E., & Bochner, A. P. (2011). Autoethnography: An overview. Historical Social Research. *Historische Sozialforschung*, *36*(4 (138)), 273–290.

Ellis, C., & Bochner, A. P. (1992). Telling and performing personal stories: The constraints of choice in abortion. In C. Ellis & M. G. Flaherty (Eds.), *Investigating subjectivity: Research on lived experience* (pp. 79–101). Sage.

Farrelly, T., & Baker, N. (2023). Generative artificial intelligence: Implications and considerations for higher education practice. *Education Sciences*, *13*(11), 1109. doi:10.3390/educsci13111109

Firat, M. (2023). What ChatGPT means for universities: Perceptions of scholars and students. *Journal of Applied Learning and Teaching*, *6*(1), 57–63.

Glesne, C. (2011). *Becoming qualitative researchers: An introduction* (4th ed.). Pearson.

Grassini, S. (2023). Shaping the future of education: Exploring the potential and consequences of AI and ChatGPT in educational settings. *Education Sciences, 13*(7), 1–13. doi:10.3390/educsci13070692

Guo, Y., & Lee, D. (2023). Leveraging ChatGPT for enhancing critical thinking skills. *Journal of Chemical Education, 100*(12), 4876–4883. doi:10.1021/acs.jchemed.3c00505

Hariri, W. (2023). Unlocking the potential of ChatGPT: A comprehensive exploration of its applications, advantages, limitations, and future directions in natural language processing. arXiv preprint arXiv:2304.02017.

Hornberger, M., Bewersdorff, A., & Nerdel, C. (2023). What do university students know about Artificial Intelligence? Development and validation of an AI literacy test. *Computers and Education: Artificial Intelligence, 5*, 1–12. doi:10.1016/j.caeai.2023.100165

Huang, J., & Tan, M. (2023). The role of ChatGPT in scientific communication: Writing better scientific review articles. *American Journal of Cancer Research, 13*(4), 1148–1154. PMID:37168339

Ibna Seraj, P. M., & Oteir, I. (2022). Playing with AI to investigate human-computer interaction technology and improving critical thinking skills to pursue 21st century age. *Education Research International.*

Ifelebuegu, A. O., Kulume, P., & Cherukut, P. (2023). Chatbots and AI in Education (AIEd) tools: The good, the bad, and the ugly. *Journal of Applied Learning and Teaching, 6*(2), 332–345.

Lapadat, J. C. (2017). Ethics in autoethnography and collaborative autoethnography. *Qualitative Inquiry, 23*(8), 589–603. doi:10.1177/1077800417704462

Laupichler, M. C., Aster, A., Schirch, J., & Raupach, T. (2022). Artificial intelligence literacy in higher and adult education: A scoping literature review. Computers and Education: Artificial Intelligence, 100101.

Leavy, P. (2023). *Research design: Quantitative, qualitative, mixed methods, arts-based, and community-based participatory research approaches.* Guilford Publications.

Limna, P., Kraiwanit, T., Jangjarat, K., Klayklung, P., & Chocksathaporn, P. (2023). The use of ChatGPT in the digital era: Perspectives on chatbot implementation. *Journal of Applied Learning and Teaching*, 6(1), 64–74.

Marechal, G. (2010). Autoethnography. In A. J. Mills, G. Durepos, & E. Wiebe (Eds.), *Encyclopedia of Case Study Research* (pp. 43–45).

McAdoo, T. (2023, April 7). How to cite ChatGPT. APA Style. https://apastyle.apa.org/blog/how-to-cite-chatgpt

Megawati, R., Listiani, H., Pranoto, N. W., Akobiarek, M., & Megahati S, R. R. P. (2023). The Role of GPT Chat in Writing Scientific Articles: A Systematic Literature Review. *Jurnal Penelitian Pendidikan IPA*, 9(11), 1078–1084. doi:10.29303/jppipa.v9i11.5559

Meurers, D. (2012). Natural language processing and language learning. Encyclopedia of Applied Linguistics, 4193-4205. doi:10.1002/9781405198431.wbeal0858

Mhlanga, D. (2023). Open AI in education, the responsible and ethical use of ChatGPT towards lifelong learning. Education, the Responsible and Ethical Use of ChatGPT Towards Lifelong Learning (February 11, 2023).

Ng, D. T. K., Leung, J. K. L., Chu, S. K. W., & Qiao, M. S. (2021). Conceptualizing AI literacy: An exploratory review. *Computers and Education: Artificial Intelligence*, 2, 1–11.

Ngunjiri, F. W., Hernandez, K. A. C., & Chang, H. (2010). Living autoethnography: Connecting life and research. *Journal of Research Practice*, 6(1), E1–E1.

Raheem, B. R., Anjum, F., & Ghafar, Z. N. (2023). Exploring the Profound Impact of Artificial Intelligence Applications (Quillbot, Grammarly and ChatGPT) on English Academic Writing: A Systematic Review. *International Journal of Integrative Research*, 1(10), 599–622.

Rahman, A., Santosa, T. A., Ilwandri, I., Suharyat, Y., Aprilisia, S., & Suhaimi, S. (2023). The effectiveness of AI based blended learning on student scientific literacy: Meta-analysis. LITERACY: International Scientific Journals of Social, Education. *Humanities (Washington)*, 2(1), 141–150.

Rasul, T., Nair, S., Kalendra, D., Robin, M., de Oliveira Santini, F., Ladeira, W. J., ... Heathcote, L. (2023). The role of ChatGPT in higher education: Benefits, challenges, and future research directions. *Journal of Applied Learning and Teaching*, 6(1), 41–56.

Robinson, S. C. (2020). Trust, transparency, and openness: How inclusion of cultural values shapes Nordic national public policy strategies for artificial intelligence (AI). *Technology in Society*, *63*, 101421. doi:10.1016/j.techsoc.2020.101421

Rudolph, J., Tan, S., & Tan, S. (2023a). ChatGPT: Bullshit spewer or the end of traditional assessments in higher education? *Journal of Applied Learning and Teaching*, *6*(1), 342–363.

Rudolph, J., Tan, S., & Tan, S. (2023b). War of the chatbots: Bard, Bing Chat, ChatGPT, Ernie and beyond. The new AI gold rush and its impact on higher education. Journal of Applied Learning and Teaching, 6(1), 364-389.

Savin-Baden, M., & Niekerk, L. V. (2007). Narrative inquiry: Theory and practice. *Journal of Geography in Higher Education*, *31*(3), 459–472. doi:10.1080/03098260601071324

Sawyer, R. D., & Norris, J. (2012). *Duoethnography*. Oxford University Press. doi:10.1093/acprof:osobl/9780199757404.001.0001

Spector, C. (2023, October 31). What do Ai Chatbots really mean for students and cheating? Stanford Graduate School of Education. https://ed.stanford.edu/news/what-do-ai-chatbots-really-mean-students-and-cheating

Sullivan, M., Kelly, A., & McLaughlan, P. (2023). ChatGPT in higher education: Considerations for academic integrity and student learning. *Journal of Applied Learning & Teaching*, *6*(1), 31–40.

Taecharungroj, V. (2023). "What can ChatGPT do?" Analyzing early reactions to the innovative AI Chatbot on twitter. *Big Data and Cognitive Computing.*, *7*(35), 35. Advance online publication. doi:10.3390/bdcc7010035

Tanveer, M., Hassan, S., & Bhaumik, A. (2020). Academic policy regarding sustainability and artificial intelligence (AI). *Sustainability (Basel)*, *12*(22), 9435. doi:10.3390/su12229435

Throne, R. (2019). *Autoethnography and heuristic inquiry for doctoral-level researchers: Emerging research and opportunities*. IGI Global. 9365-2 doi:10.4018/978-1-5225-9365-2

Toyosaki, S., Pensoneau-Conway, S. L., Wendt, N. A., & Leathers, K. (2009). Community autoethnography: Compiling the personal and resituating whiteness. Cultural Studies? *Cultural Studies, Critical Methodologies*, *9*(1), 56–83. doi:10.1177/1532708608321498

Tran, T. N., & Tran, H. P. (2023, November). Exploring the Role of ChatGPT in Developing Critical Digital Literacies in Language Learning: A Qualitative Study. In *Proceedings of the AsiaCALL International Conference* (Vol. 4, pp. 1-17). 10.54855/paic.2341

University of North Georgia. (2023). Student Code of Conduct Policy. https://northgeorgia.policystat.com/policy/13881254/latest/

Wang, H., Dang, A., Wu, Z., & Mac, S. (2023). Seeing ChatGPT through universities' policies, resources and guidelines. arXiv preprint arXiv:2312.05235.

Webster, L., & Mertova, P. (2007). *Using narrative inquiry as a research method: An introduction to using critical event narrative analysis in research on learning and teaching.* Routledge. doi:10.4324/9780203946268

Wibowo, G. A., Rahman, A., & Anis, M. (2023). The impact of ChatGPT use on the quality of academic support for students. *Technology and Society Perspectives, 1*(3), 132–138. doi:10.61100/tacit.v1i3.69

Xames, M. D., & Shefa, J. (2023). ChatGPT for research and publication: Opportunities and challenges. *SSRN, 6*(1), 390–395. doi:10.2139/ssrn.4381803

Xiong, W., Litman, D., & Schunn, C. (2012). Natural language processing techniques for researching and improving peer feedback. *Journal of Writing Research, 4*(2), 155–176. doi:10.17239/jowr-2012.04.02.3

Zou, M., & Huang, L. (2023). To use or not to use? Understanding doctoral students' acceptance of ChatGPT in writing through technology acceptance model. *Frontiers in Psychology, 14*, 14. doi:10.3389/fpsyg.2023.1259531 PMID:37954179

KEY TERMS AND DEFINITIONS

Academic Integrity: The ethical policy or moral code of academia that sets boundaries for determining authenticity in writing, or conversely, plagiarism.

Academic Writing: A style of writing used in academic settings, characterized by evidence-based arguments, precision, formality, and objectivity.

AI Literacy: The knowledge, skills, and competencies required to understand, assess, and use AI technologies effectively.

Artificial Intelligence (AI): Computer programs that are designed with the intention of mimicking human intelligence.

Bias: Prejudice in favor of or against one thing, person, or group compared with another, usually considered to be unfair.

ChatGPT (Generative Pre-trained Transformer): A popular NLP developed by OpenAI, designed to understand and generate human-like text based on the input it receives.

Critical Thinking: The objective analysis and evaluation of an issue in order to form a judgment.

Digital Literacy: The ability to find, evaluate, utilize, share, and create content using information technologies and the Internet.

Natural Language Processing (NLP): A type of AI that relies on human language for input commands and outputs.

Plagiarism: The practice of taking someone else's work or ideas and passing them off as one's own.

Writing Literacy: The ability to effectively communicate ideas in writing, including the proficiency in grammar, spelling, and structure, to convey messages clearly and efficiently.

Chapter 9
A GenAI Ontology for Academic Literacies Teaching and Learning Practices

Oscar Oliver Eybers

ⓘ https://orcid.org/0000-0002-2693-3955
University of Pretoria, South Africa

ABSTRACT

In the ever-evolving higher education landscape, the integration of AI, particularly Generative AI (GenAI), is causing a profound shift. This chapter explores how GenAI is reshaping teaching, learning, and academic literacies. Academic literacies facilitators now navigate a diverse terrain, bridging traditional materials, digital resources, and AI-enhanced texts. They cultivate scholars' proficiency in GenAI tools and pioneer innovative teaching methods. This chapter introduces a GenAI ontology to support this transformative journey. It equips facilitators and students to use GenAI effectively, fostering tailored teaching methods and personalised literacies assessments. In summary, this chapter presents GenAI's potential to innovate, enhance accessibility, and elevate academic prowess in higher education.

INTRODUCTION

Undeniably, GenAI, as well as non-Generative AI, are increasingly prominent in pedagogic discourses (Escotet, 2023). In this context, academic literacy facilitators positioned at the intersection of disciplinary knowledge and the tools scholars apply to contemplate, interpret and express new knowledge, are equally confronted with GenAI technologies thrusting our field into the future. Consequently, new

DOI: 10.4018/979-8-3693-1054-0.ch009

discourses are emerging in the field of academic literacy prompting practitioners and researchers to incorporate AI ethically and practically into the ways students interact with disciplinary knowledge. Given public rhetoric and scholarly outputs examining the impact of GenAI in disciplinary spaces, the voices around academic literacy appear to be of hope and innovation combined with dread and fear.

On the one hand, there is the acknowledgement that AI is beneficial for developing scholars as novice disciplinary members. In de Souza et al. (2024), GenAI capabilities to create images are identified as effective pedagogical tools for enhancing scholars' mastery of complex physics concepts. Li (2023) reasons that GenAI, including ChatGPT, is enabling the development of students' self-efficacy, academic motivation and critical creative thinking. In this light, GenAI presents benefits for teachers and learners alike. Inversely, there are also cohorts of educators who bemoan perceptions of GenAI's threat to the academic project.

As exemplification of the aforementioned concerns, a senior director of academic affairs at Wits University in South Africa proposed that when students craft academic texts, they should reference specific sections within their work that have been bolstered by Large Language Models like ChatGPT and Google's Bard (Lebuso, 2023). While the practice of citation is an unavoidable convention for senior and junior scholars, the director's proposition poses further questions. For instance, akin to novice students, senior scholars are also frequent users of ChatGPT and other Large Language Models (LLMs) in their research endeavors.

According to de Silva and El-Ayoubi (2023), ChatGPT's capability to produce summaries of research methodology and evaluate both qualitative and quantitative data speeds up the process from conceptualizing research to its actual implementation and validation. As is evident, there are benefits in ChatGPT for seasoned researchers and scholars. In Chen et al. (2023), novice scholars report learning benefits that mirror the analytical profits identified by de Silva and El-Ayoubi (2023). Some of the intellectual advantages highlighted from novice scholars' outlooks include ChatGPT's utility in forming disciplinary ideas (Chen et al., 2023).

Early university entrants distinguish between the extended logical process of constructing ideas through Google's search engine and ChatGPT's rapid interpretation of students' questions around discipline-specific topics (Chen et al., 2023). Although the critical thinking abilities of junior and senior students may vary when attempting to use GenAI for knowledge production, all students, regardless of experience level, have similar goals when it comes to communicating in disciplines.

CHALLENGES IN IMPLEMENTING GENAI FOR ACADEMIC LITERACY DEVELOPMENT

While there are a multitude of methods for incorporating GenAI into disciplinary academic literacy development, it would be unwise to approach the new technologies as being problem-free. For illustration, some of the main concerns around academic literacy and novice scholars' development include addressing language barriers, cultivating critical thinking skills, promoting effective and ethical research and writing practices, and ensuring equitable access to educational resources and support. In Southern Africa, Africa and across economically developing regions, the aforementioned issues resonate within disciplinary contexts, suggesting the need for an ontology, or conceptual framework, to effectively integrate academic literacies with GenAI technologies.

Currently, the majority of GenAI technologies are mostly functional in languages related to the Global North and English. In this way, massive databases are used to train GenAI interfaces, such as ChatGPT, Bard and Microsoft Autopilot. In other words, predominantly English knowledge archives and the Internet are the sources of information included in GenAI tools. That so, it is reasonable to argue that most contemporary online writings—that is, the texts being uploaded to new GenAI technologies—reflect the languages of the Global North rather than indigenous African tongues. African academic literacy facilitators are therefore faced with the challenge of integrating GenAI technologies that may involve epistemic, cultural biases as a result of the uneven inclusion of African linguistic mediums, as languages reflect cultures and communities' knowledge systems and vice versa. As a result, an inclusive academic literacy ontology that incorporates GenAI should consider linguistic diversity.

As with linguistic imbalances, there are also arguments among some educators that when students produce new knowledge with GenAI technologies, their critical, higher-order thinking is impeded. Literacy facilitators who adopt this stance are concerned that GenAI capabilities will stunt students' readiness to participate in higher order reasoning, thinking and writing. These claims and their counterarguments require scrutiny. Firstly, it is necessary to distinguish between higher and lower thinking in academic literacy contexts. Qaswari and BeniAbdelrahman (2020) differentiate between higher and lower thinking, in reference to Bloom's taxonomy, by associating the first with critical and creative literacies that involve analysis, evaluation and creative responses to questions in processes of solving problems. In contrast, lower order thinking is displayed through students' repetition, or mimicking teachers' literacies, remembering facts, and regurgitating information in an uncritical fashion.

The stance of this chapter is that, as with all technologies, there is the risk of passive and lower-order practices with GenAI. Nonetheless, academic literacy facilitators' incorporation of GenAI tools and technologies into the curriculum need not emphasize lower order cognition. In contrast, GenAI technologies are primable to enhance students' higher order cognition through multiple pedagogical methods. To reiterate, higher education practitioners, including literacy facilitators - are currently situated at the nexus of new argumentation modes, courtesy of GenAI and Large Language Models.

While the inception of the Internet fundamentally altered the ways in which academic literacies were theoretically constructed, researched, and practiced in higher education, GenAI is catalyzing even more transformations in these domains (Bates et al., 2020). Hence, the principal aim of this chapter is to articulate an ontology for academic literacies facilitators, enabling them to delineate their teaching, learning, and assessment practices with GenAI pedagogic tools in a manner that enhances scholars' higher order literacies, disciplinary argumentation, critical thinking, reading, writing and creativity.

ROLES OF ACADEMIC LITERACIES FACILITATORS IN THE GENAI AGE

Throughout human history, the oncoming generation has been taught how to use tools and technologies that are necessary for survival by adults. Senior clan members of the ancient Khoi and San in southern Africa, for instance, taught young people how to make hunting bows and arrows and how to reach underground roots in order to assess their nutritional and therapeutic worth (Seroto, 2011). In a similar vein, senior academics at universities nowadays are responsible for providing junior scholars with the practical, cognitive, and epistemological tools they need to use digital, GenAI technology. Specifically, facilitators of contemporary academic literacies need to nurture in emerging scholars the abilities and knowledge needed to apply GenAI to forge their disciplinary identities and survive communicatively in their disciplines.

In the GenAI age, academic literacy facilitators assume three crucial roles, as detailed in this chapter. Firstly, literacy developers assist novice scholars in decoding ethical principles, logical guidelines, and potential fallacies encountered by senior scholars when integrating Artificial Intelligence (AI) into disciplinary communication. In so doing, academic literacy facilitators contribute toward developing novice disciplinary members' discoursal identities (Qi & Zhoo, 2023).

Secondly, academic literacies facilitators spearhead the adaptation of conventional teaching and learning methodologies to digital innovations, ensuring effective integration of AI for faculty and students. Integration involves bridging the gap between established and AI infused epistemologies. In accord, Vemula (2022, p. 1) describes interplays between humans and AI as "a collaborative approach". Finally, academic literacy facilitators serve as innovation catalysts in their faculties, guiding colleagues and students in harnessing AI for pedagogical purposes.

In this chapter, the primary emphasis is on developing an AI ontology using GenAI tools to support educators in cultivating advanced cognitive abilities among novice disciplinary learners, encompassing critical thinking, reading comprehension, and writing of an argumentative, critical nature. Additionally, the chapter addresses the criticality of integrating higher order thinking skills to bridge traditional and GenAI-infused teaching methods, while also considering the implications of lower order thinking processes on academic literacy learning outcomes.

Need for an Academic Literacies GenAI Ontology

In the context of the increasing prominence of AI in higher education, the author aims to present an ontology as a pedagogic framework for integrating AI into academic literacies and disciplinary development. As AI continues to gain visibility, voice and agency in higher education, the imperative for universities to establish comprehensive frameworks becomes evident. AI pedagogical frameworks can serve as the bedrock on which instructors and students effectively harness the capabilities of emerging GenAI technologies. According to Chan (2023), AI frameworks in education are necessary for upholding ethical, teaching and learning principles when engaging with new technologies. Chan (2023) suggests five key principles for developing AI frameworks: human centricity, inclusivity, sustainability, fairness, and accountability. By adhering to these principles, academic literacy facilitators and students can ethically advance the intellectual project with the assistance of GenAI.

The evolving digital landscape necessitates that GenAI frameworks not only inspire students in their disciplinary journeys but also empower instructors to creatively align their teaching methodologies with courses' teaching and learning outcomes. In the academic literacy domain, GenAI powered pedagogical tools, virtual teaching assistants, tutors, and conversational agents powered by LLMs are already a reality in some higher education institutions (McMurtrie, 2018). Consequently, new GenAI frameworks and policies require a focus on teaching, learning, and assessment precepts. Academic literacies facilitators, as the custodians of communication and disciplinary discourses within faculties, emerge as key stakeholders whose voices and agency are vital in this digital paradigm shift.

Academic literacy developers' positions within faculties enable them to guide and support universities in articulating comprehensive policies and frameworks around GenAI. These frameworks can empower disciplinary instructors to enhance their pedagogical methods by leveraging the enabling features of GenAI. Goodier and Parkinson (2005) highlight how literacy facilitators operate at the meeting point of intellectual communication, course materials, skills, disciplinary genres and discourses which novice scholars must master to attain degrees. Hence, by collaborating with faculty to formulate human-centric and ethically sound GenAI frameworks and teaching and learning policies, literacies facilitators can contribute to improving graduation rates, enhancing research productivity, and pioneering teaching methodologies in disciplines that draw on GenAI capacities.

In summary, the integration of GenAI into higher education demands the establishment of critical frameworks and ethical guidelines. These strategic conceptualizations serve to not only elevate the disciplinary journeys of students but also to empower academic literacy facilitators and disciplinary instructors to push boundaries of pedagogical possibilities. Positioned at the heart of this transformative process, academic literacies facilitators are poised to take the helm through guiding universities toward superior outcomes, fostering innovation and cultivating a more dynamic community of disciplines grounded in critical pedagogic practices, digital innovation and ethical considerations.

The Evolving Academic Literacies Landscape

It is crucial to make a clear distinction between early academic literacies, digital literacies, and AI-infused literacies. This distinction allows for a nuanced understanding of how literacy practices have evolved in response to the digital age and the integration of AI in contemporary disciplines. Academic literacy has historically been associated with activities like reading books, scholarly papers, and other disciplinary writings in the setting of higher education. As such, the earliest uses of literacies revolved around interactions with hard copy records of historical events, religious doctrine as well as philosophical, agricultural, economic and scientific developments. To illustrate, consider the fact that priests, scribes, and merchants in ancient Kemet (Egypt) documented some of the world's earliest systemic written records (Regulski, 2016). Hence, in ancient Africa, scholars' academic literacies were assessed by evaluating their reading and writing abilities through the examination of physical texts like papyrus scrolls or inscriptions found on temple walls and burial sites (Amen, 2010).

In the present age, academic literacy facilitators need to be mindful of the historical progression from ancient African literacy practices to present times. Understanding the link between ancient African epistemologies, reading traditions, writing materials, and present-day literacies in the digital era is crucial. Such examination is of paramount importance as it sheds light on how choices made today by literacy facilitators, including the selection of teaching, learning, and reading methods, written genres, modes of knowledge dissemination, and assessment techniques, are influenced by ideological perspectives with roots tracing back to the ancient scribes of Africa. Street's (2003) ideological framework provides insights into how disciplinary discourses, methodologies of facilitators, and the evolution of past literacies contribute to the development of pedagogies in the digital and AI-infused era. According to Street, literacies are always shaped by dominant cultures in society and educational institutions.

In line with Street's (2003) ideological theory, literacy is not only a mechanical or generic skill but a social undertaking which is deeply embedded in the cultural and knowledge systems of local communities. In ancient Ethiopia and Kemet, priests and scribes cultivated systemic, alphabetic, scripted literacies as a means to record their epistemologies and maintain governance by articulating laws and precedents on behalf of the greater society. In a similar fashion, literacies in higher education are entwined with epistemic systems of disciplinary communities, including those of literacies facilitators (Harb & Thomure, 2020; Street, 2003). The enduring epistemic thread woven through African history reveals shared characteristics between ancient and contemporary academic literacies. This continuum of historical literacies, as mentioned earlier, emphasizes how present-day disciplinary communities, reminiscent of ancient Africa's priestly, scribal, and royal clusters, continue to influence knowledge construction in the contemporary digital, Gen AI age.

The Impact of the Internet of Things on Higher Education

In 2012, Tianbo highlighted the transformative impact of the Internet of Things (IoT) on higher education. The digital revolution reshaped interactions in personal, public, and educational spheres, fundamentally changing educational technologies, teaching methods, and learning processes. Previously, academic literacies centered around physical libraries and face-to-face interactions; however, the Internet era enabled students to access global information through various digital platforms like journal databases, eBooks, videos, discussion boards, and learning management systems. Face-to-face learning became optional as online resources expanded.

Moreover, the Internet revolutionized learning styles in higher education by shifting from teacher-centered to student-centered approaches, offering vast digital resources and interactive tools tailored to different disciplines. This transformation in pedagogies was crucial for maintaining the academic project during the COVID-19 pandemic. Yet, the emergence of GenAI has further revolutionized teaching, learning, and assessment in higher education, potentially surpassing the Internet's impact. GenAI provides new avenues for accessing, interpreting, and generating disciplinary knowledge, reshaping how educators, evaluators, and students engage in face-face dialogues, argumentation and academic literacies.

Possibilities and Challenges Posed by Generative AI

It is important to first examine new GenAI structures where literacy events occur and where literacies take place before venturing into how GenAI is changing academic literacies teaching, learning, and evaluation in higher education. The following GenAI teaching and learning structures, which are pertinent to developing academic literacies in the present age, will now be analyzed: simulated professional environments, intelligent tutoring systems, audio processing, immersive instruction and augmented realities (see Ontology 1).

Ontology 1: GenAI structural ontology for academic literacies

While past educational methods before the digital age necessitated that educators physically bring students to laboratories or natural settings for physiological sciences, or to the community and workplaces for social sciences, GenAI has introduced novel ways of offering simulated environments that align with the focal areas of academic disciplines. GenAI simulated environments propel academic literacy facilitators and aspiring scholars into innovative teaching and learning events and practices. Social simulation in educational contexts involves the replication of disciplinary, social activities with the aid of GenAI.

One significant benefit of social simulation is its ability to help scientists understand the intricacies of human worlds and cultures (Chen, Gao, Lan, Lu, Mao, Piao, Wang, Jin, & Li, 2023). Integrating chatbots into simulated, social environments is a promising method. With the assistance of GenAI, academic literacy facilitators and disciplinary experts can utilize the capabilities of Large Language Models (LLMs) alongside visual and auditory tools, such as chatbots, to create simulated, disciplinary environments.

In research conducted by Chen et al. (2023), a Large Language Model (LM) was used to help scholars participate in simulated conversations on topics including gender equality and perspectives on nuclear energy. The advantage of employing GenAI to simulate social, discipline-specific settings became apparent when the researchers enabled the system's chatbots to observe their surroundings and imitate human responses. Simulated agents cultivated students' observations of population-level phenomena, such as the spread of information, attitudes and emotions, within the simulations (Chen et al., 2023). Chen et al. (2023) conclude that there are benefits to incorporating LLMs into simulated learning environments. These advantages include helping scholars create explanations for social phenomena, analyzing large amounts of quantitative data, locating and reproducing patterns seen in the social domains that disciplines study.

Intelligent tutoring systems, like simulated learning demonstrated in the Chen et al. (2023) analysis, were transforming academic literacies before the emergence of GenAI, including ChatGPT (Ballantyne, Livingston, & Garraway, 2021; Mousavinasab, Zarifsanaiey, Niakan Kalhori, Rakhshan, Keikha, & Ghazi Saeedi, 2021). However, similar to their impact on simulated learning, LLMs are ushering in innovations within the sphere of intelligent tutoring systems. Briefly, an intelligent tutoring system is an educational tool designed to provide personalized and interactive support to learners, facilitating their understanding of disciplinary content and mastery of affiliated literacies (Le & Jia, 2022).

Large Language Models have expanded the pedagogic reach of intelligent tutoring systems and altered how they operate in the present era. To demonstrate, pre-LLM intelligent tutoring systems were designed around a structured knowledge base and rule-based algorithms. A structured knowledge base is an organized repository of information, while rule-based algorithms consist of predefined instructions or rules that guide computer applications in decision-making processes (Gao, Takanobu, Bosselut, & Huang, 2022; Zhu, Wang, Chen, & Dong, 2022). Accordingly, pre-LLM intelligent tutoring systems offered personalized instruction and feedback but were limited by their reliance on manually crafted rules and a fixed knowledge base. The introduction of LLMs has expanded the capabilities of intelligent tutoring systems. Large Language Models permit intelligent tutoring systems, including chatbots, to understand and generate natural language while accessing multiple knowledge bases curated from all industrial and disciplinary domains.

Describing the myriad of ways education has transformed in virtual settings within a single chapter's length poses a challenge. Nevertheless, the emergence of the metaverse highlights how GenAI can revolutionize learning in augmented and virtual realms, particularly benefiting academic literacy development. Students and academic literacy facilitators presently have the opportunity to enhance their disciplinary membership not only through traditional textbooks and classrooms but within augmented and virtual settings, where chatbots fulfill agential roles of tutors, textual peer reviewers, and critics. As such, the metaverse is capable of serving as a transdisciplinary ecosystem where scholars from diverse fields can collaborate, exchange knowledge, and display their multiliteracies (Ahuja, Polascik, Doddapaneni, Byrnes, & Sridhar, 2023). Here, multiliteracies encompass all communication modes essential for generating, challenging, and refining knowledge in disciplinary domains.

Critically, multiliteracies encompass computational thinking. Computational cognitive literacies involve problem-solving, algorithmic logic, data analysis, and abstraction, allowing scholars to analyze complex problems by using the capacities of computers and digital devices (Li, Schoenfeld, diSessa, Graesser, Benson, English, & Duschl, 2020). Algorithmic logic, as practiced among first-year scholars, requires skill in problem-solving and logical reasoning to formulate knowledge and solutions.

In this context, computational literacies are fundamental for navigating physical and disciplinary spaces in the metaverse where Large Language Models regularly apply algorithms while interacting with humans. Similarly, academic literacies facilitators apply computational thinking to design scaffold learning experiences and problem-solving strategies.

Novice students acquire computational and algorithmic literacies through active engagement of disciplinary concepts, theories, quantitative data and problems in the metaverse while interacting with the priming that literacy facilitators inject into chatbots. Here, priming, a vital skill for contemporary academic literacy developers, is the process of preparing chatbots and LLMs with relevant information or data to enhance their performance and accuracy in responding to academic students' queries, textual productions and interactions. In sync, Go and Sundar (2019) suggest that academic literacy facilitators can influence disciplines' psychological, behavioral, and attitudinal outcomes based on the types of data, instructions, and algorithmic interactions used to prime chatbots for scholarly interactions.

Stressing the pedagogical possibilities of academic literacy facilitators and educators who prime their own chatbots to develop novice scholars' competencies, Ojha (2021) metaphorically suggests that students routinely engage in an algorithmic aspect of computational thinking when addressing textual or data-based matters, particularly within social science disciplines. In the realm of humanities, students regularly analyze multimodal texts, statistics and visuals, systematically assess them and convey their interpretations through writing and alternative forms of knowledge representation. Therefore, Ojha's (2021) concept of knowledge construction as internal algorithmic cognition is relevant for academic literacies facilitators. The reasoning implies that literacies involve algorithmic cognitive processes intertwined with written and diverse records, texts and disciplinary genres.

GenAI and Shifting Roles of Academic Literacies Facilitators

Similar to the revolutionary effects of the Internet during its initial phase, GenAI is transforming and expanding the roles of academic literacy facilitation through applications of intelligent tutoring systems and primed chatbots, leading to permanent alterations in how the curriculum is organized to familiarize students with disciplinary knowledge. In the academic literacy landscape, emerging technologies such as intelligent tutoring systems and primed chatbots present pedagogical benefits which demand that literacy facilitators receive training to transform their methods to operate effectively in novel learning environments, including chatbots and the metaverse. This paradigm shift from traditional classroom settings to meta spaces equally requires academic literacies facilitators in higher education to actively contribute to the transformation of academic text production and interpretation.

Chatbot and Metaverse Domains	Affiliated Academic Literacies
Simulated Professional Environments	• Digital communication literacy. • Critical thinking literacy.
Intelligent Tutoring Systems	• Adaptability skills. • Autonomous learning. • Questioning skills.
Immersive Instruction	• Navigation literacies. • Interactive skills.
Audio Processing	• Sound editing literacies. • Audio recording skills.
Metaverse	• Digital spatial literacies. • Digital identity literacy.

Academic literacies facilitators play a pivotal role in facilitating the transformation and maintenance of essential functions in literacies, as delineated in Ontology 1.

In the realm of chatbots and metaverses, it is imperative to literacy facilitators to develop new modes and mediums to strengthen students' interaction with and presentation of computational data in higher education disciplines. This transformation in curriculum and instructional design, which stresses algorithmic and critical analysis on the students' part, exposes the metamorphosing nature of literacies within chatbots and the metaverse, much as previous literacies have adapted and evolved throughout African and global histories. At the same time existing literacies are evolving, with traditional modes being adapted and improved by incorporating new AI tools and technologies. In this pedagogic sphere, the transformation of literacy facilitation reflects the ongoing evolution of pedagogic technologies and knowledge construction in higher education's ever-changing digital frontier.

Ontology 2: Interplays of chatbot and metaverse domains with academic literacies.

Academic Literacies Facilitators Paving the Way With GenAI

Currently, there are academic literacies facilitators worldwide who are actively integrating GenAI technologies into their instructional practices to enhance the knowledge, abilities, and skills of novice scholars across disciplines. For instance, Irfan, Murray and Ali's (2023) study provides an example of how ChatGPT is applied to bolster students' journalistic literacies, fostering critical thinking and writing abilities. In this particular project, students' critical thinking was evaluated by way of a pre-test without ChatGPT support and a post-test involving ChatGPT interactions. Irfan et al. (2023) found that GenAI significantly enhanced students' critical reasoning and journalistic writing literacies subsequent to the use of ChatGPT.

Participants in the Irfan et al. (2023) study report that ChatGPT aided their generation of fresh ideas, saved time during research and improved their writing. Moreover, ChatGPT prompted critical dialogues and interactive brainstorming in the learning process (Irfan et al., 2023). The findings of the aforementioned analysis indicate integrating scholars' learning in the metaverse, with the support of ChatGPT into disciplines such as journalism can advance their acquisition of academic literacies. Moreover, in disciplinary domains ChatGPT's pedagogic capacities extend across literacies and modes, as illustrated in Ontology 2.

Similar to the transformative impact of the Internet in its early stages, GenAI is revolutionizing literacy facilitation through intelligent tutoring systems and primed chatbots. This integration is leading to fundamental shifts in instructional methodologies around academic literacies, particularly in familiarizing students with disciplinary subjects. Within the realm of academic literacy, emerging technologies like intelligent tutoring systems and primed chatbots offer pedagogical advantages, necessitating literacy facilitators to adapt to new roles in novel educational settings, including chatbots and the metaverse. The shift from conventional classrooms to developing meta spaces poses a dilemma for academic literacy facilitators in higher education as they strive to play an active role in progressing academic text creation and comprehension. That is, academic literacies facilitators play a crucial role in fostering the transformation and sustainability of essential literacy functions by way of emerging GenAI technologies and pedagogic ecospheres.

Drawing from Sample's (2020) research, which explores the applications of augmented and virtual realities in information literacy instruction, particularly aiming to alleviate academic anxiety among non-English speaking scholars from Global South backgrounds, it becomes evident that GenAI technologies hold promise in reducing reading anxiety through immersive learning. According to Sample, virtual and augmented learning ecologies enhance knowledge accessibility and mitigate intimidation sometimes experienced in actual library settings. Furthermore, Sample (2020) suggests that augmented and virtual realities promote active learning by immersing scholars in disciplinary epistemes, fostering authentic literacies in information systems, and augmented environments.

The implications of Sample's study highlight how augmented realities, which complement traditional instruction, and virtual realities fully integrate into the metaverse, thereby creating new disciplinary domains of interaction for appropriately primed literacy chatbots; these reach beyond conventional textbooks and e-text interactions. Therefore, new academic literacy facilitators' roles involve integrating the priming capacities of Large Language Models with virtual and augmented environments to enhance students' academic literacy development. This integration offers immersive experiences that promote a deeper understanding and engagement with disciplinary subjects and literacies.

Transforming Argumentation Logic and Fallacies Through GenAI

The methods by which established argumentation fallacies and logic are preserved and rendered accessible to inexperienced disciplinary scholars are transforming due to the advancing GenAI ontology within which academic literacies facilitators operate. In this context, argumentation refers to generation of new knowledge through analysis of significant claims and counterarguments in academic disciplines (Eybers, 2021; Eybers & Paulet, 2022). Before the emergence of GenAI and the Internet, literacy instructors encountered challenges in teaching novice disciplinary members and writers how to reason logically, recognise fallacies and align with disciplinary epistemologies.

Due to valid concerns surrounding plagiarism and dishonesty among African scribes and scholars date back in time, and in the current era, GenAI has altered textual production by introducing new modes through which inexperienced students may inadvertently overlook fallacies and logic, which are crucial for understanding how senior disciplinary members argue with integrity and ethics. Consequently, contemporary academic literacies facilitators' new roles include instilling in students an awareness of logic and fallacies that are acceptable within disciplines, particularly through the utilization of GenAI tools.

The impact of GenAI logic and fallacies on the production of original academic literacies is significant. In the pre-Internet era, plagiarism involved borrowing ideas from experts in hard copy texts without citation. With the Internet, students gained easy access to vast quantities of data that could readily be copied and pasted into their own work, leading to plagiarism. In the GenAI age plagiarism has evolved. Unethical academic writing now involves generating academic genres, such as reports, essays, literature reviews, and analytical texts, without formal referencing. Hence, academic literacy facilitators are leading the way in cultivating students referencing, citational and original text generation through GenAI platforms. These evolving roles include introducing students to the ethical use of emerging technologies and assisting novice disciplinary members in mastering research literacies and generating original academic texts in the GenAI era.

To effectively cultivate students as disciplinary knowers and communicators, academic literacy facilitators require futuristic methodologies. The acceleration of knowledge production, exemplified by the integration of GenAI tools among disciplinary staff and students, reveals the significance of this transformation. Furthermore, the rapid evolution of the Internet, including the meta sphere and advancements in chatbots, demand a shift in academic literacy facilitators' argumentation methods from inductive to deductive modes.

To effectively adapt to digital learning environments and enhance students' capacity to critically engage with disciplinary content, from a knowledge production perspective, previous technologies necessitated that scholars induce knowledge through the accumulation of empirical data and theory in academic texts. This argumentative process mirrors grounded theory, wherein novice scholars construct knowledge by uncovering recurring themes, categories, and concepts during analysis. However, GenAI has the potential to disrupt inductive epistemological traditions and transform the ways scholars engage through deductive cognitive and written literacies.

Deductive reasoning occurs when academic writers begin with a broad premise and then derive conclusions or predictions from it. In this context, a premise serves as the foundation for an argument, theory or claim. According to Johnson-Laird (2010), deductive reasoning requires scholars' cognitive, logical inferences which are a fundamental aspect of constructing knowledge in disciplines. Computational, algorithmic literacies play a significant role in scholars' deductive processes since they enable us to analyze and manipulate data more fluidly to arrive at logical conclusions. In line with the perspective presented in this chapter, it can be metaphorically suggested that when students interact with Large Language Models such as ChatGPT to develop disciplinary understanding, they engage in deductive logic.

Similar to experienced researchers who work with big data to draw conclusions, GenAI empowers novice students to access vast amounts of information across genres to generate new knowledge while engaging in deductive argumentation. GenAI Chatbots are capable of being primed to incorporate diverse literacies including dialogues, prose, emails, narratives, summaries, visual mind-maps, essays, literature reviews and more. As such, students' literacies can be developed when they employ deductive reasoning to argue, specifically through interactions with GenAI augmented texts and ecosystems.

By utilizing GenAI prompted texts to engage with disciplinary premises and articulate original, logical reasoning and conclusions, students can actively employ deductive reasoning. The matter of adopting or combining deductive and inductive argumentation methodologies is vital for academic literacy curriculum developers, especially those working with Large Language Models that shape how students interact with knowledge and reproduce it through written texts.

Situating Informal Logic, Fallacies in a GenAI Ontology

Considering how students interact with GenAI texts and data as a deductive process is distinct from a perspective that sees their actions as shortcuts, intentional plagiarism or cheating. While this chapter does not endorse novice scholars' utilization of experts' data and insights without the literacy of citing, shifting interpretive paradigms of novice scholars' academic writing toward deductive reasoning may increase understanding of students' plagiarism and possibly failure rates resulting from this teaching and learning hurdle. In this light, the thesis of this chapter holds that novice scholars need to be introduced to disciplines' argumentation norms, including informal logic and fallacies early in the academic year. Within this paradigm, informal logic comprises negotiated and acceptable strategies for arguing and building knowledge. Fallacies, inversely, include ideas that justify plagiarism, are unacceptable and un-negotiated in scholarly communities of practice.

This chapter advocates for a deductive academic literacy developmental approach to solidify novice scholars' awareness of logic and fallacies, which can help reduce plagiarism and promote the creation of original knowledge. By integrating computational and algorithmic literacies into teaching and learning through GenAI, educators can enhance students' skills in navigating deductive reasoning processes, identify logical fallacies, and produce original texts. This holistic method can lead to fostering critical thinking skills and equipping students with the literacies necessary to engage meaningfully with disciplinary content and contribute critically to their fields of study.

To cultivate novice academic literacy students as computational thinkers aware of disciplines' informal logic and fallacies, this chapter introduces an argumentation ontology. Educators can modify the ontology to align with their fields of instruction. The GenAI argumentation ontology identifies key logical principles and fallacies impacting students' writing, supported by Large Language Models. Additionally, the argumentation ontology articulates three methodological pathways for integrating logic and fallacies into the development of novice scholars as critical, original readers and writers. This GenAI argumentation ontology is intended to aid academic literacies facilitators' critical reflection on how they introduce novice scholars to ethical textual production in higher education. Consequently, the ontology illustrates literacies facilitators' deficits in understanding various factors shaping novice disciplinary thinkers' navigation of Large Language Models aid in representing their understandings of disciplinary fields and genres.

Ontology 3: Argumentation logic, fallacies and teaching standards for GenAI.

As asserted above, GenAI is transforming the landscape of learning and teaching much like the advent of writing in ancient Ethiopia and Egypt, typewriters, and the Internet. Despite these changes, ancient principles of textual production, including argumentation logic and fallacies around recording knowledge in texts persist. In the present, researchers and authors still must think deductively, computationally to evaluate data sources while honing skills in stimulating new knowledge. Contemporary academic literacy facilitators equally bear responsibilities of equipping new university entrants with the tools to leverage GenAI technologies ethically, safeguarding their critical thinking, reading, and writing abilities. Accordingly with newly emerging GenAI instructional methods, there is a need for facilitators to recognize that students are not only exposed to vast archives of knowledge but also engage in valuable dialogic exchanges facilitated by chatbots within digital domains and the meta sphere.

In recent years, chatbots have gained popularity in academia, with platforms like Google's Gemini, Bing's chat application, Microsoft's CoPilot and ChatGPT revolutionizing how students brainstorm, create mind maps, draft and brainstorm academic texts within chatbots. Previously, students relied on inducing knowledge through source combination and genre design. Currently, with the emergence of Large Language Models, students are able to deductively access knowledge in the form of completed academic texts, including citation conventions. This access highlights the importance of cultivating deductive reasoning in academic disciplines, since literacies facilitators and evaluators need to be aware of the reality that novice scholars now possess capabilities that were previously unavailable to understand academic genres, despite potential logical, accuracy and stylistic discrepancies - with GenAI. Evidently, innovative teaching methods are crucial for guiding novice scholars in critical thinking, reasoning and original academic literature production with the support of GenAI.

To advance the academic pursuit of knowledge generation in the GenAI age, academic literacy facilitators can employ multiple strategies to ensure students think critically and do not attempt to replace computation with technology in the meta sphere and Internet domains. Similarly, methods exist to increase novice scholars' awareness of ethics governing original writing and fallacies that can lead to plagiarism and cheating. These methodologies will now be detailed.

Novice scholars require training in the informal logic and fallacies that are common to academic literacies and higher education. Such training is especially crucial since present-day novice scholars have access to educational tools that very recently were not available in higher education. Research shows that logic is closely tied to academic literacy, as stressed by scholars such as Macagno and Rapanta (2019). These researchers emphasize how argumentative structures in various genres, interactions with audiences and the use of citations, quotes and references demonstrate the logic of academic writing.

Academic literacy facilitators can devise formative and summative tasks that utilize GenAI to scaffold students' argument structuring by leveraging computational and algorithmic thinking. This approach can entail including Large Language Models in students' brainstorming, data analysis and integration of disciplinary premises into their original writing. The proposed method stresses computational and algorithmic thinking to develop students' skill to critically analyze and construct coherent arguments, academic texts in digital ecospheres.

Involving students in peer reviews and collaborative dialogues, akin to practices among senior scholars, facilitates the identification of originality, plagiarism, fallacies and critical thinking within the meta sphere and through chatbots. GenAI can be harnessed by providing aiding students' constructive feedback to each other, thereby developing their inferential and analytical thinking skills by critiquing each other's texts (Cho & Cho, 2010). Additionally, literacy facilitators can foster scholars' deductive logic by teaching them to offer constructive feedback rooted in disciplinary data. In this process, knowledge is deduced, literacy facilitators aid students in accessing each other's original writing, engaging in dialogic interactions through a computational and algorithmic curriculum.

Ultimately, when facilitators scaffold academic literacies with a foundation in logic and fallacies, students' reviews of each other's texts are grounded in disciplinary ethics. Ontology 4 provides a structured framework for implementing this approach to ensure alignment between disciplinary teaching and learning objectives with methods of cultivating students' inferential and analytical literacies.

For academic literacy facilitators working within generic modules, integrating interpretive and evaluative thinking alongside applications of disciplinary informal logic and fallacies, including deductive reasoning, poses a challenge in achieving smooth cohesion. As such, this chapter advocates for incorporating trans-disciplinarity into generic literacy modules using artificial intelligence capabilities. An effective method involves developing literacy curricula tailored to specific academic disciplines by leveraging LLMs like ChatGPT. This deductive approach requires aligning the literacies curriculum with the learning objectives of disciplines by accessing mainstream curricula, genres for communicating knowledge, theories and concepts when priming chatbots that interact with students' original writing and argumentation generation (see Ontology 4). This method encourages students to engage in interpretive and algorithmic thinking, enabling them to evaluate and analyze diverse data sources in their disciplines.

Ontology 4: Deductive logic for writing with GenAI

CONCLUSION

The criticality of academic literacies in higher education disciplines cannot be overstated, as they provide epistemological access to powerful information, data and enable novice scholars to participate in intellectual discourses. Equally important is the agency of global academic literacy facilitators in cultivating knowledge in multiple levels throughout higher education institutions. However, as in ancient times in Ethiopia and Kemet (Egypt), when institutionalized knowledge was limited to a select few clusters of individuals - academic literacy remains elusive for many in African and developed nations today. Nonetheless, historically, elite scribes and priests in Africa mentored scholars, imparting knowledge and literacies inherited from their ancestors. In a historical continuum, the current chapter holds that the legacy of exclusivity continues to shape how academic literacy facilitators introduce students to ethical premises and academic writing, deductive logic and GenAI technologies. To reiterate, academic literacy facilitators possess agency to design inclusive disciplinary ecosystems through GenAI.

The transformative powers of GenAI are reshaping scholarly engagement, promoting new debates surrounding original textual production, underlying causes of plagiarism and the role of senior scholars in developing novice students' capabilities in contributing new knowledge to fields of practice. Academic literacy facilitators, in this context, play a pivotal role in guiding students to master disciplinary epistemologies and genres by incorporating AI tools into the curriculum. The critical functions of computational and algorithmic thinking cannot be overlooked in the contemporary digital age. Educators in higher education need to master the capabilities of new GenAI tools to develop students' communication proficiency in their academic disciplines through priming their own chatbots. Despite these advantages, resistance to technological changes in faculties poses a challenge. Yet, by empowering faculties, educators and academic literacy facilitators with GenAI teaching skills and addressing their epistemic and ethical concerns, higher education can facilitate an unavoidable transformation of knowledge production.

REFERENCES

Ahuja, A. S., Polascik, B. W., Doddapaneni, D., Byrnes, E. S., & Sridhar, J. (2023). The Digital Metaverse: Applications in Artificial Intelligence, Medical Education, and Integrative Health. *Integrative Medicine Research*, *12*(1), 1–19. doi:10.1016/j.imr.2022.100917 PMID:36691642

Amen, R. (2010). *The Writing System of Medu Neter*. The Institute of Kemetic Philology.

Ballantyne, D., Livingston, C., & Garraway, J. (2021). Cultural-historical activity theory as a framework for exploring pre-service teachers' use of an intelligent tutoring system for English language proficiency. *Africa Education Review*, *18*(3-4), 1–24. doi:10.1080/18146627.2022.2150245

Bates, T., Cobo, C., Mariño, O., & Wheeler, S. (2020). Can artificial intelligence transform higher education? *International Journal of Educational Technology in Higher Education, 17*(42), 1–12.

Brannon, L., Courtney, J. P., Urbanski, C. P., Woodward, S. V., Reynolds, J. M., Iannone, A. E., Haag, K. D., Mach, K., Manship, L. A., & Kendrick, M. (2008). The Five-Paragraph Essay and the Deficit Model of Education. *English Journal, 98*(2), 16–21. doi:10.58680/ej20086823

Chan, C. K. Y. (2023). A comprehensive AI policy education framework for university teaching and learning. *International Journal of Educational Technology in Higher Education, 20*(38), 1–25. doi:10.1186/s41239-023-00408-3

Cho, Y. H., & Cho, K. (2011). Peer reviewers learn from giving comments. *Instructional Science, 39*(5), 629–643. doi:10.1007/s11251-010-9146-1

Cope, B., & Kalantzis, M. (Eds.). (2015). *Pedagogy of Multiliteracies: Learning by Design*. Palgrave Macmillan.

De Silva, D., & El-Ayoubi, M. (2023, June 20). Three ways to leverage ChatGPT and other generative AI in research: A guide to three key uses of generative AI tools like ChatGPT in developing and enhancing research. *Times Higher Education*. https://www.timeshighereducation.com/campus/three-ways-leverage-chatgpt-and-other-generative-ai-research

De Souza, M. G., Won, M., Treagust, D., & Serrano, A. (2024). Visualising relativity: Assessing high school students' understanding of complex physics concepts through AI-generated images. *Physics Education, 59*(2), 025018. doi:10.1088/1361-6552/ad1e71

Escotet, M. Á. (2023). The optimistic future of Artificial Intelligence in higher education. *Prospects*, 1–10. doi:10.1007/s11125-023-09642-z

Eybers, O. (2021). *A realist approach towards student application of agency, culture, and social structures in the demonstration of competency in argumentative writing* (PhD thesis). University of Pretoria. doi:10.13140/RG.2.2.30245.22242

Eybers, O., & Paulet, E. (2022). Sociocultural theory for academic literacy research involving argumentation in institutions of higher learning. *South African Journal of Higher Education, 36*(2), 115–132. doi:10.20853/36-2-4683

Gao, C., Lan, X., Lu, Z., Mao, J., Piao, J., Wang, H., Jin, D., & Li, Y. (2023). S3: Social-network simulation system with large language model-empowered agents. arXiv preprint arXiv:2307.14984.

Gao, S., Takanobu, R., Bosselut, A., & Huang, M. (2022). End-to-end task-oriented dialog modeling with semi-structured knowledge management. *IEEE/ACM Transactions on Audio, Speech, and Language Processing*, *30*, 2173–2187. Advance online publication. doi:10.1109/TASLP.2022.3153255

Go, E., & Sundar, S. S. (2019). Humanizing chatbots: The effects of visual, identity, and conversational cues on humanness perceptions. *Computers in Human Behavior*, *97*, 304–316. doi:10.1016/j.chb.2019.01.020

Goodier, C., & Parkinson, J. (2005). Discipline-based academic literacy in two contexts. *Journal for Language Teaching* = Ijenali Yekufundzisa Lulwimi =. *Tydskrif vir Taalonderrig*, *39*(1), 66–79. doi:10.4314/jlt.v39i1.6050

Haque, Islam, & Mikalef. (2023). Explainable Artificial Intelligence (XAI) from a user perspective: A synthesis of prior literature and problematizing avenues for future research. *Technological Forecasting and Social Change*, 186(Part A), 1-19. doi:10.1016/j.techfore.2022.122120

Harb, M., & Taha Thomure, H. (2020). Connecting literacy to curriculum ideologies. *Curriculum Perspectives*, *40*(1), 27–33. doi:10.1007/s41297-020-00099-0

Heaven, W. D. (2023, April 6). ChatGPT is going to change education, not destroy it. *MIT Technology Review*. https://www.technologyreview.com/2023/04/06/1071059/chatgpt-change-not-destroy-education-openai/

Islam, M., Sarker, M., & Islam, M. (2021). Promoting student-centred blended learning in higher education: *A model. E-Learning and Digital Media*, *19*(1), 36–54. doi:10.1177/20427530211027721

Johnson-Laird, P. (2010). Deductive reasoning. *Wiley Interdisciplinary Reviews: Cognitive Science*, *1*(1), 8–17. doi:10.1002/wcs.20 PMID:26272833

Katz, S., Albacete, P., Chounta, I. A., Jordan, P., McLaren, B. M., & Zapata-Rivera, D. (2021). Linking Dialogue with Student Modelling to Create an Adaptive Tutoring System for Conceptual Physics. *International Journal of Artificial Intelligence in Education*, *31*(3), 397–445. doi:10.1007/s40593-020-00226-y

Le, H., & Jia, J. (2022). Design and implementation of an intelligent tutoring system in the view of learner autonomy. *Interactive Technology and Smart Education*, *19*(4), 510–525. doi:10.1108/ITSE-12-2021-0210

Learning, E. L. M. (2022). Adaptive Learning vs. Personalized Learning: A Guide to Both. *ELM Learning*. https://elmlearning.com/blog/personalized-learning-vs-adaptive-learning/

Lebuso, S. (2023, February 2). How SA universities plan to deal with ChatGPT. Accreditation. *News24*. https://www.news24.com/citypress/news/how-sa-universities-plan-to-deal-with-chatgpt-20230202

Li, H. F. (2023). Effects of a ChatGPT-based flipped learning guiding approach on learners' courseware project performances and perceptions. *Australasian Journal of Educational Technology*, *39*(5), 40–58. doi:10.14742/ajet.8923

Macagno, F., & Rapanta, C. (2020). *The Logic of Academic Writing*. Wessex Press.

McMurtrie, B. (2018). How artificial intelligence is changing teaching. *The Chronicle of Higher Education*. Retrieved from https://www.chronicle.com/article/How-ArtificialIntelligence-Is/244231

Mousavinasab, E., Zarifsanaiey, N., & Niakan Kalhori, R., S., Rakhshan, M., Keikha, L., & Ghazi Saeedi, M. (. (2021). Intelligent tutoring systems: A systematic review of characteristics, applications, and evaluation methods. *Interactive Learning Environments*, *29*(1), 142–163. doi:10.1080/10494820.2018.1558257

Ojha, S. S. (2021). Computational Thinking and Social Science Education. *Academia Letters*, *1-5*. Advance online publication. doi:10.20935/AL1577

Qasrawi, R., & BeniAndelrahman, A. (2020). The higher and lower-order thinking skills (HOTS and LOTS) in Unlock English textbooks (1st and 2nd editions) based on Bloom's Taxonomy: An analysis study. International Online Journal of Education and Teaching, 7(3), 744–758.

Qi, Q., & Zhao, C. G. (2023). Discoursal scholarly identity in research writing. *Journal of Second Language Writing*, *62*, 1–12. doi:10.1016/j.jslw.2023.101052

Regulski, I. (2016). The Origins and Early Development of Writing in Egypt. In The Oxford Handbook of Topics in Archaeology (pp. 1-32). Oxford University Press. doi:10.1093/oxfordhb/9780199935413.013.61

Sample, A. (2020). Using Augmented and Virtual Reality in Information Literacy Instruction to Reduce Library Anxiety in Non-Traditional and International Students. *Information Technology and Libraries*, *39*(1), 1–33. doi:10.6017/ital.v39i1.11723

Schoenfeld, A. H., diSessa, A. A., Graesser, A. C., Benson, L. C., English, L. D., & Duschl, R. A. (2020). Computational thinking is more about thinking than computing. *Journal for STEM Education Research*, *3*(1), 1–18. doi:10.1007/s41979-020-00030-2 PMID:32838129

Seroto, J. (2011). Indigenous education during the pre-colonial period in southern Africa. *Indilinga*, *10*(1), 77–88.

Street, B. (2003). What's "new" in New Literacy Studies? Critical approaches to literacy in theory and practice. *Current Issues in Comparative Education*, *5*(2), 77–91.

Tegegne, H. M. (2015). Recordmaking, Recordkeeping and Landholding – Chanceries and Archives in Ethiopia (1700–1974). *History in Africa*, *42*, 433–461. doi:10.1017/hia.2014.23

Thaheem, S. K., Zainol Abidin, M. J., Mirza, Q., & Pathan, H. U. (2022). Online teaching benefits and challenges during pandemic COVID-19: A comparative study of Pakistan and Indonesia. *Asian Education and Development Studies*, *11*(2), 311–323. doi:10.1108/AEDS-08-2020-0189

Tianbo, Z. (2012). *The Internet of Things Promoting Higher Education Revolution*. In *2012 Fourth International Conference on Multimedia Information Networking and Security* (pp. 790-793). 10.1109/MINES.2012.231

Vemula, S. (2022). *Human-Centered Explainable Artificial Intelligence for Anomaly Detection in Quality Inspection: A Collaborative Approach to Bridge the Gap between Humans and AI* (Doctoral dissertation, University of the Incarnate Word). ProQuest Dissertations Publishing. (Accession No. 29069196)

Watty, K., McKay, J., & Ngo, L. (2016). Innovators or inhibitors? Accounting faculty resistance to new educational technologies in higher education. *Journal of Accounting Education*, *36*, 1–15. doi:10.1016/j.jaccedu.2016.03.003

Zhu, Y., Wang, Z., Chen, C., & Dong, D. (2022). Rule-Based Reinforcement Learning for Efficient Robot Navigation With Space Reduction. *IEEE/ASME Transactions on Mechatronics*, *27*(2), 846–857. doi:10.1109/TMECH.2021.3072675

Compilation of References

Abedjan, Z. (2022). Enabling data-centric AI through data quality management and data literacy. *It - Information Technology, 64*(1–2), 67–70. doi:10.1515/itit-2021-0048

Adams, T. E., Ellis, C., & Jones, S. H. (2017). Autoethnography. The International Encyclopedia of Communication Research Methods, 1-11.

Adamson, D., Ashe, C., Jang, H., Yaron, D., & Rosé, C. P. (2014). Intensification of group knowledge exchange with academically productive talk agents. In *Proceedings of the 10th International Conference on Computer Supported Collaborative Learning* (pp. 10-17). Academic Press.

Adams, T. E., Jones, S. L. H., & Ellis, C. (2015). *Autoethnography. Understanding qualitative research*. Oxford University Press.

Ahuja, A. S., Polascik, B. W., Doddapaneni, D., Byrnes, E. S., & Sridhar, J. (2023). The Digital Metaverse: Applications in Artificial Intelligence, Medical Education, and Integrative Health. *Integrative Medicine Research*, *12*(1), 1–19. doi:10.1016/j.imr.2022.100917 PMID:36691642

Aldoseri, A., Al-Khalifa, K. N., & Hamouda, A. M. (2023). Re-Thinking Data Strategy and Integration for Artificial Intelligence: Concepts, Opportunities, and Challenges. *Applied Sciences (Basel, Switzerland)*, *13*(12), 7082. doi:10.3390/app13127082

Aleedy, M., Atwell, E., & Meshoul, S. (2022). Using AI chatbots in education: recent advances challenges and use case. In Algorithms for intelligent systems (pp. 661–675). doi:10.1007/978-981-19-1653-3_50

Alex Press. (2021). Microworkers are disempowered to a degree previously unseen in capitalist history. *Jacobin, Science and Technology, 22*.

Alhawiti, K. M. (2014). Natural language processing and its use in education. *International Journal of Advanced Computer Science and Applications*, 5(12), 72–76.

Alison & Eltham. (2001). *Creativity in Crisis: Rebooting Australia's Arts and Entertainment Sector After COVID*. The Centre for Future Work at the Australia Institute. https://apo.org.au/sites/default/files/resource-files/2021-07/apo-nid313299.pdf

Alkaissi, H., & McFarlane, S. I. (2023). *Artificial Hallucinations in ChatGPT: Implications in Scientific Writing*. doi:10.7759/cureus.35179

Allington, R. L., & Cunningham, P. M. (2002). *Schools that work: Where all children read and write*. Allyn & Bacon.

Almusaed, A., Almssad, A., Yitmen, İ., & Homod, R. Z. (2023). Enhancing Student Engagement: Harnessing "AIED"'s Power in Hybrid Education—A Review analysis. *Education Sciences*, *13*(7), 632. doi:10.3390/educsci13070632

Amen, R. (2010). *The Writing System of Medu Neter*. The Institute of Kemetic Philology.

American Library Association. (1989). ALA Presidential Committee on Information Literacy: Final Report, released January 10, 1989. https://www.ala.org/acrl/publications/whitepapers/presidential

Anders, B. A. (2024, March 4). The AI Literacy Imperative: Empowering Instructors & Students. TeachOnline.CA. Contact North/Contact Nord. https://bit.ly/4a2hzqO

Anis, S., & French, J. A. (2023). Efficient, Explicatory, and Equitable: Why Qualitative Researchers Should Embrace AI, but Cautiously. *Business & Society*, *62*(6), 1139–1144. doi:10.1177/00076503231163286

Annamalai, N., Eltahir, M. E., Zyoud, S. H., Soundrarajan, D., Zakarneh, B., & Alsalhi, N. R. (2023). Exploring English language learning via Chabot: A case study from a self-determination theory perspective. Computers & Education. *Artificial Intelligence*, *5*, 100148. doi:10.1016/j.caeai.2023.100148

Anthony, L. (2023). *AntConc (Version 4.2.4)* [Computer Software]. Waseda University. Available from https://www.laurenceanthony.net/software

Anunobi, C., & Udem, O. K. (2014). Information literacy competencies: A conceptual analysis. *Journal of Applied Information Science and Technology*, *7*(2), 64–80.

Apartheid Education - New Learning online. (n.d.). https://newlearningonline.com/new-learning/chapter-5/supproting-materials/apartheid-education

Applebee, A. N., & Langer, J. A. (2006). *The state of writing instruction in America's schools: What existing data tell us*. Center on English Learning and Achievement.

Applebee, A. N., & Langer, J. A. (2009). EJ extra: What is happening in the teaching of writing? *English Journal*, *98*(5), 18–28. doi:10.58680/ej20097117

Aradau, C. (2023). Algorithmic Security and Conflict in a Datafied World. In C. Bjola & M. Kornprobst (Eds.), *Digital International Relations: Technology, Agency and Order* (1st ed.). Routledge. doi:10.4324/9781003437963-11

Association of College & Research Libraries. (2000). Information Literacy Competency Standards for Higher Education. https://alair.ala.org/ handle/11213/7668

Astle, J. (2018). Do schools really 'kill creativity'? *RSA Journal*. https://www.thersa.org/blog/2018/04/do-schools-kill-creativity

Atenas, J., Havemann, L., & Timmermann, C. (2020). Critical literacies for a datafied society: Academic development and curriculum design in higher education. *Research in Learning Technology, 28*(0). Advance online publication. doi:10.25304/rlt.v28.2468

Attali, Y. (2013). Validity and reliability of automated essay scoring. In *Handbook of automated essay evaluation* (pp. 181–198). Routledge.

Attali, Y., & Burstein, J. (2006). Automated essay scoring with e-rater®; V. 2. *The Journal of Technology, Learning, and Assessment, 4*(3).

Azamfirei, R., Kudchadkar, S. R., & Fackler, J. (2023). Large language models and the perils of their hallucinations. *Critical Care, 27*(1), 1–2. doi:10.1186/s13054-023-04393-x PMID:36945051

Bacha, N. N. (2002). Developing Learners' Academic Writing Skills in Higher Education: A Study for *Educational Reform. Language and Education, 16*(3), 161–177. doi:10.1080/09500780208666826

Badenhorst, C. (2018). Citation practices of postgraduate students writing literature reviews. *London Review of Education, 16*(1), 121–135. doi:10.18546/LRE.16.1.11

Bader, M. W. (2016). Reign of the Algorithms: How 'artificial intelligence' is threatening our freedom. *Herrschaft der Algorithmen, 8*(22). https://stiftung-media.de/web/wp-content/uploads/2016/06/Herrschaft_der_Algorithmen_V08_22_06_16_EN-mb04.pdf

Baffour, P. (2023, January 25). AI can strengthen student writing, not weaken it. *Language Magazine Improving Literacy & Communication*. https://www.languagemagazine.com/2023/01/25/ai-can-strengthen-student-writing-not-weaken-it/

Baker, S., Bangeni, B., Burke, R., & Hunma, A. (2019). The invisibility of academic reading as social practice and its implications for equity in higher education: A scoping study. *Higher Education Research & Development, 38*(1), 142–156. doi:10.1080/07294360.2018.1540554

Ballantyne, D., Livingston, C., & Garraway, J. (2021). Cultural-historical activity theory as a framework for exploring pre-service teachers' use of an intelligent tutoring system for English language proficiency. *Africa Education Review, 18*(3-4), 1–24. doi:10.1080/18146627.2022.2150245

Bandura, A. (1971). *Social learning theory*. General Learning Press.

Baron, L. J. (1985). Television Literacy Curriculum in Action: A long-term study. *Journal of Educational Television, 11*(1), 49–55. doi:10.1080/0260741850110107

Bass, D. (2023). Microsoft Invests $10 Billion in ChatGPT Maker OpenAI. Retrieved from Bloomberg: https://www. bloomberg. com/news/articles/2023-01-23/microsoft-makes-multibillion-dollar-investment-in-openai# xj4y7vzkg

Bates, T., Cobo, C., Mariño, O., & Wheeler, S. (2020). Can artificial intelligence transform higher education? *International Journal of Educational Technology in Higher Education, 17*(42), 42. Advance online publication. doi:10.1186/s41239-020-00218-x

Bela, V., & Peng, D. (2024, January 5). China unveils new artificial intelligence guidelines for scientists and bans use in funding applications. *South China Morning Post*. https://www.scmp.com/news/china/science/article/3206531/china-unveils-new-artificial-intelligence-guidelines-scientists-and-bans-use-funding-applications

Bengt-Åke, L. (2008). Innovation and creativity - the crisis as opportunity for change. https://www.researchgate.net/publication/237833821_Innovation_and_creativity_-_the_crisis_as_opportunity_for_change

Benharrak, K., Zindulka, T., Lehmann, F., Heuer, H., & Buschek, D. (2023). Writer-defined AI personas for on-demand feedback generation. *arXiv preprint arXiv:2309.10433*.

Benichou, L. (2023). The role of using ChatGPT AI in writing medical scientific articles. *J Stomatol Oral Maxillofac Surg., 124*(5), 101456. doi:10.1016/j.jormas.2023.101456

Benjamin. (2021). Delivering food on bikes: Between machine subordination and autonomy in the algorithmic workplace. In *Augmented Exploitation: Artificial Intelligence, Automation and Work*. Pluto Press.

Bertrand, R. (1940). *An Inquiry into Meaning and Truth*. George Allen and Unwen Ltd. https://archive.org/details/in.ernet.dli.2015.458710

Bertrand, R. (1905). On Denoting. *Mind, 14*(56), 479–493.

Betty, K. (2022). Research shows need for training of staff and students on online learning. https://news.mak.ac.ug/2022/09/research-shows-need-for-training-of-staff-and-students-on-online-learning/

Bhatia, P. (2023). ChatGPT for academic writing: A game changer or a disruptive tool? *Journal of Anaesthesiology, Clinical Pharmacology, 39*(1), 1–2. doi:10.4103/joacp.joacp_84_23 PMID:37250265

Biswas, G., Segedy, J. R., & Bunchongchit, K. (2016). From design to implementation to practice a learning by teaching system: Betty's Brain. *International Journal of Artificial Intelligence in Education, 26*(1), 350–364. doi:10.1007/s40593-015-0057-9

Blalock, A. E., & Akehi, M. (2018). Collaborative autoethnography as a pathway for transformative learning. *Journal of Transformative Education, 16*(2), 89–107. doi:10.1177/1541344617715711

Bob, S., & Wayne, K. (2004). Markov Model of Natural Language. https://www.cs.princeton.edu/courses/archive/spring05/cos126/assignments/markov.html

Bouchrika, I., Harrati, N., Mahfouf, Z., & Gasmallah, N. (2018). Evaluating the Acceptance of e-Learning Systems via Subjective and Objective Data Analysis. In S. Caballé & J. Conesa (Eds.), *Software Data Engineering for Network eLearning Environments: Analytics and Awareness Learning Services* (pp. 199–219). Springer International Publishing. doi:10.1007/978-3-319-68318-8_10

Bozkurt, A. (2023). Unleashing the potential of generative AI, conversational agents and chatbots in educational praxis: A systematic review and bibliometric analysis of GenAI in education. http://hdl.handle.net/20.500.12424/4299873

Brannon, L., Courtney, J. P., Urbanski, C. P., Woodward, S. V., Reynolds, J. M., Iannone, A. E., Haag, K. D., Mach, K., Manship, L. A., & Kendrick, M. (2008). The Five-Paragraph Essay and the Deficit Model of Education. *English Journal*, 98(2), 16–21. doi:10.58680/ej20086823

Branson, S. M. (2023). Chasing a Moving Target: Examining Shifts in Elementary Teachers' Language and Conceptions of Digital Literacy During Professional Learning. Academic Press.

Bretag, T., & Mahmud, S. (2016). A conceptual framework for implementing exemplary academic integrity policy in Australian higher education. In T. Bretag (Ed.), *Handbook of Academic Integrity* (pp. 463–480). Springer. doi:10.1007/978-981-287-098-8_24

Brian, B. (2023). How Hyperautomation and AI in Accounts Payable Can Increase Profits. https://www.kofax.com/learn/blog/how-hyperautomation-and-ai-in-accounts-payable-can-increase-profits

Bringsjord, S., & Ferrucci, D. (1999). *Artificial Intelligence and Literary Creativity: Inside the Mind of Brutus, A Storytelling Machine*. Psychology Press. doi:10.4324/9781410602398

Brown, T., Mann, B., Ryder, N., Subbiah, M., Kaplan, J. D., Dhariwal, P., Neelakantan, A., Shyam, P., Sastry, G., Askell, A., & Agarwal, S. (2020). Language models are few-shot learners. *Advances in Neural Information Processing Systems*, 33, 1877–1901.

Buckingham Shum, S. J., & Luckin, R. (2019). Learning analytics and AI: Politics, pedagogy and practices. *British Journal of Educational Technology*, 50(6), 2785–2793. doi:10.1111/bjet.12880

Buckingham, D. (2004). Children Talking Television: The Making of Television Literacy. Taylor & Francis. https://books.google.co.za/books?id=kKBlAgAAQBAJ

Butterfuss, R., Roscoe, R. D., Allen, L. K., McCarthy, K. S., & McNamara, D. S. (2022). Strategy uptake in writing pal: Adaptive feedback and instruction. *Journal of Educational Computing Research*, 60(3), 696–721. doi:10.1177/07356331211045304

Calle-Arango, L., & Ávila Reyes, N. (2023). Obstacles, facilitators, and needs in doctoral writing: A systematic review. *Studies in Continuing Education*, 45(2), 133–151. doi:10.1080/0158037X.2022.2026315

Carr, N. G. (2010). *The Shallows: What the Internet Is Doing to Our Brains*. W.W. Norton & Co.

Carvalho, L., Martinez-Maldonado, R., Tsai, Y. S., Markauskaite, L., & De Laat, M. (2022). How can we design for learning in an AI world? *Computers and Education: Artificial Intelligence*, 3, 100053. doi:10.1016/j.caeai.2022.100053

Casal-Otero, L., Catala, A., Fernández-Morante, C., Taboada, M., Cebreiro, B., & Barro, S. (2023). AI literacy in K-12: A systematic literature review. *International Journal of STEM Education*, 10(1), 29. doi:10.1186/s40594-023-00418-7

Casey, E. (2023). Pathways to Academic Integrity: Supporting Students through a Community of Practice Approach. *European Conference on Ethics and Integrity in Academia 2023*. https://hiberniacollege.com/news/a-community-of-practice-on-academic-integrity/

Catts, H. W., & Kamhi, A. G. (Eds.). (2005). *The connections between language and reading disabilities*. Psychology Press. doi:10.4324/9781410612052

Centre for Teaching and Learning. (2023a). *Beginning University Survey of Student Engagement: North-West University* [Unpublished report]. University of the Free State.

Centre for Teaching and Learning. (2023b). *South African Survey of Student Engagement: North-West University Institutional Report* [Unpublished report]. University of the Free State.

Chaka, C. (2023). Detecting AI content in responses generated by ChatGPT, YouChat, and Chatsonic: The case of five AI content detection tools. *Journal of Applied Learning and Teaching*, *6*(2). Advance online publication. doi:10.37074/jalt.2023.6.2.12

Chan, B. S. K., Churchill, D., & Chiu, T. K. F. (2017). Digital Literacy Learning in Higher Education Through Digital Storytelling Approach. *Journal of International Education Research*, *13*(1), 1–16. https://files.eric.ed.gov/fulltext/EJ1144564.pdf. doi:10.19030/jier.v13i1.9907

Chan, C. K. Y. (2023). A comprehensive AI policy education framework for university teaching and learning. *International Journal of Educational Technology in Higher Education*, *20*(1), 38. doi:10.1186/s41239-023-00408-3

Chang, H. (2008). *Autoethnography as method*. Left Coast.

Chang, H., Ngunjiri, F., & Hernandez, K. A. C. (2016). *Collaborative autoethnography* (Vol. 8). Routledge. doi:10.4324/9781315432137

Chase, S. (2005). Narrative inquiry. The Sage handbook of qualitative research, 651-679.

Chen, H. (2023). A lexical network approach to second language development. *Humanities & Social Sciences Communications*, *10*(1), 735. doi:10.1057/s41599-023-02151-6

Chen, J., Zhuo, Z., & Lin, J. (2023). Does ChatGPT play a double-edged sword role in the field of higher education? An in-depth exploration of the factors affecting student performance. *Sustainability (Basel)*, *15*(24), 1–18. doi:10.3390/su152416928

Chen, K., Shao, A., Burapacheep, J., & Li, X. (2024). Conversational AI and equity through assessing GPT-3's communication with diverse social groups on contentious topics. *Scientific Reports*, *14*(1561), 1561. Advance online publication. doi:10.1038/s41598-024-51969-w PMID:38238474

Chester, M. V., & Allenby, B. R. (2020). Perspective: The Cyber Frontier and Infrastructure. *IEEE Access: Practical Innovations, Open Solutions*, *8*, 28301–28310. doi:10.1109/ACCESS.2020.2971960

Chi, M. T., Bassok, M., Lewis, M. W., Reimann, P., & Glaser, R. (1989). Self-explanations: How students study and use examples in learning to solve problems. *Cognitive Science*, *13*(2), 145–182.

Chiu, T. K. (2024). Future research recommendations for transforming higher education with generative AI. *Computers and Education: Artificial Intelligence, 6*, 100197. doi:10.1016/j.caeai.2023.100197

Chiu, T. K., Xia, Q., Zhou, X., Chai, C. S., & Cheng, M. (2023). Systematic literature review on opportunities, challenges, and future research recommendations of artificial intelligence in education. *Computers and Education: Artificial Intelligence, 4*, 100118. doi:10.1016/j.caeai.2022.100118

Cho, K., & MacArthur, C. (2010). Student revision with peer and expert reviewing. *Learning and Instruction, 20*(4), 328–338. doi:10.1016/j.learninstruc.2009.08.006

Chomsky, N., Roberts, I., & Watumull, J. (2023, March 8). Noam Chomsky: The False Promise of ChatGPT. *New York Times.* https://www.nytimes.com/2023/03/08/opinion/noam-chomsky-chatgpt-ai.html

Chou, C. Y., Chan, T. W., & Lin, C. J. (2003). Redefining the learning companion: The past, present, and future of educational agents. *Computers & Education, 40*(3), 255–269. doi:10.1016/S0360-1315(02)00130-6

Cho, Y. H., & Cho, K. (2011). Peer reviewers learn from giving comments. *Instructional Science, 39*(5), 629–643. doi:10.1007/s11251-010-9146-1

Ciampa, K., Wolfe, Z. M., & Bronstein, B. (2023). ChatGPT in education: Transforming digital literacy practices. *Journal of Adolescent & Adult Literacy, 67*(3), 186–195. doi:10.1002/jaal.1310

CIPIT. (2023). *The State of AI in Africa Report – 2023.* Strathmore University.

Clandinin, D. J. (2013). Living, telling, and retelling: Processes of narrative inquiry. In *Engaging in Narrative Inquiry* (pp. 9–31). Routledge.

Clandinin, D. J. (Ed.). (2006). *Handbook of narrative inquiry: Mapping a methodology.* Sage Publications.

Clandinin, D. J., & Caine, V. (2013). Narrative inquiry. In *Reviewing qualitative research in the social sciences* (pp. 166–179). Routledge.

Clandinin, D. J., & Connelly, F. M. (2000). *Narrative inquiry: Experience and story in qualitative research.* Jossey-Bass.

Clandinin, D., & Caine, V. (2008). Narrative inquiry. In L. M. Given (Ed.), *The Sage Encyclopedia of Qualitative Research Methods* (pp. 542–545). Sage Publications.

Cobourn, A. B., Brown, J. C., Warga, E., & Louis, L. (2022). Toward Metaliteracy and Transliteracy in the History Classroom: A Case Study Among Underserved Students. *The American Archivist, 85*(2), 587–608. doi:10.17723/2327-9702-85.2.587

Cohen, E. G., & Lotan, R. A. (2014). *Designing groupwork: Strategies for the heterogeneous classroom* (3rd ed.). Teachers College Press.

Cohen, P. A., Kulik, J. A., & Kulik, C. L. C. (1982). Educational outcomes of tutoring: A meta-analysis of findings. *American Educational Research Journal, 19*(2), 237–248. doi:10.3102/00028312019002237

Coiro, J., Knobel, M., Lankshear, C., & Leu, D. J. (2014). Central issues in new literacies and new literacies research. In *Handbook of research on new literacies* (pp. 1–22). Routledge. doi:10.4324/9781410618894-7

Committee on Publication Ethics. (n.d.). Artificial Intelligence and Authorship. https://publicationethics.org/news/artificial-intelligence-and-authorship

Conroy, G. (2023). Scientists used ChatGPT to generate an entire paper from scratch — But is it any good? Nature. *Nature, 619*(7970), 443–444. doi:10.1038/d41586-023-02218-z PMID:37419951

Cook-Sather, A. (2016). Creating brave spaces within and through student-faculty pedagogical partnerships. *Teaching and Learning Together in Higher Education, 1*(18), 1.

Cope, B., & Kalantzis, M. (Eds.). (2015). *Pedagogy of Multiliteracies: Learning by Design.* Palgrave Macmillan.

Coursera. (2023, November 29). *What Is Artificial Intelligence? Definition, Uses, and Types.* Https://Www.Coursera.Org/Articles/What-Is-Artificial-Intelligence

Crabtree, M. (2023). What is AI Literacy? A Comprehensive Guide for Beginners. https://www.datacamp.com/blog/what-is-ai-literacy-a-comprehensive-guide-for-beginners

Crabtree, M. (2023, May). *The Future of Data Literacy: A Fundamental Skill Shaping Society: Uncover the role of data literacy in the 21st century.* Https://Www.Datacamp.Com/Blog/the-Future-of-Data-Literacy-a-Fundamental-Skill-Shaping-Society

Creelman, D. (2023). Embrace generative AI. *HR Future, 5*, 54. doi:10.10520/ejc-om_hrf_v2023_n5_a19

Creely, E., Apps, T., Beckman, K., & McKnight, L. (2023). Chat about ChatGPT. *Literacy Learning, 31*(2), 35–39.

Creswell, J. W., & Poth, C. N. (2018). *Qualitative inquiry and research design: Choosing among five approaches* (4th ed.). Sage.

Cronin, C. (2017). Openness and Praxis: Exploring the Use of Open Educational Practices in Higher Education. *International Review of Research in Open and Distance Learning, 18*(5). Advance online publication. doi:10.19173/irrodl.v18i5.3096

Cronje, J. (2023). Exploring the Role of ChatGPT as a Peer Coach for Developing Research Proposals: Feedback Quality, Prompts, and Student Reflection. *Electronic Journal of e-Learning.* Advance online publication. doi:10.34190/ejel.21.5.3042

Culp, W. C. (2023). Artificial Intelligence and ChatGPT: Bane or boon for academic writing? *The Journal of Education in Perioperative Medicine : JEPM*, *25*(2), E702–E702. doi:10.46374/VolXXV_Issue2_Culp PMID:37377506

Cunningham-Nelson, S. (2024, February 12). A review of chatbots in education: Practical steps forward. QUT ePrints. https://eprints.qut.edu.au/134323/

Dai, Y. (2020). How many ways can we teach data literacy? *IASSIST Quarterly*, *43*(4), 1–11. doi:10.29173/iq963

Dale, H. (1994). Collaborative writing interactions in one ninth-grade classroom. *The Journal of Educational Research*, *87*(6), 334–344. doi:10.1080/00220671.1994.9941264

Davis, A. (2024, January 24). A new collaboration with OpenAI charts the future of AI in higher education. *ASU News*. https://news.asu.edu/20240118-university-news-new-collaboration-openai-charts-future-ai-higher-education

De Maio, C. (2024). Institutional responses to ChatGPT. *Journal of Academic Language and Learning*, *18*(1), T1–T8. https://journal.aall.org.au/index.php/jall/article/view/917

De Silva, D., & El-Ayoubi, M. (2023, June 20). Three ways to leverage ChatGPT and other generative AI in research: A guide to three key uses of generative AI tools like ChatGPT in developing and enhancing research. *Times Higher Education*. https://www.timeshighereducation.com/campus/three-ways-leverage-chatgpt-and-other-generative-ai-research

De Souza, M. G., Won, M., Treagust, D., & Serrano, A. (2024). Visualising relativity: Assessing high school students' understanding of complex physics concepts through AI-generated images. *Physics Education*, *59*(2), 025018. doi:10.1088/1361-6552/ad1e71

Dempere, J., Modugu, K., Hesham, A., & Ramasamy, L. K. (2023). The impact of ChatGPT on higher education. *Frontiers in Education*, *8*, 1206936. Advance online publication. doi:10.3389/feduc.2023.1206936

DentellaV.MurphyE.MarcusG.LeivadaE. (2023) Testing ai performance on less frequent aspects of language reveals insensitivity to underlying meaning. arXiv:2302.12313.

Denzin, N. K. (2014). *Interpretive autoethnography* (2nd ed.). Sage. doi:10.4135/9781506374697

Dergaa, I., Chamari, K., Zmijewski, P., & Ben Saad, H. (2023). From human writing to artificial intelligence generated text: Examining the prospects and potential threats of ChatGPT in academic writing. *Biology of Sport*, *40*(2), 615–622. doi:10.5114/biolsport.2023.125623 PMID:37077800

Dhungana, S. (2022). Dialogic storying: A narrative research methodology in English language education. *Qualitative Research Journal*, *22*(2), 173–187. doi:10.1108/QRJ-05-2021-0057

DiCerbo, K. E., Behrens, J. T., & Barber, M. (2014). *Impacts of the digital ocean on education*. Pearson.

Dillenbourg, P. (1999). What do you mean by collaborative learning? Elbow, P. (2013). High stakes and low stakes in assigning and responding to writing. In *Dialogue on Writing* (pp. 289–298). Routledge.

Donnellan, K.S. (1966). Reference and Definite Descriptions. *The Philosophical Review*, *75*(3), 281–304.

Douglas, R. S., & Landry, M. H. (2021). English for Academic Purposes Programs: Key trends across Canadian universities. *Comparative and International Education*, *50*(1), 49–73. doi:10.5206/cieeci.v50i1.10925

Downes, S. (2023, October 21). Three frameworks for data literacy. *20th International Conference on Cognition and Exploratory Learning in the Digital Age (CELDA 2023)*.

Drennan, L. M. (2017). Engaging Students through Writing: A Collaborative Journey. *South African Journal of Higher Education*, *31*(3), 63–81. doi:10.20853/31-3-1041

Duah, J. E., & McGivern, P. (2024). How generative artificial intelligence has blurred notions of authorial identity and academic norms in higher education, necessitating clear university usage policies. *The International Journal of Information and Learning Technology*. doi:10.1108/IJILT-11-2023-0213

Dwivedi, Y. K., Kshetri, N., Hughes, L., Slade, E. L., Jeyaraj, A., Kar, A. K., Baabdullah, A. M., Koohang, A., Raghavan, V., Ahuja, M., Albanna, H., Albashrawi, M. A., Al-Busaidi, A. S., Balakrishnan, J., Barlette, Y., Basu, S., Bose, I., Brooks, L., Buhalis, D., ... Wright, R. (2023). Opinion Paper: "So what if ChatGPT wrote it?" Multidisciplinary perspectives on opportunities, challenges and implications of generative conversational AI for research, practice and policy. *International Journal of Information Management*, *71*, 102642. doi:10.1016/j.ijinfomgt.2023.102642

Eager, B., & Brunton, R. (2023). Prompting Higher Education Towards AI-Augmented Teaching and Learning Practice. *Journal of University Teaching & Learning Practice*, *20*(5), 1–19. doi:10.53761/1.20.5.02

Elkhatat, A. M., Elsaid, K., & Almeer, S. (2023). Evaluating the efficacy of AI content detection tools in differentiating between human and AI-generated text. *International Journal for Educational Integrity*, *19*(17), 17. Advance online publication. doi:10.1007/s40979-023-00140-5

Ellis, C. (2004). *The ethnographic I: A methodological novel about autoethnography* (Vol. 13). Rowman Altamira.

Ellis, C., Adams, T. E., & Bochner, A. P. (2011). Autoethnography: An overview. Historical Social Research. *Historische Sozialforschung*, *36*(4 (138)), 273–290.

Ellis, C., & Bochner, A. P. (1992). Telling and performing personal stories: The constraints of choice in abortion. In C. Ellis & M. G. Flaherty (Eds.), *Investigating subjectivity: Research on lived experience* (pp. 79–101). Sage.

Equal Education Law Centre. (2023). Joint statement: The 2021 Progress in International Reading Literacy Study (Pirls) results confirm a schooling system in crisis and the extent of learning losses created by COVID-19. https://equaleducation.org.za/2023/05/23/joint-statement-the-2021-progress-in-international-reading-literacy-study-pirls-results-confirm-a-schooling-system-in-crisis-and-the-extent-of-learning-losses-created-by-covid-19/#:~:text=On%20Tuesday%20 16%20May%202023,language%2C%20including%20their%20home%20languages

Escotet, M. Á. (2023). The optimistic future of Artificial Intelligence in higher education. *Prospects*, 1–10. doi:10.1007/s11125-023-09642-z

Eshet, Y. (2012). Thinking in the digital era: A revised model for digital literacy. *Issues in Informing Science and Information Technology, 9*(2), 267-276.

Evanick, J. (2023, November 4). *Ethical Dilemmas In Student Data Privacy: Navigating EdTech Safeguards.* Https://Elearningindustry.Com/Ethical-Dilemmas-in-Student-Data-Privacy-Navigating-Edtech-Safeguards

Eybers, O. (2021). *A realist approach towards student application of agency, culture, and social structures in the demonstration of competency in argumentative writing* (PhD thesis). University of Pretoria. doi:10.13140/RG.2.2.30245.22242

Eybers, O., & Paulet, E. (2022). Sociocultural theory for academic literacy research involving argumentation in institutions of higher learning. *South African Journal of Higher Education, 36*(2), 115–132. doi:10.20853/36-2-4683

Ezen-Can, A., Boyer, K. E., Kellogg, S., & Booth, S. (2015). Unsupervised modeling for understanding MOOC discussion forums: A learning analytics approach. *In Proceedings of the Fifth International Conference on Learning Analytics and Knowledge* (pp. 146-150). 10.1145/2723576.2723589

Fall, J. (2019). Create a digital workforce with robotic process automation. https://www.linkedin.com/pulse/create-digital-workforce-robotic-process-automation-jason-miracle

Fariani, R. I., Junus, K., & Santoso, H. B. (2023). A Systematic Literature Review on Personalised Learning in the Higher Education Context. *Tech Know Learn, 28*(2), 449–476. doi:10.1007/s10758-022-09628-4

Farrell, M. (2023, January 6). *Data and Intuition: Good Decisions Need Both.* Harvard Business Publishing Corporate Learning.

Farrelly, T., & Baker, N. (2023). Generative artificial intelligence: Implications and considerations for higher education practice. *Education Sciences, 13*(11), 1109. doi:10.3390/educsci13111109

Fazackerly, A. (2023, March 19). AI makes plagiarism harder to detect, argue academics – in paper written by chatbot. *The Guardian.* https://www.theguardian.com/technology/2023/mar/19/ai-makes-plagiarism-harder-to-detect-argue-academics-in-paper-written-by-chatbot

Fecher, B., Hebing, M., Laufer, M., Pohle, J., & Sofsky, F. (2023). Friend or Foe? Exploring the Implications of Large Language Models on the Science System. *arXiv preprint arXiv:2306.09928.*

Firat, M. (2023). What ChatGPT means for universities: Perceptions of scholars and students. *Journal of Applied Learning and Teaching*, *6*(1), 57–63.

Florida, R. (2004, October). America's looming creativity crisis. *Harvard Business Review*. PMID:15559581

Floridi, L., Cowls, J., Beltrametti, M., Chatila, R., Chazerand, P., Dignum, V., ... Vayena, E. (2021). An ethical framework for a good AI society: Opportunities, risks, principles, and recommendations. *Ethics, Governance, and Policies in Artificial Intelligence*, 19-39.

Fowler, S., Korolkiewicz, M., & Marrone, R. (2023). First 100 days of ChatGPT at Australian universities: An analysis of policy landscape and media discussions about the role of AI in higher education. *Learning Letters*, *1*, 1–1. doi:10.59453/JMTN6001

Francis. (2021). Huawei Uganda offers free artificial intelligence training. *The New Vision*.

Gao, C., Lan, X., Lu, Z., Mao, J., Piao, J., Wang, H., Jin, D., & Li, Y. (2023). S3: Social-network simulation system with large language model-empowered agents. arXiv preprint arXiv:2307.14984.

Gao, S., Takanobu, R., Bosselut, A., & Huang, M. (2022). End-to-end task-oriented dialog modeling with semi-structured knowledge management. *IEEE/ACM Transactions on Audio, Speech, and Language Processing*, *30*, 2173–2187. Advance online publication. doi:10.1109/TASLP.2022.3153255

Gee, J. P. (2008). A sociocultural perspective on opportunity to learn. *Assessment, Equity, and Opportunity to Learn*, 76-108.

Gee, J. P. (2000). Teenagers in new times: A new literacy studies perspective. *Journal of Adolescent & Adult Literacy*, *43*(5), 412–420.

Gee, J. P. (2008). *Social Linguistics and literacies: Ideology in discourses* (3rd ed.). Routledge.

Ghodoosi, B., Torrisi-Steele, G., West, T., & Li, Q. (2023). An Exploration of the Definition of Data Literacy in the Academic and Public Domains. *International Journal of Adult Education and Technology*, *14*(1), 1–16. doi:10.4018/IJAET.325218

Ghodoosi, B., West, T., Li, Q., Torrisi-Steele, G., & Dey, S. (2023). A systematic literature review of data literacy education. *Journal of Business & Finance Librarianship*, *28*(2), 112–127. doi:10.1080/08963568.2023.2171552

Gibson, D., & de Freitas, S. (2016). Exploratory analysis in learning analytics. *Technology. Knowledge and Learning*, *21*(1), 5–19. doi:10.1007/s10758-015-9249-5

Gielen, S., Peeters, E., Dochy, F., Onghena, P., & Struyven, K. (2010). Improving the effectiveness of peer feedback for learning. *Learning and Instruction*, *20*(4), 304–315. doi:10.1016/j.learninstruc.2009.08.007

Gillespie, A., & Graham, S. (2014). A meta-analysis of writing interventions for students with learning disabilities. *Exceptional Children*, *80*(4), 454–473. doi:10.1177/0014402914527238

Gillies, R. M. (2016). Cooperative learning: Review of research and practice. *The Australian Journal of Teacher Education, 41*(3), 39–54. doi:10.14221/ajte.2016v41n3.3

Gilmore, D., Crain Soudien, C., & Donald, D. (1999). Post-Apartheid Policy and Practice: Educational Reform in South Africa. In M. Kas, M. Winzer, & C. Majorek (Eds.), *Education in a Global Society: A Comparative Perspective* (pp. 341–350). Allyn and Bacon.

Gilster, P. (1997). *Digital literacy.* Wiley Computer Pub.

GimpelH.HallK.DeckerS.EymannT.LämmermannL.MädcheA.RöglingerM.RuinerC.SchochM. SchoopM.UrbachN.VandirkS. (2023). Unlocking the Power of Generative AI Models and Systems such as GPT-4 and ChatGPT for Higher Education: A Guide for Students and Lecturers. University of Hohenheim, March 20, 2023. doi:10.13140/RG.2.2.20710.09287/2

Glesne, C. (2011). *Becoming qualitative researchers: An introduction* (4th ed.). Pearson.

Go, E., & Sundar, S. S. (2019). Humanizing chatbots: The effects of visual, identity, and conversational cues on humanness perceptions. *Computers in Human Behavior, 97*, 304–316. doi:10.1016/j.chb.2019.01.020

Goel, A. K., & Polepeddi, L. (2016). *Jill Watson: A virtual teaching assistant for online education.* Georgia Tech Library.

Gonzalez, B. (2021). Automated and Autonomous? Technologies mediating the exertion and perception of labour control. In *Augmented Exploitation: Artificial Intelligence, Automation and Work.* Pluto Press. doi:10.2307/j.ctv1h0nv3d.13

Goodier, C., & Parkinson, J. (2005). Discipline-based academic literacy in two contexts. *Journal for Language Teaching*= Ijenali Yekufundzisa Lulwimi=. *Tydskrif vir Taalonderrig, 39*(1), 66–79. doi:10.4314/jlt.v39i1.6050

Gosu, V. K. (2023, October). Navigating ethical AI and the future of automation. *Forbes*, 13.

Graesser, A. C. (2011). Learning, thinking, and emoting with discourse technologies. *The American Psychologist, 66*(8), 746–757. doi:10.1037/a0024974 PMID:22082403

Graesser, A. C., Hu, X., Nye, B. D., VanLehn, K., Kumar, R., Heffernan, C., Heffernan, N., Woolf, B., Olney, A. M., Rus, V., Andrasik, F., Pavlik, P., Cai, Z., Wetzel, J., Morgan, B., Hampton, A. J., Lippert, A. M., Wang, L., Cheng, Q., ... Baer, W. (2018). ElectronixTutor: An intelligent tutoring system with multiple learning resources for electronics. *International Journal of STEM Education, 5*(1), 1–21. doi:10.1186/s40594-018-0110-y PMID:30631705

Graesser, A., & McNamara, D. (2010). Self-regulated learning in learning environments with pedagogical agents that interact in natural language. *Educational Psychologist, 45*(4), 234–244. doi:10.1080/00461520.2010.515933

Graham, S., & Hebert, M. (2010). Writing to read: Evidence for how writing can improve reading. *A Report from Carnegie Corporation of New York.*

Graham, S., & Perin, D. (2007). Writing next-effective strategies to improve writing of adolescents in middle and high schools. Academic Press.

Graham, S., & Hebert, M. (2011). Writing to read: A meta-analysis of the impact of writing and writing instruction on reading. *Harvard Educational Review*, *81*(4), 710–744. doi:10.17763/haer.81.4.t2k0m13756113566

Grassini, S. (2023). Shaping the future of education: Exploring the potential and consequences of AI and ChatGPT in educational settings. *Education Sciences*, *13*(7), 692. Advance online publication. doi:10.3390/educsci13070692

Grimes, D., & Warschauer, M. (2010). Utility in a fallible tool: A multi-site case study of automated writing evaluation. *The Journal of Technology, Learning, and Assessment*, *8*(6).

Gu, H. (2023). Data, Big Tech, and the New Concept of Sovereignty. *Journal of Chinese Political Science*. Advance online publication. doi:10.1007/s11366-023-09855-1 PMID:37359767

GuoB. (2023). How close is chatgpt to human experts? comparison corpus, evaluation, and detection. arXiv:2301.07597.

Guo, Y., & Lee, D. (2023). Leveraging ChatGPT for enhancing critical thinking skills. *Journal of Chemical Education*, *100*(12), 4876–4883. doi:10.1021/acs.jchemed.3c00505

Gweon, G., Jun, S., Finger, S., & Rosé, C. P. (2017). Towards effective group work assessment: Even what you don't see can bias you. *International Journal of Technology and Design Education*, *27*(1), 165–180. doi:10.1007/s10798-015-9332-1

Haleem, A., Javaid, M., & Singh, R. P. (2022). An era of ChatGPT as a significant futuristic support tool: A study on features, abilities, and challenges. BenchCouncil Transactions on Benchmarks. *Standards and Evaluations*, *2*(4), 100089. doi:10.1016/j.tbench.2023.100089

Halliday, M. A. K. (1994). *An Introduction to Functional Grammar*. Edward Arnold.

Hanegan, K. (2023, November 1). *From Data Literacy to AI Literacy. The Evolution of Critical Thinking in the Digital Age*. Turning Data into Wisdom. https://www.turningdataintowisdom.com/from-data-literacy-to-ai-literacy/

Hanegan, K. (2021). *Turning Data into Wisdom: How We Can Collaborate with Data to Change Ourselves*. Our Organizations, and Even the World.

Hanemann, U., & Scarpino, C. (2016). *Literacy in multilingual and multicultural contexts: Effective approaches to adult learning and education*. UNESCO Institute for Lifelong Learning.

Haque, Islam, & Mikalef. (2023). Explainable Artificial Intelligence (XAI) from a user perspective: A synthesis of prior literature and problematizing avenues for future research. *Technological Forecasting and Social Change*, 186(Part A), 1-19. doi:10.1016/j.techfore.2022.122120

Harb, M., & Taha Thomure, H. (2020). Connecting literacy to curriculum ideologies. *Curriculum Perspectives*, *40*(1), 27–33. doi:10.1007/s41297-020-00099-0

Compilation of References

Hariri, W. (2023). Unlocking the potential of ChatGPT: A comprehensive exploration of its applications, advantages, limitations, and future directions in natural language processing. arXiv preprint arXiv:2304.02017.

Hattie, J., & Timperley, H. (2007). The power of feedback. *Review of Educational Research*, *77*(1), 81–112. doi:10.3102/003465430298487

Heaven, W. D. (2023, April 6). ChatGPT is going to change education, not destroy it. *MIT Technology Review*. https://www.technologyreview.com/2023/04/06/1071059/chatgpt-change-not-destroy-education-openai/

Heck, T., Weisel, L., & Kullmann, S. (2021). Information literacy and its interplay with AI. In A. Botte, P. Libbrecht, & M. Rittberger (Eds.), *Learning Information Literacy across the Globe* (pp. 129–131). Leibniz-Institut für Bildungsforschung und Bildungsinformation. doi:10.25656/01:17891

Hegelheimer, V., & Lee, J. (2013). The role of technology in teaching and researching writing. In M. Thomas, H. Reinders, & M. Warschauer (Eds.), *Contemporary Computer-Assisted Language Learning* (pp. 287–302). Bloomsbury Academic.

Hendershott, A., Drinan, P., & Cross, M. (2000). Toward enhancing a culture of academic integrity. *NASPA Journal*, *37*(4), 587–598. doi:10.2202/1949-6605.1119

Herbold, S., Hautli-Janisz, A., Heuer, U., Kikteva, Z., & Trautsch, A. (2023). A large-scale comparison of human-written versus ChatGPT-generated essays. *Scientific Reports*, *13*(1), 18617. doi:10.1038/s41598-023-45644-9 PMID:37903836

Holmes, W., Bialik, M., & Fadel, C. (2023). *Artificial intelligence in education*. Globethics Publications.

Hong, J.-Y., & Kim, Y. (2020). Development of AI Data Science Education Program to Foster Data Literacy of Elementary School Students. *Journal of The Korean Association of Information Education*, *24*(6), 633–641. doi:10.14352/jkaie.2020.24.6.633

Hornberger, M., Bewersdorff, A., & Nerdel, C. (2023). What do university students know about Artificial Intelligence? Development and validation of an AI literacy test. *Computers and Education: Artificial Intelligence*, *5*, 1–12. doi:10.1016/j.caeai.2023.100165

Hossain, Z. (2022). University freshmen recollect their academic integrity literacy experience during their K-12 years: Results of an empirical study. *International Journal for Educational Integrity*, *18*(4), 4. Advance online publication. doi:10.1007/s40979-021-00096-4

Hruby, G., & Burns, L. D. (2020). The Science of Adolescent Literacy. *Journal of Adolescent & Adult Literacy*, *63*(6), 693–696. doi:10.1002/jaal.1054

Huang, J., & Tan, M. (2023). The role of ChatGPT in scientific communication: Writing better scientific review articles. *American Journal of Cancer Research*, *13*(4), 1148–1154. PMID:37168339

Huddleston, T., Jr. (2023, April 22). Bill Gates says A.I. chatbots will teach kids to read within 18 months: You'll be "stunned by how it helps." CNBC. https://www.cnbc.com/2023/04/22/bill-gates-ai-chatbots-will-teach-kids-how-to-read-within-18-months.html

Hutchinson, B., Prabhakaran, V., Denton, E., Webster, K., Zhong, Y., & Denuyl, S. (2020). Social biases in NLP models as barriers for persons with disabilities. *arXiv preprint arXiv:2005.00813.* doi:10.18653/v1/2020.acl-main.487

Hyland, K. (1999). Academic attribution: Citation and the construction of disciplinary knowledge. *Applied Linguistics, 20*(3), 341–367. doi:10.1093/applin/20.3.341

Ibna Seraj, P. M., & Oteir, I. (2022). Playing with AI to investigate human-computer interaction technology and improving critical thinking skills to pursue 21st century age. *Education Research International.*

Ifelebuegu, A. O., Kulume, P., & Cherukut, P. (2023). Chatbots and AI in Education (AIEd) tools: The good, the bad, and the ugly. *Journal of Applied Learning and Teaching, 6*(2), 332–345.

Imran, M., & Almusharraf, N. (2023). Analyzing the role of ChatGPT as a writing assistant at higher education level: A systematic review of the literature. *Contemporary Educational Technology, 15*(4), ep464. doi:10.30935/cedtech/13605

International Center for Academic Integrity. (2021). The fundamental values of academic integrity (3rd ed.). www.academicintegrity.org/the-fundamental-valuesof-academic-integrity

Inter-University Council of East Africa (IUCEA). (2023). *Exploring the Potential of AI for Teaching and Learning in East Africa - TESCEA Phase 2.* IUCEA. https://www.inasp.info/sites/default/files/2023-08/AI%20event%20summary%20July%202023.pdf

Ippolito, J., Steele, J. L., & Samson, J. F. (2008). Introduction: Why adolescent literacy matters now. *Harvard Educational Review, 78*(1), 1–6.

Islam, M., Sarker, M., & Islam, M. (2021). Promoting student-centred blended learning in higher education: A model. *E-Learning and Digital Media, 19*(1), 36–54. doi:10.1177/20427530211027721

Jack, C. (1993). *Artificial Intelligence: A Philosophical Introduction.* John Wiley & Sons.

Jackson, G. T., Boonthum, C., & McNamara, D. S. (2009). iSTART-ME: Situating extended learning within a game-based environment. In *Proceedings of the Workshop on Intelligent Educational Games at the 14th Annual Conference on Artificial Intelligence in Education* (pp. 59-68). Academic Press.

Jacobs, C. (2013). Academic literacies and the question of knowledge. *Tydskrif vir Taalonderrig, 47*(2), 127–140. doi:10.4314/jlt.v47i2.7

Janine, B. (1997). *Biomimicry: Innovation Inspired by Nature.* Reed Business Information, Inc.

Jarrahi, M. H., Lutz, C., & Newlands, G. (2022). Artificial intelligence, human intelligence and hybrid intelligence based on mutual augmentation. *Big Data & Society, 9*(2). Advance online publication. doi:10.1177/20539517221142824

Jia, J. (2004). The study of the application of a web-based chatbot system on the teaching of foreign languages. In *Society for Information Technology & Teacher Education International Conference* (pp. 1201-1207). Association for the Advancement of Computing in Education (AACE).

Johnson, D. W., & Johnson, R. T. (2009). An educational psychology success story: Social interdependence theory and cooperative learning. *Educational Researcher, 38*(5), 365–379. doi:10.3102/0013189X09339057

Johnson-Laird, P. (2010). Deductive reasoning. *Wiley Interdisciplinary Reviews: Cognitive Science, 1*(1), 8–17. doi:10.1002/wcs.20 PMID:26272833

Joint Information Systems Committee. (2014). Developing digital literacies. https://www.jisc.ac.uk/guides/developing-digital-literacies

Jones, P. (2021, Oct. 27). Big tech's push for automation hides the grim reality of 'microwork'. *The Guardian.*

KaddourJ.JoshuaH.MaximilianM.BradleyγH.RaileanuR.McHardyR. (2023). Challenges and applications of Large Language Models. arXiv:2307.10169v1 [cs.CL]. https://arxiv.org/pdf/2307.10169.pdf

Kanarek, J. (2021). The tortoise and the hare: A new moral for an old fable. *The Intellectual Standard, 2*(1). https://digitalcommons.iwu.edu/tis/vol2/iss1/1

Karaali, G. (2023). Artificial Intelligence, Basic Skills, and Quantitative Literacy. Numeracy: Advancing Education in Quantitative Literacy, 16(1).

Kardan, S., & Conati, C. (2012). Exploring gaze data for determining user learning with an interactive simulation. *User Modeling, Adaptation, and Personalization: 20th International Conference, UMAP 2012, Montreal, Canada, July 16-20, 2012 Proceedings, 20*, 126–138.

Kativhu, S. (2021). Covid-19 as a Catalyst for Digital Transformation in Higher Education: Insights for Rural-based Universities in South Africa. *African Renaissance, 18*(4), 285–304.

Katz, S., Albacete, P., Chounta, I. A., Jordan, P., McLaren, B. M., & Zapata-Rivera, D. (2021). Linking Dialogue with Student Modelling to Create an Adaptive Tutoring System for Conceptual Physics. *International Journal of Artificial Intelligence in Education, 31*(3), 397–445. doi:10.1007/s40593-020-00226-y

Kersley, A. (2022, October 5). Clickwork and labour exploitation in the digital economy. *Computer Weekly.*

Kim, J., Hong, L., Evans, S., Oyler-Rice, E., & Ali, I. (2023). Development and Validation of a Data Literacy Assessment Scale. *Proceedings of the Association for Information Science and Technology, 60*(1), 620–624. doi:10.1002/pra2.827

Kim, M. K., Kim, N. J., & Heidari, A. (2022). Learner experience in artificial intelligence-scaffolded argumentation. *Assessment & Evaluation in Higher Education, 47*(8), 1301–1316. doi:10.1080/02602938.2022.2042792

Kim, M. S., & Yu, F. (2023). 'Teacher data literacies practice' meets 'pedagogical documentation': A scoping review. *Review of Education, 11*(2), e3414. Advance online publication. doi:10.1002/rev3.3414

Kimmons, R., & Veletsianos, G. (2016). Education scholars' evolving uses of twitter as a conference backchannel and social commentary platform. *British Journal of Educational Technology, 47*(3), 445–464. doi:10.1111/bjet.12428

Kinash, S. (2013). MOOCing about MOOCs. *Education Technology Solutions, 57*, 56–58.

King, M. R. (2023). A Conversation on Artificial Intelligence, Chatbots, and Plagiarism in Higher Education. [A conversation on artificial intelligence, chatbots, and plagiarism in higher education]. *Cellular and Molecular Bioengineering, 16*(1), 1–2. doi:10.1007/s12195-022-00754-8 PMID:36660590

Kirschner, F., Paas, F., & Kirschner, P. A. (2011). Task complexity as a driver for collaborative learning efficiency: The collective working-memory effect. *Applied Cognitive Psychology, 25*(4), 615–624. doi:10.1002/acp.1730

Kong, S. C., Cheung, W. M. Y., & Zhang, G. (2023). Evaluating an artificial intelligence literacy programme for developing university students' conceptual understanding, literacy, empowerment and ethical awareness. *Journal of Educational Technology & Society, 26*(1), 16–30.

Korzyński, P., Mazurek, G., Krzypkowska, P., & Kurasinski, A. (2023). Artificial intelligence prompt engineering as a new digital competence: Analysis of generative AI technologies such as ChatGPT. *Entrepreneurial Business and Economics Review, 11*(3), 25–37. doi:10.15678/EBER.2023.110302

KreinsenM.SchulzS. (2023). Towards the triad of digital literacy, data literacy and AI literacy in teacher education – A discussion in light of the accessibility of novel generative AI. doi:10.35542/osf.io/xguzk

Kyndt, E., Raes, E., Lismont, B., Timmers, F., Cascallar, E., & Dochy, F. (2013). A meta-analysis of the effects of face-to-face cooperative learning. Do recent studies falsify or verify earlier findings? *Educational Research Review, 10*, 133–149. doi:10.1016/j.edurev.2013.02.002

Lakhani, K. (2023, August 4). Humans will not be replaced by artificial intelligence, but humans with AI will eventually take the place of humans without AI. *Harvard Business Review*.

Landauer, T. K., Laham, D., & Foltz, P. W. (2003). Automated scoring and annotation of essays with the intelligent essay assessor. Automated essay scoring: A cross-disciplinary perspective, 87–112.

Lankshear, C., & Knobel, M. (2006). *New literacies: Everyday practices and classroom learning.* Open University Press.

Compilation of References

Lapadat, J. C. (2017). Ethics in autoethnography and collaborative autoethnography. *Qualitative Inquiry*, *23*(8), 589–603. doi:10.1177/1077800417704462

Larson, L. C. (2009). e-Reading and e-responding: New tools for the next generation of readers. *Journal of Adolescent & Adult Literacy*, *53*(3), 255–258. doi:10.1598/JAAL.53.3.7

Laupichler, M. C., Aster, A., Schirch, J., & Raupach, T. (2022). Artificial intelligence literacy in higher and adult education: A scoping literature review. Computers and Education: Artificial Intelligence, 100101.

Laupichler, M. C., Aster, A., Schirch, J., & Raupach, T. (2022). Artificial intelligence literacy in higher and adult education: A scoping literature review. *Computers and Education: Artificial Intelligence*, *3*, 100101. doi:10.1016/j.caeai.2022.100101

Lauterbach, A., & Bonime-Blanc, A. (2018). *The Artificial Intelligence Imperative: A Practical Roadmap for Business*. Praeger. doi:10.5040/9798400614835

Lax, J. (2002). Academic writing for international graduate students. 32nd ASEE/IEEE Frontiers in Education Conference, November 6 – 9, 2002, Boston, MA. http://fie2012.fie-conference.org/sites/fie2012.fie-conference.org/history/fie2002/papers/ 1301.pdf

Leal Filho, W., Yang, P., Eustachio, J. H. P. P., Azul, A. M., Gellers, J. C., Gielczyk, A., Dinis, M. A. P., & Kozlova, V. (2023). Deploying digitalisation and artificial intelligence in sustainable development research. *Environment, Development and Sustainability*, *25*(6), 4957–4988. doi:10.1007/s10668-022-02252-3 PMID:35313685

Lea, M. R., & Street, B. V. (2006). The "Academic Literacies" Model: Theory and Applications. *Theory into Practice*, *45*(4), 368–377. doi:10.1207/s15430421tip4504_11

Learning, E. L. M. (2022). Adaptive Learning vs. Personalized Learning: A Guide to Both. *ELM Learning*. https://elmlearning.com/blog/personalized-learning-vs-adaptive-learning/

Leavy, P. (2023). *Research design: Quantitative, qualitative, mixed methods, arts-based, and community-based participatory research approaches*. Guilford Publications.

Lebuso, S. (2023, February 2). How SA universities plan to deal with ChatGPT. Accreditation. *News24*. https://www.news24.com/citypress/news/how-sa-universities-plan-to-deal-with-chatgpt-20230202

Lee, H. (2023, March 14). The rise of ChatGPT: Exploring its potential in medical education. *Anatomical Sciences Education*, ase.2270. Advance online publication. doi:10.1002/ase.2270 PMID:36916887

Le, H., & Jia, J. (2022). Design and implementation of an intelligent tutoring system in the view of learner autonomy. *Interactive Technology and Smart Education*, *19*(4), 510–525. doi:10.1108/ITSE-12-2021-0210

Leu, D. J., Kinzer, C. K., Coiro, J., Castek, J., & Henry, L. A. (2018). New literacies: A dual-level theory of the changing nature of literacy, instruction, and assessment. In *Theoretical Models and Processes of Literacy* (pp. 319–346). Routledge. doi:10.4324/9781315110592-19

Lew, R. (2023). ChatGPT as a COBUILD lexicographer. *Humanities & Social Sciences Communications*, *10*(1), 704. doi:10.1057/s41599-023-02119-6

Li, D. (2022). A review of academic literacy research development: from 2002 to 2019. *Asian-Pacific Journal of Second and Foreign Language Education*, *7*(1), 1–22. doi:10.1186/s40862-022-00130-z

Li, H. F. (2023). Effects of a ChatGPT-based flipped learning guiding approach on learners' courseware project performances and perceptions. *Australasian Journal of Educational Technology*, *39*(5), 40–58. doi:10.14742/ajet.8923

Limna, P., Kraiwanit, T., Jangjarat, K., Klayklung, P., & Chocksathaporn, P. (2023). The use of ChatGPT in the digital era: Perspectives on chatbot implementation. *Journal of Applied Learning and Teaching*, *6*(1), 64–74.

Liu, L., Liu, Q., Li, Y., Li, J., Li, H., & Zhao, H. (2019). Teacher perceptions and attitudes towards artificial intelligence in education: A survey study. *Educational Technology Research and Development*, *67*(3), 9–20.

Li, Z., Makarova, V., & Wang, Z. (2023). Developing literature review writing skills through an online writing tutorial series: Corpus-based evidence. *Frontiers in Communication*, *8*, 1035394. Advance online publication. doi:10.3389/fcomm.2023.1035394

Luckin, R. (2018). The AI revolution: The road to superintelligence. https://www.researchgate.net/publication/324319843_The_AI_Revolution_The_Road_to_Superintelligence

Luckin, R., & Holmes, W. (2016). Intelligence unleashed: An argument for AI in education. Academic Press.

Luckin, R., Holmes, W., Griffiths, M., & Forcier, L. B. (2016). Intelligence unleashed: An argument for AI in education. Academic Press.

Lukman, & Wahyudin. (2020). Statistical literacy of undergraduate students in Indonesia: Survey studies. Journal of Physics: Conference Series, 1521(3). doi:10.1088/1742-6596/1521/3/032050

Luo, J. (2024). A critical review of GenAI policies in higher education assessment: A call to reconsider the "originality" of students' work. *Assessment & Evaluation in Higher Education*, 1–14. https://www.tandfonline.com/doi/full/10.1080/02602938.2024.2309963

Lynn, B. (2020). Elon Musk demonstrates technology linking computer to brain. *VOA News*. https://learningenglish.voanews.com/a/elon-musk-demonstrates-technology-linking-computer-to-brain/5565332.html

Macagno, F., & Rapanta, C. (2020). *The Logic of Academic Writing*. Wessex Press.

Compilation of References

Makala, B., Schmitt, M., & Caballero, A. (2021). How Artificial Intelligence Can Help Advance Post-Secondary Learning in Emerging Markets. Academic Press.

Malmstedt, G. (2021). Spells and Charms. In Premodern Beliefs and Witch Trials in a Swedish Province. Palgrave Macmillan. doi:10.1007/978-3-030-76120-2_8

Marechal, G. (2010). Autoethnography. In A. J. Mills, G. Durepos, & E. Wiebe (Eds.), *Encyclopedia of Case Study Research* (pp. 43–45).

Markauskaite, L., Rebecca Marrone, R., Poquet, O., Knight, S., Martinez-Maldonado, R., Howard, S., Tondeur, J., De Laat, M., Buckingham Shum, S., Gašević, D., & Siemens, G. (2022). Rethinking the entwinement between artificial intelligence and human learning: What capabilities do learners need for a world with AI? *Computers and Education: Artificial Intelligence*, *3*(100056), 100056. Advance online publication. doi:10.1016/j.caeai.2022.100056

Martinez-Maldonado, R., Schneider, B., Charleer, S., Buckingham Shum, S., Klerkx, J., & Duval, E. (2016). Interactive surfaces and learning analytics: Data, orchestration aspects, pedagogical uses, and challenges. In *Proceedings of the Sixth International Conference on Learning Analytics & Knowledge* (pp. 124-133). 10.1145/2883851.2883873

Marzuki, M., Widiati, U., Rusdin, D., & Indrawati, I. (2023). The impact of AI writing tools on the content and organization of students' writing: EFL teachers' perspective. *Cogent Education*, *10*(2), 2236469. Advance online publication. doi:10.1080/2331186X.2023.2236469

Masenya, T. M. (2021). Digital Literacy Skills As Prerequisite for Teaching and Learning in Higher Education Institutions. *Mousaion: South African Journal of Information Studies*, *39*(2), 1–20. doi:10.25159/2663-659X/8428

Ma, W., Adesope, O. O., Nesbit, J. C., & Liu, Q. (2014). Intelligent tutoring systems and learning outcomes: A meta-analysis. *Journal of Educational Psychology*, *106*(4), 901–918. doi:10.1037/a0037123

Mawere, J., Mukonza, R. M., & Kugara, S. L. (2021). Re-envisioning the Education System for 4IR: Exploring the Experiences Faced by First Entering Students from Rural-based Institutions on the Use of Digital Learning during the Coronavirus Pandemic in Limpopo province, South Africa. *Journal of African Education*, *2*(2), 43–65. doi:10.31920/2633-2930/2021/v2n2a2

Mazzone, M., & Elgammal, A. (2019). Art, Creativity, and the Potential of Artificial Intelligence. *Arts*, *8*(1), 26. doi:10.3390/arts8010026

McAdoo, T. (2023, April 7). How to cite ChatGPT. APA Style. https://apastyle.apa.org/blog/how-to-cite-chatgpt

McFarland, A. (2024, February 28). *10 Best AI Tools for Education*. Unite.AI. https://www.unite.ai/10-best-ai-tools-for-education/

McMurtrie, B. (2018). How artificial intelligence is changing teaching. *The Chronicle of Higher Education*. Retrieved from https://www.chronicle.com/article/How-ArtificialIntelligence-Is/244231

McNamara, D. S., Allen, L., Crossley, S., Dascalu, M., & Perret, C. A. (2017). Natural language processing and learning analytics. In Handbook of Learning Analytics (pp. 93). doi:10.18608/hla17.008

McNamara, D. S., Levinstein, I. B., & Boonthum, C. (2004). iSTART: Interactive strategy training for active reading and thinking. *Behavior Research Methods, Instruments, & Computers*, *36*(2), 222–233. doi:10.3758/BF03195567 PMID:15354687

Megawati, R., Listiani, H., Pranoto, N. W., Akobiarek, M., & Megahati S, R. R. P. (2023). The Role of GPT Chat in Writing Scientific Articles: A Systematic Literature Review. *Jurnal Penelitian Pendidikan IPA*, *9*(11), 1078–1084. doi:10.29303/jppipa.v9i11.5559

Meurers, D. (2012). Natural language processing and language learning. Encyclopedia of Applied Linguistics, 4193-4205. doi:10.1002/9781405198431.wbeal0858

Mhlanga, D. (2023). Open AI in education, the responsible and ethical use of ChatGPT towards lifelong learning. Education, the Responsible and Ethical Use of ChatGPT Towards Lifelong Learning (February 11, 2023).

Michal, K. (2023). Theory of Mind might have spontaneously emerged in Large Language Models. arXiv preprint arXiv: 2302.02083. https://arxiv.org/ftp/arxiv/papers/2302/2302.02083.pdf

Michos, K., Schmitz, M.-L., & Petko, D. (2023). Teachers' data literacy for learning analytics: A central predictor for digital data use in upper secondary schools. *Education and Information Technologies*, *28*(11), 14453–14471. doi:10.1007/s10639-023-11772-y PMID:37361815

Mittelstadt, B., Russell, C., & Wachter, S. (2019). Explaining explanations in AI. In *Proceedings of the Conference on Fairness, Accountability, and Transparency* (pp. 279-288). 10.1145/3287560.3287574

Moonasamy, A. R., & Naidoo, G. M. (2022). Digital Learning: Challenges experienced by South African university students' during the COVID-19 pandemic. *The Independent Journal of Teaching and Learning, 17*(2), 76-90.

Morrow, W. E. (1990). Aims of Education in South Africa. International Review of Education/Internationale Zeitschrift fur Erziehunswissenschaft/Revue Internationale de l'Education 36, 171–181. doi:10.1007/BF01874882

Mostow, J. (2001). Evaluating tutors that listen: An overview of Project LISTEN. Academic Press.

Mousavinasab, E., Zarifsanaiey, N., & Niakan Kalhori, R., S., Rakhshan, M., Keikha, L., & Ghazi Saeedi, M. (. (2021). Intelligent tutoring systems: A systematic review of characteristics, applications, and evaluation methods. *Interactive Learning Environments*, *29*(1), 142–163. doi:10.1080/10494820.2018.1558257

Murtarellia, G., Gregory, A., & Romentia, S. (2021). A conversation-based perspective for shaping ethical human–machine interactions: The particular challenge of chatbots. *Journal of Business Research*, *129*, 927–935. doi:10.1016/j.jbusres.2020.09.018

Naidoo, S., & Raju, J. (2012). Impact of the digital divide on information literacy training in a higher education context. *South African Journal of Library and Information Science*, *78*(1), 34–44. doi:10.7553/78-1-46

Naidu, K., & Sevnarayan, K. (2023). ChatGPT: An ever-increasing encroachment of artificial intelligence in online assessment in distance education. *Online Journal of Communication and Media Technologies*, *13*(3), e202336. Advance online publication. doi:10.30935/ojcmt/13291

Nayar, P. B. (1997). ESL/EFL dichotomy today: Language politics or pragmatics. *TESOL Quarterly*, *31*(1), 9–37. doi:10.2307/3587973

Nedungadi, P., & Raj, H. (2014). Unsupervised word sense disambiguation for automatic essay scoring. *Advanced Computing Networking and Informatics*, *1*, 437–443.

Neumann & Kurzweil. (2012), *The Computer and the Brain*. Yale University Press.

Neumann, M., Rauschenberger, M., & Schon, E.-M. (2023). *"We Need To Talk About ChatGPT": The Future of AI and Higher Education* [Paper Presentation]. IEEE/ACM 5th International Workshop on Software Engineering Education for the Next Generation (SEENG), Melbourne, Australia. https://doi-org.nwulib.idm.oclc.org/10.1109/SEENG59157.2023.00010

Newell, S. (2023). ChatGPT the homework machine. *HERDSA Connect*, 26–26.

Ng, D. T. K., Leung, J. K. L., Chu, S. K. W., & Qiao, M. S. (2021). Conceptualizing AI Literacy: An Exploratory Review. *Computers and Education: Artificial Intelligence*, *2*(100041), 100041. Advance online publication. doi:10.1016/j.caeai.2021.100041

Ng, D. T. K., Leung, J. K. L., Chu, S. K. W., & Qiao, M. S. (2021). Conceptualizing AI literacy: An exploratory review. *Computers and Education: Artificial Intelligence*, *2*, 100041.

Ngunjiri, F. W., Hernandez, K. A. C., & Chang, H. (2010). Living autoethnography: Connecting life and research. *Journal of Research Practice*, *6*(1), E1–E1.

Nicholas, W. (2011, Fall). Within language, through language, beyond language: The portmanteau-word neologism as agent and emblem of contingent change. *Journal of South Texas English Studies*, *3*(1), 1–28.

Nicol, D. (2014). Guiding principles for peer review: Unlocking learners' evaluative skills. In Advances and Innovations in University Assessment and Feedback (pp. 197-224). Academic Press.

Nicol, D., Thomson, A., & Breslin, C. (2014). Rethinking feedback practices in higher education: A peer review perspective. *Assessment & Evaluation in Higher Education*, *39*(1), 102–122. doi:10.1080/02602938.2013.795518

Nikou, S., & Aavakare, M. (2021). An assessment of the interplay between literacy and digital Technology in Higher Education. *Education and Information Technologies*, *26*(4), 3893–3915. Advance online publication. doi:10.1007/s10639-021-10451-0

Nilsson, N. J. (2009). *The Quest for Artificial Intelligence.* Cambridge University Press. doi:10.1017/CBO9780511819346

Nix, J. (2023, November 30). The year ChatGPT changed almost everything. Bloomberg. com. https://www.bloomberg.com/news/articles/2023-11-30/the-year-chatgpt-changed-almost-everything

Nordling, L. (2023). How ChatGPT is transforming the postdoc experience. *Nature, 622*(7983), 655–657. doi:10.1038/d41586-023-03235-8 PMID:37845528

Nyamupangedengu, E. (2017). Investigating factors that impact the success of students in a Higher Education classroom: A case study. *Journal of Education, 68,* 113–130.

O'Dea, X. (2023). Teaching AI literacy: how to begin. *Times Higher Education.* https://www.timeshighereducation.com/campus/teaching-ai-literacy-how-begin

O'Neil, C. (2017). *Weapons of Math Destruction: How Big Data Increases Inequality and Threatens Democracy.* Crown.

Ogan, A., Walker, E., Baker, R., Rodrigo, M. M. T., Soriano, J. C., & Castro, M. J. (2015). Towards understanding how to assess help-seeking behavior across cultures. *International Journal of Artificial Intelligence in Education, 25*(2), 229–248. doi:10.1007/s40593-014-0034-8

Ojha, S. S. (2021). Computational Thinking and Social Science Education. *Academia Letters, 1-5.* Advance online publication. doi:10.20935/AL1577

Okuda, T., & Anderson, T. (2018). Second-language graduate students' experiences at the writing center: A language socialization perspective. *TESOL Quarterly, 52*(2), 391–413. doi:10.1002/tesq.406

Olari, V. (2023). Data Literacy as a Fundamental Component of Artificial Intelligence Education in Schools (Doctoral Consortium). *Proceedings of the 23rd Koli Calling International Conference on Computing Education Research,* 1–2. 10.1145/3631802.3631839

Olari, V., Zoppke, T., Reger, M., Samoilova, E., Kandlhofer, M., Dagiene, V., Romeike, R., Lieckfeld, A. S., & Lucke, U. (2023). Introduction of Artificial Intelligence Literacy and Data Literacy in Computer Science Teacher Education. *Proceedings of the 23rd Koli Calling International Conference on Computing Education Research,* 1–2. 10.1145/3631802.3631851

Olney, A. M., Graesser, A. C., & Person, N. K. (2012). Question generation from concept maps. *Dialogue & Discourse, 3*(2), 75–99. doi:10.5087/dad.2012.204

Ottonicar, S., Manhique, I., & Mosconi, E. (2021). Ethical Aspects of Information Literacy in Artificial Intelligence. In B. Vassileva & M. Zwilling (Eds.), *Responsible AI and Ethical Issues for Businesses and Governments* (pp. 179–201). doi:10.4018/978-1-7998-4285-9.ch010

Ou, A. W., Stöhr, C., & Malmström, H. (2024). Academic communication with AI-powered language tools in higher education: From a post-humanist perspective. *System, 121*(103225), 103225. Advance online publication. doi:10.1016/j.system.2024.103225

Ounnas, A., Davis, H. C., & Millard, D. E. (2009). A framework for semantic group formation in education. *Journal of Educational Technology & Society, 12*(4), 43–55.

Page, E. B. (2003). Project essay grade: PEG. Automated essay scoring: A cross-disciplinary perspective, 43–54.

Palinscar, A. S., & Brown, A. L. (1984). Reciprocal teaching of comprehension-fostering and comprehension-monitoring activities. *Cognition and Instruction, 1*(2), 117–175. doi:10.1207/s1532690xci0102_1

Panitz, T. (1999). Collaborative versus cooperative learning: A comparison of the two concepts which will help us understand the underlying nature of interactive learning. Academic Press.

Papert, S. (2020). *Mindstorms: Children, computers, and powerful ideas.* Basic Books.

Patrickson, B. L. (2019). The reflective muse. *Student Engagement in Higher Education Journal, 2*(3), 77–83.

Paul, T. E. (1995). *Why Fly? A Philosophy of Creativity.* Bloomsbury Academic.

Pavlik, G. (2024, January 16). What is generative AI? How does it work? https://www.oracle.com/za/artificial-intelligence/generative-ai/what-is-generative-ai/ doi:10.1007/978-3-030-77584-1_15

Perkins, M. (2023). Academic Integrity considerations of AI Large Language Models in the post-pandemic era: ChatGPT and beyond. *Journal of University Teaching & Learning Practice, 20*(2). Advance online publication. doi:10.53761/1.20.02.07

PhenomenalPancake. (n.d.). Why are people talking about kids not being able to read anymore? r/OutOfTheLoop. https://www.reddit.com/r/OutOfTheLoop/comments/18igdho/why_are_people_talking_about_kids_not_being_able/?rdt=59203

Pineteh, E. M. (2014). The academic writing challenges of undergraduate students: A South African case study. *International Journal of Higher Education, 3*(1), 12–22.

Pinto, M., Caballero-Mariscal, D., García-Marco, F.-J., & Gómez-Camarero, C. (2023). A strategic approach to information literacy: Data literacy. A systematic review. *El Profesional de la Información*, e320609. Advance online publication. doi:10.3145/epi.2023.nov.09

Pllana, D. (2019). Creativity in modern education. *World Journal of Education, 9*(2), 136–140. doi:10.5430/wje.v9n2p136

Po, B., & Merryman, A. (2010). The Creativity Crisis. *Newsweek Education.* https://www.newsweek.com/2010/07/10/the-creativity-crisis.html

Prillaman, M. (2024, February 28). Is ChatGPT making scientists hyper-productive? The highs and lows of using AI. *Nature, 627*(8002), 16–17. Advance online publication. doi:10.1038/d41586-024-00592-w PMID:38418736

Prince, R. N., Frith, V., Steyn, S., & Cliff, A. F. (2021). Academic and quantitative literacy in higher education: Relationship with cognate school-leaving subjects. *South African Journal of Higher Education*, *35*(3). Advance online publication. doi:10.20853/35-3-3943

Prolifics. (2023, June 23). *Foster a culture of data literacy*. Prolifics. https://prolifics.com/us/stream-articles/category/data-analysis/6839209/02/25/2024/foster-a-culture-of-data-literacy

Proscovia. (2023). Google invests US$1.5M in Mak Ocular: An AI Automated Mobile Microscopic Diagnosis of Malaria, Cancer & Tuberculosis. *Mak News*. bit.ly/3ZWQb9K

Puaschunder, J. M. (2020). On Freedom in the Artificial Age. *RAIS Conference Proceedings*, 75-80.

Qasrawi, R., & BeniAndelrahman, A. (2020). The higher and lower-order thinking skills (HOTS and LOTS) in Unlock English textbooks (1st and 2nd editions) based on Bloom's Taxonomy: An analysis study. International Online Journal of Education and Teaching, 7(3), 744–758.

Qi, Q., & Zhao, C. G. (2023). Discoursal scholarly identity in research writing. *Journal of Second Language Writing*, *62*, 1–12. doi:10.1016/j.jslw.2023.101052

Radford, A., Wu, J., Child, R., Luan, D., Amodei, D., & Sutskever, I. (2019). Language models are unsupervised multitask learners. *OpenAI blog, 1*(8), 9.

Raheem, B. R., Anjum, F., & Ghafar, Z. N. (2023). Exploring the Profound Impact of Artificial Intelligence Applications (Quillbot, Grammarly and ChatGPT) on English Academic Writing: A Systematic Review. *International Journal of Integrative Research*, *1*(10), 599–622.

Rahman, A., Santosa, T. A., Ilwandri, I., Suharyat, Y., Aprilisia, S., & Suhaimi, S. (2023). The effectiveness of AI based blended learning on student scientific literacy: Meta-analysis. LITERACY: International Scientific Journals of Social, Education. *Humanities (Washington)*, *2*(1), 141–150.

Ramandanis, D., & Xinogalos, S. (2023). Investigating the support provided by chatbots to educational institutions and their students: A systematic literature review. *Multimodal Technologies and Interaction*, *7*(11), 103. doi:10.3390/mti7110103

Rasul, T., Nair, S., Kalendra, D., Robin, M., de Oliveira Santini, F., Ladeira, W. J., ... Heathcote, L. (2023). The role of ChatGPT in higher education: Benefits, challenges, and future research directions. *Journal of Applied Learning and Teaching*, *6*(1), 41–56.

Regulski, I. (2016). The Origins and Early Development of Writing in Egypt. In The Oxford Handbook of Topics in Archaeology (pp. 1-32). Oxford University Press. doi:10.1093/oxfordhb/9780199935413.013.61

Reynolds, A., & Wiggill, C. (2022). LandyBot: Learner support. https://chats.landbot.io/v3/H-1050800-XBXSFK7IKLM0J5NT/index.html

Ridley, M., & Pawlick-Potts, D. (2021). Algorithmic literacy and the role for libraries. *Information Technology and Libraries*, *40*(2). Advance online publication. doi:10.6017/ital.v40i2.12963

Robinson, J. A., & Glanzer, P. L. (2017). Building a culture of academic integrity: What students perceive and need. *College Student Journal*, *51*(2), 209–221.

Robinson, S. C. (2020). Trust, transparency, and openness: How inclusion of cultural values shapes Nordic national public policy strategies for artificial intelligence (AI). *Technology in Society*, *63*, 101421. doi:10.1016/j.techsoc.2020.101421

Roll, I., & Wylie, R. (2016). Evolution and revolution in artificial intelligence in education. *International Journal of Artificial Intelligence in Education*, *26*(2), 582–599. doi:10.1007/s40593-016-0110-3

Ronald, C. (2015). *Language and Creativity: The Art of Common Talk*. Routledge.

Roose, K. (2022). The brilliance and weirdness of ChatGPT. The New York Times. https://www.nytimes.com/2022/12/05/technology/chatgpt-ai-twitter.html

Roscoe, R. D., Allen, L. K., Weston, J. L., Crossley, S. A., & McNamara, D. S. (2014). The Writing Pal intelligent tutoring system: Usability testing and development. *Computers and Composition*, *34*, 39–59. doi:10.1016/j.compcom.2014.09.002

Roscoe, R. D., & Chi, M. T. (2007). Understanding tutor learning: Knowledge-building and knowledge-telling in peer tutors' explanations and questions. *Review of Educational Research*, *77*(4), 534–574. doi:10.3102/0034654307309920

Roscoe, R. D., Kugler, D., Crossley, S. A., Weston, J. L., & McNamara, D. S. (2012). Developing pedagogically-guided threshold algorithms for intelligent automated essay feedback. *International FLAIRS Conference*.

Roscoe, R. D., & McNamara, D. S. (2013). Writing Pal: Feasibility of an intelligent writing strategy tutor in the high school classroom. *Journal of Educational Psychology*, *105*(4), 1010–1025. doi:10.1037/a0032340

Rosmawati. (2014) Dynamic development of complexity and accuracy: A case study in second language academic writing. *Australian Review of Applied Linguistics*, 37(2), 75–100. . doi:10.1075/aral.37.2.01ros

Roth, S., & de la Sota, B. (2023, April 26). ChatGPT: The start of the AI revolution. https://privatebank.jpmorgan.com/nam/en/insights/markets-and-investing/chatgpt-the-start-of-the-ai-revolution

Rudolph, J., Tan, S., & Tan, S. (2023b). War of the chatbots: Bard, Bing Chat, ChatGPT, Ernie and beyond. The new AI gold rush and its impact on higher education. Journal of Applied Learning and Teaching, 6(1), 364-389.

Rudolph, J., Tan, S., & Teaching, S. T.-J. (2023). ChatGPT: Bullshit spewer or the end of traditional assessments in higher education? *Journal of Applied Learning and Teaching*, *6*(1). Advance online publication. doi:10.37074/jalt.2023.6.1.9

Rummel, N., & Spada, H. (2005). Learning to collaborate: An instructional approach to promoting collaborative problem solving in computer-mediated settings. *Journal of the Learning Sciences*, *14*(2), 201–241. doi:10.1207/s15327809jls1402_2

Sabbati, G. (2022). Statistical and Data Literacy, a practitioner's view for policy-making: How to provide independent, objective and authoritative data and information for policy-making. *Statistical Journal of the IAOS*, *38*(2), 463–469. doi:10.3233/SJI-220942

Sample, A. (2020). Using Augmented and Virtual Reality in Information Literacy Instruction to Reduce Library Anxiety in Non-Traditional and International Students. *Information Technology and Libraries*, *39*(1), 1–33. doi:10.6017/ital.v39i1.11723

Sap, M., Gabriel, S., Qin, L., Jurafsky, D., Smith, N. A., & Choi, Y. (2019). Social bias frames: Reasoning about social and power implications of language. *arXiv preprint arXiv:1911.03891*.

Sarker, I. H. (2021). Machine Learning: Algorithms, Real-World Applications and Research Directions. *SN Computer Science*, *2*(3), 160. doi:10.1007/s42979-021-00592-x PMID:33778771

Savin-Baden, M., & Niekerk, L. V. (2007). Narrative inquiry: Theory and practice. *Journal of Geography in Higher Education*, *31*(3), 459–472. doi:10.1080/03098260601071324

Sawyer, R. D., & Norris, J. (2012). *Duoethnography*. Oxford University Press. doi:10.1093/acprof:osobl/9780199757404.001.0001

Schmarzo, B. (2023). *AI & Data Literacy: Empowering Citizens of Data Science*. Packt Publishing.

Schneider, B., & Pea, R. (2017). Real-time mutual gaze perception enhances collaborative learning and collaboration quality. *Educational Media and Technology Yearbook*, *40*, 99–125. doi:10.1007/978-3-319-45001-8_7

Schoenfeld, A. H., diSessa, A. A., Graesser, A. C., Benson, L. C., English, L. D., & Duschl, R. A. (2020). Computational thinking is more about thinking than computing. *Journal for STEM Education Research*, *3*(1), 1–18. doi:10.1007/s41979-020-00030-2 PMID:32838129

Schüller, K. (2022). Data and AI literacy for everyone. *Statistical Journal of the IAOS*, *38*(2), 477–490. doi:10.3233/SJI-220941

Selwyn, N. (2019). *Should robots replace teachers?: AI and the future of education*. John Wiley & Sons.

Seroto, J. (2011). Indigenous education during the pre-colonial period in southern Africa. *Indilinga*, *10*(1), 77–88.

Shermis, M. D. (2014). State-of-the-art automated essay scoring: Competition, results, and future directions from a United States demonstration. *Assessing Writing*, *20*, 53–76. doi:10.1016/j.asw.2013.04.001

Shermis, M. D., & Hamner, B. (2013). Contrasting state-of-the-art automated scoring of essays. In *Handbook of Automated Essay Evaluation* (pp. 313–346). Current Applications and New Directions.

Shidarta & Martinelli, I. (2023). Should Indonesia Block ChatGPT? E3S Web of Conferences, 426, 2046. doi:10.1051/e3sconf/202342602046

Shi, L., & Dong, Y. (2015). Graduate writing assignments across faculties in a Canadian university. *Canadian Journal of Higher Education*, *45*(4), 123–142. doi:10.47678/cjhe.v45i4.184723

Shripad, D. S. (2023, July 3). Top Artificial Intelligence (AI) Trends to Watch in 2023—MarkTechPost. Marktechpost. https://www.marktechpost.com/2023/01/07/top-artificial-intelligence-ai-trends-to-watch-in-2023/

Singh, M. (2023). Maintaining the integrity of the South African university: The impact of ChatGPT on plagiarism and scholarly writing. *South African Journal of Higher Education*, *37*(5). Advance online publication. doi:10.20853/37-5-5941

Sirna, G. (2022). Can Artificial Intelligence replace human creativity? An essay on Borges, Artificial Intelligence, DALL-E 2.0 and the future of work. https://medium.com/@guidosirna/can-artificial-intelligence-replace-human-creativity-b5e96ccd356a

Slater, W. H., & Horstman, F. R. (2002). Teaching reading and writing to struggling middle school and high school students: The case for reciprocal teaching. *Preventing School Failure*, *46*(4), 163–166. doi:10.1080/10459880209604416

SlimiZ.CarballidoB. V. (2023). Systematic Review: AI's Impact on Higher Education - Learning, Teaching, and Career Opportunities. *TEM Journal*, 1627–1637. https://doi.org/ doi:10.18421/TEM123-44

Smith, A. L., Greaves, F., & Panch, T. (2023). Hallucination or confabulation? Neuroanatomy as metaphor in large language models. *PLOS Digital Health*, *2*(11), e0000388. doi:10.1371/journal.pdig.0000388 PMID:37910473

Sokolow, A. (2020). *South Africa's Fourth Industrial Revolution limited by lack of computer literacy, access*. https://news.medill.northwestern.edu/chicago/south-africas-fourth-industrial-revolution-limited-by-lack-of-computer-literacy-access/

Southworth, Migliaccio, Glover, Glover, Reed, McCarty, Brendemuhl, & Thomas. (2023). Developing a model for AI Across the curriculum: Transforming the higher education landscape via innovation in AI literacy. *Computers and Education: Artificial Intelligence*, *4*, 1-10.

Southworth, J., Migliaccio, K., Glover, J., Glover, J., Reed, D., McCarty, C., Brendemuhl, J., & Thomas, A. (2023). Developing a model for AI Across the curriculum: Transforming the higher education landscape via innovation in AI literacy. *Computers and Education: Artificial Intelligence*, *4*(100127), 100127. Advance online publication. doi:10.1016/j.caeai.2023.100127

Spector, C. (2023, October 31). What do Ai Chatbots really mean for students and cheating? Stanford Graduate School of Education. https://ed.stanford.edu/news/what-do-ai-chatbots-really-mean-students-and-cheating

Spiliotopoulos, V., Wallace, A., & Ilieva, R. (2023). Diffusing Innovation to Support Faculty Engagement in the Integration of Language and Content across the Disciplines in an Internationalized Canadian University. *Higher Education Research & Development*, *42*(2), 453–467. doi:10.1080/07294360.2022.2052813

Spiro, R. J., Bruce, B. C., & Brewer, W. F. (Eds.). (2017). *Theoretical issues in reading comprehension: Perspectives from cognitive psychology, linguistics, artificial intelligence, and education* (Vol. 11). Routledge. doi:10.4324/9781315107493

Stack, M. (2023). *E-Journal of Humanities, Arts and Social Sciences (EHASS) Investigating an Assessment Design that Prevents Students from Using ChatGPT as the Sole Basis to Pass Assessment at the Tertiary Level.* doi:10.38159/ehass.20234127

Statista. (2024, February 26). Internet access by device in South Africa 2024. https://www.statista.com/statistics/1312851/internet-access-by-device-in-south-africa/

Storch, N., & Tapper, J. (2009). The impact of an EAP course on postgraduate writing. *Journal of English for Academic Purposes*, *8*(3), 207–223. doi:10.1016/j.jeap.2009.03.001

Street, B. (2003). What's "new" in New Literacy Studies? Critical approaches to literacy in theory and practice. *Current Issues in Comparative Education*, *5*(2), 77–91.

Strzelecki, A. (2023). To use or not to use ChatGPT in higher education? A study of students' acceptance and use of technology. *Interactive Learning Environments*, 1–14. Advance online publication. doi:10.1080/10494820.2023.2209881

Sullivan, M., Kelly, A., & McLaughlan, P. (2023). ChatGPT in higher education: Considerations for academic integrity and student learning. *Journal of Applied Learning & Teaching*, *6*(1), 31–40.

Swales, J., & Feak, C. (2012). *Academic writing for graduate students: Essential tasks and skills* (3rd ed.). University of Michigan Press. doi:10.3998/mpub.2173936

Tableu. (n.d.). *Top data literacy skills for becoming data literate.* Tableu.Com. https://www.tableau.com/data-insights/data-literacy/skills

Taecharungroj, V. (2023). "What can ChatGPT do?" Analyzing early reactions to the innovative AI Chatbot on twitter. *Big Data and Cognitive Computing.*, *7*(35), 35. Advance online publication. doi:10.3390/bdcc7010035

Tambiah, S. J. (2017). The magical power of words. In Ritual. Routledge. doi:10.4324/9781315244099-20

Tanveer, M., Hassan, S., & Bhaumik, A. (2020). Academic policy regarding sustainability and artificial intelligence (AI). *Sustainability (Basel)*, *12*(22), 9435. doi:10.3390/su12229435

Compilation of References

Tarisayi, K. S. (2024). ChatGPT use in universities in South Africa through a socio-technical lens. *Cogent Education, 11*(1), 2295654. Advance online publication. doi:10.1080/233118 6X.2023.2295654

Tegegne, H. M. (2015). Recordmaking, Recordkeeping and Landholding – Chanceries and Archives in Ethiopia (1700–1974). *History in Africa, 42*, 433–461. doi:10.1017/hia.2014.23

Tegos, S., Demetriadis, S., & Karakostas, A. (2015). Promoting academically productive talk with conversational agent interventions in collaborative learning settings. *Computers & Education, 87*, 309–325. doi:10.1016/j.compedu.2015.07.014

Tegos, S., Demetriadis, S., Papadopoulos, P. M., & Weinberger, A. (2016). Conversational agents for academically productive talk: A comparison of directed and undirected agent interventions. *International Journal of Computer-Supported Collaborative Learning, 11*(4), 417–440. doi:10.1007/s11412-016-9246-2

Tegos, S., Demetriadis, S., & Tsiatsos, T. (2014). A configurable conversational agent to trigger students' productive dialogue: A pilot study in the CALL domain. *International Journal of Artificial Intelligence in Education, 24*(1), 62–91. doi:10.1007/s40593-013-0007-3

Tenopir, C., Rice, N. M., Allard, S., Baird, L., Borycz, J., Christian, L., Grant, B., Olendorf, R., & Sandusky, R. J. (2020). Data sharing, management, use, and reuse: Practices and perceptions of scientists worldwide. *PLoS One, 15*(3), e0229003. doi:10.1371/journal.pone.0229003 PMID:32160189

Thaheem, S. K., Zainol Abidin, M. J., Mirza, Q., & Pathan, H. U. (2022). Online teaching benefits and challenges during pandemic COVID-19: A comparative study of Pakistan and Indonesia. *Asian Education and Development Studies, 11*(2), 311–323. doi:10.1108/AEDS-08-2020-0189

Thomas, A., & Van Zyl, A. (2012). Understanding of and attitudes to academic ethics among first-year university students. *African Journal of Business Ethics, 6*(2), 143–155. doi:10.4103/1817-7417.111028

Thorp, H. H. (2023). ChatGPT is fun, but not an author. *Science, 379*(6630), 313. doi:10.1126/science.adg7879 PMID:36701446

Throne, R. (2019). *Autoethnography and heuristic inquiry for doctoral-level researchers: Emerging research and opportunities*. IGI Global. 9365-2 doi:10.4018/978-1-5225-9365-2

Tianbo, Z. (2012). *The Internet of Things Promoting Higher Education Revolution*. In *2012 Fourth International Conference on Multimedia Information Networking and Security* (pp. 790-793). 10.1109/MINES.2012.231

Tlili, A., Shehata, B., Adarkwah, M. A., Bozkurt, A., Hickey, D. T., Huang, R., & Agyemang, B. (2023). What if the devil is my guardian angel: ChatGPT as a case study of using chatbots in education. *Smart Learning Environments, 10*(1), 1–24. https://link.springer.com/article/10.1186/s40561-023-00237-x

Toncic, J. (2020). Teachers, AI Grammar Checkers, and the Newest Literacies: Emending Writing Pedagogy and Assessment. Digital Culture &amp. *Education*, *12*(1), 26–51. https://doaj.org/toc/1836-8301

Toyosaki, S., Pensoneau-Conway, S. L., Wendt, N. A., & Leathers, K. (2009). Community autoethnography: Compiling the personal and resituating whiteness. Cultural Studies? *Cultural Studies, Critical Methodologies*, *9*(1), 56–83. doi:10.1177/1532708608321498

Tran, T. N., & Tran, H. P. (2023, November). Exploring the Role of ChatGPT in Developing Critical Digital Literacies in Language Learning: A Qualitative Study. In *Proceedings of the AsiaCALL International Conference* (Vol. 4, pp. 1-17). 10.54855/paic.2341

Tse, C. (2023, August 7). An AI on the Future. Goldman Sachs Asset Management. https://www.gsam.com/content/gsam/us/en/individual/market-insights/gsam-insights/perspectives/2023/artificial-intelligence-future.html

Turing, A. M. (1950). Computing Machinery and Intelligence. *Mind. New Series*, *59*(236), 433–460. doi:10.1093/mind/LIX.236.433

Twinomurinzi, H., & Gumbo, S. (2023). ChatGPT in Scholarly Discourse: Sentiments and an Inflection Point. *Communications in Computer and Information Science, 1878 CCIS*, 258–272. https://link.springer.com/chapter/10.1007/978-3-031-39652-6_17

UCT. (2023). *Senate Ethics in Research Committee (EiRc) Guidelines and recommendations for the use of generative artificial intelligence (AI) tools in research*. https://uct.ac.za/sites/default/files/media/documents/uct_ac_za/87/EiRC_GenerativeAI_guideline_Oct2023_final.pdf

UJPress. (2023). *Artificial Intelligence and Generative AI Policy*. https://ujonlinepress.uj.ac.za/index.php/ujp/AI

United Nations Educational Scientific and Cultural Organisation. (2002). Open and distance learning: trends, policy and strategy considerations. Paris: UNESCO. https://unesdoc.unesco.org/ark:/48223/pf0000128463

University of Johannesburg. (2023). *UJ practice note: Generative artificial intelligence in teaching, learning and research*. https://www.uj.ac.za/wp-content/uploads/2023/08/uj-ai-practice-guide-2023.pdf

University of Johannesburg. (n.d.). Staff guide: Generative artificial intelligence in teaching, learning and research. https://www.uj.ac.za/wp-content/uploads/2023/08/uj-ai-guidelines-staff.pdf

University of North Georgia. (2023). Student Code of Conduct Policy. https://northgeorgia.policystat.com/policy/13881254/latest/

University of Pretoria. (2023a). *Guide for ChatGPT usage in teaching and learning*. https://www.up.ac.za/media/shared/391/pdfs/up-guide-for-chatgtp-for-teaching-and-learning.zp233629.pdf

University of Pretoria. (2023b). *Leveraging Generative Artificial Intelligence for Teaching and Learning Enhancement at the University of Pretoria.* https://www.up.ac.za/media/shared/391/pdfs/up-student-guide_-leveraging-generative-artificial-intelligence-for-learning.zp242396.pdf

University of the Witwatersrand. (2023). *Approach to the use of AI in teaching and learning at Wits – Jan 2023.* https://www.wits.ac.za/media/wits-university/learning-and-teaching/cltd/documents/AI-in-teaching-and-learning-at-Wits.pdf

Usova, T., & Laws, R. (2021). Teaching a one-credit course on data literacy and data visualisation. *Journal of Information Literacy, 15*(1). Advance online publication. doi:10.11645/15.1.2840

Utami, S., Andayani, A., Winarni, R., & Sumarwati, S. (2023). Utilization of artificial intelligence technology in an academic writing class: How do Indonesian students perceive? *Contemporary Educational Technology, 14*(4), ep450. Advance online publication. doi:10.30935/cedtech/13419

Vajjala, S. (2018). Automated Assessment of Non-Native Learner Essays: Investigating the Role of Linguistic Features. *International Journal of Artificial Intelligence in Education, 28*(1), 79–105. doi:10.1007/s40593-017-0142-3

Van Dijk, T. A. (1994). Academic nationalism. *Discourse & Society, 5*(3), 275–276. doi:10.1177/0957926594005003001

VanLehn, K. (2011). The relative effectiveness of human tutoring, intelligent tutoring systems, and other tutoring systems. *Educational Psychologist, 46*(4), 197–221. doi:10.1080/00461520.2011.611369

Vasile-Daniel, P., & Sabina-Cristiana, N. (2023). Artificial Intelligence as a Disruptive Technology - A Systematic Literature Review. *Electronics (Basel), 12*(5), 1102. doi:10.3390/electronics12051102

Vaswani, A., Shazeer, N., Parmar, N., Uszkoreit, J., Jones, L., Gomez, A. N., Kaiser, Ł., & Polosukhin, I. (2017). Attention is all you need. Advances in neural information processing systems [Paper Presentation]. *31st Conference on Neural Information Processing Systems*, Long Beach, CA, United States.

Vemula, S. (2022). *Human-Centered Explainable Artificial Intelligence for Anomaly Detection in Quality Inspection: A Collaborative Approach to Bridge the Gap between Humans and AI* (Doctoral dissertation, University of the Incarnate Word). ProQuest Dissertations Publishing. (Accession No. 29069196)

Venkatesh, V., Morris, M. G., Davis, G. B. D. F. D., & Davis. (2003). User acceptance of information Technology: Toward a unified view. *Management Information Systems Quarterly, 27*(3), 425–478. . doi:10.2307/30036540

Verma, N. (2023, February 9). How Effective is AI in Education? 10 Case Studies and Examples. Axon Park. https://axonpark.com/how-effective-is-ai-in-education-10-case-studies-and-examples/ Volume doi:10.1002/rrq.494

Vinall, K., & Hellmich, E. (2022). Do you speak translate?: Reflections on the nature and role of translation. *Journal of Linguistics and Language Teaching*, *14*(1). Advance online publication. doi:10.5070/L214156150

Vinichenko, M. V., Melnichuk, A. V., & Karácsony, P. (2020). Technologies of improving the university efficiency by using artificial intelligence: Motivational aspect. *Entrepreneurship and Sustainability Issues*, *7*(4), 2696–2714. doi:10.9770/jesi.2020.7.4(9)

Vinuesa, R., & Sirmacek, B. (2021). Interpretable deep-learning models to help achieve the Sustainable Development Goals. *Nature Machine Intelligence*, *3*(11), 926–926. doi:10.1038/s42256-021-00414-y

Vygotsky, L. S., & Cole, M. (1978). *Mind in society: The development of higher psychological processes*. Harvard University Press.

Wallwey, C., & Kajfez, R. L. (2023). Quantitative research artifacts as qualitative data collection techniques in a mixed methods research study. *Methods in Psychology (Online)*, *8*, 100115. doi:10.1016/j.metip.2023.100115

Walters, W. H., & Wilder, E. I. (2023). Fabrication and errors in the bibliographic citations generated by ChatGPT. *Scientific Reports*, *13*(1), 14045. doi:10.1038/s41598-023-41032-5 PMID:37679503

Wang, H., Dang, A., Wu, Z., & Mac, S. (2023). Seeing ChatGPT through universities' policies, resources and guidelines. arXiv preprint arXiv:2312.05235.

Wang, N., & Lester, J. (2023, June). K-12 Education in the Age of AI: A Call to Action for K-12 AI Literacy. International Journal of Artificial Intelligence in Education, 33(2), 228-232.

Wang, X., Yang, D., Wen, M., Koedinger, K., & Rosé, C. P. (2015). *Investigating how students' cognitive behavior in MOOC discussion forums affect learning gains*. International Educational Data Mining Society.

Warschauer, M., & Grimes, D. (2008). Automated writing assessment in the classroom. *Pedagogies*, *3*(1), 22–36. doi:10.1080/15544800701771580

Watty, K., McKay, J., & Ngo, L. (2016). Innovators or inhibitors? Accounting faculty resistance to new educational technologies in higher education. *Journal of Accounting Education*, *36*, 1–15. doi:10.1016/j.jaccedu.2016.03.003

Wayman, J. C., & Jimerson, J. B. (2014). Teacher needs for data-related professional learning. *Studies in Educational Evaluation*, *42*, 25–34. doi:10.1016/j.stueduc.2013.11.001

Webb, N. M., Nemer, K. M., & Zuniga, S. (2002). Short circuits or superconductors? Effects of group composition on high-achieving students' science assessment performance. *American Educational Research Journal*, *39*(4), 943–989. doi:10.3102/00028312039004943

Compilation of References

Weber-Wulff, D., Anohina-Naumeca, A., Bjelobaba, S., Foltýnek, T., Guerrero-Dib, J., Popoola, O., & Waddington, L. (2023). Testing of detection tools for AI-generated text. *International Journal for Educational Integrity*, *19*(1), 26. doi:10.1007/s40979-023-00146-z

Webster, L., & Mertova, P. (2007). *Using narrative inquiry as a research method: An introduction to using critical event narrative analysis in research on learning and teaching*. Routledge. doi:10.4324/9780203946268

Wei, X. (2023). Data-Driven Revolution: Advancing Scientific and Technological Innovation in Chinese A-Share Listed Companies. *Journal of the Knowledge Economy*. Advance online publication. doi:10.1007/s13132-023-01476-6

Wheatley, A., & Hervieux, S. (2022). Separating artificial intelligence from science fiction: Creating an academic library workshop series on AI literacy. In S. Hervieux & A. Wheatley (Eds.), *The Rise of AI: Implications and Applications of Artificial Intelligence in Academic Libraries*. Association of College and Research Libraries.

Wibowo, G. A., Rahman, A., & Anis, M. (2023). The impact of ChatGPT use on the quality of academic support for students. *Technology and Society Perspectives*, *1*(3), 132–138. doi:10.61100/tacit.v1i3.69

Wiggill, C. (2024). *South African Teachers' Perceptions of the Adoption of Artificial Intelligence in the Classroom. Submission of research report for part-fulfillment of MEd ICT*. University of Johannesburg.

Williamson, B., Eynon, R., & Potter, J. (2020). Pandemic politics, pedagogies, and practices: Digital technologies and distance education during the coronavirus emergency. *Learning, Media and Technology*, *45*(2), 107–114. doi:10.1080/17439884.2020.1761641

Wilson, J., & Czik, A. (2016). Automated essay evaluation software in English Language Arts classrooms: Effects on teacher feedback, student motivation, and writing quality. *Computers & Education*, *100*, 94–109. doi:10.1016/j.compedu.2016.05.004

Wise, A. F., & Cui, Y. (2018). Unpacking the relationship between discussion forum participation and learning in MOOCs: Content is key. In *Proceedings of the 8th International Conference on Learning Analytics and Knowledge* (pp. 330-339). 10.1145/3170358.3170403

Wise, A., Zhao, Y., & Hausknecht, S. (2014). Learning analytics for online discussions: Embedded and extracted approaches. *Journal of Learning Analytics*, *1*(2), 48–71. doi:10.18608/jla.2014.12.4

Wolff, A., Gooch, D., Cavero Montaner, J. J., Rashid, U., & Kortuem, G. (2016). Creating an Understanding of Data Literacy for a Data-driven Society. *The Journal of Community Informatics*, *12*(3). Advance online publication. doi:10.15353/joci.v12i3.3275

Wollscheid, S., Lødding, B., & Aamodt, P. O. (2021). Prepared for higher education? Staff and student perceptions of academic literacy dimensions across disciplines. *Quality in Higher Education*, *27*(1), 20–39. doi:10.1080/13538322.2021.1830534

Woolf, B. P., Lane, H. C., Chaudhri, V. K., & Kolodner, J. L. (2013). AI grand challenges for education. *AI Magazine*, *34*(4), 66–84. doi:10.1609/aimag.v34i4.2490

Xames, M. D., & Shefa, J. (2023). ChatGPT for research and publication: Opportunities and challenges. *SSRN*, *6*(1), 390–395. doi:10.2139/ssrn.4381803

Xiao, Y., & Lucking, R. (2008). The impact of two types of peer assessment on students' performance and satisfaction within a Wiki environment. *The Internet and Higher Education*, *11*(3-4), 186–193. doi:10.1016/j.iheduc.2008.06.005

Xiong, W., Litman, D., & Schunn, C. (2010). Assessing reviewers' performance based on mining problem localization in peer-review data. In *Educational Data Mining 2010-3rd International Conference on Educational Data Mining* (pp. 211-220). Academic Press.

Xiong, W., Litman, D., & Schunn, C. (2012). Natural language processing techniques for researching and improving peer feedback. *Journal of Writing Research*, *4*(2), 155–176. doi:10.17239/jowr-2012.04.02.3

Yang, H. (2023). How I use ChatGPT responsibly in my teaching. *Nature*. Advance online publication. doi:10.1038/d41586-023-01026-9 PMID:37045954

Yeh, C.-W., Hung, S.-H., & Chang, C.-Y. (2022). The influence of natural environments on creativity. *Frontier Psychiatry*, *13*. https://www.frontiersin.org/articles/10.3389/fpsyt.2022.895213/full

Yeh, H.-C. (2015). Facilitating metacognitive processes of academic genre-based writing using an online writing system. *Computer Assisted Language Learning*, *28*(6), 479–498. doi:10.108 0/09588221.2014.881384

Yohannes, M. Y., Demis, A. G., & Asemamaw, T. D. (2023). Factors affecting "employees' creativity": The mediating role of intrinsic motivation. *Journal of Innovation and Entrepreneurship*, *12*(31).

York, A. (2024, February 14). *Make Informed Decisions: 10 First-Class AI Tools for Data Visualization*. ClickUp. https://clickup.com/blog/ai-tools-for-data-visualization/

Yusuf. (2023). AI poses new threat to integrity of Kenyan university students' work. *Voice of America*.

Zhang, H., Lee, I., & Safinah, A. (2023, June). Integrating Ethics and Career Futures with Technical Learning to Promote AI Literacy for Middle School Students: An Exploratory Study. International Journal of Artificial Intelligence in Education, 33(2), 290-324.

Zhao, T., & Eskenazi, M. (2018). Zero-shot dialog generation with cross-domain latent actions. *arXiv preprint arXiv:1805.04803*. doi:10.18653/v1/W18-5001

Zhao, L., Wu, X., & Luo, H. (2022). Developing AI Literacy for Primary and Middle School Teachers in China: Based on a Structural Equation Modeling Analysis. *Sustainability (Basel)*, *14*(21), 14549. doi:10.3390/su142114549

Zhu, Y., Wang, Z., Chen, C., & Dong, D. (2022). Rule-Based Reinforcement Learning for Efficient Robot Navigation With Space Reduction. *IEEE/ASME Transactions on Mechatronics*, *27*(2), 846–857. doi:10.1109/TMECH.2021.3072675

Zou, M., & Huang, L. (2023). To use or not to use? Understanding doctoral students' acceptance of ChatGPT in writing through technology acceptance model. *Frontiers in Psychology*, *14*, 14. doi:10.3389/fpsyg.2023.1259531 PMID:37954179

Related References

To continue our tradition of advancing academic research, we have compiled a list of recommended IGI Global readings. These references will provide additional information and guidance to further enrich your knowledge and assist you with your own research and future publications.

Aburezeq, I. M., & Dweikat, F. F. (2017). Cloud Applications in Language Teaching: Examining Pre-Service Teachers' Expertise, Perceptions and Integration. *International Journal of Distance Education Technologies*, *15*(4), 39–60. doi:10.4018/IJDET.2017100103

Acharjya, B., & Das, S. (2022). Adoption of E-Learning During the COVID-19 Pandemic: The Moderating Role of Age and Gender. *International Journal of Web-Based Learning and Teaching Technologies*, *17*(2), 1–14. https://doi.org/10.4018/IJWLTT.20220301.oa4

Adams, J. L., & Thomas, S. K. (2022). Non-Linear Curriculum Experiences for Student Learning and Work Design: What Is the Maximum Potential of a Chat Bot? In S. Ramlall, T. Cross, & M. Love (Eds.), *Handbook of Research on Future of Work and Education: Implications for Curriculum Delivery and Work Design* (pp. 299–306). IGI Global. https://doi.org/10.4018/978-1-7998-8275-6.ch018

Adera, B. (2017). Supporting Language and Literacy Development for English Language Learners. In J. Keengwe (Ed.), *Handbook of Research on Promoting Cross-Cultural Competence and Social Justice in Teacher Education* (pp. 339–354). Hershey, PA: IGI Global. doi:10.4018/978-1-5225-0897-7.ch018

Ahamer, G. (2017). Quality Assurance for a Developmental "Global Studies" (GS) Curriculum. In I. Management Association (Ed.), Educational Leadership and Administration: Concepts, Methodologies, Tools, and Applications (pp. 438-477). Hershey, PA: IGI Global. https://doi.org/ doi:10.4018/978-1-5225-1624-8.ch023

Ahamer, G. (2017). Quality Assurance for a Developmental "Global Studies" (GS) Curriculum. In I. Management Association (Ed.), Educational Leadership and Administration: Concepts, Methodologies, Tools, and Applications (pp. 438-477). Hershey, PA: IGI Global. https://doi.org/ doi:10.4018/978-1-5225-1624-8.ch023

Akayoğlu, S., & Seferoğlu, G. (2019). An Analysis of Negotiation of Meaning Functions of Advanced EFL Learners in Second Life: Negotiation of Meaning in Second Life. In M. Kruk (Ed.), *Assessing the Effectiveness of Virtual Technologies in Foreign and Second Language Instruction* (pp. 61–85). IGI Global. https://doi.org/10.4018/978-1-5225-7286-2.ch003

Akella, N. R. (2022). Unravelling the Web of Qualitative Dissertation Writing!: A Student Reflects. In A. Zimmerman (Ed.), *Methodological Innovations in Research and Academic Writing* (pp. 260–282). IGI Global. https://doi.org/10.4018/978-1-7998-8283-1.ch014

Alegre de la Rosa, O. M., & Angulo, L. M. (2017). Social Inclusion and Intercultural Values in a School of Education. In S. Mukerji & P. Tripathi (Eds.), *Handbook of Research on Administration, Policy, and Leadership in Higher Education* (pp. 518–531). Hershey, PA: IGI Global. doi:10.4018/978-1-5225-0672-0.ch020

Alexander, C. (2019). Using Gamification Strategies to Cultivate and Measure Professional Educator Dispositions. *International Journal of Game-Based Learning*, 9(1), 15–29. https://doi.org/10.4018/IJGBL.2019010102

Anderson, K. M. (2017). Preparing Teachers in the Age of Equity and Inclusion. In I. Management Association (Ed.), Medical Education and Ethics: Concepts, Methodologies, Tools, and Applications (pp. 1532-1554). Hershey, PA: IGI Global. doi:10.4018/978-1-5225-0978-3.ch069

Awdziej, M. (2017). Case Study as a Teaching Method in Marketing. In D. Latusek (Ed.), *Case Studies as a Teaching Tool in Management Education* (pp. 244–263). Hershey, PA: IGI Global. doi:10.4018/978-1-5225-0770-3.ch013

Bakos, J. (2019). Sociolinguistic Factors Influencing English Language Learning. In N. Erdogan & M. Wei (Eds.), *Applied Linguistics for Teachers of Culturally and Linguistically Diverse Learners* (pp. 403–424). IGI Global. https://doi.org/10.4018/978-1-5225-8467-4.ch017

Banas, J. R., & York, C. S. (2017). Pre-Service Teachers' Motivation to Use Technology and the Impact of Authentic Learning Exercises. In L. Tomei (Ed.), *Exploring the New Era of Technology-Infused Education* (pp. 121–140). Hershey, PA: IGI Global. doi:10.4018/978-1-5225-1709-2.ch008

Barton, T. P. (2021). Empowering Educator Allyship by Exploring Racial Trauma and the Disengagement of Black Students. In C. Reneau & M. Villarreal (Eds.), *Handbook of Research on Leading Higher Education Transformation With Social Justice, Equity, and Inclusion* (pp. 186–197). IGI Global. https://doi.org/10.4018/978-1-7998-7152-1.ch013

Benhima, M. (2021). Moroccan English Department Student Attitudes Towards the Use of Distance Education During COVID-19: Moulay Ismail University as a Case Study. *International Journal of Information and Communication Technology Education*, 17(3), 105–122. https://doi.org/10.4018/IJICTE.20210701.oa7

Beycioglu, K., & Wildy, H. (2017). Principal Preparation: The Case of Novice Principals in Turkey. In I. Management Association (Ed.), Educational Leadership and Administration: Concepts, Methodologies, Tools, and Applications (pp. 1152-1169). Hershey, PA: IGI Global. https://doi.org/ doi:10.4018/978-1-5225-1624-8.ch054

Bharwani, S., & Musunuri, D. (2018). Reflection as a Process From Theory to Practice. In M. Khosrow-Pour, D.B.A. (Ed.), Encyclopedia of Information Science and Technology, Fourth Edition (pp. 1529-1539). Hershey, PA: IGI Global. doi:10.4018/978-1-5225-2255-3.ch132

Bhushan, A., Garza, K. B., Perumal, O., Das, S. K., Feola, D. J., Farrell, D., & Birnbaum, A. (2022). Lessons Learned From the COVID-19 Pandemic and the Implications for Pharmaceutical Graduate Education and Research. In C. Ford & K. Garza (Eds.), *Handbook of Research on Updating and Innovating Health Professions Education: Post-Pandemic Perspectives* (pp. 324–345). IGI Global. https://doi.org/10.4018/978-1-7998-7623-6.ch014

Bintz, W., Ciecierski, L. M., & Royan, E. (2021). Using Picture Books With Instructional Strategies to Address New Challenges and Teach Literacy Skills in a Digital World. In L. Haas & J. Tussey (Eds.), *Connecting Disciplinary Literacy and Digital Storytelling in K-12 Education* (pp. 38–58). IGI Global. https://doi.org/10.4018/978-1-7998-5770-9.ch003

Bohjanen, S. L., Cameron-Standerford, A., & Meidl, T. D. (2018). Capacity Building Pedagogy for Diverse Learners. In J. Keengwe (Ed.), *Handbook of Research on Pedagogical Models for Next-Generation Teaching and Learning* (pp. 195–212). Hershey, PA: IGI Global. doi:10.4018/978-1-5225-3873-8.ch011

Related References

Brewer, J. C. (2018). Measuring Text Readability Using Reading Level. In M. Khosrow-Pour, D.B.A. (Ed.), Encyclopedia of Information Science and Technology, Fourth Edition (pp. 1499-1507). Hershey, PA: IGI Global. doi:10.4018/978-1-5225-2255-3.ch129

Brookbanks, B. C. (2022). Student Perspectives on Business Education in the USA: Current Attitudes and Necessary Changes in an Age of Disruption. In A. Zhuplev & R. Koepp (Eds.), *Global Trends, Dynamics, and Imperatives for Strategic Development in Business Education in an Age of Disruption* (pp. 214–231). IGI Global. doi:10.4018/978-1-7998-7548-2.ch011

Brown, L. V., Dari, T., & Spencer, N. (2019). Addressing the Impact of Trauma in High Poverty Elementary Schools: An Ecological Model for School Counseling. In K. Daniels & K. Billingsley (Eds.), *Creating Caring and Supportive Educational Environments for Meaningful Learning* (pp. 135–153). IGI Global. https://doi.org/10.4018/978-1-5225-5748-7.ch008

Brown, S. L. (2017). A Case Study of Strategic Leadership and Research in Practice: Principal Preparation Programs that Work – An Educational Administration Perspective of Best Practices for Master's Degree Programs for Principal Preparation. In V. Wang (Ed.), *Encyclopedia of Strategic Leadership and Management* (pp. 1226–1244). Hershey, PA: IGI Global. doi:10.4018/978-1-5225-1049-9.ch086

Brzozowski, M., & Ferster, I. (2017). Educational Management Leadership: High School Principal's Management Style and Parental Involvement in School Management in Israel. In V. Potocan, M. Üngan, & Z. Nedelko (Eds.), *Handbook of Research on Managerial Solutions in Non-Profit Organizations* (pp. 55–74). Hershey, PA: IGI Global. doi:10.4018/978-1-5225-0731-4.ch003

Cahapay, M. B. (2020). Delphi Technique in the Development of Emerging Contents in High School Science Curriculum. *International Journal of Curriculum Development and Learning Measurement, 1*(2), 1–9. https://doi.org/10.4018/IJCDLM.2020070101

Camacho, L. F., & Leon Guerrero, A. E. (2022). Indigenous Student Experience in Higher Education: Implementation of Culturally Sensitive Support. In P. Pangelinan & T. McVey (Eds.), *Learning and Reconciliation Through Indigenous Education in Oceania* (pp. 254–266). IGI Global. https://doi.org/10.4018/978-1-7998-7736-3.ch016

Cannaday, J. (2017). The Masking Effect: Hidden Gifts and Disabilities of 2e Students. In P. Dickenson, P. Keough, & J. Courduff (Eds.), *Preparing Pre-Service Teachers for the Inclusive Classroom* (pp. 220–231). Hershey, PA: IGI Global. doi:10.4018/978-1-5225-1753-5.ch011

Cederquist, S., Fishman, B., & Teasley, S. D. (2022). What's Missing From the College Transcript?: How Employers Make Sense of Student Skills. In Y. Huang (Ed.), *Handbook of Research on Credential Innovations for Inclusive Pathways to Professions* (pp. 234–253). IGI Global. https://doi.org/10.4018/978-1-7998-3820-3.ch012

Cockrell, P., & Gibson, T. (2019). The Untold Stories of Black and Brown Student Experiences in Historically White Fraternities and Sororities. In P. Hoffman-Miller, M. James, & D. Hermond (Eds.), *African American Suburbanization and the Consequential Loss of Identity* (pp. 153–171). IGI Global. https://doi.org/10.4018/978-1-5225-7835-2.ch009

Cohen, M. (2022). Leveraging Content Creation to Boost Student Engagement. In T. Driscoll III, (Ed.), *Designing Effective Distance and Blended Learning Environments in K-12* (pp. 223–239). IGI Global. https://doi.org/10.4018/978-1-7998-6829-3.ch013

Contreras, E. C., & Contreras, I. I. (2018). Development of Communication Skills through Auditory Training Software in Special Education. In M. Khosrow-Pour, D.B.A. (Ed.), Encyclopedia of Information Science and Technology, Fourth Edition (pp. 2431-2441). Hershey, PA: IGI Global. doi:10.4018/978-1-5225-2255-3.ch212

Cooke, L., Schugar, J., Schugar, H., Penny, C., & Bruning, H. (2020). Can Everyone Code?: Preparing Teachers to Teach Computer Languages as a Literacy. In J. Mitchell & E. Vaughn (Eds.), *Participatory Literacy Practices for P-12 Classrooms in the Digital Age* (pp. 163–183). IGI Global. https://doi.org/10.4018/978-1-7998-0000-2.ch009

Cooley, D., & Whitten, E. (2017). Special Education Leadership and the Implementation of Response to Intervention. In F. Topor (Ed.), *Handbook of Research on Individualism and Identity in the Globalized Digital Age* (pp. 265–286). Hershey, PA: IGI Global. doi:10.4018/978-1-5225-0522-8.ch012

Cosner, S., Tozer, S., & Zavitkovsky, P. (2017). Enacting a Cycle of Inquiry Capstone Research Project in Doctoral-Level Leadership Preparation. In I. Management Association (Ed.), Educational Leadership and Administration: Concepts, Methodologies, Tools, and Applications (pp. 1460-1481). Hershey, PA: IGI Global. doi:10.4018/978-1-5225-1624-8.ch067

Crawford, C. M. (2018). Instructional Real World Community Engagement. In M. Khosrow-Pour, D.B.A. (Ed.), Encyclopedia of Information Science and Technology, Fourth Edition (pp. 1474-1486). Hershey, PA: IGI Global. doi:10.4018/978-1-5225-2255-3.ch127

Related References

Crosby-Cooper, T., & Pacis, D. (2017). Implementing Effective Student Support Teams. In P. Dickenson, P. Keough, & J. Courduff (Eds.), *Preparing Pre-Service Teachers for the Inclusive Classroom* (pp. 248–262). Hershey, PA: IGI Global. doi:10.4018/978-1-5225-1753-5.ch013

Curran, C. M., & Hawbaker, B. W. (2017). Cultivating Communities of Inclusive Practice: Professional Development for Educators – Research and Practice. In C. Curran & A. Petersen (Eds.), *Handbook of Research on Classroom Diversity and Inclusive Education Practice* (pp. 120–153). Hershey, PA: IGI Global. doi:10.4018/978-1-5225-2520-2.ch006

Dass, S., & Dabbagh, N. (2018). Faculty Adoption of 3D Avatar-Based Virtual World Learning Environments: An Exploratory Case Study. In I. Management Association (Ed.), Technology Adoption and Social Issues: Concepts, Methodologies, Tools, and Applications (pp. 1000-1033). Hershey, PA: IGI Global. https://doi.org/ doi:10.4018/978-1-5225-5201-7.ch045

Davison, A. M., & Scholl, K. G. (2017). Inclusive Recreation as Part of the IEP Process. In C. Curran & A. Petersen (Eds.), *Handbook of Research on Classroom Diversity and Inclusive Education Practice* (pp. 311–330). Hershey, PA: IGI Global. doi:10.4018/978-1-5225-2520-2.ch013

DeCoito, I. (2018). Addressing Digital Competencies, Curriculum Development, and Instructional Design in Science Teacher Education. In M. Khosrow-Pour, D.B.A. (Ed.), Encyclopedia of Information Science and Technology, Fourth Edition (pp. 1420-1431). Hershey, PA: IGI Global. https://doi.org/ doi:10.4018/978-1-5225-2255-3.ch122

DeCoito, I., & Richardson, T. (2017). Beyond Angry Birds™: Using Web-Based Tools to Engage Learners and Promote Inquiry in STEM Learning. In I. Levin & D. Tsybulsky (Eds.), *Digital Tools and Solutions for Inquiry-Based STEM Learning* (pp. 166–196). Hershey, PA: IGI Global. doi:10.4018/978-1-5225-2525-7.ch007

Delmas, P. M. (2017). Research-Based Leadership for Next-Generation Leaders. In R. Styron Jr & J. Styron (Eds.), *Comprehensive Problem-Solving and Skill Development for Next-Generation Leaders* (pp. 1–39). Hershey, PA: IGI Global. doi:10.4018/978-1-5225-1968-3.ch001

Demiray, U., & Ekren, G. (2018). Administrative-Related Evaluation for Distance Education Institutions in Turkey. In K. Buyuk, S. Kocdar, & A. Bozkurt (Eds.), *Administrative Leadership in Open and Distance Learning Programs* (pp. 263–288). Hershey, PA: IGI Global. doi:10.4018/978-1-5225-2645-2.ch011

Dickenson, P. (2017). What do we Know and Where Can We Grow?: Teachers Preparation for the Inclusive Classroom. In P. Dickenson, P. Keough, & J. Courduff (Eds.), *Preparing Pre-Service Teachers for the Inclusive Classroom* (pp. 1–22). Hershey, PA: IGI Global. doi:10.4018/978-1-5225-1753-5.ch001

Ding, Q., & Zhu, H. (2021). Flipping the Classroom in STEM Education. In J. Keengwe (Ed.), *Handbook of Research on Innovations in Non-Traditional Educational Practices* (pp. 155–173). IGI Global. https://doi.org/10.4018/978-1-7998-4360-3.ch008

Dixon, T., & Christison, M. (2021). Teaching English Grammar in a Hybrid Academic ESL Course: A Mixed Methods Study. In K. Kelch, P. Byun, S. Safavi, & S. Cervantes (Eds.), *CALL Theory Applications for Online TESOL Education* (pp. 229–251). IGI Global. https://doi.org/10.4018/978-1-7998-6609-1.ch010

Donne, V., & Hansen, M. (2017). Teachers' Use of Assistive Technologies in Education. In L. Tomei (Ed.), *Exploring the New Era of Technology-Infused Education* (pp. 86–101). Hershey, PA: IGI Global. doi:10.4018/978-1-5225-1709-2.ch006

Donne, V., & Hansen, M. A. (2018). Business and Technology Educators: Practices for Inclusion. In I. Management Association (Ed.), Business Education and Ethics: Concepts, Methodologies, Tools, and Applications (pp. 471-484). Hershey, PA: IGI Global. https://doi.org/ doi:10.4018/978-1-5225-3153-1.ch026

Dos Santos, L. M. (2022). Completing Student-Teaching Internships Online: Instructional Changes During the COVID-19 Pandemic. In M. Alaali (Ed.), *Assessing University Governance and Policies in Relation to the COVID-19 Pandemic* (pp. 106–127). IGI Global. https://doi.org/10.4018/978-1-7998-8279-4.ch007

Dreon, O., Shettel, J., & Bower, K. M. (2017). Preparing Next Generation Elementary Teachers for the Tools of Tomorrow. In M. Grassetti & S. Brookby (Eds.), *Advancing Next-Generation Teacher Education through Digital Tools and Applications* (pp. 143–159). Hershey, PA: IGI Global. doi:10.4018/978-1-5225-0965-3.ch008

Durak, H. Y., & Güyer, T. (2018). Design and Development of an Instructional Program for Teaching Programming Processes to Gifted Students Using Scratch. In J. Cannaday (Ed.), *Curriculum Development for Gifted Education Programs* (pp. 61–99). Hershey, PA: IGI Global. doi:10.4018/978-1-5225-3041-1.ch004

Egorkina, E., Ivanov, M., & Valyavskiy, A. Y. (2018). Students' Research Competence Formation of the Quality of Open and Distance Learning. In V. Mkrttchian & L. Belyanina (Eds.), *Handbook of Research on Students' Research Competence in Modern Educational Contexts* (pp. 364–384). Hershey, PA: IGI Global. doi:10.4018/978-1-5225-3485-3.ch019

Related References

Ekren, G., Karataş, S., & Demiray, U. (2017). Understanding of Leadership in Distance Education Management. In I. Management Association (Ed.), Educational Leadership and Administration: Concepts, Methodologies, Tools, and Applications (pp. 34-50). Hershey, PA: IGI Global. https://doi.org/ doi:10.4018/978-1-5225-1624-8.ch003

Elmore, W. M., Young, J. K., Harris, S., & Mason, D. (2017). The Relationship between Individual Student Attributes and Online Course Completion. In K. Shelton & K. Pedersen (Eds.), *Handbook of Research on Building, Growing, and Sustaining Quality E-Learning Programs* (pp. 151–173). Hershey, PA: IGI Global. doi:10.4018/978-1-5225-0877-9.ch008

Ercegovac, I. R., Alfirević, N., & Koludrović, M. (2017). School Principals' Communication and Co-Operation Assessment: The Croatian Experience. In I. Management Association (Ed.), Educational Leadership and Administration: Concepts, Methodologies, Tools, and Applications (pp. 1568-1589). Hershey, PA: IGI Global. https://doi.org/ doi:10.4018/978-1-5225-1624-8.ch072

Everhart, D., & Seymour, D. M. (2017). Challenges and Opportunities in the Currency of Higher Education. In K. Rasmussen, P. Northrup, & R. Colson (Eds.), *Handbook of Research on Competency-Based Education in University Settings* (pp. 41–65). Hershey, PA: IGI Global. doi:10.4018/978-1-5225-0932-5.ch003

Farmer, L. S. (2017). Managing Portable Technologies for Special Education. In V. Wang (Ed.), *Encyclopedia of Strategic Leadership and Management* (pp. 977–987). Hershey, PA: IGI Global. doi:10.4018/978-1-5225-1049-9.ch068

Farmer, L. S. (2018). Optimizing OERs for Optimal ICT Literacy in Higher Education. In J. Keengwe (Ed.), *Handbook of Research on Mobile Technology, Constructivism, and Meaningful Learning* (pp. 366–390). Hershey, PA: IGI Global. doi:10.4018/978-1-5225-3949-0.ch020

Ferguson, B. T. (2019). Supporting Affective Development of Children With Disabilities Through Moral Dilemmas. In S. Ikuta (Ed.), *Handmade Teaching Materials for Students With Disabilities* (pp. 253–275). IGI Global. doi:10.4018/978-1-5225-6240-5.ch011

Fındık, L. Y. (2017). Self-Assessment of Principals Based on Leadership in Complexity. In I. Management Association (Ed.), Educational Leadership and Administration: Concepts, Methodologies, Tools, and Applications (pp. 978-991). Hershey, PA: IGI Global. https://doi.org/ doi:10.4018/978-1-5225-1624-8.ch047

Flor, A. G., & Gonzalez-Flor, B. (2018). Dysfunctional Digital Demeanors: Tales From (and Policy Implications of) eLearning's Dark Side. In I. Management Association (Ed.), The Dark Web: Breakthroughs in Research and Practice (pp. 37-50). Hershey, PA: IGI Global. https://doi.org/ doi:10.4018/978-1-5225-3163-0.ch003

Floyd, K. K., & Shambaugh, N. (2017). Instructional Design for Simulations in Special Education Virtual Learning Spaces. In T. Kidd & L. Morris Jr., (Eds.), *Handbook of Research on Instructional Systems and Educational Technology* (pp. 202–215). Hershey, PA: IGI Global. doi:10.4018/978-1-5225-2399-4.ch018

Freeland, S. F. (2020). Community Schools: Improving Academic Achievement Through Meaningful Engagement. In R. Kronick (Ed.), *Emerging Perspectives on Community Schools and the Engaged University* (pp. 132–144). IGI Global. https://doi.org/10.4018/978-1-7998-0280-8.ch008

Ghanbarzadeh, R., & Ghapanchi, A. H. (2019). Applied Areas of Three Dimensional Virtual Worlds in Learning and Teaching: A Review of Higher Education. In I. Management Association (Ed.), *Virtual Reality in Education: Breakthroughs in Research and Practice* (pp. 172-192). IGI Global. https://doi.org/10.4018/978-1-5225-8179-6.ch008

Giovannini, J. M. (2017). Technology Integration in Preservice Teacher Education Programs: Research-based Recommendations. In M. Grassetti & S. Brookby (Eds.), *Advancing Next-Generation Teacher Education through Digital Tools and Applications* (pp. 82–102). Hershey, PA: IGI Global. doi:10.4018/978-1-5225-0965-3.ch005

Good, S., & Clarke, V. B. (2017). An Integral Analysis of One Urban School System's Efforts to Support Student-Centered Teaching. In J. Keengwe & G. Onchwari (Eds.), *Handbook of Research on Learner-Centered Pedagogy in Teacher Education and Professional Development* (pp. 45–68). Hershey, PA: IGI Global. doi:10.4018/978-1-5225-0892-2.ch003

Guetzoian, E. (2022). Gamification Strategies for Higher Education Student Worker Training. In C. Lane (Ed.), *Handbook of Research on Acquiring 21st Century Literacy Skills Through Game-Based Learning* (pp. 164–179). IGI Global. https://doi.org/10.4018/978-1-7998-7271-9.ch009

Hamidi, F., Owuor, P. M., Hynie, M., Baljko, M., & McGrath, S. (2017). Potentials of Digital Assistive Technology and Special Education in Kenya. In C. Ayo & V. Mbarika (Eds.), *Sustainable ICT Adoption and Integration for Socio-Economic Development* (pp. 125–151). Hershey, PA: IGI Global. doi:10.4018/978-1-5225-2565-3.ch006

Related References

Hamim, T., Benabbou, F., & Sael, N. (2022). Student Profile Modeling Using Boosting Algorithms. *International Journal of Web-Based Learning and Teaching Technologies*, *17*(5), 1–13. https://doi.org/10.4018/IJWLTT.20220901.oa4

Henderson, L. K. (2017). Meltdown at Fukushima: Global Catastrophic Events, Visual Literacy, and Art Education. In R. Shin (Ed.), *Convergence of Contemporary Art, Visual Culture, and Global Civic Engagement* (pp. 80–99). Hershey, PA: IGI Global. doi:10.4018/978-1-5225-1665-1.ch005

Hudgins, T., & Holland, J. L. (2018). Digital Badges: Tracking Knowledge Acquisition Within an Innovation Framework. In I. Management Association (Ed.), Wearable Technologies: Concepts, Methodologies, Tools, and Applications (pp. 1118-1132). Hershey, PA: IGI Global. https://doi.org/ doi:10.4018/978-1-5225-5484-4.ch051

Hwang, R., Lin, H., Sun, J. C., & Wu, J. (2019). Improving Learning Achievement in Science Education for Elementary School Students via Blended Learning. *International Journal of Online Pedagogy and Course Design*, *9*(2), 44–62. https://doi.org/10.4018/IJOPCD.2019040104

Jančec, L., & Vodopivec, J. L. (2019). The Implicit Pedagogy and the Hidden Curriculum in Postmodern Education. In J. Vodopivec, L. Jančec, & T. Štemberger (Eds.), *Implicit Pedagogy for Optimized Learning in Contemporary Education* (pp. 41–59). IGI Global. https://doi.org/10.4018/978-1-5225-5799-9.ch003

Janus, M., & Siddiqua, A. (2018). Challenges for Children With Special Health Needs at the Time of Transition to School. In I. Management Association (Ed.), Autism Spectrum Disorders: Breakthroughs in Research and Practice (pp. 339-371). Hershey, PA: IGI Global. doi:10.4018/978-1-5225-3827-1.ch018

Jesus, R. A. (2018). Screencasts and Learning Styles. In M. Khosrow-Pour, D.B.A. (Ed.), Encyclopedia of Information Science and Technology, Fourth Edition (pp. 1548-1558). Hershey, PA: IGI Global. doi:10.4018/978-1-5225-2255-3.ch134

John, G., Francis, N., & Santhakumar, A. B. (2022). Student Engagement: Past, Present, and Future. In S. Ramlall, T. Cross, & M. Love (Eds.), *Handbook of Research on Future of Work and Education: Implications for Curriculum Delivery and Work Design* (pp. 329–341). IGI Global. https://doi.org/10.4018/978-1-7998-8275-6.ch020

Karpinski, A. C., D'Agostino, J. V., Williams, A. K., Highland, S. A., & Mellott, J. A. (2018). The Relationship Between Online Formative Assessment and State Test Scores Using Multilevel Modeling. In M. Khosrow-Pour, D.B.A. (Ed.), Encyclopedia of Information Science and Technology, Fourth Edition (pp. 5183-5192). Hershey, PA: IGI Global. doi:10.4018/978-1-5225-2255-3.ch450

Kats, Y. (2017). Educational Leadership and Integrated Support for Students with Autism Spectrum Disorders. In I. Management Association (Ed.), *Educational Leadership and Administration: Concepts, Methodologies, Tools, and Applications* (pp. 101-114). Hershey, PA: IGI Global. https://doi.org/ doi:10.4018/978-1-5225-1624-8.ch007

Kaya, G., & Altun, A. (2018). Educational Ontology Development. In M. Khosrow-Pour, D.B.A. (Ed.), *Encyclopedia of Information Science and Technology, Fourth Edition* (pp. 1441-1450). Hershey, PA: IGI Global. doi:10.4018/978-1-5225-2255-3.ch124

Keough, P. D., & Pacis, D. (2017). Best Practices Implementing Special Education Curriculum and Common Core State Standards using UDL. In P. Dickenson, P. Keough, & J. Courduff (Eds.), *Preparing Pre-Service Teachers for the Inclusive Classroom* (pp. 107–123). Hershey, PA: IGI Global. doi:10.4018/978-1-5225-1753-5.ch006

Kilburn, M., Henckell, M., & Starrett, D. (2018). Factors Contributing to the Effectiveness of Online Students and Instructors. In M. Khosrow-Pour, D.B.A. (Ed.), *Encyclopedia of Information Science and Technology, Fourth Edition* (pp. 1451-1462). Hershey, PA: IGI Global. doi:10.4018/978-1-5225-2255-3.ch125

Koban Koç, D. (2021). Gender and Language: A Sociolinguistic Analysis of Second Language Writing. In E. Hancı-Azizoglu & N. Kavaklı (Eds.), *Futuristic and Linguistic Perspectives on Teaching Writing to Second Language Students* (pp. 161–177). IGI Global. https://doi.org/10.4018/978-1-7998-6508-7.ch010

Konecny, L. T. (2017). Hybrid, Online, and Flipped Classrooms in Health Science: Enhanced Learning Environments. In I. Management Association (Ed.), *Flipped Instruction: Breakthroughs in Research and Practice* (pp. 355-370). Hershey, PA: IGI Global. https://doi.org/ doi:10.4018/978-1-5225-1803-7.ch020

Kupietz, K. D. (2021). Gaming and Simulation in Public Education: Teaching Others to Help Themselves and Their Neighbors. In N. Drumhiller, T. Wilkin, & K. Srba (Eds.), *Simulation and Game-Based Learning in Emergency and Disaster Management* (pp. 41–62). IGI Global. https://doi.org/10.4018/978-1-7998-4087-9.ch003

Kwee, C. T. (2022). Assessing the International Student Enrolment Strategies in Australian Universities: A Case Study During the COVID-19 Pandemic. In M. Alaali (Ed.), *Assessing University Governance and Policies in Relation to the COVID-19 Pandemic* (pp. 162–188). IGI Global. https://doi.org/10.4018/978-1-7998-8279-4.ch010

Related References

Lauricella, S., & McArthur, F. A. (2022). Taking a Student-Centred Approach to Alternative Digital Credentials: Multiple Pathways Toward the Acquisition of Microcredentials. In D. Piedra (Ed.), *Innovations in the Design and Application of Alternative Digital Credentials* (pp. 57–69). IGI Global. https://doi.org/10.4018/978-1-7998-7697-7.ch003

Llamas, M. F. (2019). Intercultural Awareness in Teaching English for Early Childhood: A Film-Based Approach. In E. Domínguez Romero, J. Bobkina, & S. Stefanova (Eds.), *Teaching Literature and Language Through Multimodal Texts* (pp. 54–68). IGI Global. https://doi.org/10.4018/978-1-5225-5796-8.ch004

Lokhtina, I., & Kkese, E. T. (2022). Reflecting and Adapting to an Academic Workplace Before and After the Lockdown in Greek-Speaking Cyprus: Opportunities and Challenges. In A. Zhuplev & R. Koepp (Eds.), *Global Trends, Dynamics, and Imperatives for Strategic Development in Business Education in an Age of Disruption* (pp. 126–148). IGI Global. https://doi.org/10.4018/978-1-7998-7548-2.ch007

Lovell, K. L. (2017). Development and Evaluation of Neuroscience Computer-Based Modules for Medical Students: Instructional Design Principles and Effectiveness. In J. Stefaniak (Ed.), *Advancing Medical Education Through Strategic Instructional Design* (pp. 262–276). Hershey, PA: IGI Global. doi:10.4018/978-1-5225-2098-6.ch013

Maher, D. (2019). The Use of Course Management Systems in Pre-Service Teacher Education. In J. Keengwe (Ed.), *Handbook of Research on Blended Learning Pedagogies and Professional Development in Higher Education* (pp. 196–213). IGI Global. https://doi.org/10.4018/978-1-5225-5557-5.ch011

Makewa, L. N. (2019). Teacher Technology Competence Base. In L. Makewa, B. Ngussa, & J. Kuboja (Eds.), *Technology-Supported Teaching and Research Methods for Educators* (pp. 247–267). IGI Global. https://doi.org/10.4018/978-1-5225-5915-3.ch014

Mallett, C. A. (2022). School Resource (Police) Officers in Schools: Impact on Campus Safety, Student Discipline, and Learning. In G. Crews (Ed.), *Impact of School Shootings on Classroom Culture, Curriculum, and Learning* (pp. 53–70). IGI Global. https://doi.org/10.4018/978-1-7998-5200-1.ch004

Marinho, J. E., Freitas, I. R., Leão, I. B., Pacheco, L. O., Gonçalves, M. P., Castro, M. J., Silva, P. D., & Moreira, R. J. (2022). Project-Based Learning Application in Higher Education: Student Experiences and Perspectives. In A. Alves & N. van Hattum-Janssen (Eds.), *Training Engineering Students for Modern Technological Advancement* (pp. 146–164). IGI Global. https://doi.org/10.4018/978-1-7998-8816-1.ch007

McCleskey, J. A., & Melton, R. M. (2022). Rolling With the Flow: Online Faculty and Student Presence in a Post-COVID-19 World. In S. Ramlall, T. Cross, & M. Love (Eds.), *Handbook of Research on Future of Work and Education: Implications for Curriculum Delivery and Work Design* (pp. 307–328). IGI Global. https://doi.org/10.4018/978-1-7998-8275-6.ch019

McCormack, V. F., Stauffer, M., Fishley, K., Hohenbrink, J., Mascazine, J. R., & Zigler, T. (2018). Designing a Dual Licensure Path for Middle Childhood and Special Education Teacher Candidates. In D. Polly, M. Putman, T. Petty, & A. Good (Eds.), *Innovative Practices in Teacher Preparation and Graduate-Level Teacher Education Programs* (pp. 21–36). Hershey, PA: IGI Global. doi:10.4018/978-1-5225-3068-8.ch002

McDaniel, R. (2017). Strategic Leadership in Instructional Design: Applying the Principles of Instructional Design through the Lens of Strategic Leadership to Distance Education. In V. Wang (Ed.), *Encyclopedia of Strategic Leadership and Management* (pp. 1570–1584). Hershey, PA: IGI Global. doi:10.4018/978-1-5225-1049-9.ch109

McKinney, R. E., Halli-Tierney, A. D., Gold, A. E., Allen, R. S., & Carroll, D. G. (2022). Interprofessional Education: Using Standardized Cases in Face-to-Face and Remote Learning Settings. In C. Ford & K. Garza (Eds.), *Handbook of Research on Updating and Innovating Health Professions Education: Post-Pandemic Perspectives* (pp. 24–42). IGI Global. https://doi.org/10.4018/978-1-7998-7623-6.ch002

Meintjes, H. H. (2021). Learner Views of a Facebook Page as a Supportive Digital Pedagogical Tool at a Public South African School in a Grade 12 Business Studies Class. *International Journal of Smart Education and Urban Society*, *12*(2), 32–45. https://doi.org/10.4018/IJSEUS.2021040104

Melero-García, F. (2022). Training Bilingual Interpreters in Healthcare Settings: Student Perceptions of Online Learning. In J. LeLoup & P. Swanson (Eds.), *Handbook of Research on Effective Online Language Teaching in a Disruptive Environment* (pp. 288–310). IGI Global. https://doi.org/10.4018/978-1-7998-7720-2.ch015

Related References

Meletiadou, E. (2022). The Use of Peer Assessment as an Inclusive Learning Strategy in Higher Education Institutions: Enhancing Student Writing Skills and Motivation. In E. Meletiadou (Ed.), *Handbook of Research on Policies and Practices for Assessing Inclusive Teaching and Learning* (pp. 1–26). IGI Global. https://doi.org/10.4018/978-1-7998-8579-5.ch001

Memon, R. N., Ahmad, R., & Salim, S. S. (2018). Critical Issues in Requirements Engineering Education. In I. Management Association (Ed.), Computer Systems and Software Engineering: Concepts, Methodologies, Tools, and Applications (pp. 1953-1976). Hershey, PA: IGI Global. doi:10.4018/978-1-5225-3923-0.ch081

Mendenhall, R. (2017). Western Governors University: CBE Innovator and National Model. In K. Rasmussen, P. Northrup, & R. Colson (Eds.), *Handbook of Research on Competency-Based Education in University Settings* (pp. 379–400). Hershey, PA: IGI Global. doi:10.4018/978-1-5225-0932-5.ch019

Mense, E. G., Griggs, D. M., & Shanks, J. N. (2018). School Leaders in a Time of Accountability and Data Use: Preparing Our Future School Leaders in Leadership Preparation Programs. In E. Mense & M. Crain-Dorough (Eds.), *Data Leadership for K-12 Schools in a Time of Accountability* (pp. 235–259). Hershey, PA: IGI Global. doi:10.4018/978-1-5225-3188-3.ch012

Mense, E. G., Griggs, D. M., & Shanks, J. N. (2018). School Leaders in a Time of Accountability and Data Use: Preparing Our Future School Leaders in Leadership Preparation Programs. In E. Mense & M. Crain-Dorough (Eds.), *Data Leadership for K-12 Schools in a Time of Accountability* (pp. 235–259). Hershey, PA: IGI Global. doi:10.4018/978-1-5225-3188-3.ch012

Mestry, R., & Naicker, S. R. (2017). Exploring Distributive Leadership in South African Public Primary Schools in the Soweto Region. In I. Management Association (Ed.), Educational Leadership and Administration: Concepts, Methodologies, Tools, and Applications (pp. 1041-1064). Hershey, PA: IGI Global. doi:10.4018/978-1-5225-1624-8.ch050

Monaghan, C. H., & Boboc, M. (2017). (Re)Defining Leadership in Higher Education in the U.S. In V. Wang (Ed.), *Encyclopedia of Strategic Leadership and Management* (pp. 567–579). Hershey, PA: IGI Global. doi:10.4018/978-1-5225-1049-9.ch040

Morall, M. B. (2021). Reimagining Mobile Phones: Multiple Literacies and Digital Media Compositions. In C. Moran (Eds.), *Affordances and Constraints of Mobile Phone Use in English Language Arts Classrooms* (pp. 41-53). IGI Global. https://doi.org/10.4018/978-1-7998-5805-8.ch003

Mthethwa, V. (2022). Student Governance and the Academic Minefield During COVID-19 Lockdown in South Africa. In M. Alaali (Ed.), *Assessing University Governance and Policies in Relation to the COVID-19 Pandemic* (pp. 255–276). IGI Global. https://doi.org/10.4018/978-1-7998-8279-4.ch015

Muthee, J. M., & Murungi, C. G. (2018). Relationship Among Intelligence, Achievement Motivation, Type of School, and Academic Performance of Kenyan Urban Primary School Pupils. In M. Khosrow-Pour, D.B.A. (Ed.), Encyclopedia of Information Science and Technology, Fourth Edition (pp. 1540-1547). Hershey, PA: IGI Global. https://doi.org/ doi:10.4018/978-1-5225-2255-3.ch133

Naranjo, J. (2018). Meeting the Need for Inclusive Educators Online: Teacher Education in Inclusive Special Education and Dual-Certification. In D. Polly, M. Putman, T. Petty, & A. Good (Eds.), *Innovative Practices in Teacher Preparation and Graduate-Level Teacher Education Programs* (pp. 106–122). Hershey, PA: IGI Global. doi:10.4018/978-1-5225-3068-8.ch007

Nkabinde, Z. P. (2017). Multiculturalism in Special Education: Perspectives of Minority Children in Urban Schools. In J. Keengwe (Ed.), *Handbook of Research on Promoting Cross-Cultural Competence and Social Justice in Teacher Education* (pp. 382–397). Hershey, PA: IGI Global. doi:10.4018/978-1-5225-0897-7.ch020

Nkabinde, Z. P. (2018). Online Instruction: Is the Quality the Same as Face-to-Face Instruction? In J. Keengwe (Ed.), *Handbook of Research on Digital Content, Mobile Learning, and Technology Integration Models in Teacher Education* (pp. 300–314). Hershey, PA: IGI Global. doi:10.4018/978-1-5225-2953-8.ch016

Nugroho, A., & Albusaidi, S. S. (2022). Internationalization of Higher Education: The Methodological Critiques on the Research Related to Study Overseas and International Experience. In H. Magd & S. Kunjumuhammed (Eds.), *Global Perspectives on Quality Assurance and Accreditation in Higher Education Institutions* (pp. 75–89). IGI Global. https://doi.org/10.4018/978-1-7998-8085-1.ch005

Nulty, Z., & West, S. G. (2022). Student Engagement and Supporting Students With Accommodations. In P. Bull & G. Patterson (Eds.), *Redefining Teacher Education and Teacher Preparation Programs in the Post-COVID-19 Era* (pp. 99–116). IGI Global. https://doi.org/10.4018/978-1-7998-8298-5.ch006

O'Connor, J. R. Jr, & Jackson, K. N. (2017). The Use of iPad® Devices and "Apps" for ASD Students in Special Education and Speech Therapy. In Y. Kats (Ed.), *Supporting the Education of Children with Autism Spectrum Disorders* (pp. 267–283). Hershey, PA: IGI Global. doi:10.4018/978-1-5225-0816-8.ch014

Related References

Okolie, U. C., & Yasin, A. M. (2017). TVET in Developing Nations and Human Development. In U. Okolie & A. Yasin (Eds.), *Technical Education and Vocational Training in Developing Nations* (pp. 1–25). Hershey, PA: IGI Global. doi:10.4018/978-1-5225-1811-2.ch001

Pack, A., & Barrett, A. (2021). A Review of Virtual Reality and English for Academic Purposes: Understanding Where to Start. *International Journal of Computer-Assisted Language Learning and Teaching*, *11*(1), 72–80. https://doi.org/10.4018/IJCALLT.2021010105

Pashollari, E. (2019). Building Sustainability Through Environmental Education: Education for Sustainable Development. In L. Wilson, & C. Stevenson (Eds.), *Building Sustainability Through Environmental Education* (pp. 72-88). IGI Global. https://doi.org/10.4018/978-1-5225-7727-0.ch004

Paulson, E. N. (2017). Adapting and Advocating for an Online EdD Program in Changing Times and "Sacred" Cultures. In I. Management Association (Ed.), *Educational Leadership and Administration: Concepts, Methodologies, Tools, and Applications* (pp. 1849-1876). Hershey, PA: IGI Global. https://doi.org/doi:10.4018/978-1-5225-1624-8.ch085

Petersen, A. J., Elser, C. F., Al Nassir, M. N., Stakey, J., & Everson, K. (2017). The Year of Teaching Inclusively: Building an Elementary Classroom for All Students. In C. Curran & A. Petersen (Eds.), *Handbook of Research on Classroom Diversity and Inclusive Education Practice* (pp. 332–348). Hershey, PA: IGI Global. doi:10.4018/978-1-5225-2520-2.ch014

Pfannenstiel, K. H., & Sanders, J. (2017). Characteristics and Instructional Strategies for Students With Mathematical Difficulties: In the Inclusive Classroom. In C. Curran & A. Petersen (Eds.), *Handbook of Research on Classroom Diversity and Inclusive Education Practice* (pp. 250–281). Hershey, PA: IGI Global. doi:10.4018/978-1-5225-2520-2.ch011

Phan, A. N. (2022). Quality Assurance of Higher Education From the Glonacal Agency Heuristic: An Example From Vietnam. In H. Magd & S. Kunjumuhammed (Eds.), *Global Perspectives on Quality Assurance and Accreditation in Higher Education Institutions* (pp. 136–155). IGI Global. https://doi.org/10.4018/978-1-7998-8085-1.ch008

Preast, J. L., Bowman, N., & Rose, C. A. (2017). Creating Inclusive Classroom Communities Through Social and Emotional Learning to Reduce Social Marginalization Among Students. In C. Curran & A. Petersen (Eds.), *Handbook of Research on Classroom Diversity and Inclusive Education Practice* (pp. 183–200). Hershey, PA: IGI Global. doi:10.4018/978-1-5225-2520-2.ch008

Randolph, K. M., & Brady, M. P. (2018). Evolution of Covert Coaching as an Evidence-Based Practice in Professional Development and Preparation of Teachers. In V. Bryan, A. Musgrove, & J. Powers (Eds.), *Handbook of Research on Human Development in the Digital Age* (pp. 281–299). Hershey, PA: IGI Global. doi:10.4018/978-1-5225-2838-8.ch013

Rell, A. B., Puig, R. A., Roll, F., Valles, V., Espinoza, M., & Duque, A. L. (2017). Addressing Cultural Diversity and Global Competence: The Dual Language Framework. In L. Leavitt, S. Wisdom, & K. Leavitt (Eds.), *Cultural Awareness and Competency Development in Higher Education* (pp. 111–131). Hershey, PA: IGI Global. doi:10.4018/978-1-5225-2145-7.ch007

Richards, M., & Guzman, I. R. (2020). Academic Assessment of Critical Thinking in Distance Education Information Technology Programs. In I. Management Association (Ed.), *Learning and Performance Assessment: Concepts, Methodologies, Tools, and Applications* (pp. 1-19). IGI Global. https://doi.org/10.4018/978-1-7998-0420-8.ch001

Riel, J., Lawless, K. A., & Brown, S. W. (2017). Defining and Designing Responsive Online Professional Development (ROPD): A Framework to Support Curriculum Implementation. In T. Kidd & L. Morris Jr., (Eds.), *Handbook of Research on Instructional Systems and Educational Technology* (pp. 104–115). Hershey, PA: IGI Global. doi:10.4018/978-1-5225-2399-4.ch010

Roberts, C. (2017). Advancing Women Leaders in Academe: Creating a Culture of Inclusion. In S. Mukerji & P. Tripathi (Eds.), *Handbook of Research on Administration, Policy, and Leadership in Higher Education* (pp. 256–273). Hershey, PA: IGI Global. doi:10.4018/978-1-5225-0672-0.ch012

Rodgers, W. J., Kennedy, M. J., Alves, K. D., & Romig, J. E. (2017). A Multimedia Tool for Teacher Education and Professional Development. In C. Martin & D. Polly (Eds.), *Handbook of Research on Teacher Education and Professional Development* (pp. 285–296). Hershey, PA: IGI Global. doi:10.4018/978-1-5225-1067-3.ch015

Romanowski, M. H. (2017). Qatar's Educational Reform: Critical Issues Facing Principals. In I. Management Association (Ed.), Educational Leadership and Administration: Concepts, Methodologies, Tools, and Applications (pp. 1758-1773). Hershey, PA: IGI Global. https://doi.org/ doi:10.4018/978-1-5225-1624-8.ch080

Ruffin, T. R., Hawkins, D. P., & Lee, D. I. (2018). Increasing Student Engagement and Participation Through Course Methodology. In M. Khosrow-Pour, D.B.A. (Ed.), Encyclopedia of Information Science and Technology, Fourth Edition (pp. 1463-1473). Hershey, PA: IGI Global. doi:10.4018/978-1-5225-2255-3.ch126

Sabina, L. L., Curry, K. A., Harris, E. L., Krumm, B. L., & Vencill, V. (2017). Assessing the Performance of a Cohort-Based Model Using Domestic and International Practices. In I. Management Association (Ed.), Educational Leadership and Administration: Concepts, Methodologies, Tools, and Applications (pp. 913-929). Hershey, PA: IGI Global. https://doi.org/ doi:10.4018/978-1-5225-1624-8.ch044

Samkian, A., Pascarella, J., & Slayton, J. (2022). Towards an Anti-Racist, Culturally Responsive, and LGBTQ+ Inclusive Education: Developing Critically-Conscious Educational Leaders. In E. Cain-Sanschagrin, R. Filback, & J. Crawford (Eds.), *Cases on Academic Program Redesign for Greater Racial and Social Justice* (pp. 150–175). IGI Global. https://doi.org/10.4018/978-1-7998-8463-7.ch007

Santamaría, A. P., Webber, M., & Santamaría, L. J. (2017). Effective School Leadership for Māori Achievement: Building Capacity through Indigenous, National, and International Cross-Cultural Collaboration. In I. Management Association (Ed.), Educational Leadership and Administration: Concepts, Methodologies, Tools, and Applications (pp. 1547-1567). Hershey, PA: IGI Global. https://doi.org/ doi:10.4018/978-1-5225-1624-8.ch071

Santamaría, L. J. (2017). Culturally Responsive Educational Leadership in Cross-Cultural International Contexts. In I. Management Association (Ed.), Educational Leadership and Administration: Concepts, Methodologies, Tools, and Applications (pp. 1380-1400). Hershey, PA: IGI Global. https://doi.org/ doi:10.4018/978-1-5225-1624-8.ch064

Segredo, M. R., Cistone, P. J., & Reio, T. G. (2017). Relationships Between Emotional Intelligence, Leadership Style, and School Culture. *International Journal of Adult Vocational Education and Technology*, 8(3), 25–43. doi:10.4018/IJAVET.2017070103

Shalev, N. (2017). Empathy and Leadership From the Organizational Perspective. In Z. Nedelko & M. Brzozowski (Eds.), *Exploring the Influence of Personal Values and Cultures in the Workplace* (pp. 348–363). Hershey, PA: IGI Global. doi:10.4018/978-1-5225-2480-9.ch018

Siamak, M., Fathi, S., & Isfandyari-Moghaddam, A. (2018). Assessment and Measurement of Education Programs of Information Literacy. In R. Bhardwaj (Ed.), *Digitizing the Modern Library and the Transition From Print to Electronic* (pp. 164–192). Hershey, PA: IGI Global. doi:10.4018/978-1-5225-2119-8.ch007

Siu, K. W., & García, G. J. (2017). Disruptive Technologies and Education: Is There Any Disruption After All? In I. Management Association (Ed.), *Educational Leadership and Administration: Concepts, Methodologies, Tools, and Applications* (pp. 757-778). Hershey, PA: IGI Global. https://doi.org/ doi:10.4018/978-1-5225-1624-8.ch037

Slagter van Tryon, P. J. (2017). The Nurse Educator's Role in Designing Instruction and Instructional Strategies for Academic and Clinical Settings. In J. Stefaniak (Ed.), *Advancing Medical Education Through Strategic Instructional Design* (pp. 133–149). Hershey, PA: IGI Global. doi:10.4018/978-1-5225-2098-6.ch006

Slattery, C. A. (2018). Literacy Intervention and the Differentiated Plan of Instruction. In *Developing Effective Literacy Intervention Strategies: Emerging Research and Opportunities* (pp. 41–62). Hershey, PA: IGI Global. doi:10.4018/978-1-5225-5007-5.ch003

Smith, A. R. (2017). Ensuring Quality: The Faculty Role in Online Higher Education. In K. Shelton & K. Pedersen (Eds.), *Handbook of Research on Building, Growing, and Sustaining Quality E-Learning Programs* (pp. 210–231). Hershey, PA: IGI Global. doi:10.4018/978-1-5225-0877-9.ch011

Souders, T. M. (2017). Understanding Your Learner: Conducting a Learner Analysis. In J. Stefaniak (Ed.), *Advancing Medical Education Through Strategic Instructional Design* (pp. 1–29). Hershey, PA: IGI Global. doi:10.4018/978-1-5225-2098-6.ch001

Spring, K. J., Graham, C. R., & Ikahihifo, T. B. (2018). Learner Engagement in Blended Learning. In M. Khosrow-Pour, D.B.A. (Ed.), Encyclopedia of Information Science and Technology, Fourth Edition (pp. 1487-1498). Hershey, PA: IGI Global. doi:10.4018/978-1-5225-2255-3.ch128

Storey, V. A., Anthony, A. K., & Wahid, P. (2017). Gender-Based Leadership Barriers: Advancement of Female Faculty to Leadership Positions in Higher Education. In V. Wang (Ed.), *Encyclopedia of Strategic Leadership and Management* (pp. 244–258). Hershey, PA: IGI Global. doi:10.4018/978-1-5225-1049-9.ch018

Stottlemyer, D. (2018). Develop a Teaching Model Plan for a Differentiated Learning Approach. In *Differentiated Instructional Design for Multicultural Environments: Emerging Research and Opportunities* (pp. 106–130). Hershey, PA: IGI Global. doi:10.4018/978-1-5225-5106-5.ch005

Related References

Stottlemyer, D. (2018). Developing a Multicultural Environment. In *Differentiated Instructional Design for Multicultural Environments: Emerging Research and Opportunities* (pp. 1–27). Hershey, PA: IGI Global. doi:10.4018/978-1-5225-5106-5.ch001

Swagerty, T. (2022). Digital Access to Culturally Relevant Curricula: The Impact on the Native and Indigenous Student. In E. Reeves & C. McIntyre (Eds.), *Multidisciplinary Perspectives on Diversity and Equity in a Virtual World* (pp. 99–113). IGI Global. https://doi.org/10.4018/978-1-7998-8028-8.ch006

Swami, B. N., Gobona, T., & Tsimako, J. J. (2017). Academic Leadership: A Case Study of the University of Botswana. In N. Baporikar (Ed.), *Innovation and Shifting Perspectives in Management Education* (pp. 1–32). Hershey, PA: IGI Global. doi:10.4018/978-1-5225-1019-2.ch001

Swanson, K. W., & Collins, G. (2018). Designing Engaging Instruction for the Adult Learners. In M. Khosrow-Pour, D.B.A. (Ed.), Encyclopedia of Information Science and Technology, Fourth Edition (pp. 1432-1440). Hershey, PA: IGI Global. doi:10.4018/978-1-5225-2255-3.ch123

Swartz, B. A., Lynch, J. M., & Lynch, S. D. (2018). Embedding Elementary Teacher Education Coursework in Local Classrooms: Examples in Mathematics and Special Education. In D. Polly, M. Putman, T. Petty, & A. Good (Eds.), *Innovative Practices in Teacher Preparation and Graduate-Level Teacher Education Programs* (pp. 262–292). Hershey, PA: IGI Global. doi:10.4018/978-1-5225-3068-8.ch015

Taliadorou, N., & Pashiardis, P. (2017). Emotional Intelligence and Political Skill Really Matter in Educational Leadership. In I. Management Association (Ed.), Educational Leadership and Administration: Concepts, Methodologies, Tools, and Applications (pp. 1274-1303). Hershey, PA: IGI Global. https://doi.org/doi:10.4018/978-1-5225-1624-8.ch060

Tandoh, K. A., & Ebe-Arthur, J. E. (2018). Effective Educational Leadership in the Digital Age: An Examination of Professional Qualities and Best Practices. In J. Keengwe (Ed.), *Handbook of Research on Digital Content, Mobile Learning, and Technology Integration Models in Teacher Education* (pp. 244–265). Hershey, PA: IGI Global. doi:10.4018/978-1-5225-2953-8.ch013

Tobin, M. T. (2018). Multimodal Literacy. In M. Khosrow-Pour, D.B.A. (Ed.), Encyclopedia of Information Science and Technology, Fourth Edition (pp. 1508-1516). Hershey, PA: IGI Global. doi:10.4018/978-1-5225-2255-3.ch130

Torres, K. M., Arrastia-Chisholm, M. C., & Tackett, S. (2019). A Phenomenological Study of Pre-Service Teachers' Perceptions of Completing ESOL Field Placements. *International Journal of Teacher Education and Professional Development*, 2(2), 85–101. https://doi.org/10.4018/IJTEPD.2019070106

Torres, M. C., Salamanca, Y. N., Cely, J. P., & Aguilar, J. L. (2020). All We Need is a Boost! Using Multimodal Tools and the Translanguaging Strategy: Strengthening Speaking in the EFL Classroom. *International Journal of Computer-Assisted Language Learning and Teaching*, 10(3), 28–47. doi:10.4018/IJCALLT.2020070103

Torres, M. L., & Ramos, V. J. (2018). Music Therapy: A Pedagogical Alternative for ASD and ID Students in Regular Classrooms. In P. Epler (Ed.), *Instructional Strategies in General Education and Putting the Individuals With Disabilities Act (IDEA) Into Practice* (pp. 222–244). Hershey, PA: IGI Global. doi:10.4018/978-1-5225-3111-1.ch008

Toulassi, B. (2017). Educational Administration and Leadership in Francophone Africa: 5 Dynamics to Change Education. In S. Mukerji & P. Tripathi (Eds.), *Handbook of Research on Administration, Policy, and Leadership in Higher Education* (pp. 20–45). Hershey, PA: IGI Global. doi:10.4018/978-1-5225-0672-0.ch002

Umair, S., & Sharif, M. M. (2018). Predicting Students Grades Using Artificial Neural Networks and Support Vector Machine. In M. Khosrow-Pour, D.B.A. (Ed.), Encyclopedia of Information Science and Technology, Fourth Edition (pp. 5169-5182). Hershey, PA: IGI Global. doi:10.4018/978-1-5225-2255-3.ch449

Vettraino, L., Castello, V., Guspini, M., & Guglielman, E. (2018). Self-Awareness and Motivation Contrasting ESL and NEET Using the SAVE System. In M. Khosrow-Pour, D.B.A. (Ed.), Encyclopedia of Information Science and Technology, Fourth Edition (pp. 1559-1568). Hershey, PA: IGI Global. doi:10.4018/978-1-5225-2255-3.ch135

Wiemelt, J. (2017). Critical Bilingual Leadership for Emergent Bilingual Students. In I. Management Association (Ed.), Educational Leadership and Administration: Concepts, Methodologies, Tools, and Applications (pp. 1606-1631). Hershey, PA: IGI Global. doi:10.4018/978-1-5225-1624-8.ch074

Wolf, F., Seyfarth, F. C., & Pflaum, E. (2018). Scalable Capacity-Building for Geographically Dispersed Learners: Designing the MOOC "Sustainable Energy in Small Island Developing States (SIDS)". In U. Pandey & V. Indrakanti (Eds.), *Open and Distance Learning Initiatives for Sustainable Development* (pp. 58–83). Hershey, PA: IGI Global. doi:10.4018/978-1-5225-2621-6.ch003

Related References

Woodley, X. M., Mucundanyi, G., & Lockard, M. (2017). Designing Counter-Narratives: Constructing Culturally Responsive Curriculum Online. *International Journal of Online Pedagogy and Course Design*, 7(1), 43–56. doi:10.4018/IJOPCD.2017010104

Yell, M. L., & Christle, C. A. (2017). The Foundation of Inclusion in Federal Legislation and Litigation. In C. Curran & A. Petersen (Eds.), *Handbook of Research on Classroom Diversity and Inclusive Education Practice* (pp. 27–52). Hershey, PA: IGI Global. doi:10.4018/978-1-5225-2520-2.ch002

Zinner, L. (2019). Fostering Academic Citizenship With a Shared Leadership Approach. In C. Zhu & M. Zayim-Kurtay (Eds.), *University Governance and Academic Leadership in the EU and China* (pp. 99–117). IGI Global. https://doi.org/10.4018/978-1-5225-7441-5.ch007

About the Contributors

Oscar Eybers is an academic literacy facilitator in the Unit for Academic Literacy at the University of Pretoria in southern Africa. He has taught various levels of literacy, spanning from pre-school children to scholars enrolled in higher education. Eybers is passionate about the roles academic literacy plays in cultivating students' wellbeing, confidence and development in various scholarly disciplines. His current research focus areas include visual literacy, multilingualism and discourse analysis. Eybers's PhD focused on interactions between social structures, culture and agency in novice science scholars mastering argumentative writing. He is keen to collaborate with transdisciplinary and international academics and activists.

Alan Muller is a lecturer and PhD candidate at the University of Pretoria where teaches academic literacy. His research interests include, AI in the Humanities, science and speculative fiction, and academic literacy. He is a co-editor of *Cities in Flux: Metropolitan Spaces in South African Literary and Visual Texts* (2017). His most recent publications are 'Cultural Entanglement, Displacement and Contemporary Durban in Imraan Coovadia's *High Low In-between*' (2023) and 'Left, Right then Left Again: Educators at the Intersection of Global Citizenship Education, Technology and Academic Literacies' (2024).

* * *

Katherine Rose Adams is an Associate Professor in the College of Education at the University of North Georgia. Katherine received her Ph.D. in Adult Education, where her focus was on community boundary spanners within university-community partnerships. She also obtained a M.Ed. in Human Resources/Occupational Development, a GC in Interdisciplinary Qualitative Research, and a B.S. in Psychology all from The University of Georgia. Dr. Adams has been working in higher education administration roles since 2005 prior to joining UNG in August 2018 as an assistant professor. Katherine became the Higher Education Leadership and Practice program coordinator in 2019 and immediately began creating programing for graduate students such as a grant writing academy, peer mentoring program for adult learners, and program workshop series. Teaching in UNG's first dissertation-based doctoral program, Katherine facilitates coursework on higher education leadership, qualitative methodology research, student affairs administration, supporting underrepresented students, high impact teaching, and law and ethics in higher education. Katherine's research interests are in the areas of boundary spanning, higher education leadership, minority-serving institutions, and college homelessness. She is also the Community Voice and Student Perspectives Associate Editor for the Journal of Community Engagement and Scholarship.

Retha Alberts is a lecturer at the University of Pretoria with a Master's in Translation and Interpreting. Her thesis explored the potential of translated literature to contribute to renewing South Africa's national narrative. Retha has over 15 years of experience teaching academic literacy and language-related subjects at the University of Pretoria and other institutions. Retha's expertise spans editing, translation, and the responsible integration of generative AI in academic contexts.

Ágnes Hajdu Barát is a full professor of the Library Science Department at ELTE Eötvös Loránd University, Budapest, Hungary. She was the president of the Association of Hungarian Librarians 2015-2023. She is Stichting IFLA Global Libraries Foundation member 2023-, IFLA's European Regional Division Committee member, Standing Committee member of Knowledge Management Section, Building Strong Library and Information Science Education (BSLISE) Working Group member. She is the Executive Committee member of the Universal Decimal Classification Consortium. She is the author of twenty books, more chapters of books and articles (about 230).

Jacqualine Batchelor from the University Johannesburg is, first and foremost is a teacher, a recognized innovative teacher within the boundaries of teaching and learning with varieties of ICT and a facilitator in innovative teacher development. She has received accolades on local, national and international forums for her innovative teaching practices. She is a mobile learning specialist who conceptualizes and executes learning events that pilot new technologies in formal teaching environments in collaboration with research institutes and research partners.

Aulia Puspaning Galih is a doctoral student at the Institute of Library and Information Science, ELTE Eötvös Loránd University, Budapest, Hungary. She is also an assistant professor at the Library Science program, Universitas Brawijaya,

Malang, Indonesia. She has a Master of Science in Information Management degree from National Yang Ming Chiao Tung University, Taiwan. She wrote several scientific articles, books and book chapters during her career. She is also a reviewer and editorial board member for several Indonesian and international journals.

Mirna Ibrahim is a dynamic and passionate early career researcher dedicated to advancing the fields of business and sustainability. Mirna explores sustainable supply chain practices while also delving into emerging technologies such as artificial intelligence and blockchain to optimize supply chain processes. Mirna is an advocate for interdisciplinary collaboration. She actively engages with professionals from diverse fields, recognizing the interconnected nature of modern business challenges. In addition, Mirna's commitment to the adoption and impact of adaptive learning technologies in higher education. She explores how these technologies can be tailored to individual learning styles to enhance student engagement, improve academic performance, and boost motivation and participation.

Zander Janse van Rensburg is a lecturer and Writing Centre Manager in the School of Languages at North-West University (NWU), South Africa. In 2018, he was appointed as the University's subject specialist on academic integrity. His work in this regard focusses on forensic investigations of misconduct at all levels of academic practice, development of proactive academic integrity strategies, and an active contribution to the NWU's strategic response to the emergence of AI. His research interests include the development of academic writing, academic integrity, and philosophical inquiry.

Dickson Kanakulya is a lecturer in the College of Humanities and Social Sciences at Makerere University. He holds a PhD in philosophy, (Makerere University - Uganda); a Licentiate in Applied Ethics (Linköping university - Sweden); MA Philosophy in Bioethics (University of Bergen - Norway) and BA in philosophy and political science (Makerere University - Uganda).

Helena Kruger-Roux is a senior language practitioner at the University of Pretoria's Unit for Academic Literacy. She holds a PhD in English focused on subtitler training in South Africa, a multilingual developing country. She has extensive experience teaching academic literacy and applied linguistics and has developed and presented courses for diverse literacies. Her research interests include human language technology, language support for multilingual students, and the integration of generative AI in higher education.

Zhi Li is an Associate Professor in the Department of Linguistics, University of Saskatchewan. His areas of research specialization are applied linguistics, corpus linguistics, language assessment, computational linguistics, systemic functional linguistics, computer-assisted language learning (CALL).

Kelly Long teaches quantitative research methods and courses focused on social justice. Prior to UNG, Dr. Long worked in Institutional Research, most recently as the Assistant Vice President at a private college for three years and she held a similar role at a community college for six years. Dr. Long is a peer reviewer for the Community College Journal of Research and Practice and a peer reviewer for the Higher Learning Commission. She holds an M.S. in Survey Methodology from the University of Michigan and has a Ph.D. in Education Leadership from Oakland University. She currently researches in the field of QuantCrit, focusing on the ways researchers use racial statistics to promote racial justice and disrupt racism.

Veronika Makarova is a Professor at the Department of Linguistics, University of Saskatchewan, Canada. Prior to taking her position in the University of Saskatchewan and establishing the Department of Linguistics there, she worked in universities of Russia, Japan, and UK. She has published over 100 articles and 5 books. Her research interests include applied linguistics (including extracurricular activities), adult and child/youth bilingualism/multilingualism, immigrant, and heritage languages, Russian, Ukrainian, and Canadian Doukhobor (Spirit Wrestlers) language and culture.

Sonja van der Westhuizen is an academic advisor at the Centre for Teaching and Learning (CTL), North-West University (NWU). Her professional commitment involves Student Academic Development and Support, where she has actively co-ordinated various peer learning support programs, most notably the Academic Peer Mentoring and Peer Assisted Learning Support for Distance Learning Students-programs. She furthermore coordinates the NWU CTL First Year Experience initiative. Her research interests include collaborative teaching as instructional strategy to enhance inclusive teaching and learning and improving digital literacy and academic integrity among higher education students.

Charles Wiggill is an innovative educator and education manager passionate about transformational educational leadership, leveraging digital media and the power of ICT's, and how this all intersects with our humanity. He is fascinated by innovation and creative problem-solving, and how this emerges and is implemented in educational institutions. He holds a BEd Honours from Stellenbosch in Education Management and Innovative Leadership and has submitted the dissertation for

MEd ICT, focusing on artificial intelligence in South African schools through the University of Johannesburg. In K12 schools, both primary and high, he has filled roles of teacher, head of department, deputy principal, and head of school, and has also previously lectured at an independent higher education institution while heading up the PGCE Department. He currently lectures at the Stadio School of Education in Musgrave, Durban, South Africa.

Zhengxiang Wang is a PhD student in Linguistics at Stony Brook University, specializing in Natural Language Processing, Computational Linguistics, Computational Social Science, and Machine Learning. His research focuses on large-scale language use analysis, data augmentation techniques, neural network learning and generalization, and Large Language Model capabilities. With a keen interest in understanding the intricacies of language processing, Zhengxiang is dedicated to advancing knowledge in the field and contributing to cutting-edge research initiatives.

Index

A

B

C

  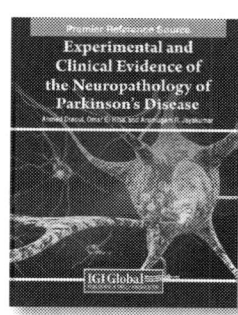 

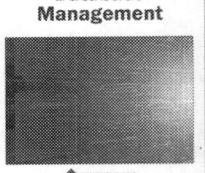